China's Capital Markets

ADVANCES IN CHINESE ECONOMIC STUDIES

Series Editor: Yanrui Wu, *Associate Professor in Economics, University of Western Australia, Australia*

The Chinese economy has been transformed dramatically in recent years. With its rapid economic growth and accession to the World Trade Organization, China is emerging as an economic superpower. China's development experience provides valuable lessons to many countries in transition.

Advances in Chinese Economic Studies aims, as a series, to publish the best work on the Chinese economy by economists and other researchers throughout the world. It is intended to serve a wide readership including academics, students, business economists and other practitioners.

Titles in the series include:

The Evolution of the Stock Market in China's Transitional Economy
Chien-Hsun Chen and Hui-Tzu Shih

Financial Reform and Economic Development in China
James Laurenceson and Joseph C.H. Chai

China's Telecommunications Market
Entering a New Competitive Age
Ding Lu and Chee Kong Wong

Banking and Insurance in the New China
Competition and the Challenge of Accession to the WTO
Chien-Hsun Chen and Hui-Tzu Shih

The Chinese Stock Market
Efficiency, Predictability and Profitability
Nicolaas Groenewold, Yanrui Wu, Sam Hak Kan Tang and Xiang Mei Fan

High-Tech Industries in China
Chien-Hsun Chen and Hui-Tzu Shih

Economic Growth, Transition and Globalization in China
Yanrui Wu

The Chinese Business Environment
An Annotated Bibliography
Fuming Jiang and Bruce W. Stening

China's Capital Markets
Challenges from WTO Membership
Kam C. Chan, Hung-gay Fung and Qingfeng 'Wilson' Liu

China's Capital Markets

Challenges from WTO Membership

Edited by

Kam C. Chan

Western Kentucky University, USA

Hung-gay Fung

University of Missouri – St. Louis, USA

and

Qingfeng 'Wilson' Liu

James Madison University, USA

ADVANCES IN CHINESE ECONOMIC STUDIES

Edward Elgar

Cheltenham, UK • Northampton, MA, USA

Published by
Edward Elgar Publishing Limited
Glensanda House
Montpellier Parade
Cheltenham
Glos GL50 1UA
UK

Edward Elgar Publishing, Inc.
William Pratt House
9 Dewey Court
Northampton
Massachusetts 01060
USA

A catalogue record for this book
is available from the British Library

Library of Congress Cataloging in Publication Data
China's capital markets : challenges from WTO membership / edited by Kam C. Chan, Hung-gay Fung, and Qingfeng 'Wilson' Liu.
p. cm. – (Advances in Chinese economic studies series)
Includes bibliographical references and index.
1. Finance–China. 2. World Trade Organization–China. I. Chan, Kam C., 1959– II. Fung, Hung-gay. III. Liu, Qingfeng 'Wilson'.
HG187.C6C4353 2007
332′.04150951–dc22 2006021898

ISBN 978 1 84542 656 9

Printed and bound in Great Britain by MPG Books Ltd, Bodmin, Cornwall

Contents

Contributors

Kam C. Chan, is the Leon and Ruby Mai Page Professor of Finance at Gordon Ford College of Business, Western Kentucky University. Dr Chan received his bachelor's degree in economics at the Chinese University of Hong Kong (1984), MA in economics (1987), MA in finance (1989), and PhD in finance (1990) at the University of Alabama. His teaching interests are investments and international finance. Research interests include derivative securities, mutual funds, fixed income, and Chinese financial markets. He has published more than 70 journal articles in leading finance journals. He is also a Chartered Financial Analyst (CFA) charter holder and currently serving a three-year term as a director of Midwest Finance Association (2004–2006).

Alan V. S. Douglas completed his PhD in Finance and Economics at Queen's University in Kingston, Canada in 1994. His first appointment was at Clemson University in South Carolina USA, and he is currently an Associate Professor at the University of Waterloo in Canada. His primary research interests include the theory of the firm and information asymmetries, particularly as related to financial markets. He has published papers on topics including the dividend puzzle, capital structure, corporate control, managerial incentives, and the role of accounting information in security design, in journals such as the *Review of Financial Studies*, *Journal of Empirical Finance*, *Journal of Corporate Finance*, *European Finance Review* and *Contemporary Accounting Research*.

Hung-gay Fung, is Dr Y. S. Tsiang Chair Professor of Chinese studies at the College of Business Administration and Center of International Studies, University of Missouri – St Louis. Dr Fung's research covers a wide range of international finance and Chinese financial markets. He has published over 100 scholarly articles and books. He is a recipient of many grants and academic awards. As a senior expert of Chinese studies, Dr Fung has frequently organized many international conferences and symposiums.

Ying Han is a graduate student in economics at the University of Missouri – St Louis. She earned her bachelor's degree in finance at Sun Yat-sen University, Guangzhou, China.

Alan Guoming Huang is currently an Assistant Professor of Finance at the University of Waterloo, Canada. His research focuses on the asset pricing implications of dynamic risk aversion and corporate earnings volatility, as well as issues related to emerging markets, especially the Chinese markets. He was an investment banker in China. Alan Huang holds a PhD in finance from the University of Colorado at Boulder, and a master's degree from Shanghai University of Finance and Economics.

Mary Ip is a member of the faculty at the University of Sydney with a research interest in Chinese commercial law. Her comparative research approach is regarded as conducive to the recent legal reform in China. She has been invited to speak to Chinese officials both in Australia and overseas on many occasions. In 2003, she carried out research at Peking University and Nanjing University as a visiting scholar and has obtained a number of universities' research grants. She has published extensively in internationally referred journals.

Julia S. Kwok is an Assistant Professor of Finance in the Department of Accounting and Finance, College of Business and Technology, Northeastern State University – Broken Arrow. She obtained her doctoral degree in finance from Virginia Polytechnic Institute and State University. Her research interests include corporate governance, venture financing, equity offering, telecommunication policies, and small and high-tech businesses. Prior to joining the academics, she was involved in strategic planning and telecommunication technical standards development. Currently she serves as a director of the Southwestern Finance Association.

Fei Liu is a research scholar in the Institute of Finance and Banking at the Chinese Academy of Social Science, China. She came to the University of Missouri – St Louis as a visiting scholar in 2004. Her research focuses primarily on China's insurance industry and she has published extensively on Chinese insurance issues.

Qingfeng 'Wilson' Liu is Assistant Professor of Finance at the College of Business, James Madison University in Virginia. His research interests include financial derivatives, investments, statistical forecasting and international finance. He has published articles in China's banking and securities markets, the real estate market, the emerging venture capital, and poverty-alleviating microfinance programmes. He received his PhD in finance from the University of Oklahoma.

Congsheng Wu is an Associate Professor of Finance at the University of Bridgeport. He is the co-author of two books about international corporate finance, both of which are published in Chinese. He has also published many articles in the area of global equity offerings and cross-listing.

Xiaoqing Xu is an Associate Professor of Finance at the Stillman School of Business at Seton Hall University and a Chartered Financial Analyst. Her research interests are in hedge funds, venture capital, emerging markets, security market microstructure and mortgage-backed securities. She has published over 20 research articles in journals such as *Journal of Banking and Finance, Real Estate Economics, Financial Analysts Journal, Journal of Futures Markets, Financial Review, Review of Quantitative Finance and Accounting, International Review of Economics and Finance, Journal of Investing* and *Journal of Alternative Investments.*

Yanda Xu graduated from the Accounting and Management Information Systems Department of the University of Missouri – St Louis. He is currently working as an analyst in the finance department of BJC Healthcare System. Prior to studying in the USA, he had many years of experience in the banking industry of China.

Jot Yau is Chair and Professor of Finance at the Department of Finance at Seattle University, WA. He holds a PhD in finance from the University of Massachusetts Amherst and is a CFA charterholder. He was a co-founder and company director of Strategic Options Investment Advisory Ltd in Hong Kong.

Gaiyan Zhang is Assistant Professor of Finance at the University of Missouri – St Louis. She received her PhD from the University of California, Irvine. Her research interests include credit risk, financial risk management, international finance, and China finance.

Preface

China's economy has been growing rapidly over the last two and a half decades and is expected to maintain this momentum in the foreseeable future. Because of the huge foreign direct investments and domestic entrepreneurships, China's economic growth has been largely fueled by the expansion of the industrial sector, which has helped China earn the nickname 'Workshop of the World' and represented more than half of its GDP.[1] This economic structure, however, is in sharp contrast with those of developed economies, in which the service sector invariably constitutes an overwhelming share.

Because China has the biggest population in the world with ongoing urbanization trends, there is tremendous growth potential for China's underdeveloped service sector, especially the capital markets and financial services industry, which are pivotal in meeting the ever-increasing financing needs of the manufacturing sectors to ensure the continued development of the economy. As a member of the World Trade Organization, China's accession promises to open up the financial sector to foreign competition by the end of 2006. Thus, China affords endless lucrative opportunities to domestic as well as international institutional and individual investors. Nevertheless, there also exist tremendous risks and challenges. They include the changing nature of the financial markets, inadequate and fast-changing regulations and laws, excessive governmental influence, the lack of transparency in accounting and corporate governance, and all the other problems associated with the transition economy with financial market liberalization.

A handbook on China's capital market that systematically documents and analyses its current and future development while integrating the banking system and legal issues is desirable and will certainly help investors, practitioners, researchers and policymakers to understand these perplexing and intertwined issues. The experience of China's capital market is also a valuable lesson for other transitional economies. This handbook is one of the first available in the market to cover a wide range of topics including China's stock market, bond market and other securities markets (for example the futures market and over-the-counter markets), as well as regulatory issues that shape the direction of the development of the financial markets. We will also discuss the development and roles of financial institutions, such as brokerage firms, banks and insurance companies, in China's capital markets. Banks dominate corporate financing needs in China's bank-based economy, but the development of the capital markets would provide additional avenues for firms to raise external capitals and change the dynamics of fund flows in the economy. We will examine the recent performance of the equity markets, the emergence of the small-medium enterprise market, the state banks' bids to be listed in overseas stock exchanges, and other current issues that are timely and of interest to readers. The book will shed light on China's overall economic growth as it is well-recognized that finance and economic growth are closely linked.

NOTE

1. *China Economic Times*, 8 May 2005, http://finance.sina.com.cn/g/20050508/23521569498.shtml.

Introduction: development and challenges of Chinese financial markets

Kam C. Chan, Hung-gay Fung and Qingfeng 'Wilson' Liu

INTRODUCTION

China's capital market grew substantially in the decade after the Shanghai Stock Exchange market opened in 1990. Despite China's impressive economic performance, the development of its capital market has encountered various hurdles. As China has evolved from a planned economy to a market-oriented economy in which the stock and bond markets have enabled Chinese corporations to raise external funds, the Chinese economy today is still dominated by banks. China is a bank-based economy overall.

Panel A of Table I.1 shows the importance of banks in China and other countries as compared to the stock market capitalization. Bank credits in China account for 141 percent of its GDP, a very high figure in comparison to other countries in East Asia and the US, implying the importance of bank loans to the Chinese economy. The numbers point to the fact that China is a bank-based economy. At the same time, China's stock market capitalization is about 39 percent of its GDP, a low figure compared to Japan (79 percent), Euro area (55 percent) and the US (129 percent). These figures suggest that China's capital structure (that is, the relations between the equity market and the bank loans market) remains unbalanced and underdeveloped due to limited equity financing for corporations when compared to developed countries including the traditional banking-dominated European economies (55 percent), or even with Korea (57 percent of GDP) and other emerging markets (61 percent of GDP).

It is apparent that Chinese investors primarily put their money into banks instead of investing it directly in the stock market. Savings in banks in China exceeded US$1 trillion as of late 2005. The reliance in banks by investors and market participants to scrutinize investments in firm projects is the result of excessive noises/confounding signals in the market if they

Table I.1 Financial structure comparison

Panel A Bank Credit versus Stock Market, 2004		
Country	Bank credit (%) of GDP	Stock Market capitalization (%) of GDP
China	141	39
Euro area	104	55
Japan	94	79
South Korea	80	57
Emerging markets	65	61
US	46	129
India	37	56

Source: *Wall Street Journal*, 13 October 2005.

Panel B Local Currency Bond Markets, 1997 versus 2003				
	1997		2003	
	US$ billion	% GDP	US$ billion	% GDP
China	116.4	12.9	440.4	31.3
Korea	45.1	29.1	445.7	73.6
Singapore	23.8	24.9	67.2	73.6
Thailand	9.6	6.1	58.4	40.7
Japan	355.5	19.1	1202.8	44.3
US	11 997.5	144.5	17 644.8	160.3
EU15	7095.7	85.8	10 357.3	98.6

Source: *Asia Bond Monitor*, November 2004, Asian Development Bank.

would invest directly in firm projects. Thus, market reforms need to stress and improve the transparency, credibility and liquidity of the capital markets.

In terms of bond market development, Panel B of Table I.1 shows the size of China's bond market is about 31.3 percent of its GDP in 2003. This figure again is low when compared to Singapore (73.6 percent), Japan (44.3 percent) and the US (160.3 percent). The result indicates that China's bond market is relatively underdeveloped in comparison to other countries. The bond market is another dimension that market participants can monitor and discipline in firm behavior. For the Chinese economy to achieve sustained and healthy growth, the development of its bond market is important.

All in all, this chapter provides an overview of the development and challenges in China's capital market, while the detailed structure and components will be presented in later chapters. In a review paper of the finance literature, Chan *et al.* (2006) discuss the various underlying factors leading to the development of China's capital market, including the imperfect market and segmentation, regulation and stages of financial development. We will provide an updated examination of China's capital market that includes equity market, bond market, foreign exchange market and futures market. This chapter serves as a building block for readers to better understand the overall development of China's capital market.

STOCK MARKET

Institutional Structure

The Shanghai Stock Exchange and Shenzhen Stock Exchange are the two major stock exchanges in China. As of the end of 2005, there were about 1400 listed companies on the two exchanges. Since the stock market was established in the early 1990s, there have been various types of shares issued to the public: A shares, B shares, H shares and N shares. The A-share market trades the shares of Chinese companies limited primarily to domestic Chinese investors. The B-share market is for shares of Chinese companies traded on the exchange and they are issued to foreign investors or for Chinese investors who have foreign currencies (US or Hong Kong dollars). Some Chinese companies issue both A shares and B shares provided that they satisfy the listing requirements, such as compliance with the International Accounting Standards, a more stringent standard than the domestic counterpart. H shares are shares of Chinese companies traded on the Hong Kong Stock Exchange and thus these companies need to satisfy the listing requirements of the Hong Kong Stock Exchange. N shares are shares traded in the US stock exchanges, including the NYSE and the Nasdaq. These shares are basically American depositary receipts for the stocks of Chinese companies. Chinese companies issue B shares, H shares, and N shares to foreign investors in order to raise foreign capital.

In recent years, a mutual fund market has emerged and developed in China, which expands the landscape of China's capital market and offers more investment options to investors with both open-ended and closed-ended funds (Xu 2005). On 23 February 2005, China started the first exchange-traded fund, ETF, on the Shanghai Stock Exchange (Ling and Yau 2005). An ETF is similar to a mutual fund but it can be traded like a stock listed on the exchange. China 50 ETF, issued by China Asset

Management Co., sponsored by State Street Global, tracks the 50 largest Chinese stocks on the Shanghai Stock Exchange. Foreign investors can buy China 50 ETF through the QFII (Qualified Financial Institutional Investor) program. In addition, there are several Chinese exchange traded funds available in the US and elsewhere.

The A-share market is apparently the most important component of the Chinese stock market system. This Introduction primarily focuses on this segment of the market. The growth and changes of the A-share market shape the growth of China's stock market.

Policy Changes and Implications

The Chinese government initially created the A- and B-share markets in order to maintain control because the B-share market is for foreign investors while the A-share market is for domestic investors. Thus, the segmentation of the A-share and B-share market is artificial, resulting in a considerable premium for the A-share market relative to the B-share for the same companies (Fung, Lee and Leung 2000). As the Chinese government relaxed the restrictions for domestic investors to invest in the B-share market in 2001, the barriers between the two markets gradually broke down, moving toward one market regime, although there are still differences in investor clientele between the two markets.

One thorny issue in the Chinese stock market development is the distinction between non-tradable shares and tradable shares within the A-share market. Non-tradable shares are shares held by financial institutions (called legal person shares) or by the state (called state shares). About two-thirds of Chinese shares are non-tradable shares. Non-tradable shares can be exchanged between market participants at the book value, which is substantially below the market price (Huang and Fung 2004).

The current challenge for the Chinese government is to convert all non-tradable shares into tradable shares. Over recent years, the sluggish price performance of the Chinese stock have been primarily due to: (a) the likely dilution of shares whenever the Chinese government expressed intention to convert the non-tradable shares into tradable shares; and (b) the overpricing of the A-shares relative to their intrinsic values. The overpricing of the Chinese shares is probably the result of limited investment opportunities for Chinese residents who have accumulated a large amount of savings. The Chinese government has implemented, within recent years, several measures in hopes to boost its bearish stock market, including the following by the China Securities Regulatory Commission (CSRC) in reforming the stock market.

First, the CSRC allows controlling shareholders to buy stocks in the open market to stabilize the price, sending a signal to the market that large shareholders of the companies are, instead of cashing out, serious about the pricing of the stock. Similarly, companies are allowed to start a series of stock repurchase programs if they feel the stock prices are excessively depressed and undervalued.

Second, the CSRC has started the conversion of non-tradable shares to tradable shares, initially from certain types of companies. There has been a general policy allowing the conversion of non-tradable shares into tradable shares provided that the board of the companies and the public shareholders approve the deal. The conversion of non-tradable shares has important implications on Chinese corporate governance issue, and on the further growth of the stock market. As non-tradable shares, including state shares, represent the majority control rights, sales of these non-tradable shares signal to the market that the Chinese government no longer wants to retain control of the listed companies. This policy can potentially reduce the tension between major and minority shareholders and alleviate the conflict of interest issue. When all shares are tradable, the companies will be free to issue derivatives such as warrants and options.

Third, a rule has recently been implemented that requires approval from the majority of minority shareholders for key projects to be undertaken by firms. This policy allows the minority stockholders to have influence on corporate decisions with the goal of mitigating the conflict between majority and minority stockholders that has been prevalent in Chinese firms. The new rule can potentially change the dynamics of corporate governance, providing valuable experiences to firms around the world.

Finally, the Qualified Financial Institutional Investor (QFII) programs were launched in December 2002. Foreign institutional investors can now invest in the A-share market, which had been off limits to them before. As QFIIs have more experience and better skills for screening stocks and making investments, they will exert pressures on domestic firms for better performance. At the same time, their investments will likely boost the Chinese stock market. The Chinese government initially allows QFIIs to have a quota of $4 billion for their Chinese investment. As of late 2005, the Chinese government has doubled the stock quota to about $10 billion for foreign investors in order to stimulate the stock markets.

The Over-the-Counter Stock Markets

In the late 1990s and early 2000s, the government was prepared to set up a NASDAQ-type over-the-counter stock market under the Shenzhen Stock Exchange that would have allowed high-tech companies to be listed to raise equity capital with relaxed listing requirements. The proposed market, called 'the second board' by investors, was intially named the Growth Enterprise Board in May 2000. However, the preparation work was halted by the authorities in light of the ensuing market crash of the NASDAQ and other regional growth-oriented stock markets.

The preparation for the new board resumed in early 2004. On 17 May 2004, the CSRC issued the Implementation Scheme of the Establishment of the Small- and Medium-Enterprise Block (SMEB) in the Shenzhen Stock Exchange. On 27 May 2004, the SMEB was formally launched. It was deemed widely as the beginning of the second board in Chinese stock market history. The SMEB was meant to be a component of the main board but it allows high-growth and high-tech companies to be listed.

As of December 2005, 50 companies had been approved to go public and get listed on the SMEB. About 80 percent of these firms are privately-held and the rest state-owned. The SMEB basically followed the strict listing requirements of the main board with few information technology companies (for example, dot-com's) listed. Many listed companies are from the traditional industries such as pharmacy, utilities, appliances and machinery.

All companies listed on the SMEB have tradable shares after converting all non-tradable shares into tradable shares by December 2005. The announcements of the policy change of conversion appeared to have a positive effect on the market in general. When the SMEB index was first compiled and released on 1 December 2005, it was 43.9 percent higher than the base date of 7 June 2005. The price appreciation indicated the market optimism for the SMEB in light of all the listed stocks having resolved the stock circulation problem. The complete conversion of non-tradable shares to tradable shares in this market section ahead of the main board also suggested that the authorities were willing to allow the SMEB to experiment new reform measures, which might help it develop into a NASDAQ-type second board with relaxed listing requirements in the future.

By comparison, the second board has not materialized yet to become a similar market to NASDAQ in the US. There is actually a 'third board' in China's stock markets (Wang 2005). Its official name is 'the Proxy Shares Exchange System', which was set up on 16 July 2001 and traded ten stocks as of late 2005. These ten stocks are mostly stocks de-listed from the main board. If any stock on the third board is able to meet the listing requirements again, it will be transferred back to the main board. As such, this third board serves as an essential component of the delisting mechanism in China's stock markets (similar to the bulletin board in the US). On the other hand, this third board is truly an over-the-counter stock market, because it only exists among six securities brokerage firms – Shenyin

Wanguo, Guotai Junan, Dapeng, Guoxin, Liaoning and Minfa. Investors can open a non-listed shares exchange account and trade these shares in any one of the 318 branches of the six brokerage firms. Although this third board is not related to financing technology firms, it does provide valuable experience in conducting over-the-counter trading on a separate stock trading system in China's stock markets.

In 2003, China also established a new equity exchange called the China Technology and Equity Exchange (CTEE) in Zhonguancun, Beijing (see Fung and Liu 2006). The market is primarily developed for high-tech firms because Zhonguancun, also known as 'China's Silicon Valley', is the location of many technology companies. In this market, some special types of securities, including private equity and non-performing loans, were traded, adding another layer of flexibility to high-tech firms to finance their projects. The CTEE merged with the Beijing Equity and Assets Exchange in 2004 to form the China Beijing Equity Exchange in Beijing. The exchange serves as a major equity transaction platform for the transfer of ownership and assets among high-tech firms (*China Daily*, 5 April 2004, http://www.chinadaily.com.cn). Similarly, Shanghai also opened the Shanghai Technology Stock Exchange in the late 1990s, which provides similar functions for technology firms in Shanghai.

CHINA'S BOND MARKET

China's bond market primarily consists of an inter-bank market, an over-the-counter (OTC) market, and a stock exchange market. Government bonds are listed in three markets while corporate bonds are mainly traded on the stock exchanges. The regulations and trading of the two markets differ, causing market segmentation in terms of non-uniform liquidity and pricing. Thus, there is a need to unify the two markets for future development.

The inter-bank market involves over-the-counter transactions among banks, institutional investors, enterprises and individual investors. Participating banks use the inter-bank market to adjust liquidity and asset structures, while the People's Bank of China (PBOC), the central bank, conducts open market operations for monetary policies in this market.

There are spot and repurchase transactions in the inter-bank market. Generally speaking, the repurchase transactions are more active than the spot transactions. Bond repurchase is a short term financing method involving both parties of the transaction taking bonds as pledges. The borrower (the repurchaser) agrees with the lender to return the borrowed funds as specified in the agreement to the lender (counter repurchaser) who will return the pledged bonds as collaterals to the borrower on a certain day in the future. Spot transaction involves the transfer of bond ownership based on an agreed-upon price.

Corporate bonds can be categorized into general corporate bonds and convertible bonds. They are listed and traded on the two stock exchanges (Shanghai and Shenzhen Stock Exchanges). The Ministry of Finance issues treasury bonds in either market or in both markets simultaneously. Joint venture companies in which foreign firms have partial ownership can engage in securities investment and fund management, and thus they can trade either Chinese government or corporate bonds.

Treasury and Corporate Bonds

Table I.2 shows the distribution of different types of bonds in China and other Asian countries. Several implications are noteworthy. First, the growth of China's bond market has been impressive. The growth rate was around 25 percent per year from 1997 to 2003, higher than those of Korea and Singapore, and only lower than that of Thailand. Second, the size of the Chinese bond market, which is about 31.3 percent of the GDP, is still the lowest percentage among all Asian countries in question. Korea's bond

Table I.2 Sizes of local currency bond markets

	Annual growth rate (%) 1997–2003	Amount in 2003	
		$ billion	% GDP
China	**24.8**	**440.4**	**31.3**
Government	27.3	287.4	20.4
Corporate	11.6	12.2	0.9
Financial Institutions	22.0	140.8	10.0
Korea	**22.7**	**445.7**	**73.6**
Government	30.3	124.3	20.5
Corporate	19.8	157.3	26.0
Financial Institutions	21.2	164.1	27.1
Singapore	**18.9**	**67.2**	**73.6**
Government	19.0	37.1	40.6
Corporate & Fin Inst.	18.8	30.1	33.0
Thailand	**35.2**	**58.4**	**40.7**
Government	116.3	30.7	21.4
Corporate	13.5	19.3	13.5
Financial Institutions	83.0	8.4	5.8

Source: *Asia Bond Monitor*, November 2004, Asian Development Bank (http://asianbonds online adb.org).

market is about 73.6 percent of its GDP, while Singapore is also 73.6 percent, more than double the percentage in China. Third, the corporate bonds in China account for 0.9 percent of GDP, which is by far the lowest and points to an underdeveloped corporate bond market. In contrast, the corporate bond markets are 26.0 percent of GDP in Korea and 33.0 percent in Singapore. Currently, the interest in the convertible bond market has been growing rapidly and it has the potential to become a major component of China's bond market in the future.

Bonds from financial institutions (10 percent of GDP) and Treasury bonds (20.4 percent) were the key components of the Chinese bond market in 2003. Financial institution bonds in China are called F-bonds. There are two main kinds of financial institution bonds: policy financial institution bonds (policy F-bond) and special financial institution bonds (special F-bond) for special financial needs. Policy F-bonds are issued by three policy banks, which are State Development Bank, China Export-Import Bank and China Agricultural Development Bank. These bonds are used by the Chinese government to help carry out monetary policies. In comparison, special financial institution bonds include investment fund bonds, trust income securities, certificate of deposits and bonds issued by the Ministry of Finance. Investment fund bonds were issued by state-owned investment companies to support key construction projects but they had been stopped by 1992. The Ministry of Finance issues different types of bonds such as Special Purchase bonds, Price Index Bonds and Special Bonds for different purposes.

Treasury bonds can be grouped into four categories: (a) book-entry bonds, which are paperless with lower administration costs; (b) paper-face T-bond, traded on both the OTC market and the exchanges; (c) voucher T-bonds or saving bonds for owners; and (d) Special Purchase bonds for pension funds and insurance funds (Zhang and Liu 2001).

The challenges in reforming China's bond market are many-fold. First, China needs to develop a sound legal and regulatory framework for bond issues that define property rights for investors. This framework would include the standardization of bond issues in both stock exchanges and the OTC market. Second, there is an urgent need to improve the bond issuing process and pricing mechanism. As of late 2005, there are various offering processes such as open auction and syndicated underwriting. The Chinese government has to evaluate the merits of each option and provide related rules to avoid potential pricing problems. Third, the government needs to stimulate investor demand for bonds. Currently, QFIIs are allowed to invest in the convertible bond and Treasury bond markets, which will help increase bond demands. But better transparency is needed for bond issues and bond ratings to promote investor confidence and demand in the market. Finally, for economies of scale purposes, it is desirable to promote regional cooperation among Asian countries to develop regional bond markets. But apparently, the denomination currency is an issue to be resolved as there is no consensus right now as to which currency should be used as the benchmark.

Panda Bonds and Foreign Investors

On 18 February 2005, the PBOC, Ministry of Finance, National Development and Reform Commission, and CSRC jointly issued the *Provisional Measures for the Administration of Renminbi-Denominated Bonds* in China's domestic market. The measures require the international development institutions that want to issues renminbi bonds in China to have: (a) double A or better credit ranking; and (b) more than US$1 billion in loans and equity investments in China.

There are restrictions on handling the bond yield, proceeds and interest. The bond issuer will set the interest rate of these bonds based on the prevailing yield of the Chinese bonds verified by the PBOC. The proceeds of the bond issue cannot be converted into foreign exchange for remittance out of China. In addition, the funds should be used for medium or long-term asset loans or equity investment for construction projects in China.

The Ministry of Finance has approved several international institutions to operate in the market, including the International Finance Corporation of the World Bank, Asian Development Bank, and the Japan Bank for International Cooperation. Underwriting and distribution of the bonds are to be handled solely by domestic Chinese firms.

The Asian Development Bank (ADB), based in Manila, has launched renminbi-denominated bonds, called Panda Bonds, in the interbank market through a syndicate of underwriters with the Bank of China serving as the lead manager. The ADB has Triple A ratings by Fitch, Moody's and S&P and thus can provide domestic investors the highest quality investment opportunities, and standard international services and practices. The sale of domestic-currency bonds by a foreign multilateral institution signals to the market the level of maturity of China's capital market. The nickname for the bonds, panda, is similar to the US dollar denominated 'dragon bonds' that were sold around Asia during the 1990s.

The QFII program came into effect on 1 December 2002. Since then, foreign investors are allowed to purchase China's T-bonds through the QFIIs. In addition, in May 2005, the PBOC allowed the first foreign institutional investor, the Pan-Asia Bond Index Fund (PAIF), to participate in the interbank bond market. If more foreign institutions are allowed to enter this market, the interbank market is expected to grow rapidly.

Future Bond Market Development

China's bond forward market started trading in June, 2005. This represents a positive first step toward the development of financial derivatives markets. It would help traders to hedge risks and improve liquidity in the bond markets. The forward market will also provide a pricing discovery function for the bonds and help form a market-oriented bond pricing system.

Following a 1995 bond futures trading scandal, China closed down its bond futures market and barred the trade of financial derivatives, limiting China's exchanges to handling futures based on commodities. In light of the T-bond futures experience, the regulator has issued strict rules on margins and delivery to minimize the default risk of the forward contracts. For instance, the rules for the forward trade limit the contract terms to no more than 365 days and limit the funds for net purchases by market participants to the buyers' existing managed assets, working capital or net assets in order to prevent default.

FINANCIAL INSTITUTIONS

Domestic Institutions

Three types of financial institutions in China are important and they have played an important role in the development of the capital markets since the early 1990s. They are banks, insurance companies, and securities firms. We will discuss each one briefly in the following sections and the subsequent chapters will provide more details about these financial intermediaries.

The banking industry

Chinese banks have received much attention because of their monopolistic characteristics and colossal non-performing loans resulting from policy loans under the central-planning economic system. China's four big state banks, the Bank of China, China Construction Bank, Industrial and Commercial Bank of China, and Agricultural Bank of China, account for 57 percent of all corporate loans, which go mostly to state enterprises and have a bad debt ratio of approximately 10 percent (*Business Week*, 22/29 August 2005).

The Chinese banking structure includes: (a) the four big state banks discussed above; (b) three state policy banks (the State Development Bank, China Export-Import Credit Bank, and China Agricultural Development Bank); (c) shareholding banks; (d) city commercial banks; (e) rural banks; and (f) foreign banks.

The Chinese government has created four asset management companies corresponding to the four state banks respectively to deal with the non-performing loan problem. The Great Wall asset management company was set up for the Agricultural Bank of China, Dongfang asset management company for the Bank of China, Cinda asset management company for China Construction Bank, and the Huarong asset management company for the Industrial and Commercial Bank of China (Fung and Liu 2006).

Table I.3 reports the aggregate assets and liabilities for four major types of banking institutions in China. Panel A shows that the debt ratio (total debt to total asset) of the banking institutions on average was about 96 percent in 2003–2004, indicating the capital adequacy ratio in China is well below the global standard rate of 8 percent, as specified by the International Basel Standards for banks. Thus the Chinese banks may not be able to provide adequate capital protection for depositors. Similar patterns of inadequate equity capital persist across all four types of banks (state-owned banks, joint stock commercial banks, city commercial banks and other banking institutions, including rural credit operatives and postal savings).

Panel B of Table I.3 shows the amount of non-performing loans purchased by the four asset management corporations (AMCs) in 2004. The four AMCs have purchased over US$150 billion of non-performing assets from the four big banks. The average cash recovery ratio for four AMCs is about 20 percent while the disposal ratio is about 54 percent.

Despite the large non-performing loans in the banking sector, it appears that the banking sector is not threatening the stability of the Chinese economy given the ability of the government to issue more bonds in case of emergency. In addition, Chinese government plans to privatize some state banks so that they can raise more new equity capital.

The important challenges for the Chinese banks are to manage the assets and loans efficiently (that is to mitigate the non-performing loans problems and maintain healthy profit margins) and at the same time compete effectively with the foreign banks after entry barriers to the Chinese market will be removed after 2006 in accordance with the WTO entrance agreements. In addition, Chinese banks have to cope with new technologies such as credit card processing, credit analysis, internet banking and the development of a mortgage backed securities market.

The insurance industry

As the insurance industry is an important component of China's capital market, it used to be protected by the Chinese government and shielded from foreign competition. However, as a WTO member, China has to open its domestic market doors for foreign insurers. It is conceivable that the

Table I.3 Banking institutions

Panel A: Assets (Liabilities) of China's domestic banking institutions (billion yuan)

	2003	2004
All banking institutions	27.6	31.6
	(26.6)	(30.3)
Debt/asset	96%	95.9%
State-owned banks	15.2	16.9
	(14.6)	(16.2)
JSCBs	3.8	4.7
	(3.7)	(4.5)
City commercial banks	1.5	1.7
	(1.4)	(1.6)
Other banking institutions	7.3	8.3
	(7.0)	(7.9)

Note: The banking institutions include policy banks, state-owned commercial banks (four big banks), joint stock commercial banks (JSCBs), city commercial banks, and other banking institutions (rural commercial banks, urban credit cooperatives, rural credit cooperatives, postal savings, foreign banks and non-bank financial institutions).

Panel B: Non-performing loans of four Asset Management Corporations (AMC), 2004 (US$ billion, using 1US$ = 8.27 yuan)

	Non-performing assets purchased	Total disposal	Cash recovered
Huarong	43.39	25.34	5.00
Great Wall	41.00	25.38	2.61
Dongfang	30.52	12.64	2.82
Cinda	37.35	18.27	6.14
Total	150.06	63.93	16.57
Average recovery ratio		53.96%	20.29%

Note: Disposal recovery ratio = disposal/asset purchased; Cash discovery ratio = cash recovered/total disposal.

Source: China Banking Regulatory Commissions, http://www.cbrc.gov.cn

insurance industry will undergo substantial changes as more foreign insurance companies enter the domestic market.

Table I.4, Panel A, shows the operating performance of China's insurance industry. Insurance premiums received have been increasing over

Table I.4 China's insurance industry

Panel A: Operating performance (in billion yuan)

	2000	2001	2002	2003	2004
Premiums	**159.6**	**210.9**	**305.3**	**388.0**	**431.8**
Property and casualty	59.8	68.5	77.8	86.9	109.0
Life and health	99.7	142.4	227.4	301.1	322.8
Compensation	**52.7**	**59.8**	**70.7**	**84.1**	**100.4**
Property and casualty	30.6	33.3	40.5	47.6	56.8
Life and health	22.1	26.5	30.2	36.5	43.7
Business expenses	21.7	25.8	31.4	36.1	43.6
Bank deposits	123.5	193.1	302.6	455.0	496.9
Investments	**130.3**	**171.3**	**250.4**	**382.9**	**571.2**
T-bonds	95.6	79.6	110.8	140.7	265.2
Investment funds	13.4	20.9	30.8	46.3	67.3
Total assets	337.4	459.1	649.4	912.3	118.5
Pre-tax profits	*85.2*	*125.3*	*203.2*	*267.8*	*287.8*

Note: Pre-tax Profits = Premiums – Compensation – Business Expenses.

Panel B: Structure of Insurance Industry, December 2005

	No. of companies
Domestic insurers	44
Foreign invested insurers	41
Foreign insurance representative offices	188
Joint venture companies	271

Source: China Insurance Regulatory Commission, http://www.circ.gov.cn/assay

time. In 2004, the total insurance premium has reached 431 billion yuan as compared to 159.6 billion yuan in 2000, with an average annual growth rate of 42.6 percent. In particular, life and health insurance premiums rise faster than property and casualty premiums, reflecting the fast-growing concerns for individual well-being among Chinese consumers.

Most of the insurance companies have invested their premium in Treasury bonds and investment funds. With more premium received and a relatively slow rate of compensation, the Chinese insurance industry is making healthy profits. The pre-tax profits were 287.8 billion yuan in 2004, more than triple the 85.2 billion yuan in 2000.

Table I.5 The number of securities and futures intermediaries

	2000	2001	2002	2003
Securities companies	100	109	127	133
Fund management companies	10	15	21	34
Futures brokerage houses	178	200	179	186
Investment advising firms	143	137	167	111

Source: *China Securities Regulatory Commission*, April 2004.

The total number of domestic insurance companies is small, 44 as of the end of 2005. Although the number of foreign invested insurance is only 41, there are a large number of joint venture insurance companies (271). Although China will still not allow foreign insurance companies to set up wholly-owned branches, their presence will inevitably grow as China gradually relaxes its restrictive policies.

The securities industry

The number of securities firms is relatively small in China. Table I.5 shows that the number of securities companies stands at 133 in 2003 as compared to 100 in 2000. This result reflects China's tight control on its securities industry, and the industry's monopolistic status. Investment advising firms dropped to 111 in 2003 from 143 in 2000. This downward trend coincides with the disappointing performance of China's stock market in recent years after the Asian financial crisis. And fund management companies grew from 10 to 34, reflecting growing interest among investors in professionally-managed funds in a bearish market.

Regarding the reforms of the securities industry, the Chinese government has implemented two new measures to revitalize the industry, which has been plagued by liquidity problems and bankruptcy threats. First, the government has injected capital into the ailing securities firms with liquidity problems. Many local securities brokerage firms have suffered heavy losses because they offered guarantees for high returns to investors, which proved to be impossible to honor when the stock market fell consistently for eight years in the wake of the Asian financial crisis. If the securities firms' liquidity becomes a concern among investors, there will be credibility problems in the financial markets which will further depress stock market performance. Injecting a huge amount of capital into the brokerage firms will prop up the confidence of Chinese investors and help boost the stock markets. As the first stage of a broad package of government support for the securities industry, the PBOC provided loans to Shenyin & Wanguo Securities and Huaan Securities in mid-2005 (*Financial Times*, 14 June 2005).

Second, under the new rules, at the end of December 2005, foreign ownership limit in fund management firms was raised from 33 percent to 49 percent. Chinese regulators have started approving fund management ventures between commercial banks, such as the Industrial and Commercial Bank of China's joint venture with Credit Suisse Frist Boston. The new rules were aimed to increase competition and make existing fund management firms, local or joint ventures, more streamlined and effective in meeting investor needs.

Globalization

China's financial industry has been subject to global forces in various aspects. In accordance with the WTO requirements, China has to open up to global competition by allowing foreign banks, brokerage firms and insurance companies to operate in China. Second, China has also implemented rules such as the QFII program to speed up financial reforms. Third, privatization of the banks and joint ventures of the brokerage firms lead to changes in Chinese financial industries.

In addition, the China Insurance Regulatory Commission (CIRC) allowed local insurance companies to invest their foreign currency in common stocks listed on overseas exchanges that are deemed to be mature. Initially, insurance companies will be allowed to invest only in Chinese company stocks listed abroad, but the restriction could be relaxed, depending on the insurers' management capability and international stock market environment. Chinese insurers hold an estimated $10 billion in foreign currencies. There are restrictions for these equity investments – insurers are required to use less than 10 percent of the total foreign exchange investment quota allotted by regulators to invest in overseas Chinese company stocks, with the rest invested in various types of bonds (*Wall Street Journal*, 20 June 2005).

THE FOREIGN EXCHANGE MARKET

China adopted a managed exchange rate regime in 1994, allowing the exchange rates to fluctuate within a tight range. The yuan's exchange rate has been pegged to the US dollar with $US1 to 8.28 yuan. In July 2005, China allowed its currency to appreciate 2.1 percent in value in light of the pressures from the US and other Western countries. Since then, China has linked its currency to a basket of currencies that are closely tied to its international trade.

Although under the QFII program, investors can repatriate their profits and capital back to their home countries, China still maintains tight control on its capital account. When foreign investors trade with China, they get their renminbi earnings in other tradable currencies.

A new development of the Chinese currency has taken place between China and Hong Kong recently. Banks in Hong Kong allow deposits of Chinese currencies and credit cards in Chinese currencies. At the same time, Chinese currencies can be freely converted into Hong Kong dollars. This development basically allows partial float of the Chinese currency because Hong Kong dollars are freely converted into other currencies. In addition, some Southeast Asian countries such as Singapore, Thailand and Laos, have widely accepted Chinese currencies for business transactions.

Offshore trading on Chinese currencies has been growing in recent years. In light of the unconvertible Chinese currencies, derivatives such as non-deliverable forward contracts and currency options have been developed (Fung *et al.* 2004). The continual liberalization of the foreign exchange market in China and off-shore market trading will inevitably speed up the reforms in China's foreign exchange system.

FUTURES MARKETS

The first commodity futures market in China was the Zhengzhou Grain Wholesale Market, which introduced its first futures contract in October 1990. Between 1990 and 1993, there were about 50 futures exchanges in China, marked by a period of huge speculation and chaos. In 1994, the CSRC restructured the futures markets and reorganized all futures exchanges into three futures markets. They are Shanghai Futures Exchange (SHFE), Zhengzhou Commodity Exchange (ZCE) and Dalian Commodity Exchange (DCE). Apparently, the standardization and integration of the futures market create more uniform rules and healthy practices in the industry.

Transactions in overseas futures contracts by Chinese firms are possible, but they have to be first approved by both State Council and CSRC. The regulation stipulates that this overseas trading must be used for hedging purposes only. The goal is to preempt the speculation motive. However, some Chinese firms have violated the rule and thus created news in the financial markets.

During the development of the Chinese futures markets in the early 1990s, Chinese officials solicited advice from the Chicago Board of Trade (CBOT) executives to help set up its first futures exchange (Williams *et al.* 1998). Instead of the open outcry system in CBOT, China adopted an electronic trading system, which appeared to be more transparent and appropriate for China.

In the literature, several studies have examined the behavior of futures markets in China (see Chan *et al.* 2004). Two aspects regarding the development of China's futures markets should be noted. First, it seems that government plays a critical role in developing the futures market by Chinese government, such as information disclosure. Second, the Chinese futures markets will emulate the developed financial markets over time. For example, Fung *et al.* (2003) investigate the pricing patterns of information flows for three commodity futures: copper, soybeans, and wheat traded in US and Chinese markets. The US futures market seems to play a dominant role in transmitting information to the Chinese market for two commodities (copper and soybeans) that are subject to less government regulation and fewer import restrictions in China. The heavily regulated and subsidized wheat commodity futures contracts are highly segmented in pricing, although there is some information transmission via volatility spillover across markets.

In Chan *et al.* (2004), they examine the intraday volatility of four futures contracts (copper, mungbeans, soybeans, and wheat) in China. They find that negative returns have more of an effect on volatility than positive returns do, while volume is positively related to volatility; open interest is negatively related to volatility. The large volume traders' participation is also positively related to volatility. The strong relationship of volatility to open interest, volume, and returns is more pronounced in recent periods than earlier periods. The volatility behavior of the Chinese futures market is quite similar to the developed financial market in the more recent period, a result indicating maturity of the market. The reason is likely due to the government policies that make the futures market more transparent through more information disclosure to the market.

The future development of China's futures may need to launch more commodity oriented futures contracts as China still has a large agricultural sector, where hedging against price fluctuations is important. In addition, China has become a key importer of metals such as copper and iron, as well as petroleum. Development of these futures markets would help prepare China for large price shocks. Historically, China once had the T-bond futures market, which was stopped in the late 1990s. Given the development of the T-bond market in recent years, it is important to reopen the T-bond futures market to benefit the growth of the T-bond market.

RISK MANAGEMENT

As China evolves from a central-planning economy to a market economy, we find that many concepts related to market risks are new to the institutions and practitioners. Without proper measures to avoid market price volatility resulting from speculation and noise, various market participants, including investors, firms and the government, may incur substantial losses. Therefore, it is important for the Chinese government to implement policies to help develop sound risk management practices among Chinese companies and financial intermediaries.

Various events illuminate the problems China has been facing in its financial reforms. For example, the Treasury bond futures market began trading on the Shanghai Stock Exchange in 1993. On 23 February 1995, the trading volume of the T-bond futures surged ten times to 100 billion yuan with the falling spot prices because short positions piled up. After a series of scandals and speculative trading, the CSRC closed down the T-bond futures market (Poon *et al.* 1998).

In December 2004, five executives of China Aviation Oil, a state-owned company, were arrested after its Singapore branch recorded losses of $554 million in speculative oil derivatives trading. Although the Chinese government has rules on derivatives trading, these rules were obviously not properly enforced and implemented.

In November 2005, Liu Qibing, a trader for China's State Reserve Bureau (SRB) had accumulated massive short positions in copper on the London Metal Exchange (LME). The short-selling (sales of copper, he did not own, in hopes of buying it back later at a lower price) has left China short of copper by some 100 000–200 000 tonnes (*The Economist*, 18 November 2005).

Problems at China's securities brokerages have been a major obstacle to the development of the capital markets. About 90 percent of the securities firms are believed to be losing money and many have inadequate equity capital. In addition, the industry uses a mixture of reckless proprietary trading and poor risk management practices, which inevitably led to heavy losses. Securities firms lost about $1.8 billion in 2004 (*Financial Times*, 18 November 2005).

In light of the ever-increasing market volatility, the Chinese government needs to implement policies to encourage Chinese firms to adopt good risk management practices. As a first step, CSRC, China's capital markets regulator, has allowed 31 companies to trade foreign financial derivatives to hedge their exposure in commodity prices.

Another important aspect of risk management in the financial sector, to a large extent, depends on rules and laws governing the operations of financial firms and how these rules and laws are implemented. A sound regulatory framework of the capital market is critical in the future development of China's capital market. At the same time, China will have to balance and safeguard the national interests of the financial services sectors in light of external shocks and its WTO commitments to removing restrictive barriers to help the economy.

CONCLUDING REMARKS

This chapter introduces and examines the development and challenges in China's capital markets. It serves as a building block for the following chapters on various aspects of China's capital markets such as stock market, bond market, financial intermediations, foreign exchange market and futures markets. As China's capital market emerges, it shares many characteristics with other emerging financial markets. Our analysis echoes the review study of Chan *et al.* (2006), which discusses various underlying factors in the development and growth of China's capital market.

In this chapter, we present a broad perspective on the overall development of China's capital market and compare it with some other emerging markets. China's capital market faces tremendous challenges during the development stage and it will continue to evolve over time. It serves as an interesting experiment for other emerging markets to evaluate. The limited growth in China's bond market and its future development also present us with interesting lessons to be learned. Certain issues deserve further review, such as how to balance the T-bond market with the corporate bond markets, and what types of futures markets should be developed.

Determining the proper roles financial intermediaries should play in an emerging market requires a deeper understanding of finance theories. China's reforms of its capital market and financial industries through a trial-and-error approach provide a unique learning opportunity for finance researchers. It is an important experiment that financial economists cannot ignore.

ACKNOWLEDGMENT

We thank Jennifer Dennis for editorial assistance.

REFERENCES

Chan, Kam, C., H. G. Fung and W. K. Leung (2004), 'Intraday volatility behavior in Chinese futures markets', *Journal of International Financial Markets, Institutions, and Money*, **14**, 491–505.

Chan, Kam, C., H. G. Fung and Samanta Thapa (forthcoming), 'China financial research: a review and synthesis', *International Review of Economics and Finance.*

China Securities Regulatory Commission (2004), 'China's securities and futures markets', working paper, April.

Fung, H. G., W. K. Leung and X. E. Xu (2003), 'Information flows between the US and China commodity futures trading', *Review of Quantitative Finance and Accounting*, **21**, 267–85.

Fung, H. G., W. K. Leung and J. Zhu (2004), 'Non-deliverable forward market for Chinese RMB: a first look', *China Economic Review*, **15**(3), 348–52.

Fung, Hung-Gay and Qingfeng Liu (2006), 'China's financial reform in banking and securities markets', in H. G. Fung, C. H. Pei and Kevin Zhang (eds), *China and the Challenge of Economic Globalization: The Impact of WTO Membership*, New York: M. E. Sharpe, pp. 145–63.

Fung, Hung-Gay, Wai Lee and W. K. Leung (2000), 'Segmentation of the A- and B-share Chinese equity markets', *Journal of Financial Research*, **23**, 178–95.

Huang, A. G. and H. G. Fung (2004), 'Stock ownership segmentation, floatability and constraints on investment banking in China', *China and World Economy*, **12**(2), 66–78.

Ling, Teresa and Jot Yau (2005), 'China' state share reform and exchange traded funds', *China and World Economy*, **13**(16), 52–65.

Poon, Winnie, Michael Firth and Hung-Gay Fung (1998), 'The spillover effects of the trading suspension of the treasury bond futures markets in China', *Journal of International Financial Markets, Institutions, and Money*, **8**, 205–18.

Wang, Li (2005), *A Guide to Listing on and Investment in the Small- and Medium-Enterprise Board*, Beijing: The China Machine Press.

Williams, Jeffrey, Anne Peck, Albert Park and Scott Rozelle (1998), 'The emergence of a futures market: mungbeans on the China Zhengzhou Commodity Exchange', *Journal of Futures Markets*, **18**(4), 427–48.

Xu, Xiaoqing (2005), 'Performance of securities investment funds in China', *Emerging Markets Finance and Trade*, **41**(5), 27–42.

Zhang, Mingli and Hui Liu (2001), 'People's Republic of China', in Yun-Hwan Kim (ed.), *Government Bond Market Development in Asia*, Manila: Asian Development Bank, Chapter 5.

PART I

Financial markets

1. Chinese stock market: perspectives in institutional structure, regulations and performance

Kam C. Chan, Hung-gay Fung and Julia S. Kwok

INTRODUCTION

To facilitate economic reforms and to help state-owned enterprise raising capital, China began its capital market reform in the late 1980s. A big step taken was to launch its two stock exchanges (Shanghai Stock Exchange and Shenzhen Stock Exchange) and allowed state-owned enterprises to have their shares listed on two stock exchanges. Shanghai Stock Exchange was founded on 26 November 1990 and Shenzhen Stock Exchange was officially established later on 1 December 1990. Over 15 years, the Chinese stock markets came a long way. By 2001, the total market capitalization of Chinese stock markets was ranked second in Asia (Jingu 2002, p. 3).

There are many events and policy changes throughout the economic reforms. We present some of these major events and changes in Appendix 1.1. These events and policy changes reflect the development of an equity market in China and they offer valuable lessons and policies for China and other emerging markets. While there have been a number of studies on Chinese stock markets in recent years, the discussion of institutional structure and regulations in the Chinese stock market is rather limited. This chapter will shed some lights on China's institutional structure and regulations. Moreover, the Chinese stock market experienced a downturn beginning in the early 2000s. We also offer some discussions and examine how the Chinese government reacts to the recent poor performance of its stock market.

INSTITUTIONAL STRUCTURE

Types of Shares

Not surprisingly, the Chinese government was cautious with its new stock market in early 1990. From the start, China imposed ownership restrictions on the publicly traded companies using different classes of shares. In general, Chinese publicly traded companies currently have two classes of shares: tradable and non-tradable shares. For non-tradable shares, the shareholders are provinces, cities, or central government. Typically, the non-tradable shares constitute a minimum of two-thirds of the ownership of the companies. The non-tradable shares allow the government to continue maintaining ownership control of the companies. Non-tradable shares are also called state-owned shares or 'legal person' shares. Because non-tradable shares are not circulated among the public, there are few studies done on the pricing behavior of the value of these shares. These non-tradable shares typically changed hands among government entities at a discount from the market price (Huang and Fung 2004).

For tradable shares, there are four types of shares to be issued to the public: A- shares, B-shares, H-shares and N-shares. Originally, the A-share market trades the shares of Chinese companies limited to domestic Chinese investors. Started in May 2000, foreign investors are allowed to participate gradually in the A-share market. The B-share market is for shares of Chinese companies traded on the exchange and they are issued to foreign investors or for Chinese investors who have foreign currencies (US or Hong Kong dollars). H-shares are shares of Chinese companies traded on the Hong Kong stock exchange and thus these companies need to satisfy the listing requirements of the Hong Kong Stock Exchange. N-shares are shares traded in the US stock exchanges, including the NYSE and the NASDAQ. Chinese companies issue B-shares, H-shares, and N-shares to foreign investors in order to raise foreign capital. There are a number of studies on A-shares, the relation between A-shares and B-shares, A-shares and H-shares (for example Chan *et al.* 2001; Chan *et al.* 2004; Chong and Su 2006) and few studies are on N-shares. From the perspectives of market capitalization, A- shares have the largest market, and hence, it is apparently the most important component of the Chinese stock market system.

Shares of some Chinese companies in Hong Kong are also called 'red-chips'. These companies have close ties with mainland operations and companies, but they are registered in Hong Kong for their operations. These Chinese companies satisfy the listing requirements of the Hong Kong Stock Exchange for listing their shares to be traded in Hong Kong. The 'red-chips', while they are de facto Chinese companies, are legally Hong

Kong companies. Given the development of qualified domestic institutional investors (QDII), there will be more Chinese companies setting up their offices in Hong Kong and elsewhere (in the US or other nations), it seems clear that more Chinese companies will list their shares overseas similar to red-chips.

Listing and Raising Additional Capital Requirements

In terms of listing requirements, both Shanghai and Shenzhen Stock Exchanges establish the procedures that are comparable with other emerging equity markets. As of January 2006, the listing requirements are:[1]

- IPO granted by the China Securities Regulatory Commission;
- a minimum three-year operating history;
- positive earnings in each of the past three years;
- public holding of no less than 25 percent;
- gross capital stock of 50 million shares; and
- good credit records in the past three years.

The listing requirements bring along some issues. Specifically, the 'positive earnings' requirement leads to a wide spread earnings management phenomenon among companies that apply for IPOs (initial public offerings). For IPO-applying companies, in order to meet or exceed the listing requirements, they often engage in earnings management so as to put together a betting listing application package. To study the widespread earnings management phenomenon, Haw *et al.* (2005) examine a sample of the IPO application firms during 1996–1998. They find that managers manipulate transactions to generate positive returns on equity (ROE) of their companies so as to meet the listing regulation of three consecutive year positive earnings requirement. Interestingly, Haw *et al.* also find that companies with denied-IPO applications had more aggressive earnings management practices than the approved-IPO companies. On one hand, the listing requirements unintentionally encourage companies to engage in earnings management. On the other hand, it appears that the Chinese regulatory authority is also able to exercise some rational adjustments to the earnings manipulations (Haw *et al.* 2005, p. 94). Nonetheless, Chi and Padgett (2006) and Chen *et al.* (2006) find that the post-IPO operating performance of the newly listed firms, on average, are poor. The poor post-IPO operating performance is no surprise given the widespread earnings management practices.

Before 2000, most of the listed companies used rights offerings to raise additional capital (Fung *et al.* 2006). Originally, rights offerings require successive three-year ROEs of 10 percent on average before they are allowed to apply for rights offering. The latest regulation was in 1999 and companies cannot have additional shares issued more than 30 percent of the outstanding shares. Starting in 2000, seasoned equity offering began to pick up as restrictions for additional equity financing are lifted.

Trading Mechanism

In terms of trading mechanism, the stock exchanges in China are modern and use neither dealers nor market makers. The stock trading is order-driven and fully automated with electronic trading. Both Exchanges are able to handle high volume. Shenzhen Stock Exchange uses a computer system that can handle 20 millions transactions in any given day.[2] For Shanghai Stock Exchange, its computer system is able to process 60 million transactions each day.[3] According to Areddy (2006), Shanghai Stock Exchange is upgrading its new trading system so that the system can potentially handle an array of financial products such as options, futures, and other derivatives in addition to stock trading. Similar to other emerging markets, there is a daily price limit, which currently is 10 percent for common stocks in a given trading day.[4]

The trading hours are 9:30–11:30 a.m. and 1:00–3:00 p.m. Settlement period is $T+1$ for securities traded in the local currency and $T+3$ for B-shares. Both Exchanges impose a 0.1 percent stamp duty, 0.1 percent of transaction processing fee, and no more than 0.3 percent on the commission charged by brokerage firm on each transaction as of 31 December 2005.

REGULATIONS

Basics

Compared to other emerging equity markets, the Chinese stock market also features a pattern of heavy regulations, which is also a common characteristic of capital markets in socialist economies. The most updated version of the regulations was set in December 2003. There are eight major laws governing the stock market as of 8 December 2003:

- Company Law of the People's Republic of China;
- Securities Law of the People's Republic of China;
- Interim Measures for the Administration of Securities Investment Funds;

- Interim Measures for the Administration of Securities and Futures Investment Consultancy;
- Measures for the Administration of Stock Exchanges;
- Regulations of the State Council on Foreign Capital Stocks Listed in China by Joint-stock Companies;
- Special Regulations of the State Council Concerning Issuing and Listing of Shares Overseas by Company; and
- Circular of the State Council Concerning Further Strengthening the Administration of Share Issuance.

These regulations are initiated by the China Securities Regulatory Commission (CSRC) and State Council and are executed by the CSRC and respective stock exchanges. Regulations range from basic company regulations, brokerage firm operations, listing requirements to initial public offerings procedures and new product rules. To conserve space, we do not list every law and rule nor their details. Instead, we highlight some of the procedures in terms of executing these regulations by referring to the practices at Shenzhen Stock Exchange.[5] Shenzhen Stock Exchange has three dimensions of regulations, which consists of company listing compliance, market surveillance, and exchange member supervision.

First, for company listing compliance, the stock exchange requires listing companies meeting the initial listing requirements continuously. Specifically, if a company incurs operating losses for three consecutive years, the exchange will suspend the trading of its stocks for six months. With another six months of operating loss, the company is then delisted. In addition, the publicly traded company is required to disclose price-sensitive information in a timely manner including issues related to its financial integrity, corporate governance, and business developments. Its annual financial statements must be audited by certified public accountants. In early 2005, the CSRC also directed an obligated electronic voting system for when significant corporate issues that may create conflict of interest between majority and minority shareholders arises.

Second, the stock exchange also has a team of analysts examining any unusual price movement of listed companies. The stock watch team makes additional inquiries and files reports to CSRC for further action, if necessary.

Third, the stock exchange also regulates the licenced securities houses. For securities houses with at least RMB500 million capitals, they can engage in a full range of securities business. For smaller securities houses with less than RMB500 million capitals, they can only do brokerage business. To ensure the integrity of the security houses, the exchange conducts regular random inspection of its members to ensure financial health and integrity.

Consequences

By the book, these regulations are sound and the regulatory system is well designed. However, in terms of executions and implementation, the regulators continue to encounter regulatory debacles. Several high profile corporate scandals broke out that brought negative publicity to the stock market.[6] We conjecture that the regulators, perhaps lacking regulatory experiences in a stock market within a socialist economic system, are implementing piece-meal solutions instead of having a thorough long-term plan. Thus those marginal changes in regulations over time appear to be reactive instead of proactive. The reactive approach also reflects the attitude of 'groping the stones to cross the river', that is, a trial-and-error perspective in solving problems.

There were many regulatory changes during 1990–2005. While some changes reflect the equity market development, some changes, in fact, represent policy reversals in terms of tightening or relaxing the control of the stock market. Moreover, these reversals bring unintended consequences to the stock market. Because of numerous reversals, investors find it difficult to follow and that hinders stock market growth. The literature calls that phenomenon policy risk, which is defined as the incremental uncertainty of a firm's cash flows because of the changes in government policies and regulations, according to Lam *et al.* (2005) (for example Perotti 1995; Lam *et al.* forthcoming).

Lam *et al.* (2005) document 43 major occurrences of policy and regulation reversals. Their study shows that policy and regulations reversals in China, whether it is apparently negative, neutral, or positive news to the stock market, on average, drive down the stock prices of companies traded on the Chinese stock exchanges during the period of 1991–2005. Moreover, Lam *et al.* (2005) find that companies with a relative higher percentage of non-tradable shares tend to receive larger adverse impact on price changes. The research findings in Lam *et al.* (2005) expose the issue of having a large percentage of non-tradable shares among state-owned enterprises that issue publicly traded stocks. Apparently, the inherited non-tradable shares design is one of the major factors in contributing to poor corporate governance and inflexibilities in altering corporate strategic directions. The presence of non-tradable block-holders makes it difficult for firms to implement changes in response to fluctuations of market conditions. All this contributes to the recent poor stock market performance in China since 2001 (see Figure 1.1).

As part of the stock market regulatory reform, the Chinese government also gradually began to convert non-tradable shares into tradable shares in 2005. Converting non-tradable shares into tradable shares has several merits. First, the process lessens the government control of the companies and accelerates the state-owned enterprises' privatization process. Thus, it can result in better-managed publicly traded companies and consequently help overall equity market growth in China (see for example, Tong and Sun 2003). Second, converting non-tradable shares into more tradable shares help increase the stock ownership among the private investors and make the large (tradable) shareholders more difficult to enrich themselves through entrenching behavior. In terms of reducing agency costs and improving corporate governance, the process is a major step towards the right direction. Bai *et al.* (2004) find that high concentration of non-controlling shareholding and foreign investors holding are positively correlated with market valuation of the stock, a result supporting the conversion of non-tradable shares to tradable shares.

PERFORMANCE

Prices of A and B, and A and H Shares

China's different classes of common stock lead to stock market segmentation. A-share, B-share, H-share, and N-share all represent the same claims on a company's assets but they are trading on different prices due to the Chinese government's capital flow restriction and possible additional regulations by other Exchanges. For instance, Poon and Fung (2000) point out that Chinese firms listed on the Hong Kong exchange in the form of H-shares must also meet even more stringent accounting and disclosure requirements in Hong Kong. A number of studies (for example Sun and Tong, 2000; Karolyi and Li, 2003), suggest that B-shares and H-shares typically trade at a discount to their A-share counterpart although all classes of shares have the same dividend and voting rights.

Some recent studies suggest that the price differential between the A- and B-share markets appears to disappear over time for a variety of reasons. Fung and Leung (2002) and Karolyi and Li (2003) find evidence to suggest that investors may find effective ways to arbitrage between the A- and B-share markets after the Chinese government allowed domestic investors with foreign currency to invest in the market since February 2001. In addition, while it is too early to conclude Qualified Financial Institutional Investor (QFII) program in early 2003 may contribute to the disappearing price discount, it is expected that the QFII also let foreign institutional investors to invest gradually in the A-share market, which allow them to effectively arbitrage among different classes of stocks.

China Accounting Standards, International Accounting Standards and Stock Price Performance

Per the Chinese company laws, Chinese companies are required to follow the People's Republic of China's generally accepted accounting principles (PRC GAAP) when preparing accounting statements. In addition, for companies also listing B-shares, they also need to convert their accounting statements to international accounting standards (IAS) and have their books audited by major international audit firms.[7] The general perception is that IAS is a tougher standard to meet relative to PRC GAAP for Chinese companies.

According to Chen *et al.* (1999), the reported earnings of the listed companies under PRC GAAP standards, on average, are 20–30 percent higher than earnings reported under IAS for the same companies. The differential is mainly due to different treatments of bad debt allowances, depreciation, inventory valuation, long-term investment, and foreign currency translation between the two standards. Moreover, after reinstatement (adjustment from PRC GAAP to IAS), 15 percent of B-share companies are changed from reported profits to reported losses. Nonetheless, Chen *et al.* also point out that the differences between the standards will likely be reduced significantly after the PRC GAAP revision in 1998.

We may ask if the accounting results under PRC GAAP are useful despite the suggestions that the PRC GAAP standards yield less reliable accounting statements from the perspectives of international investors. Interestingly, the findings in Haw *et al.* (1999), Chen *et al.* (2001), Gao and Tse (2004), and Lin and Chen (2005) all suggest that the earnings announcements based on IAS and PRC GAAP are both value relevant, that is there was a significant response of market-adjusted stock return to earning changes and announcements. Hence, the earnings calculated under the PRC GAAP are useful to stock market investors. Chen *et al.* (2001) suggest that the Chinese stock market is rather new and it lacks alternative information sources other than the published accounting reports and thus the earning announcements, even under the less reliable PRC GAAP standards, are still useful to investors.

Current Development

We discuss the stock market performance in two aspects: stock market development and investment returns. Table 1.1 presents the stock market summary statistics of Shanghai and Shenzhen Stock Exchanges over 1991–2005. Several interesting findings emerge from Table 1.1.

First, the stock market exhibited tremendous growth in early years. Both exchanges experienced tremendous growth in terms of turnover, number of listed companies, and market capitalization in the first few years. If we only

Table 1.1 *Stock market summary statistics of Shanghai and Shenzhen Stock Exchanges (1991–2005)*

Year	Market capitalization at end year (billion RMB)		Annual turnover (billion RMB)		Number of listed companies at year end	
	Shanghai	Shenzhen	Shanghai	Shenzhen	Shanghai	Shenzhen
1991	2.9	7.9	4.57	3.53	8	6
1992	55	49	32.38	43.41	30	24
1993	221	133	260.89	128.67	106	77
1994	260	109	2548.24	239.26	171	120
1995	252	95	5515.38	93.30	188	135
1996	548	436	2766.15	1221.74	293	237
1997	922	831	2984.25	1695.87	383	362
1998	1064	888	3433.58	1115.81	438	413
1999	1458	1189	3599.21	1422.34	484	463
2000	2693	2116	4990.15	2924.90	572	514
2001	2759	1593	4414.40	1559.58	646	508
2002	2933	1297	4852.77	1103.14	715	508
2003	3517	1265	8291.16	1129.11	770	505
2004	3495	n.a.	7692.73	1586.34	827	536
2005	3807	933	4977.56	1242.48	824	544

Source: *Shanghai Stock Exchange Fact Book* and *Shenzhen Stock Exchange Fact Book*, various issues.

compare the figures in 2005 relative to 1991, the growth in market capitalization, turnover, and number of listed companies are impressive and probably one of the best among emerging equity markets. Second, behind the high growth in the early years and the last 15 years, the figures also reveal that the growth in recent years has been stagnant in terms of the number of listed companies and negative growth in terms of market capitalization and turnover. The recent poor performance in stock market growth is alarming.

We present the stock price performance in Table 1.2 and Figure 1.1. For comparison purposes, we present the composite index in Shanghai and Shenzhen Stock Exchanges as well as the Hong Kong Hang Seng index in Table 1.2. When we compare all three stock market indices of 2005 with those of 1991, the overall performance suggests positive returns (as shown in geometric and holding period returns) over the 15-year period. The indices and returns indicate that the Shanghai market performed better than the Hong Kong market and much better than the Shenzhen market.

Table 1.2 Stock price performance (1990–2005)

Year	Shenzhen: Compose index-Shenzhen (year end)	Shenzhen: Annual return (%)	Shanghai: Compose index-Shanghai (year end)	Shanghai: Annual return (%)	Hong Kong: Hong Kong Hang Seng Index (year end)	Hong Kong: Annual return (%)
1990	NA	NA	127.61	NA	3243.00	17.86
1991	110.37	NA	292.75	129.41	4601.80	41.90
1992	241.21	118.55	780.39	166.57	5751.40	24.98
1993	238.28	−1.21	833.80	6.84	11 487.00	99.73
1994	140.63	−40.98	647.87	−22.30	7342.70	−36.08
1995	113.24	−19.48	555.29	−14.29	11 359.70	54.71
1996	327.45	189.16	917.01	65.14	13 321.80	17.27
1997	381.29	16.44	1194.10	30.22	9252.40	−30.55
1998	343.85	−9.82	1146.70	−3.97	9506.90	2.75
1999	402.18	16.96	1366.58	19.18	15 532.34	63.38
2000	635.73	58.07	2073.48	51.73	16 102.35	3.67
2001	475.94	−25.13	1645.97	−20.62	10 725.30	−33.39
2002	388.76	−18.32	1357.65	−17.52	9258.95	−13.67
2003	378.63	−2.61	1497.04	10.27	13 289.37	43.53
2004	315.81	−16.59	1266.50	−15.40	13 721.69	3.25
2005	278.75	−11.73	1161.06	−8.33	15 753.14	14.80
Geometric mean return (1992–2005)		6.84		10.34		9.19
Holding period return (1991–2005)		152.56		296.60		242.33
Standard deviation (1992–2005)		63.69		50.75		39.49

Source: For Chinese stock market indices, the data are from *Shanghai Stock Exchange Fact Book* and *Shenzhen Stock Exchange Fact Book*, various issues. For Hang Seng Index, the data are from Yahoo finance.

In terms of risk (as represented by standard deviation of annual returns), however, both the Shanghai and Shenzhen markets exhibit higher risk than the Hong Kong market. In terms of annual returns, the Shenzhen market had negative annual returns in nine out of 14 years, Shanghai market had negative annual returns seven out of 15 years, and Hong Kong market had negative annual returns only four out of 15 years. More importantly, for the last five years, annual returns in both Shanghai and

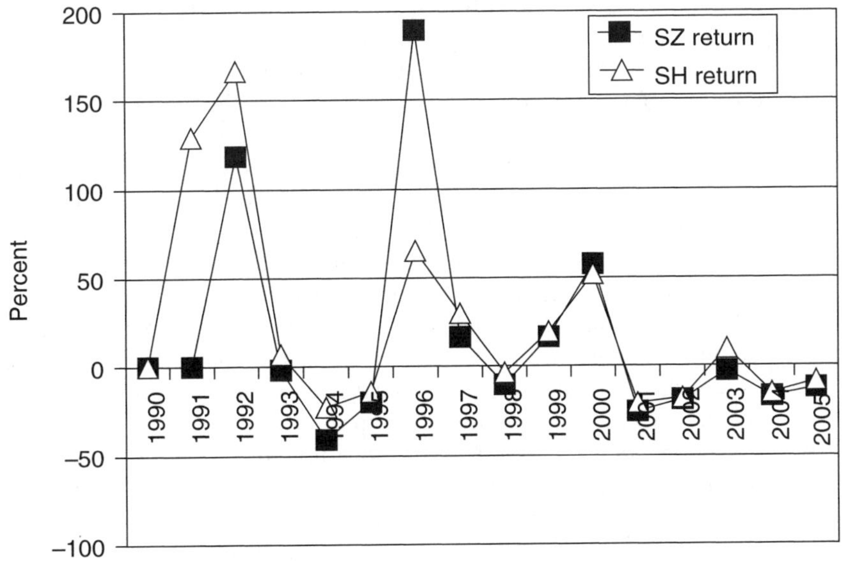

Figure 1.1 *Stock price performance of Shanghai and Shenzhen composite index (1991–2005)*

Shenzhen markets were mostly negative (with the exception of Shanghai stock return in 2003).

To the majority of investors, the recent poor performance in Chinese stock markets was discouraging. Not surprisingly, there were fewer investors excited about the stock market and hence the market turnover statistics from 2001–2005 in both exchanges did not show much increase (as shown in Table 1.1).

In light of the recent poor stock market performance, the Chinese government has implemented, within recent years, several measures to boost its bearish stock market. The measures include:

- *Share repurchase*. The CSRC allows open market repurchases by controlling shareholders and companies. The repurchase program allows flexibilities of controlling shareholders and companies to use their funds without being accused of manipulating stock prices of their own companies.
- *Boost corporate governance*. CSRC also realizes the need to promote corporate governance to strengthen investor confidence. As discussed earlier, there are rules in place now that require: (a) price-sensitive information disclosure; (b) tightening financial statement audits;

(c) obligated electronic voting system when there are significant corporate issues; and (d) independent outside directors serving on boards.

- *Non-tradable shares reform.* The CSRC has started the conversion of non-tradable shares to tradable shares; initially the conversion is limited to certain types of companies. As of the end of March, 2006, more than half of the listed companies have made the conversion of non-tradable shares to tradable shares. While the conversion may temporary increase the supply of shares on the market, the process reduces agency costs and improves corporate governance.[8] Thus, in the long run, the conversion helps companies to sustain, increase or stabilize the value of company stocks. In addition, once more shares become tradable, warrants and options on company stocks will become closer to market values because controlling shareholders are less likely to be able to manipulate stock prices.
- *Institutional investors.* The Chinese government launched the Qualified Financial Institutional Investor (QFII) programs in December 2002. The QFII programs, in essence, allow institutional investors to participate in stock trading. Specifically, foreign institutional investors can now invest in the A-share market, which had been off limits to them before. It is believed that these institutional investors (QFIIs) have more experience and better skills to perform monitoring on the Chinese companies. The Chinese government initially allows QFIIs to have a quota of $4 billion for their Chinese investment. As of late 2005, the Chinese government had doubled the stock quota to about $10 billion for foreign investors in order to stimulate the stock markets. The specific rules that govern the QFII programs are shown in Appendix 1.2.
- *Dividend tax.* On 13 June 2005, the Minister of Finance and the State Administration of Taxation announced that the tax on stock dividends was cut from 20 percent to 10 percent. While it is still early to know the impact of such a dividend tax cut, there is no doubt that the move will encourage investors to invest in dividend-paying stocks.
- *Investor protection.* On 30 August 2005, the China government established the China Securities Investor Protection Fund Corporation Limited. The company was formed by State Council with initial funding of RMB 6.3 billion. The objective of the company is to compensate investors when losses to investors are due to frauds. The protection fund is meant to restore investor confidence in light of several visible accounting frauds and criminal acts by major shareholders.
- *Second Board.* The Shenzhen Stock Exchange launched the Small- and Medium-Enterprise Bloc (SME Board) in Shenzhen Stock Exchange on 27 May 2004. As of 31 December 2005, there were

50 companies listed. The objective of the SME Board is to offer investors more investment choices through a growth-oriented stock market that attracts and lists high-growth and high-tech companies.
- *New products*. There are various new products developed in recent years to allow investors more investment choices. These include China-based mutual funds and closed-end funds, exchange traded funds (China 50 ETF) and warrants.

Overall, all these measures represent proactive approaches by the Chinese government and regulators to restore the investor confidence and to attract local and foreign investors' participation. While it is too early to conclude if these measures are able to jump-start the Chinese stock market, some of the early results suggest the measures are helping the stock market performance. For instance, the SMEB index, which was first compiled and released on 1 December 2005, was 43.9 percent higher than that on the base date of 7 June 2005.

CONCLUDING REMARKS

There have been significant developments and changes to the Chinese stock exchanges since they were launched in late 1990. The stock trading in China is fully automated with electronic trading and it is order-driven. Both Shanghai and Shenzhen stock exchanges experienced tremendous growth in terms of turnover, number of listed companies and market capitalization despite recent setbacks. As of 2005, the Shanghai Exchange has 824 companies listed with an annual turnover of approximately RMB6.22 trillion and RMB4.74 trillion market capitalization. Chinese investors in China, using average returns from Shanghai and Shenzhen Stock Exchanges, earn 8.59 percent return per year (57 percent standard deviation of annual returns) during the period 1992–2005. The Chinese stock market indices fare well when they are compared to a 9.19 percent return from the Hong Kong Hang Seng Index that has a 40 percent standard deviation of returns. The success of these exchanges comes from hard-learned lessons.

Despite the impressive growth, the growth of the Chinese stock market has been stagnant in recent years. The setbacks of the development of two exchanges stem mainly from frequent policy reversals as well as the institutional structure of the stock market. There are 43 major occurrences of policy and regulation reversals in 1990–2005. Too many policy reversals not only damage the well-functioning of the Chinese stock market, but also the effectiveness of policy implementation. The negative stock prices reaction to policy announcement irrespective of the nature of the information contents reflects investor sentiments toward those reactive (instead of proactive) marginal changes.

Institutionally, the structure of ownership classes and non-IAS Chinese accounting standards also contribute to the recent poor stock market performance. Ownership restrictions of A, B, H and N classes of common stocks effectively prevented arbitraging price differentials prior to the QFII program in 2002. China also imposed trading restrictions among non-tradable shares, which represented at least 67 percent of the ownership of the company. These non-tradable shares created block ownership and encouraged entrenchment problems, making exercising corporate governance practices more difficult. The CRSC recognized this problem and started converting non-tradable shares to tradable shares in 2005.

The Chinese PRC GAAP provides another source of problem. A big blow of investors' confidence is the differences between PRC GAAP and IAS prior to the PRC GAAP revision in 1998. Last but not least of the setbacks is the wide spread of earnings manipulation among those exchange-listed Chinese companies, as evidenced by poor post-IPO operating performance.

To revert the bearish trend of the Chinese stock market, CSRC, Minister of Finance and the State Administration of Taxation have implemented several proactive measures to attract investor participation and investor confidence. The latest reforms, that encourage domestic and foreign investment, include:

- conversion of non-tradable shares to tradable shares;
- reduction of dividend taxes to 10 percent;
- permission of open market repurchases;
- development of new investment choices;
- introduction of SME board for high growth and high tech companies; and
- launching of QFII programs that allow foreign institutional investors to invest in the A-share market.

All these measures, in the long run, may help to reduce artificial trading barriers, increase investment, improve and stabilize value of stocks.

Boosting investor confidence is another primary focus for reforms. Both the establishment of the China Securities Investor Protection Fund Corporation Limited and promotion of corporate governance are used to strengthen investor confidence. Investors will be compensated for their loss due to accounting frauds and misconduct by block-holders. There are also corporate governance rules that are directed to market surveillance, exchange member supervision and company compliance with respect to information disclosure, board independence, electronic voting system and tightened financial audits.

All in all, this chapter presents an evolution of the institutional structure, regulations, and governmental reforms related to the development of the Chinese stock market. The development process offers valuable lessons for Chinese regulators as well as regulators and investors in other emerging markets. The 'red-chips' phenomenon and the increasing number of Chinese companies listing their shares overseas reflect both a huge demand of equity financing from those companies and the potential growth of the Chinese economy. The Chinese stock market will continue to change and play an important role in promoting China's economic growth.

NOTES

1. See http://www.sse.org.cn/main/en/Catalog_1841.aspx (for Shenzhen Stock Exchange) and http://www.sse.com.cn/sseportal/en_us/ps/lc/lst_req.shtml (for Shanghai Stock Exchange) for details.
2. Please refer to http://www.sse.org.cn/main/en/Catalog_1842.aspx for details.
3. Please refer to http://www.sse.com.cn/en_us/cs/about/factbook/factbook_us 2004.pdf for details.
4. For companies with operating losses for two consecutive years, the price limit is 5 percent.
5. The details are in http://www.see.org.cn. Shanghai Stock Exchange has similar regulatory structures.
6. Bai *et al.* (2004) describe two high profile scandals. First, the largest shareholder of Meierya conspired with other parties to embezzle US$44.6 million, 41 percent of the company's total equity in 2001. Second, in the same year, Sanjiu Pharma's largest shareholder stole US$301.9 million, 96 percent of the listed company's total equity.
7. The regulation in 1999 explicitly asked for auditing by the 'big six' accounting firms. After a merger and the collapse of Arthur Andersen, there are only the 'big four' accounting firms left.
8. To minimize the price impact of more tradable shares, the CSRC also restricts the buyers of newly converted shares not to sell the shares for one year. After one year, these buyers are able to sell at most only 5 percent of a company's equity. For details, see *Economist* (7 May 2005, p. 70).

REFERENCES

Areddy, J. T. (2006), 'Shanghai Exchange upgrades; technological overhaul will add power, potential to diversity', *Wall Street Journal*, 28 February, C16.

Bai, C., Q. Liu, J. Lu, F. M. Song and J. Zhang (2004), 'Corporate governance and market valuation in China', *Journal of Comparative Economics*, **32**, 599–616.

Chan, K. C., L. T. W. Cheng and J. K. W. Fung (2001), 'Ownership restriction and stock price behavior in China', *Chinese Economy*, **34**, 29–48.

Chan, K., A. J. Menkveld and Z. Yang (2004), 'Are domestic investors more informed than foreign investors? Evidence from perfectly segmented market in China', Hong Kong University of Science and Technology working paper.

Chen, C., W. Chen and J. Chi (forthcoming), 'Underpricing and operating performance of Chinese B-share IPOs', *Chinese Economy*.
Chen, C. J. P., S. Chen and X. Su (2001), 'Is accounting information value-relevant in the emerging Chinese stock market?', *Journal of International Accounting, Auditing, and Taxation*, **10**, 1–22.
Chen, C. J. P., F. A. Gul and X. Su (1999), 'A comparison of reported earnings under Chinese GAAP vs. IAS: evidence from the Shanghai Stock Exchange', *Accounting Horizons*, **13**, 91–111.
Chi, J. and C. Padgett (forthcoming), 'The operating performance and its relationship with the market performance of Chinese IPOs', *Chinese Economy*.
Chong, T. T. L. and Q. Su (2006), 'On the co-movement of the A and H shares', *Chinese Economy*, June.
Economist (2005), 'Finance and economics: hangover cure; Mainland China's stock markets', **375**(82), (7 May).
Fung, H. G. and W. K. Leung (2002), 'The A- and B-share Chinese equity markets: segmentation or integration', in H. G. Fung and K. H. Zhang (eds), *Financial Markets and Foreign Direct Investments in Greater China*, New York: M.E. Sharpe Publishing Co.
Fung, H. G., W. K. Leung and S. J. Zhu (2006), 'How do Chinese firms raise capital? An international comparison', in H. G. Fung, C. H. Pei and K. H. Zhang (eds), *China and the Challenge of Economic Globalization: The Impact of WTO Membership*, New York: M.E. Sharp Publishing Co., pp. 183–206.
Gao, Y. and Y. K. Tse (2004), 'Market segmentation and information values of earnings announcements: some empirical evidence from an event study on the Chinese stock market', *International Review of Economics and Finance*, **13**, 455–74.
Haw, I., D. Qi and W. Wu (1999), 'Value relevance of earnings in an emerging capital market, the case of A-shares in China', *Pacific Economic Review*, **4**, 337–47.
Haw, I., D. Qi, D. Wu and W. Wu (2005), 'Market consequences of earnings management in response to security regulations in China', *Contemporary Accounting Research*, **22**, 95–140.
Huang, A. G. and H. G. Fung (2004), 'Stock ownership segmentation, floatability and constraints on investments banking in China', *China and World Economy*, **12**(2) 66–78.
Jingu, T. (2002), 'Moving forward in reforming China's capital market', Nomura Research Institute working paper, **40**, 1–12.
Karolyi, G. A. and L. Li (2003), 'A resolution of the Chinese discount puzzle', Ohio State University working paper.
Lam, S., C. D. Tan, R. S. Tan and W. Zhang (2005), 'Policy risk: evidence from Chinese equity market', paper presented at the 13th Annual Securities and Financial Markets Conference, Kaohsiung, Taiwan.
Lam, S., R. S. Tan and G. T. Wee (forthcoming), 'Initial public offerings of state-owned enterprises: an international study of policy risk', *Journal of Financial and Quantitative Analysis*.
Lin, Z. and F. Chen (2005), 'Value relevance of international accounting standards harmonization: evidence from A- and B-share markets in China', *Journal of International Accounting, Auditing & Taxation*, **14**, 79–103.
Perotti, E. C. (1995), 'Credible privatizations', *American Economic Review*, **85**, 847–59.

Poon, W. P. H. and H. Fung (2000), 'Red chips or H-shares: which China-backed securities process information the fastest?', *Journal of Multinational Financial Management*, **10**, 315–43.
Sun, Q. and W. H. S. Tong (2000), 'The effect of market segmentation on stock prices: the China syndrome', *Journal of Banking and Finance*, **24**, 1875–902.

APPENDIX 1: MAJOR EVENT DATES OF STOCK MARKET LIBERALIZATIONS 1990–2005

A stock market liberalization event is defined as a measure that is implemented to allow greater participation in the local stock markets.

Date	Headlines	Description
29 November 1991	'B' Shares trading begins	Shanghai Vacuum is the first listed company in China to issue 'B' shares. However trading will only begin weeks later
1 August 1994	One billion USD worth of 'B' shares to be issued	The Chairman of China Securities Regulatory Commission (CSRC) was quoted as saying that China is planning to issue US$1 billion worth of 'B' shares, with priority given to energy, transportation and telecommunications company to help them raise funds for investment. In 1993, China issued about US$115 million worth of 'B' shares
2 June 1999	All firms allowed to raise foreign currency via 'B' shares	All, except insurance firms, can now issue 'B' shares, where previously state owned enterprises (SOEs) were given priority. Now, both public and private firms can issue 'B' shares. Prior to this, private firms were discouraged from doing so. This move to open 'B' shares listings allows the private sector to raise foreign currency
3 November 1999	Insurance companies allowed access to stock markets	Insurance companies, both foreign and local are allowed access to markets via securities investment funds. Insurance firms are now allowed to purchase securities investment funds and authorities have approved 14 foreign insurers so far
19 May 2000	Foreign participation in local 'A' Share markets	The CSRC announced that China would allow gradual and limited participation by foreign investors in the 'A' share market. The vice chairperson

Date	Headlines	Description
		of the CSRC has said that the CSRC would allow foreign participation in joint venture investment funds companies, even though a timeline was not given
22 June 2000	Trading limits removed for certain companies	China initially imposed a 5 percent trading limit for companies with at least two straight years of losses. However, the 5 percent trading limits are removed and investors can now sell these shares at market price
25 October 2000	Foreign trading houses to invest directly in 'B' shares	The CSRC chairperson said that foreign trading houses would be able to invest directly in 'B' shares, as opposed to requiring foreign institutions to use domestic brokerages as agents when trading in 'B' shares, signaling that the government supports the growth of trading by foreigners
20 November 2000	Asset management firms to be given more authority	State Council passes measures permitting asset management firms to underwrite shares and bonds, recommend listings and issue bonds as well
19 February 2001	Opening of 'B' shares to local investors	China will now allow Chinese investors to trade in 'B' shares, which was previously only open to foreign investors. The CSRC commented that the opening of the 'B' share market will help promote the 'internationalization' of the stock markets. This announcement is also seen as a step closer to the merger between 'A' and 'B' share markets
1 June 2001	Trading of 'B' shares begins with local investors	Today marked the first day that the trading of 'B' shares was fully opened to domestic investors
8 November 2001	Foreign companies to list in China	The Ministry of Foreign Trade and Economic Cooperation and the CSRC have announced rules on

Date	Headlines	Description
		allowing foreign firms to list on domestic stock markets. Foreign companies that hope to list must set up a stock holding unit in China and meet profitability requirements for three years before listing. After which, the company must own a minimum of 10 percent at all times after listing
3 June 2002	Foreign participation in local firms	The CSRC issued new rules on foreign participation in local fund management and securities firms. Foreign firms can take up to a 33 percent stake in fund management companies. Foreign companies can also hold up to one third of domestic securities firms, though the Chinese party must maintain control. This can be done either through acquiring stakes in existing domestic firms or establishing new joint ventures with local companies
*1 December 2002	Qualified institutional investment plans (QFIIs)	QFII program regulations announced. The participation of institutional investors was allowed
2 December 2002	Foreign investors in Asset Management Companies	Authorities have allowed foreign investors to take controlling stakes in joint ventures in China's Asset Management Companies
27 December 2002	First foreign local joint venture fund management company	The first joint venture fund management company is established by ING Group and China Merchants Securities. ING holds 30 percent and China Merchants holds 40 percent with the remaining 30 percent held by three domestic firms. This is the first joint venture that is permitted to have access into China's $500 billion domestic share markets
25 April 2003	First joint venture securities house	China first joint venture securities house – China Europe Securities Co. Ltd, a joint venture between

Date	Headlines	Description
		Xiangcai Securities and Credit Lyonnaise Securities announced its inception
26 May 2003	Foreign brokers to trade in RMB securities	Authorities have given its approval to UBS and Nomura Securities, two foreign brokers, to trade in renminbi denominated securities for the first time. These two companies are now able to trade in the A-share market, and also in renminbi denominated bonds, participate in IPOs and other share issues
28 May 2003	First foreign institutional investors formed joint venture fund house	BMO Montreal Bank's proposal to take an equity interest in Full Goal Fund Mgt Ltd was approved by the CSRC. The case was the first where foreign institutional investors formed a joint venture fund house by purchasing shares from existing shareholders
*23 February 2005	First exchange-traded fund (ETF) launched	China 50 ETF, issued by China Asset Management Co., sponsored by State Street Global, tracks 50 largest Chinese stocks on Shanghai Stock Exchange
*9 May 2005	Sell off state owned shares	As part of a trial program, the state will begin to sell the country's state-owned shares (also called non-tradable shares or 'legal person' shares) in a small number of companies
*13 June 2005	Dividend tax cut	Ministry of Finance and the State Administration of Taxation announced the tax payable on dividends reduced to 10 percent from 20 percent
*1 August 2005	First call warrant issued	Société Générale announced to issue a call warrant on the China 50 ETF, which is listed in Singapore Stock Exchange. The instrument is the first derivative to be based on China A-shares
*30 August 2005	China Securities Investor Protection Fund Corporation	State Council funded the company with Rmb 6.3 billion (US$770 million). The objective of the company is to

Date	Headlines	Description
	Limited formed	compensate investors when securities run under
*23 October 2005	China Index Corporation Limited formed	It is a joint venture between Shenzhen Stock Exchange and Shanghai Stock Exchange. Besides serving the marketing function of stock price indices, the company is also charged with the development of index derivatives

Source: Lam *et al.* (2005) with updates in 2004 and 2005 by authors. The authors' updates are denoted by '*'.

APPENDIX 1.2: QFII PROGRAM REGULATIONS AS OF 1 DECEMBER 2002

Chapter I General Provisions

Article 1 The present Implementing Rules have been formulated on the basis of the Interim Measures for the Administration of Domestic Securities Trading of Qualified Foreign Institutional Investors (hereafter 'the Interim Measures') for the purpose of regulating the securities trading activities of the qualified foreign institutional investors at Shenzhen Stock Exchange (hereafter 'the present stock exchange') and maintain the order of the securities market.

Article 2 The trading activities of the qualified foreign institutional investors (hereafter 'the QFIIs') at the present stock exchange shall be subject to the governance of the present Implementing Rules. Where there are no corresponding provisions in the present Implementing Rules, the provisions of the Rules of Trade and other relevant provisions of the present stock exchange shall apply.

Article 3 The present stock exchange employs real-time monitoring over the securities trading activities of the QFIIs.

Article 4 A QFII shall entrust a domestic securities company that has obtained the qualifications of the present stock exchange to handle relevant securities trading activities. To participate in the securities trading at the present stock exchange, a QFII can only do the deals by way of a sense of the securities company it has entrusted.

Article 5 In case any of the following circumstances occurs to a QFII, the trustee thereof shall report to the present stock exchange for archivist purposes within five working days of the fact taking place:

a. Obtaining the permit for engaging in the securities investment business;
b. The investment tranches has been approved and having obtained a registration certificate of foreign exchange;
c. Designating or replacing trustees;
d. Designating or replacing the securities company that serves as the agent of the QFII in domestic securities trading activities;
e. Designating or replacing the trading seat of the securities

company which serves as the agent in domestic securities trading activities.

f. Changing the name of the institution or the legal representative thereof;
g. Increasing or reducing the registered capital;
h. Being involved in any litigation or being given any serious punishment abroad;
i. The permit for engagement in securities investment or the registration certificate of foreign exchange failing to pass the annual inspection;
j. Being punished by the China Securities Regulatory Commission or the People's Bank of China or the State Administration of Foreign Exchange due to violation of the Interim Measures;
k. Any other circumstance as provided by the present stock exchange.

Article 6 With regard to the proportion of shares held by a QFII when engaging in domestic securities trading activities, the A-shares of each listed company listed for trade held by each QFII shall not exceed 10 percent of the total capital stock of the company, and the total of the A-shares of an identical listed company listed for trade held by all QFIIs shall not exceed 20 percent of the total capital stock of the company.

Article 7 When the total of A-shares of an identical listed company held by all QFIIs reaches 16 percent of the total capital stock of the company and with each 2 percent increase thereafter, the present stock exchange shall, when the trading day ends, disclose the proportion of the total of A-shares held by the QFIIs in the total capital stock of the company through the webpage of the present stock exchange.

Article 8 When the business of a same day finishes and if the proportion of an individual QFII in the A-shares of an individual listed company exceeds the prescribed limit, the present stock exchange will issue a notice to the securities company entrusted thereby, and the QFII shall, within five trading days as of the day when it receives the notice of reducing its shares, close its position so as to meet the requirement of limited proportions.

Article 9 When the business of the same day finishes, and if the total of A-shares of an identical listed company held by all QFIIs exceeds the prescribed proportion, the present stock exchange will close their positions according to the principle of 'last buy, first sell', and issue a notice to the entrusted securities company and the trustee thereof. The QFIIs shall, within five trading days as of receiving the notice, handle it in appropriate ways so as to meet the requirement of limited proportions. If, within five trading days, other QFIIs voluntarily reduce their shares and their proportion of shares falls below the prescribed limit, the QFIIs that were informed to reduce their shares may apply to the present stock exchange for retaining their original shares.

Article 10 The entrusted securities companies shall work with due diligence. In case any of the QFIIs is found to be involved in any illegal trading of securities, it shall be reported to the present stock exchange in good time.

Chapter II Punishments for Violations of the Present Implementing Rules

Article 11 In case any QFII who violates any of the present Implementing Rules by failing to deal with its shares that exceed the prescribed proportion as required, the present stock exchange and the registered settlement companies shall be entitled to inform the entrusted securities company and the trustee thereof to close their positions, and may give a warning, public reprimand or other sanctions to the QFII concerned. If the circumstances are serious, it shall be subject to the investigation and punishment of the China Securities Regulatory Commission.

Article 12 In case any QFII violates the provisions of Article 5 of the present Implementing Rules by failing to make archivist filing with the present stock exchange, the present stock exchange may give a warning or public reprimand or other sanctions to the QFII concerned. If the circumstances are serious, it shall be subject to the investigation and punishment of the China Securities Regulatory Commission.

Article 13 In case any of the entrusted securities companies violates any of the provisions of the present Implementing Rules by failing to perform its duty of due diligence, the present stock exchange shall be entitled to mete out corresponding sanctions according to the relevant provisions of the business operation rules.

Chapter III Supplementary Provisions

Article 14 Due to technical problems, the QFIIs cannot participate in the counter purchase of national debts and the trading of enterprise debentures.

Article 15 The present Implementing Rules shall take effect after being ratified by the China Securities Regulatory Commission. The same shall apply to the revision of the present Implementing Rules. The Present Implementing Rules shall be implemented as of the day of promulgation.

Source: Shenzhen Stock Exchange.

2. Bond markets: introduction and analysis

Hung-gay Fung, Ying Han and Qingfeng 'Wilson' Liu

INTRODUCTION

The Chinese bond market differs substantially from other bond markets across the world, particularly the US market. The Chinese bond market is fragmented and complicated because of different regulations governing the operations of the bond issues. The Chinese bond market is made up of Government or Treasury bonds (T-bonds), financial institutional bonds (F-bonds), enterprise bonds (E-bonds), and other bond issues such as foreign bonds (Zhang and Ji 2001). China's T-bond market has been the important financial asset in its overall financial market (including stock market and futures market) in general in terms of size and the general bond market in particular.

The Chinese bonds are traded in three different markets. That is, they are traded on the exchanges (Shanghai Stock Exchange and Shenzhen Stock Exchange), in the interbank market, and in the bank-counter market. The interbank market has the largest trading volume among the three markets, and it is the most actively traded market.

Table 2.1 shows some interesting characteristics of China's bonds. Panel A of Table 2.1 lists the amount issued for the most important types of Chinese bonds in 2004 and 2005. In 2004, more than half of the bonds issued were central bank bonds (54.6 percent), followed by the T-bonds (25.1 percent), F-bonds (18.4 percent), and E-bonds (1.9 percent). In 2005, the government bond (T-bond) accounted for 16 percent of the total bond market, while the Central Bank bond accounted for about 62.3 percent of the total bond volume. Financial bonds (F-bonds) accounted for 16.6 percent and E-bonds, 18.4 percent. Other bonds include foreign bonds (such as Panda Bonds) and commercial papers. The central bank bonds have the largest amount issued. T-bonds and F-bonds each represents one-third to half of the amount of the central bank bonds. The E-bonds and other bonds represent only a small percentage of the bond market. Between

Table 2.1 Characteristic of China's Bond market

Panel A: China's Bond market 2004 and 2005 (RMB billions)

Types	2004 amount	%	2005 amount	%
Government bond	692	25.1	704	16.0
Central bank bond	1507	54.6	2746	62.3
F-bond	509	18.4	732	16.6
E-bond	53	1.9	91	2.0
Others	NA	NA	137	3.1
Total	2761	100.0	4410	100.0

Note: The numbers have been subject to rounding. 'Others' include foreign bonds in China. NA means 'not available'.

Panel B: Trading volume of Chinese bonds in the three markets, 2004 and 2005 (RMB billions)

Market	2004	2005
Interbank market	12784.9	22850
Exchange market	5014*	2660
Bank-counter market	6.217	6.568

Note: * the trading volumes of bonds on the exchange market in 2004 do not include the trading volumes of the Shenzhen Stock Exchange.

Sources: Chinese Bond Markets 2004 Annual Book, Chinese Bond Markets 2005 Annual Book, from the Department of Information of the China Government Securities Depository Trust & Clearing Co, Ltd, http://www.chinabond.com.cn, and statistics from the Ministry of Finance People's Republic of China, from http://www.mof.gov.cn

2004 and 2005, while all types of bond issues went up, central bank bonds grew by over 80 percent, increasing its weight from 54 percent to 62 percent. In contrast, government bonds grew by less than 2 percent and its weight went down from 25.1 percent to 16.0 percent among all new bond issues.

Panel B shows the total trading volume of all bonds in the three markets over 2004–2005. The interbank market had RMB12 784.9 billion trading volume in 2004, far exceeding the bond trading on the Shanghai Stock Exchange of RMB5014 billion. In the bank-counter market, there were RMB6.217 billion trading. In 2005, the interbank market had RMB22 850 billion in trading volume, almost double that of 2004. The two stock exchanges together had 2660 billion in trading volume, while the bank-counter market had RMB6.568 billion. The interbank market was the most actively traded market, followed by the stock exchanges. The bank-counter market had the smallest trading volume.

The rest of the chapter is organized as follows. First, we discuss different types of government bonds, and describe the financial institution bonds in the third section and enterprise bonds in the fourth section. In the fifth section we look into the development of the bond market, then we examine the market structure of the secondary bond market and offer some thoughts on future development of the bond market in the next two sections. The last section concludes the chapter.

GOVERNMENT BONDS

The Chinese government resumed issuing T-bonds in 1981, shortly after the economic reforms started in late 1978. The government bond market has developed rapidly ever since. In 2001, ultra long-term treasury bonds of 15 and 20 years were issued. In 2004, the authorities issued about RMB 700 billion of Treasury bonds (T-bonds), 84 percent of total financing economy wide, while the companies issued RMB 130 billion of stocks and bonds, of which 6.9 billion was the amount of bond issued. The government bond market is apparently the largest component in the Chinese financial market.

The government bonds are issued by the Ministry of Finance (MOF) of the central government. The Standing Committee of the National People's Congress determines and approves the quantity and types of bonds the government should issue. The government bonds are used to finance the government's proactive fiscal policy of investing in fixed assets to maintain its economic growth.

Most T-bonds are coupon bonds. The coupon bonds with fixed coupon rates usually have a maturity ranging from one year to 10 years. Coupon bonds may have variable interest rates, too. Coupon bonds are not common and have only limited issues. The maturity of the zero-coupon bonds typically ranges from one year to two years.

Before 1993, the treasury bonds had mainly been physical bonds on printed paper. This kind of bond disappeared in 1998. Today, there are two major government bonds (T-bonds): voucher government bonds and book-entry government bonds. We will discuss these two types of bonds in more detail in the following sections. There are other types of government bonds. For example, special government bonds are sold to social pension funds, unemployment insurance funds, and other financial institutions only.

We will also introduce the Central Bank bonds in this section. These securities are issued to commercial banks by the People's Bank of China.

They are also very important in the bond market given their market size and functions as regulatory tools.

Voucher Government Bonds

The voucher, or certificate, government bonds are sold directly to individual investors in the bank-counter market. Voucher bonds were introduced to the market in 1994 and were similar to the saving bonds in the US. Their coupon rates are predetermined by the government. The face value per bond is RMB100. The bonds are sold at face value. The maximum amount that can be bought is RMB1 million per account. Coupons are paid annually. The maturities of voucher bonds usually range from two to five years.

In the primary market of voucher government bonds, the government sells the T-bonds to investors with the help of a government bond underwriting group, consisting of 39 banks, including the four big state-owned banks,[1] ten big commercial banks, several municipal and regional banks, and the China Post Bank. When the government bonds are issued, each member of the underwriting group will inform the People's Bank of China the number of bonds they are committed to sell. The minimum number and the unit number of underwriting is RMB100 million. The People's Bank of China will then compare the underwriting numbers each member reports with the target. When the subscription is smaller than the target number, the government will assign the remaining bonds to the big four state-owned banks to underwrite.

After the government determines the quota, the underwriters will sell the bonds to the public over their own bank counters. They will earn issuance fees from the government. In 2002, for example, the issuance fees ranged from 3.2 percent and 4.0 percent of the amount sold. Individual investors will then open an account to buy government bonds from a bank.

Investors cannot trade the voucher bonds after they buy them from the bank counter, but they can use the bonds as collateral for loans. They can also sell them back to the bank six months after they bought the bonds. The MOF determines and announces the coupon rate received in different sell-back periods before issuance. Most of the investors keep voucher bonds until maturity.

Book-Entry Government Bonds

The book-entry government bonds were first issued in 1993. Book-entry bonds differ from voucher bonds in the way they are traded in the secondary market. Panel A of Table 2.2 summarizes the characteristics of voucher bonds and book-entry bonds in terms of initial distribution, secondary market trading, coupon rate determination and insurance price determination.

Book-entry bonds are initially issued to members of the government bonds underwriting group by auction in the primary market. The selling prices and the amount issued are determined by bids among institutional investors. After the initial auction, bonds will be distributed to and traded in the interbank market, on the exchanges, and in the bank-counter market.

In the interbank market, members of the Government Bonds Underwriters Group will distribute the book-entry bonds to the members who have a bond account with the Bond Registration companies but are not a member of the underwriting group. On the exchanges, the security companies will distribute some bonds to investors, who have a security account on the exchange market, while in the bank-counter market, the four big banks will distribute the bonds to investors who have a bond account with the banks.

The government determines the amount of bonds that can be sold and which market to be issued. According to a release by the MOF, of the RMB 4.4 trillion amount of book-entry bonds issued in 2004, 23.4 percent of the total was marketable only in the interbank market, 51 percent both in the interbank market and on the exchanges, 3.2 percent of the total volume was marketable in the bank-counter market, and 25.6 percent in all three markets.

Panel B of Table 2.2 shows the characteristics and amount of government bonds issued in 2004. The data indicate that for both voucher bonds and book-entry bonds, the most popular maturity is two to five years. Book-entry bonds are divided into discount bonds and coupon bonds, whereas voucher bonds only offer coupon bonds. One interesting thing to note is that book-entry bonds have higher interest rates than the corresponding voucher bond with a maturity of two to five years (3.74 percent versus 2.83 percent). As the future selling prices of the voucher bonds before maturity are certain, while those of book-entry bonds are not, the government offers higher interest rates for book-entry bonds to reflect the difference in risks.

Central Bank Bonds

We do not group central bank bonds into T-bonds; we introduce them here in the government bond section because the government uses these bonds as a policy tool. While the T-bonds are the tools for the government to finance its investment projects, the central bank bonds serve as tools for the government to achieve its monetary objectives in money and capital market operations. The central bank bonds are issued by the People's Bank of China to financial institutions in the interbank market. The financial institutions,

Table 2.2 Two major types of government bonds: voucher and the book-entry

Panel A: Characteristics of voucher and book-entry government bonds

	The voucher bonds	The book-entry bonds
Initial distribution	Over-the-counter to individuals	Government Bonds Underwriters Group
Secondary market	Not marketable on secondary market	Interbank market, exchange market, and over-the-counter market
Coupon rates	Determined by the MOF	Determined by the MOF
Issue price	RMB 100 per piece of bond	Auction

Panel B: Bond issues of government bonds in 2004 (billion RMB)

		The voucher		The book-entry	
Total amount		251.04		441.39	
		Amount	%	Amount	%
Maturities	1 year	0	0	63.48	14.4
	2–5 years	251.04	100	240.72	54.5
	5–10 years	0	0	137.19	31.1
	10 years above	0	0	0	0
Interest payment	Paid by discount	0		127.01	28.8
	Paid by coupons	2510.4		314.38	71.2

	Maturities	Average interest rate	Average interest rate
Average interest rates when initially sold	1 year	NA	2.40%
	2–5 years	2.83%	3.74%
	5–10 years	NA	4.83%
	10 years and above	NA	NA

Sources: (1) Ministry of Finance People's Republic of China, 1 March 2005; (2) Answers to reporters for the issues on Paper-Receipt government bonds (electronic registration), Ministry of Finance People's Republic of China, August, 2004; (3) Regulations for the Administration of Corporate Bonds, which took effect in 1993.

especially banks, trade the bonds on the interbank market to manage short-term liquidity. The maturities of the central bank bonds are in the range of three months, six months, and one year. In 2005, for example, 44 percent of the central bank securities were of one-year of maturity, 34 percent were of three-month maturity, 9 percent were of six-month maturity, and 13 percent were of three-year maturity. The overwhelming majority of the central bank securities are short-term securities.

FINANCIAL INSTITUTION BONDS

There are two types of financial institution bonds, both of which are called F-bonds in general. The first type is the policy bank F-bonds issued by policy banks; and the second type are commercial bank F-bonds issued by other financial institutions.

Policy Bank F-bonds

Policy F-bonds are issued by the state policy banks, which are the China Development Bank, the China Agriculture Development Bank and China Import and Export Bank. Among the policy banks, the China Development Bank is the main bond issuer, which has issued 90 percent of the policy-bank bonds. The bonds provide a capital base to support policy implementation. The money is typically used to finance medium to large national construction projects.

Prior to 1999, the People's Bank of China assigned the bonds to state-owned banks to sell to investors. After 1999, the policy F-bonds are sold by auction to investors who have opened an account in the China Government Securities Depository Trust and Clearing Company. The policy-bank bonds have maturities of three years, five years and eight years.

Commercial Bank F-bonds

Since 1985, the Chinese government has allowed commercial banks and non-bank financial institutions to issue bonds. In accordance with the regulations for issuing F-bonds in the interbank market, commercial banks that issue F-bonds need to have a leverage ratio, or capital-assets ratio, of more than 4 percent and have made positive profits in the latest three consecutive years (Decree No. 1 2005). The goal for the bond issues should be to recapitalize state-owned banks, and to improve the capital structure of the banking sector. In addition, the central bank allows commercial banks to issue these bonds for the purpose of influencing the money markets. Commercial bank bonds are subordinated to the claims of all other liabilities but before the equity of the issuer.

With approval from the People's Bank of China, commercial banks are allowed to issue commercial bank bonds to finance bad debts. Recently, some commercial bank F-bonds have been issued to finance the bad debts incurred between 1991 and 1994.

ENTERPRISE BONDS

Enterprise bonds (E-bonds) include Central Enterprise bonds, Short-term paper and Local Enterprise bonds. In China, the E-bond market developed before the appearance of the stock markets. The E-bonds first appeared in 1983. At that time, the government had no explicit regulations on the issuance and trading of E-bonds. In 1987, the first temporary regulatory rules were issued by the government. At the time there were seven types of bonds. In 1993, the Regulations for the Administration of Corporate Bonds took effect. But then in 1994, the government stopped approving corporate bond issuance when some corporate bonds defaulted (Wang 2005).

Historically, the E-bond market has had a bad image because money-losing enterprises refused to make principal or interest payments, which cooled down the interest of many investors and prompted the government to impose strict regulations on the E-bond market. Now companies need to obtain approval from various departments of the government before they can issue these bonds. The People's Bank of China examines the coupon rates of the bonds. The CSRC examines the qualifications of the prospective issuers. The National Development and Reform Commission examine the issuance quota of corporate bonds and submit the quota and issuance plans to the Standing Committee of the National People's Congress for final approval.

The government also sets limits on the coupon rates. Thus credit ratings play a relatively minor role in determining the coupon rates of these bonds. Similar to stocks, E-bonds are underwritten by securities companies. They are first issued to investors from different security brokers. After the E-bonds are approved for listing on the exchanges, investors can trade E-bonds on the exchange markets.

In recent years, there is a reviving interest among Chinese companies as an increasing number of listed firms plan to use the E-bond market to expand their financing sources. In particular, there is growing interest in convertible corporate bonds because of the potential and flexibility to convert these bonds into stocks, a valuable option when stock prices are rising. As such, we divide E-bonds into corporate bonds and convertible bonds.

Corporate and convertible bonds are two non-government bonds that are mainly traded on China's two stock exchanges. Some corporate bonds are not actively traded. In order to increase the liquidity of E-bonds, several E-bond issues have been allowed to trade in the interbank market.

Generally speaking, the issuing procedures of corporate bonds and convertible bonds are similar. But the conditions for companies to issue convertible bonds are more demanding than those to issue regular corporate bonds. Companies need to obtain approval from the corresponding departments of the State Council before they submit application to the stock exchanges and China Securities Regulatory Commission (CSRC) for examination. After the exchanges get confirmation from the CSRC, the companies can make arrangements for the issuance, complete registration, make public announcements, report these announcements to the CSRC, and sign a listing agreement with the exchange.

Although companies have the right to design the bond's indenture, the regulations of the stock exchanges set some limits on the features of the bonds. For example, the coupon rates of the E-bonds cannot exceed 40 percent of the deposit interest rates according to Article 18 of the Regulations for the Administration of Corporate Bonds, which took effect in 1993.

Table 2.3 compares the corporate bonds and convertible bonds in terms of bond features (maturity, par value, amount and options) and issuing conditions in terms of profitability, leverage, reference and guarantor. Convertible bonds can issue a large amount (RMB100 billion) as compared to the RMB50 million for the regular corporate bonds. The profitability requirement of the convertible bonds is stricter. The convertible bonds are attractive to companies because of the lower coupon rate payment from the firm's perspective. Investors can convert the bonds into shares if they think the conversion is favorable six months after the bond issue.

Table 2.4 shows relative issuing amounts of corporate bonds and convertible bonds in comparison to the stock and government bonds traded on the exchanges over 1995–2004. Corporate bond issues in China have been on the rise. There were RMB18.5 billion bonds in 2004 and RMB36.2 billion in 2005. The convertible bonds took a huge jump between 2002 and 2003 and far exceeded regular corporate bond issues in both 2003 and 2004. In 2004, there were RMB34.5 billion convertible bonds, almost doubling the regular corporate bond issues. In 2005, however, no convertible bonds were issued as the Chinese government imposed a moratorium on convertible bond issues in order to aid its efforts in transforming the non-circulating stocks into tradable shares.

Table 2.5 shows the corporate bonds traded on the exchanges. Note that the listing requirements of both exchanges are identical.

Table 2.3 Comparisons of corporate bonds and convertible bonds

	Corporate bonds	Convertible bonds
Issuer	Listed companies and non-listed limited companies	Listed companies or important state-owned companies which intend to be listed on the stock exchanges
Maturity	1 year or above	three to five years
Par value	RMB100	RMB100
Coupon rate	The coupon rate should be less than interest rates set by the State Council	Lower than the comparable deposit rate in the banking system
Amount	RMB50 million or above	RMB 100 million or above
Leverage	Amount of bonds outstanding should not exceed 40 percent of the equity	(1) After issuing convertible bonds, the debt/asset ratio should not exceed 70 percent. (2) Total amount of bond should not exceed 40 percent of the company equity
Options to issuers	No	Issuers can redeem the bonds before maturity. The measures to redeem the bonds are set by the issuers
Options to investors	No	Investors can convert the bonds to stock six months after the issuing date. The issuers set the conversion price and timing
Equity requirement	RMB30 million or above for listed companies, and RMB60 million or above for a non-listed company	RMB30 million or above
Profitability	The average profit in the recent three years is enough to pay for the annual coupon of the corporate bonds	Companies should have made profits for the latest three consecutive years, and the profit-to-equity ratio is greater than 10 percent on average. The profit-to-equity ratio can be lower than 10 percent but not less than 7 percent for the companies in energy, raw materials, or infrastructure industries.
Reference	(1) Approval from the State Council;	Prospective issuers should have provisional government or

Table 2.3: (continued)

	Corporate bonds	Convertible bonds
	(2) The underwriter, member of the stock exchange	related companies supervising departments from the State Council as reference
Guarantor	Guarantors must meet guarantee conditions set by laws and regulations with exceptions for triple A-bonds and exemption by the authorization	The important state-owned companies which are not listed on a stock exchange should have a guarantee who will be able to retire the debt instead of the issuance

Sources: (1) Regulations on listing corporate bonds, Shanghai and Shenzhen stock exchange, 2000; (2) Provisional Regulations for the Administration of Convertible Bonds, 8 March 1997, and effective from 25 March 1997.

Table 2.4 Comparison of issuing amount (million RMB) of government bonds, corporate bonds, and convertible bonds on Shanghai Stock Exchange and Shenzhen Stock Exchange (1995–2004)

Year	Book-entry government bonds	Stock	Corporate bonds	Convertible bonds
1995	36 809	13 765	0	0
1996	182 680	35 410	0	0
1997	78 483	99 534	3700	0
1998	0	79 724	0	500
1999	36 000	86 449	11 330	150
2000	26 000	152 360	7207	4200
2001	95 960	106 662	8000	0
2002	146 400	72 772	9050	5300
2003	149 380	61 750	11 500	30 357
2004	262 910	62 530	18 500	34 516
2005	504 710	37 596	36 200	0

Sources: 2001 Fact Book of Shanghai Stock Exchange, 2004 Fact Book of Shanghai Stock Exchange, and 2004 Fact Book of Shenzhen Stock Exchange, from http://www.sse.com.cn and http://www.szse.com.cn.

Table 2.6 shows the convertible bonds on both exchanges. The number of convertible bonds listed on both exchanges and the dollar amount of bonds issued have increased over time, a result consistent with those in Table 2.4.

Table 2.5 Corporate bonds traded on Shanghai and Shenzhen Exchanges (1997–2005)

Year	Bond's name	Amount (million RMB)	Listing date	Expiration date
1997	Meishan	200	29/9/1997	14/5/2000
	Jihua	1000	9/9/1997	23/2/2000
	Sanxia	1000	16/7/1997	27/2/2000
	Zhongtie	1500	31/10/1997	20/1/2002
1999	Zhongxin 983	700	30/9/1999	16/11/2001
	97 Zhongtie 5	1600	24/6/1999	10/6/2003
	98 Sanxia (3)	1000	18/6/1999	18/1/2002
	98 Sanxia (8)	1000	18/6/1999	17/1/2007
	Guodian	2907	6/5/1999	10/6/2001
2000	98 Zhongtie 1	1600	21/11/2000	14/12/2003
	98 Zhongtie 2	1000	21/11/2000	12/10/2004
	98 Zhongtie 3	2400	21/11/2000	12/10/2009
	99 Sanxia	3000	20/12/2000	25/7/2010
2001	98 Zhongxin (7)	700	15/1/2001	15/6/2006
	98 Shiyouzhai	1350	18/10/2001	8/9/2007
	99 Baogang	2000	28/9/2001	10/8/2005
	01 Zhongyidong	5000	23/10/2001	17/6/2011
2002	01 Sanxiazhai	3000	19/4/2002	8/11/2016
	01 Sanxia 10	2000	19/4/2002	8/11/2011
	01 Guanghezhai	2500	6/6/2002	10/12/2008
	02 Dianwang 3	500	10/12/2002	18/6/2005
	02 Dianwang 15	3500	10/12/2002	18/6/2017
2003	02 Sanxiazhai	5000	13/1/2003	19/9/2022
	02 Zhongyi (5)	3000	22/1/2003	27/10/2007
	02 Zhongyi (15)	5000	22/1/2003	27/10/2017
	02 Sujiaotong	1500	18/4/2003	11/12/2017
	02 Yuchengtou	1500	20/6/2003	9/12/2012
	02 Guanghezhai	4000	18/8/2003	10/11/2017
	02 Wugang (3)	500	25/9/2003	4/11/2005
	02 Wugang (7)	1500	25/9/2003	4/11/2009
	02 Jinmao	1000	21/4/2003	28/4/2012
	03 Huguidao	4000	4/9/2003	18/2/2018
	03 Suyuanjian	1000	5/12/2003	17/7/2013
2004	03 Sanxiazhai	3000	15/3/2004	31/7/2033
	03 Huaneng 1	3000	19/11/2004	8/12/2013
	03 Dianwang (1)	3000	10/9/2004	31/12/2013
	03 Dianwang (2)	2000	10/9/2004	31/12/2013

Table 2.5 (continued)

Year	Bond's name	Amount (million RMB)	Listing date	Expiration date
	04 Tongyongzhai	1000	16/9/2004	30/3/2014
	04 Zhongshihua	3500	28/9/2004	21/9/2014
	03 Zhongdiantou	3000	28/10/2004	7/12/2018
2005	03 Pufazhai	1500	16/6/2005	12/1/2013
	03 Huhangyong	1000	12/8/2005	23/1/2013
	03 Sujiaotong	1800	26/10/2005	20/11/2013
	04 Guodian (1)	2444	8/9/2005	21/9/2014
	04 Guodian (2)	1556	8/9/2005	21/9/2019
	04 Jinditie	2000	30/8/2005	14/12/2014
	04 Nanwang (1)	1000	26/10/2005	16/9/2014
	04 Nanwang (2)	2000	26/10/2005	16/9/2019
	05 Shennengzhai	1000	18/7/2005	2/2/2015
	05 Suyuanjian	1200	22/7/2005	18/5/2015
	05 Yushuiwu	1700	1/8/2005	25/4/2015
	05 Huadianzhai	2000	6/9/2005	29/6/2015
	05 Datangzhai	3000	26/8/2005	28/4/2020
	05 Tiedaozhai	5000	9/9/2005	28/7/2020
	05 Guowang (1)	3000	12/9/2005	7/7/2015
	05 Guowang (2)	1000	12/9/2005	7/7/2015
	05 Hujian (1)	2000	27/9/2005	26/7/2015
	05 Hujian (2)	1000	27/9/2005	26/7/2020
	05 Zhongdiantou	2000	26/9/2005	11/7/2015

Note: The number at the beginning of a bond's name indicates the year of issuance and the number in parentheses is the number of times at which the company issues bonds.

Sources: Statistics from the annual fact books of Shanghai Stock Exchange, www.sse.com.cn, and Shenzhen Stock Exchanges, www.szse.com.cn.

FUTURE DEVELOPMENT OF THE BOND MARKET

Given China's particular political system, only the Standing Committee of the National People's Congress has the authority to issue treasury bonds and central bank securities. Although the provincial and municipal governments cannot issue municipal bonds, they actually obtain financing from the bonds issued by the policy banks, such as those by the China Development Bank. In addition, companies owned by local governments can get financing from corporate bonds, too. Thus, policy bank bonds and corporate bonds have essentially substituted for the municipal bonds, while commercial bank bonds are mainly used to lower the bad debt level of state-owned banks.

Table 2.6 Convertible bonds issued on Shanghai Stock Exchange (SHSE) and Shenzhen Stock Exchange (SZSE), 1993–2004

Year	Bond's name	Issuing amount (million RMB)	Stock Exchange
1993	Baoan C	500	SZSE
1998	Sichou	200	SZSE
	Nanhua	150	SZSE
	NHZZ	150	SHSE
1999	Maolian	150	SZSE
2000	Jichang	1350	SZSE
	Angang	1500	SZSE
	HQZZ	1350	SHSE
2002	Yangguaong	830	SZSE
	Shuiyun	320	SZSE
	Yanjing	700	SZSE
	Sichou 2	800	SZSE
	Wanke	1500	SZSE
	SYZZ	320	SHSE
	YGZZ	830	SHSE
2003	Gangfan	1600	SZSE
	Tongdu	76	SZSE
	Fengyuan	500	SZSE
	Huaxi	400	SZSE
	Shougang	2000	SZSE
	Minsheng	4000	SZSE
	Yunhua	410	SZSE
	Sigang	490	SZSE
	Yage	1190	SZSE
	Fuxing	950	SZSE
	Guiguan	800	SZSE
	Shanying	250	SZSE
	Longdian	800	SZSE
	Guodian	2000	SZSE
	Dangang	2000	SZSE
	MSZZ	4000	SHSE
	YHZZ	410	SHSE
	XGZZ	490	SHSE
	YGZZ	1191	SHSE
	FXZZ	950	SHSE
	GGZZ	800	SHSE
	SYZZ	250	SHSE
	HDZZ	800	SHSE

Table 2.6 (*continued*)

Year	Bond's name	Issuing Amount (million RMB)	Stock Exchange
	GDZZ	2000	SHSE
	DGZZ	2000	SHSE
2004	Ganglian	1800	SZSE
	Zhaohang	6500	SZSE
	Gehua	1250	SZSE
	Nanshan	883	SZSE
	Yingang	700	SZSE
	Jianghuai	880	SZSE
	Cuangye	1200	SZSE
	Chenmin	2000	SZSE
	Haihua	1000	SZSE
	Hualin	2000	SZSE
	Wanke 2	1990	SZSE
	Jinniu	700	SZSE
	Qiaocheng	400	SZSE
	GLZZ	1800	SHSE
	ZHZZ	6500	SHSE
	GHZZ	1250	SHSE
	NSZZ	883	SHSE
	YGZZ	700	SHSE
	JHZZ	880	SHSE
	CYZZ	1200	SHSE

Resources: Statistics from the annual fact Books of Shanghai Stock Exchange, www.sse.com.cn, and Shenzhen Stock Exchange, www.szse.com.cn.

Despite the relatively large size and high growth of the T-bond, F-bond, and E-bond markets, changes and improvements in these markets are necessary. It is advisable for the Chinese government to allow different domestic companies, including private companies and branches of foreign corporations, to issue bonds in order to increase the variety of bond products to meet investor demand. In addition, the governments need to encourage the issuance of other types of bonds, such as floating rate bonds, stripped government bonds, and asset backed bonds. It seems that the first mortgage backed bonds and warrants have appeared in China's market. Finally, the government should allow investors to trade corporate bonds in all markets (that is, the interbank market, the bank-counter market, and the exchanges) to increase liquidity of the bonds.

MARKET STRUCTURE OF SECONDARY BOND MARKET

The secondary market for the T-bonds appeared in 1988. After 1990, because of the establishment of the two exchanges, T-bonds began to be used as collateral in repo transactions. In 1997, commercial banks withdrew from the exchanges and launched the interbank bonds market. T-bonds began to be traded at market price in the bank counter market in 2002. In 2004, the spot repo market of the government bonds in the interbank market and on stock exchanges was launched. In the interbank market, repos are in fact government bonds that are used as collateral for loans between banks and financial institutions. In comparison, in the exchange markets, repos are short-term loans among securities companies and other sophisticated investors and also use government bonds as collateral. Next we introduce the bond products and trading contracts available on the three markets – interbank market, exchange market and bank-counter market (Decree No. 1 2005).

Interbank Market

The interbank market has the largest trading volume among the three markets (see Panel C of Table 2.1). The interbank market is organized and regulated by the People's Bank of China. Although non-financial institutions and some foreign banks take part in the market, most of the participants of this market are domestic financial institutions. They are banks, insurance companies, funds and other financial companies, which have fulfilled the membership requirements and opened a bond account in the China Government Securities Depository Trust and Clearing Company.

The interbank market serves as primary and secondary markets for the book-entry government bonds, central bank bonds, and F-bonds. Their issuers usually use auctions to organize underwriting. Banks and securities companies selected to take part in the auction will then distribute the bonds they purchase in the auction to other financial institutions and investors.

In 2005, several E-bonds were approved to be traded in the interbank market. The representatives of each member will negotiate a trading contract with each other. There are four types of trading contracts on the interbank market – spot trading, collateral repurchase agreement trading, non-collateral repurchase agreement trading and forward trading contracts. The People's Bank of China determines which contract is to be used for which type of trading. Bonds that are not yet listed in the market cannot be traded.

In collateral repo trading, investors who buy the repos have no access to the securities used as collateral during the holding period, whereas in a non-collateral repo trading, investors who buy the repo have absolute control of the securities. They can trade them on the market during the holding period. The non-collateral repo trading actually provides a way for investors to sell bonds.

The collateral repo trading is the main type of trading on the interbank market. In 2005, the trading volume was RMB6340 billion (27.7 percent of total) for spot trading, RMB16 290 billion (71.2 percent) for collateral repo trading, RMB219.5 billion (1.0 percent) for non-collateral repos, and RMB17.7 billion (0.08 percent) for forward trading. The maximum period for collateral repo is 365 days (Decree No. 2 2000); and the maximum period for non-collateral repo is 91 days (Decree 1 2005). Most of the repos transactions were within 14 days in 2005 according to the 2005 Chinese bonds statistics provided by the China Government Securities Depository Trust and Clearing Company.

Exchanges

Shanghai and Shenzhen Stock Exchanges serve as both the primary and secondary markets for the regular corporate bonds, corporate convertible bonds and book-entry government bonds. Investors can use the money in their stocks trading account with securities brokerage companies to buy newly-issued bonds and then trade these bonds after they are listed on the exchanges. The minimum unit that investors can buy is ten bonds, which cost about RMB 1000. The buying and the selling prices are quoted by the exchanges' trading systems. Regarding the book-entry bonds, most of the trading contracts are spot trading on the exchanges. Collateral and non-collateral repo trading of book-entry bonds are also available on the exchanges.

The Bank-Counter Market

The bank-counter market serves as the primary market for voucher government bonds, and both the primary and secondary market for book-entry government bonds. The primary market for the voucher bonds is organized by 39 commercial banks. All voucher government bonds are issued to the public over the counters of the member banks of the underwriting group and they could be traded among investors afterwards. In contrast, only part of the book-entry bonds are issued to the public from the bank counters, and they cannot be traded among investors afterwards. Only the big four state-owned banks in several large cities have been allowed to participate in the primary and secondary market for book-entry bonds. Financial institutions are not allowed to take part in the trading in the bank-counter market.

Since 2004, a small proportion of book-entry bonds have been sold to individual investors on the bank-counter market (see pp. 54–5). Unlike voucher bonds, the selling prices of the bonds are determined by the market. Banks have certain flexibility in setting their own bid-ask prices. After book-entry bonds are sold by the auction system, the big four banks can resell the bonds they have acquired to individual investors, who have opened a bond account with the bank as a part of the initial issuance process. The banks can sell the book-entry bonds at any price to investors within the range set by the MOF. For example, the MOF set the range from RMB99.8 to 100.2 for the bonds sold in 2004.

The book-entry bonds that have been sold to investors through the bank counter market can be traded in the bank-counter market, where the banks act as market makers. The bid-ask spread cannot exceed 1 percent of the bid price. Prices for the same type of bonds may have different quoted prices in different banks. The government publishes the daily prices from the four banks together on the website Chinabond.com.cn.

Based on the rules set by the China Government Securities Depository Trust and Clearing Company, the bonds owned by commercial banks belong to the so-called 'first-grade' account and can be traded in the interbank market. The bonds owned by other investors and bought from the banks belong to the 'second-grade' account and can be traded in the bank-counter market but not in the interbank market.

CHALLENGES FOR THE BOND MARKET

Unification of the Markets

The tripartite structure of the secondary market for bonds in China – the interbank market, the exchange market, and the bank-counter market – is not satisfactory and creates considerable price irregularity due to significant price discrepancies and low information transparency. For example, in the government bond market, bond yield differential between the interbank and the exchange market is puzzling. It is advisable to restructure these markets into one integrated market that can provide consistent pricing information. This should be a priority in future bond market reform.

In Western countries, the government regulates the exchanges. The over-the-counter (OTC) market is for the bonds that do not fulfill the listing requirement of the exchanges. China's OTC market is different as they are closely regulated and monitored by the government. As the two exchanges have identical listing requirements, the government needs to formulate listing rules and regulations to develop a properly diversified bond market.

The OTC market is separated into the interbank market and the bank-counter market. While individual investors cannot trade in the wholesale (primary) market, the bonds in the interbank market cannot be similarly traded in the bank-counter market because interbank market and bank-counter market are segmented. As a result, the prices of the bonds do not reflect the forces of demand and supply in an integrated market. If the same bonds from different markets can be traded without unnecessary rules and regulations, the efficiency of China's bond markets will be greatly improved.

Market Interest Rate

In the corporate bond market, the deposit interest rates are used as benchmark rate for corporate yields. The practice does not reflect risk and return of the issuing companies. The government should loosen the control on the pricing and coupon rates of bonds so that the price of bonds can reflect the risks.

As of late 2005, coupon rates of the corporate bonds have not been allowed to be higher than those of government bonds. As government bonds are considered free of default risk by many investors, the coupon rates of the corporate bonds should be higher than those of the government bonds even though the government might be confident that the companies are unlikely to default.

Initial Bond Issue Process

The initial bond issue process need scrutiny and possibly changes, too. Before 1991, Treasury bonds were issued through administrative assignments due to a lack of market mechanism and high inflation. After 1991, the T-bonds (treasury bonds) were issued through syndicated underwriting. In 1995, the auction process was established, marking a step toward a more market-oriented mechanism. While book-entry bonds' initial issuance uses the auction method, voucher bonds are still issued through syndicated underwriting, in which almost all members in the syndicate are state-owned banks and securities companies. We recommend that other types of companies, such as Qualified Financial Institutional Investors, be allowed to take part in the underwriting process in order to make the initial issuance process more competitive. The E-bonds, on the other hand, are usually underwritten by security companies and guaranteed by a large state-owned bank. Due to the complicated administrative approval process, it may take a long period of time before E-bonds are finally listed on the exchange markets. Companies often point out in their issuance announcements that they cannot guarantee whether their bonds will be able to be listed on the exchanges, the main secondary market available for the corporate bonds. In view of this, we suggest that E-bonds be allowed to trade in the OTC to increase their liquidity.

Regulation Issues

An important characteristic of China's bond market is that the government strictly regulates the issuance and trading of bonds. Different regulatory bodies are involved in monitoring the tripartite market at the same time. The interbank market is governed by the People's Bank of China, the central bank, because commercial banks and other financial institutions are involved in this market. As bonds can be listed on the exchanges, they are also regulated by the CSRC. It seems that a sensible financial reform measure for China's bond market may be to create a unified regulatory body to improve efficiency and streamline the decision-making process.

Credit Rating

Credit rating started in 1987. Initially, most of the credit rating agencies were housed in a department of state-owned banks. In 1997, nine national independent credit rating agencies were granted the status of bond rating agencies. The central bank was responsible for examining the credit ratings compiled by these credit rating agencies. In 2003, five independent credit rating agencies were further recognized by the China Insurance Regulation Committee as bond rating agencies for the insurance industry (Zhang 2005).

The credit rating system in China is still quite primitive in comparison to its counterpart in Western countries. As Liu (2003) pointed out, the corporate bonds issued on the Shanghai and Shenzhen Stock Exchanges are all triple A or triple A− rated because only large state-owned companies with strong financials are allowed to issue corporate bonds. The credit ratings so far have not been applied to all types of companies, so the credit ratings are not comparable across Chinese companies. Thus the credit rating system has only limited usage in valuing a firm's cost of capital and in determining the coupon rates of corporate bonds, as the coupon rates are not allowed to exceed the current deposit interest rates in the banks. The government should remove this restriction as it inevitably results in distorted coupon interest rates. The deposit rates in the banks do not serve as a good benchmark for the bond coupon rates as the deposit rates are regulated and determined by the central bank. They do not reflect the credit risk and other factors that affect bonds' interest rates. Thus, the government needs to allow different types of companies to list their bonds on the exchanges and let bond issuers and investors decide the coupon rates.

CONCLUSIONS

This chapter introduces and analyses the characteristics of China's tripartite bond market which includes the interbank market, exchange market, and bank-counter market. We describe and compare various types of bonds – government bonds, financial bonds, central bank bonds, and enterprise bonds. In contrast to the bond markets in many Western countries, China's government is responsible for determining many features of Chinese bonds, such as the coupon rates and maturities. In general, China's bond market has four important characteristics. First, the government bonds and central bank bonds have the largest issuing volumes. Their annual issuance volume has been much larger than the total financing companies obtain from the stock markets and the corporate bond markets.

Second, the central government has controlled the insurance of all types of bonds and the operation of all market venues. As the Chinese bond market is currently heavily regulated, it is important to introduce market forces and develop a market-oriented trading system.

Third, some bonds are traded in three markets (interbank, exchanges and bank-counter). For example, the book-entry government bonds are traded on three markets at the same time. There appears to be price discrepancy among the three markets. As regulations prevents arbitrage among the three markets, it is important to reduce regulatory impediments and integrate these fragmented markets in the future to improve market efficiency.

Finally, the coupon rates of corporate bonds do not reflect the credit quality of the issuing companies as the government sets subjective administrative limits on the level of coupon rates. A sound credit rating system should be developed and used to determine the coupon rates.

NOTE

1. The four big state-owned banks refer to the Bank of China, China Construction Bank, Agricultural Bank of China, and Industrial and Commercial Bank of China. They are also called by many as the 'Big Four' as they represent an overwhelming share of the banking market.

REFERENCES

Chinese Bond Market (2004), *Annual Book*, Department of Information of the China Government Securities Depository Trust & Clearing Co., Ltd (in Chinese).

Chinese Bond Market (2005), *Annual Book*, Department of Information of the China Government Securities Depository Trust & Clearing Co., Ltd (in Chinese).

Liu, Hong (2003), 'Corporate bonds and corporate credit rating market', *Investment and Securities*, 1 (in Chinese).
Wang, Xianbao (2005), 'The development and investment opportunities of corporate bonds with the expanding supply in 2005', *Capital Market*, June (in Chinese).
Zhang, Mingli and Hui Liu (2001), 'People's Republic of China', in *Yun-Hwan Kim* (ed.), *Government Bond Market Development in Asia*, Manila: Asian Development Bank, Chapter 5.
Zhang, Kangbin and Min Ji (2005), 'An overview of China's bond markets', *China & World Economy*, **13**(6), 27–39.
Zhang, Zhen (2005), 'The development history of the China credit rating industry', accessed at www.ccn86.com (in Chinese).
'The 2001 fact book of Shanghai Stock Exchange', accessed at www.sse.com.cn (in Chinese).
'The 2004 fact book of Shanghai Stock Exchange', accessed at www.sse.com.cn (in Chinese).
'The 2004 fact book of Shenzhen Stock Exchange', accessed at www.szse.com.cn (in Chinese).
The People's Bank of China Decree No. 2 (2000), accessed at www.pbc.gov.cn
The People's Bank of China Decree, No. 1 (2004), accessed at www.pbc.gov.cn
The People's Bank of China Decree No. 1 (2005), accessed at www.pbc.gov.cn

3. Futures markets

Jot Yau

INTRODUCTION

With a growth of over 9.5 percent a year, China is one of the fastest growing economies in the world. With this growth rate comes a huge demand for raw materials and commodities. *BusinessWeek* estimates China's share of global consumption in 2005 was 47 percent in cement, 37 percent in cotton, 32 percent in rice, 30 percent in coal, 26 percent in crude steel, 21 percent in aluminum, 20 percent in copper, 16 percent in wheat and 8 percent in oil.[1] This huge consumption demand inevitably makes China a major importer in many commodities and contributes to the increasing demand and price volatility in the world commodity markets. For example, China imported 18 percent and 20 percent of the world output of wheat and aluminum, respectively, in 2004 (Table 3.1). China is the third largest oil importer and the second largest importer of wheat in the world. This great increase in demand puts pressure on commodity prices and inflation rates. The rising costs of raw materials and their volatility inevitably increase the cost of production for all manufactured products, which may eventually slow down China's growth. Moreover, political upheavals in some commodity-rich countries, new environmental regulations, and other structural changes in the global physical commodity and futures markets have all contributed to increasing price volatility. This makes hedging using various derivatives (that is, forwards, futures, options and swaps) indispensable for many sectors of the economy such as the airline industry, and strategically important for developing countries. China is no exception.

Futures markets started trading in China in 1993, with an annual trading volume of 8.9 million contracts valued at 552.2 billion yuan.[2] In 2005, China's futures market volume was 322.9 million contracts valued at 13.5 trillion yuan (US$1.6 trillion). It has been over 15 years since the first trade was made and by normal standards, the Chinese futures market is not nascent. Unfortunately, because of several trading scandals and abuses during the early years of development, China's futures market experienced a series of setbacks and the Chinese government had implemented a couple of regulatory reforms in the governance of the futures markets. Yet, the futures

Table 3.1 China's major futures exchange traded products, during the first half of 2005

Commodity	Chinese Exchange	Volume, in millions of tonnes	Dominant exchange	China trade volume as % of dominant exchange	2004 global output imported by China (%)
Rubber	Shanghai	15.0	TOCOM	131.8	14
Cotton	Zhengzhou	49.3	NYBOT	94.1	15
Copper	Shanghai	77.8	LME	30.6	18
Soybean meal	Dalian	382.5	CBOT	25.5	NA
Soybeans	Dalian	375.9	CBOT	8.6	NA
Wheat	Zhengzhou	202.2	CBOT	5.6	18
Aluminum	Shanghai	9.7	LME	2.5	20
Corn	Dalian	167.2	CBOT	1.6	20

Note: TOCOM – Tokyo Commodity Exchange; NYBOT – New York Board of Trade; LME – London Metal Exchange; CBOT – Chicago Board of Trade.

Source: Areddy (2005).

market has not caught up with the dramatic growth in the manufacturing and export sectors which could have benefited from futures trading. At present, China's futures market is not yet a complete solution to laying off the commodity price risk but a step closer toward it.[3] With the gradual opening of the Chinese economy to foreigners under the WTO agreement, developing a modern and efficient futures market has become a top priority for the nation.

In this chapter, we begin with a review of the development of futures trading in China that got started in the 1990s. In the third section, we introduce futures trading and the three futures exchanges in China. In the fourth section, we describe how futures trading is regulated by the China Securities Regulatory Commission (CSRC) and China Futures Association. In the fifth section, we review previous studies on the performance of the futures contracts and discuss the impact of government regulation/intervention on futures markets. In the sixth section, we discuss the future of China's futures market. We conclude the chapter in the final section.

THE DEVELOPMENT OF FUTURES MARKETS IN CHINA

Conceived in 1990, China's futures market started with the establishment of a wholesale grain market established in Zhengzhou as a precursor to futures trading. It experienced a quick expansion along with the development of the stock market. By 1993, there were over 1000 brokerages, more than 30 futures exchanges and over 50 products in the futures market (Table 3.2). The proliferation of regional futures exchanges in China created a flurry of chaotic trading activities as well as price irregularities during the early period of market development. Loopholes in the regulatory scheme exacerbated the situation making frauds and market manipulations commonplace. A host of trading scandals urged the authorities to consider a market clean-up, but it was the outbreak of the bond futures scandal that provided the impetus to reform.

The central government took a series of measures starting in 1994 to standardize futures trading, including the approval process in setting up an exchange, scope of products to be traded, and overall regulation of exchanges. Other regulations put a restraint on the financial prowess of big institutional players, use of public funds and likelihood of fraud in futures trading. These measures were all instituted during the period 1994–1998, known as the First Rectification of the futures market regulatory reforms. As a result, many futures exchanges and brokerages were closed down and some products were suspended from trading, including bond futures in 1995.

As abuses continued after the First Rectification, the government in 1998 further reduced the number of futures exchanges from 14 to three exchanges as the initial effort of the Second Rectification of the futures market regulatory reforms that ran from 1998–2000. In 1999, the State Council prohibited futures brokerage firms from making proprietary trading. In addition, severe penalties on illicit futures trading were imposed to discourage illicit trading and deter corruption. As the result of two rounds of rectification, market activity in the futures market was brought almost to a halt. Annual transaction, which totaled 10 trillion yuan (US$1.2 trillion) in 1995, declined to a low of 1.6 trillion yuan (US$192 billion) in 2000. It recovered to a record high of 15 trillion (US$1.8 billion) in 2004 (Table 3.2).

After the two rounds of reforms that lasted for about seven years, China's futures market has managed to grow steadily under close scrutiny by the authorities. Thus, the First Rectification can be considered as a means to reorganizing and standardizing futures trading while the Second Rectification as a means to paving the way to opening up the financial markets under the WTO agreement. A legal and regulatory framework has now been in place to facilitate futures trading while ensuring the integrity of the futures market. China is now poised to take on challenges and opportunities that are presented as the economy is opening up to the rest of the world.

Table 3.2 Futures trading in China 1993–2005

	No. of exchanges	Brokerage firms	Listed commodities	Annual turnover (RMB 100 million yuan)	Annual trading volume (10 000 lots)	Annual delivery value (RMB 100 million yuan)	Annual delivery volume (10 000 lots)
1993	32+	1000	52+	5521.99	890.69	NA	NA
1994	14	144	35	31 601.41	12 110.72	NA	NA
1995	14	330	35	100 565.30	63 612.07	181.52	83.09
1996	14	329	35	84 119.16	34 256.77	174.13	78.33
1997	14	294	35	61 170.666	15 876.32	93.75	38.18
1998	14	278	35	36 967.24	10 445.57	48.04	20.56
1999	3	313	12	22 343.01	7363.91	109.41	16.12
2000	3	718	12	16 082.29	5461.07	65.11	8.40
2001	3	159	12	30 144.98	12 046.35	57.54	64.85
2002	3	167	12	39 490.28	13 943.37	101.44	141.16
2003	3	185	12	108 396.90	27 988.57	127.46	29.10
2004	3	185	12	146 935.31	30 569.76	NA	NA
2005	3	182	12	134 463.37	32 287.41	NA	NA

Note: Trading volume figures account for both sides of the transaction (that is they are round-trip figures that include both buy and sell sides of each transaction); Delivery volume figures only account for one side of the transaction.

Source: Wang and Gorham (2002); CSRC Report (2004); Annual Reports of SHFE, DCE, and ZCE (2003, 2004, 2005).

FUTURES TRADING AND EXCHANGES

Futures exchanges in China are self-regulatory, non-profit, legal entities that perform functions as required by government regulations and stipulated in their articles of association.[4] They provide traders with venue and services for futures trading, clearing and physical delivery. At present, there are three futures exchanges in China: Shanghai Futures Exchange, Dalian Commodity Exchange and Zhengzhou Commodity Exchange. They are the survivors of the First and the Second Rectifications.[5] The futures exchanges are required to register with the State Administration of Industry and Commerce and are under the supervision of the China Securities Regulatory Commission.

Figure 3.1 and Table 3.2 present the trading volume and turnover statistics for the Chinese futures markets for the period 1993–2005. It is noted that trading volume quickly reached its record high within two years of futures trading inception in 1995 with over 636 million contracts. Volume dropped significantly during the Rectification periods to 54.6 million contracts in 2000, which is less than 10 percent of 1995's volume. Since 2000, both trading volume and turnover went up steadily. In 2005, the Chinese futures market registered a trading volume of 322.9 million contracts valued at 13.4 trillion yuan (US$1.6 trillion) (Table 3.2).

Unlike most US futures exchanges that use the open outcry-floor trading system, China's futures markets have adopted the electronic trading system, which is more transparent and more in line with other international futures markets.[6] The three exchanges were linked in 2001 electronically on a common platform sharing market data and information, barring trading. Trading and clearing are based on a time-price-priority electronic order matching system. Orders are put in the system via terminals in the trading hall and brokers' offices across the nation. Trading takes place in two

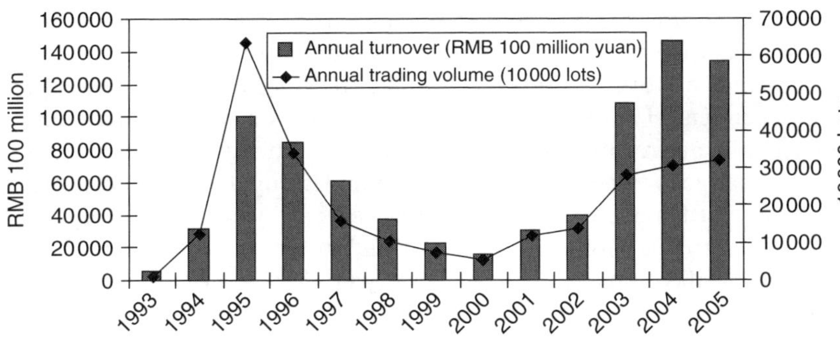

Figure 3.1 Futures trading volume and turnover (1993–2005)

sessions: 9:00 a.m.–11:30 a.m. and 1:30 p.m.–3:00 p.m. (Beijing time). All trades are denominated in Chinese Renminbi, or RMB.

At present, the Chinese regulations stipulate that only mainland citizens and companies or organizations that are organized and registered in mainland China can trade in the Chinese futures markets. All trades on behalf of domestic or foreign investors have to be executed through Chinese brokerage firms registered with the CSRC. For a subsidiary of a China-incorporated company, it must be organized as a legal person in order to trade futures in the local market. That is, a representative office or a branch office will not be allowed to trade.

Trading in overseas futures contracts by Chinese entities for the sole purpose of hedging is allowed, but prior approval must be obtained from both the State Council and the CSRC. To date, 18 state-owned enterprises are authorized to use overseas futures products for hedging purposes. Most of these companies trading metals and foodstuffs can only trade overseas futures contracts directly related to their business, and are prohibited from speculation. According to a report, despite explicit prohibition, some foreign-owned China-incorporated companies, have traded domestic futures contracts, with most of them trading copper contracts in Shanghai, either to hedge China-related price risks or to arbitrage (that is, to profit from price differences) between domestic and overseas exchanges. In addition, many companies trade in overseas exchanges on behalf of domestic enterprises both for hedging and arbitrage purposes.[7, 8]

Similar to what the US and other futures exchanges in the world used to protect the financial integrity of the futures market, China's futures exchanges have installed various risk control measures, such as daily price limits, position limits, large position reporting, margins, and marking-to-market (that is, daily settlement). In addition, the risk reserve fund is established to provide financial guarantee for maintaining normal operation of the futures markets and to make up the losses caused by unforeseeable risks whereas the settlement reserve fund is set up to guarantee the performance of futures contracts. Unlike the US futures markets where an independent clearing house is responsible for daily settlement, designated banks are responsible for clearing the exchange members' trades, while exchange members are responsible for clearing their own customers' accounts. Settlement of futures contracts is by physical delivery.[9] All expiring contracts are for physical delivery in accordance with the contract specifications in terms of delivery grade, delivery time, and point of delivery.

The Dalian Commodity Exchange

The Dalian Commodity Exchange (DCE), established in November 1993, is a nonprofit, self-regulatory legal entity. It survived the two Rectifications in 1994 and 1998 when the State Council merged the futures exchanges.[10] Today, it is one of the three futures exchanges.

At present, DCE has 195 members, 182 of whom are brokerage firm members (that is, futures commission merchants) and 13 proprietary trading members. It has five futures listed for trading on an electronic trading system: corn, soybean (No. 1 and No. 2), soy meal, and soybean oil.

The DCE has been the largest futures exchange in China by volume (number of contracts traded) since 2000.[11] Table 3.3 presents the futures trading statistics on the DCE from 2002–2005. DCE recorded an annual total of 198 million contracts in 2005, up from 96 million contracts in 2002. In terms of turnover, it went from 2 trillion yuan in 2002 to 4.74 trillion yuan (US$589 billion) in 2005. Both trading volume and turnover went up by more than 100 percent since 2002. Moreover, open interest also increased significantly since 2003 surpassing 950 000 lots in 2005 (Table 3.3).

The DCE's success is tied to soy, a major staple diet for the Chinese for thousands of years. In 2000, soybean represented 77 percent of all imported grains to China and is still the only grain import that China depends on from the US (Fung *et al.* 2003). The DCE started trading soy meal in July 2000, which was the first contract approval for trading since the First Rectification in 1998. In 2003, the soybean (No. 1) futures traded on the DCE were equivalent to 25.3 percent of those on the CBOT in the same period, and five times those at the Tokyo Grain Exchange. In 2004, soybean (No. 1) was the only commodity futures contract in the top 20 futures contract traded in the world. DCE's soy bean (No. 1) and soy meal futures were among the top ten actively traded agricultural futures contracts in the world; and the DCE was ranked 18th in terms of annual volume according to the Futures Industry Association. Although the trading volume of the soybean (No. 1) futures declined in 2005, the DCE has been the world's second largest soybean futures market as well as the largest futures market for non-transgenic soybeans (CSRC 2004). As such, the soybean futures price in the DCE has become an important benchmark for the local and foreign soybean producers, distributors, importers, and exporters.

Since 2004, corn futures contracts have been trading on the exchange, which have also generated significant trading volume for the exchange (Table 3.4). This is as expected since China is the world's second largest corn consumer and producer, which produces 120 million tonnes of corn

Table 3.3 Chinese futures market trading volume, turnover and open interest (2002–2005)

	Dalian Commodity Exchange			Shanghai Futures Exchange			Zhengzhou Commodity Exchange			Total		
	Trading volume (lots)	Turnover (100 million yuan)	Open interest (lots)	Trading volume (lots)	Turnover (100 million yuan)	Open interest (lots)	Trading volume (lots)	Turnover (100 million yuan)	Open interest (lots)	Trading volume (lots)	Turnover (100 million yuan)	Open interest (lots)
2002	96 814 808	20 836.28	907 066	24 346 166	16 401.41	398 086	18 270 000	2253.00	NA	139 430 974	39 490.69	NA
2003	149 908 412	39 895.99	526 336	80 159 500	60 539.91	627 552	49 817 800	7961.00	357 308	279 885 712	108 396.90	1 511 196
2004	176 068 306	50 968.53	719 214	81 154 746	84 326.42	437 024	48 474 548	11 640.36	314 146	305 697 600	146 935.31	1 470 384
2005	198 349 428	47 416.75	956 958	67 579 508	65 402.03	309 446	56 945 140	21 644.59	452 058	322 874 076	134 463.37	1 718 462

Note: Trading volume, turnover and open interest are round-trip figures (that is, both buy and sell sides are counted). Open interest is the number of outstanding contracts at year end.

Source: Dalian Commodity Exchange, Shanghai Futures Exchange, and Zhengzhou Commodity Exchange.

annually, accounting for about one-third of the nation's grain output (Yao 2004).

The Shanghai Futures Exchange

The Shanghai Futures Exchange (SHFE), established in December 1999, is the result of a between Shanghai Metal Exchange, Shanghai Cereal and Oils Exchange and Shanghai Commodity Exchange. As with the DCE, SHFE is also organized as a non-profit, self-regulatory legal entity. At present, SHFE has 211 members, of which 183 are brokerage firm members and the rest are proprietary trading members. SHFE is an electronic trading exchange with more than 250 distant trading terminals all over China.

While the DCE has been the largest futures exchange by volume (number of contracts traded) in China, the Shanghai Futures Exchange has been the leader in terms of turnover. SHFE was ranked 17th in 2005 in terms of trading volume among the world futures exchanges according to the Futures Industry Association.

At present, there are four contracts listed for trading: copper, aluminum, natural rubber and fuel oil. Its natural rubber futures was ranked among the top ten most actively traded agricultural futures in 2004, according to the Futures Industry Association.

Table 3.4 presents the futures trading statistics of SHFE from 2002–2005. SHFE recorded an annual total of 67.6 million contracts in 2005, up from 24.3 million contracts in 2002, representing an increase of almost 180 percent. In terms of turnover, it went from 1.6 trillion yuan in 2002 to 6.54 trillion yuan (US$824 billion) in 2005, representing an increase of almost 300 percent. The open interest in 2005, however, declined to a level below that of 2002 due to the curtailment of trading in metals.

Despite the efforts that the Shanghai Futures Exchange put to further consolidate its status as one of the three authoritative price-setting centers in the world copper market,[12] the copper trading scandal in November 2005 significantly interrupted its progress towards a global price leadership position.[13] Trading volume in Table 3.5 indicates that the decline in trading activity on the copper futures in 2005 was greater than 40 percent decline and open interest reduced by more than 65 percent than the previous year. Aluminum futures were also affected. The negative impact from the metal futures was balanced by the significant increase in trading on the other two futures listed. It should be noted from the statistics presented in Table 3.5 that natural rubber futures received great attention from traders. In addition, the trading of the fuel oil futures has heralded SHFE's exploration into energy futures.

Table 3.4 Dalian Commodity Exchange trading volume, turnover, and open interest (2002–2005)

	2002			2003			2004			2005		
	Trading volume (lots)	Turnover (100 million yuan)	Open interest (lots)	Trading volume (lots)	Turnover (100 million yuan)	Open interest (lots)	Trading volume (lots)	Turnover (100 million yuan)	Open interest (lots)	Trading volume (lots)	Turnover (100 million yuan)	Open interest (lots)
Soybean (No. 1)	25 379 870	6037.42	825 878	120 001 616	33 312.42	350 222	114 681 606	35 982.26	420 248	80 071 414	23 130.63	390 672
Soybean (No. 2)	–	–	–	–	–	–	228 694	59.56	21 158	1 082 186	291.61	25 174
Soy Meal	8 808 268	1577.76	30 816	29 906 796	6573.64	134 526	49 501 916	13 573.21	85 070	73 476 364	18 488.05	254 770
Corn	–	–	–	–	–	–	11 656 090	1353.49	192 738	43 719 464	5506.46	295 342
Soybeans	62 626 670	13 221.10	50 372	38 574	9.92	41 588	–	–	–	–	–	–
Total	96 814 808	20 836.28	907 066	149 946 986	39 895.98	526 336	176 068 306	50 968.52	719 214	198 349 428	47 416.72	965 958

Note: Trading volume, turnover and open interest are round-trip figures (that is both buy and sell sides are counted). Open interest is the number of outstanding contracts at year end.

Source: Dalian Commodity Exchange.

Table 3.5 Shanghai Futures Exchange trading volume, turnover, and open interest (2002–2005)

	2002			2003			2004			2005		
	Trading volume (lots)	Turnover (100 million yuan)	Open interest (lots)	Trading volume (lots)	Turnover (100 million yuan)	Open interest (lots)	Trading volume (lots)	Turnover (100 million yuan)	Open interest (lots)	Trading volume (lots)	Turnover (100 million yuan)	Open interest (lots)
Copper	11 592 600	9190.31	235 246	22 332 576	21 622.29	383 166	42 496 740	56 785.46	315 822	24 704 052	40 463.23	105 788
Aluminum	4 711 592	3193.27	80 840	4 310 996	3212.56	90 176	13 658 998	11 723.76	75 208	4 250 040	3714.46	78 866
Rubber	8 041 974	4017.83	82 000	53 515 928	35 705.06	154 210	19 361 298	14 580.18	14 168	19 006 316	15 601.79	56 970
Fuel oil	–	–	–	–	–	–	5 637 710	1237.02	31 826	19 619 100	5622.55	67 822
Total	24 346 166	16 401.41	398 086	80 159 500	60 539.91	627 552	81 154 746	84 326.42	437 024	67 579 508	65 402.03	309 446

Note: Trading volume, turnover and open interest are round-trip figures (that is, both buy and sell sides are counted). Open interest is the number of outstanding contracts at year end.

Source: Shanghai Futures Exchange.

The Zhengzhou Commodity Exchange

The Zhengzhou Commodity Exchange (ZCE), originally established in October 1990, is a nonprofit, self-regulatory, legal entity. It was built upon the foundation of China Zhengzhou Grain Wholesale Market (CZGWM), the first pilot futures market in China approved by the State Council which started operation in 1990. It first started with spot trading, followed by forward contract trading, and eventually made a transition to futures trading. In May 1993, CZGWM launched futures trading on five commodities: wheat, corn, soybean, mungbean and sesame under the name of China Zhengzhou Commodity Exchange (CZCE). Since then, CZGWM, a cash market, and CZCE, a futures market, operated and managed side by side by the same management team. During the First Rectification period, CZCE was approved by the central government to continue its business. In 1998, China Zhengzhou Commodity Exchange changed its name to Zhengzhou Commodity Exchange (ZCE) as one of the three exchanges approved to remain in operation at the Second Rectification. In 2001, ZCE and CZGWM became two independent organizations.

At present, ZCE has 218 member firms, including 176 brokerage firm members and 42 proprietary trading members from 27 provinces, municipalities and autonomous regions. It has offsite trading terminals in cities across the nation. Four contracts are now listed for trading: strong gluten wheat, hard white winter wheat, cotton and white sugar.

Table 3.3 presents the futures trading statistics on the ZCE from 2002–2005. ZCE recorded an annual total of 56.9 million contracts in 2005, up from 18.3 million contracts in 2002. In terms of turnover, it went from 225.3 billion yuan in 2002 to 2.16 trillion yuan (US$263 billion) in 2005. That is, the trading volume went up by more than 200 percent while the turnover went up by more than eight-fold since 2002. The open interest has been fluctuating in recent years (Table 3.3). These statistics reflect the strong growth in the wheat and cotton futures and the declining trend in the trading of the hard white winter wheat and mungbean futures. The statistics for each futures are presented in Table 3.6 for the period 2002–2005.

Although mungbean had been actively traded in Zhengzhou's futures market during 1993–1999, accounting for 50 percent of the volume of the entire Chinese futures market, it inevitably came to its demise when the margin rate for mungbean futures was raised to 20 percent in 1999, whereas the margin rate for hard white winter wheat futures was decreased from 10 percent to 5 percent. As a result, trading in mungbean futures began to fade away and wheat futures gradually became the active futures product in Zhengzhou. The listing of strong gluten wheat futures contract

Table 3.6 Zhengzhou Commodity Exchange trading volume, turnover, and open interest (2002–2005)

	2002			2003			2004			2005		
	Trading volume (lots)	Turnover (100 million yuan)	Open interest (lots)	Trading volume (lots)	Turnover (100 million yuan)	Open interest (lots)	Trading volume (lots)	Turnover (100 million yuan)	Open interest (lots)	Trading volume (lots)	Turnover (100 million yuan)	Open interest (lots)
Wheat (S)	–	–	–	19 308 856	3273.08	113 096	23 174 538	4371.42	204 926	33 240 192	5654.25	375 708
Wheat (T)	18 271 626	2252.46	300 786	30 508 942	4687.60	244 212	19 311 918	3483.77	51 292	1 963 298	305.16	1318
Cotton	–	–	–	–	–	–	5 988 092	3785.18	57 928	21 741 650	15 685.19	75 032
Mungbean	32	0.011	4	24	0.008	–	–	–	–	–	–	–
Total	18 271 658	2252.47	300 790	49 817 822	7960.68	357 308	48 474 548	11 640.37	314 146	56 945 140	21 644.60	452 058

Note: Trading volume, turnover and open interest are round-trip figures (that is, both buy and sell sides are counted). Open interest is the number of outstanding contracts at year end.

Source: Zhengzhou Commodity Exchange.

in 2003 attracted traders and promoted the inter-commodity spread trading between the two wheat futures contracts increasing the liquidity of the two markets. In 2004, both wheat contracts traded on ZCE were ranked among the top ten most actively traded agricultural futures in the world according to the Futures Industry Association, and the ZCE was ranked 19th in terms of trading volume among the world derivatives exchanges.[14] The decision to promote trading in the wheat futures in lieu of the mungbean futures has strategic significance to the national agricultural policy. The impact of this type of government intervention and its implications are discussed on pp. 87–90.

REGULATION OF FUTURES TRADING

Established in October 1992 by the State Council, the China Securities Regulatory Commission (CSRC) is responsible for regulating the securities and futures trading in China as stipulated in the *Securities Law*, *Company Law*, *Securities Investment Fund Law* and *Criminal Law.* These enacted laws provide for civil, administrative and criminal liabilities of a party guilty of securities and futures offenses and crimes, including fraudulent practices, insider dealings and market manipulations.

While the CSRC is the regulatory authority for all futures trading, the China Futures Association is a non-profit-making, self-regulatory organization incorporated in December 2000 under the *Regulations of Social Organization Registration and Management*. The China Futures Association plays the role of the self-regulator for the futures industry and is subject to the guidance, supervision and administration of the CSRC and the Ministry of Civil Affairs.

In its capacity as the industry's self-regulator, the China Futures Association helps enforce laws, regulations and policies pertaining to the futures market, liaise between the government and the futures industry, impose discipline on its members, foster the interests of its members, maintain transparency, fairness and equality in the futures market, provide training on professional ethics and uphold the professional and ethical standards.

Members of the China Futures Association include futures brokerage firms, future exchanges and licenced individual futures traders. As of the end of 2005, it had 191 institutional members including the three exchanges and 188 futures brokerage firms. Its members, who collectively represent the ultimate authority of the China Futures Association, meet every three years.

PERFORMANCE OF FUTURES CONTRACTS AND MARKETS

Unlike some developing countries, China has been quite successful in making the transition from a centrally-planned economy to a market-based economy during the last two decades. This is also true for the futures market, despite some hiccups along the way. In this section, we first review the previous studies on the performance of some futures contracts. We then examine the impact of government intervention or regulation on the development of the futures market, providing a background for understanding the prospects and problems facing the Chinese futures market today.

Performance of Futures Contracts

Previous research on the performance of China's futures contracts has been sporadic. Williams *et al.* (1998) present one of the earlier studies on China's futures markets. They document the development of the first established futures market in China – the CZCE. The exchange started with great expectations and had introduced over 11 contracts (for example, rice, soybeans, peanuts and corn) for trading in the first three years of operation. Unfortunately, by mid-1995, all but the wheat and mungbean futures were delisted due to the lack of trading.

There are several reasons for the lack of research on China's futures trading. First, there were many fragmented cash and futures markets before the Second Rectification. It was difficult to identify the central market for each commodity, if any. Second, there was no systematic collection and dissemination of trading data before the Second Rectification. Gathering good quality trading data for both the spot and futures markets is almost impossible. Third, the trading history of most contracts traded is not long enough to make any meaningful statistical inference. This deficiency, of course, will improve and disappear over time. Fourth, because of the proliferation of futures markets and contracts in the early years, most contracts did not have adequate trading and thus the scope of studies was limited. For futures contracts which had been active for some time were either subsequently delisted because of excessive speculation or replaced by other futures for different reasons. Thus, studies on the efficiency of the Chinese futures market, for example, investigation of the price discovery or hedging function, are almost non-existent for the early period.

For later periods where data are available, previous studies focus more on the macro issues (for example, volatility spillover across markets) rather than on the micro issues, such as the hedging effectiveness of a futures. For example, Fung *et al.* (2003) examine the patterns of information flows for three futures traded in both the US and China's markets during the period 1996–2001 for copper and 1995–2001 for soybeans and wheat. They find that the US futures market played a dominant role in transmitting information to the Chinese market for copper and soybeans but not for the case of wheat. They attribute this result to the fact that copper and soybeans were subject to less government regulation and fewer import restrictions than wheat in China. Their results indicate that the US–China wheat futures markets were highly segmented in pricing, although there was some information transmission via volatility spillover across markets.

Wang and Ke (2005) studied the efficiency of the Chinese wheat and soybean futures with three different cash markets and six different futures forecasting horizons ranging from one week to four months. Their results suggest a long-term equilibrium relationship between the futures and cash prices for soybeans and weak short-term efficiency in the soybean futures market. They conclude that the futures market for wheat was inefficient, which could have been caused by over-speculation and government intervention. Their finding is consistent with Fung *et al.* (2003).

Government Intervention/Regulation

Results from previous studies seem to support the notion that government intervention has impact on the futures market, particularly on the futures price volatility. However, it is not clear whether it was the direct 'regulation' or the indirect 'intervention' that caused an impact on the market. For instance, the ban on proprietary trading by futures brokerage firms in 1999 was a direct regulation which could have created an impediment to the efficiency of the futures market. Since the regulations on the futures markets in China are general regulations which focus on the trading environment and general operational structures, Chan *et al.* (2004) believe that the regulations in futures trading in China are intended to establish stability and regularity in the futures markets because trading in these markets is generally perceived to be highly speculative. They hypothesize that the daily volatility of the futures contract would be lower than that of the period before the implementation of the measures and regulations because of better information flows and lower transaction cost. They find significant reduction in daily volatility in all futures studied (copper, mungbean, soybeans and wheat) during the period 1996–2001. They also find that the strong relationship of volatility with open interest, volume and returns was more pronounced in recent than earlier years. They attribute the result to government regulations that require dissemination of more information to market participants rendering the futures market more transparent. There is no doubt that government action, as direct as special laws and regulations, or as indirect as simply moral suasion, will all affect trading in the market.

A case in point is the mungbean futures traded on the Zhengzhou Commodity Exchange between 1993 and 2003. When the ZCE was considering launching a mungbean futures market in the early 1990s, the spot market for mungbean was absent. The ZCE developed a wholesale market for mungbean prior to the establishment of the futures market with advice from the CBOT (Williams *et al.* 1998). This practice is not uncommon as the existence of an active spot market is essential for the well-functioning of the corresponding futures market.[15] The mungbean futures has had early success since its inception in 1993, through to the end of 1999 when the Exchange decided to replace it with the less actively traded wheat futures.

One probable reason for such a decision is that wheat has national strategic importance to China because China is the world number one producer and consumer of wheat (about 18 percent of the world output in 2004, see Table 3.1). The Chinese government has been protecting the wheat industry by subsidizing farmers and producers as well as restricting wheat imports. It has managed to maintain a monopoly over supply and distribution. Therefore, price volatility has not been a problem and hedging against price risk has never been done. Under the WTO agreement, China has agreed to give up its monopoly over agricultural production and distribution as well as most state controls over imports and exports. Anticipating the opening up of the agricultural markets to the rest of the world, increasing price volatility is expected. Thus, there is a need for an efficient futures market in which Chinese farmers and users of wheat can hedge against the price risk. This is no doubt a top national priority for China. To ensure an efficient and liquid wheat futures market for hedgers and users, a large pool of speculators who would be interested to trade in the market is a necessary condition for a successful futures market. Speculators trading in the mungbean futures market that could provide liquidity to the wheat futures market were a natural target participant. The Exchange and the government grasped this great opportunity and used it to their advantage.

As mentioned on pp. 77–86, it didn't take long to entice traders to switch trading from mungbean futures to wheat futures when the margin rate for mungbean futures was raised to 20 percent, while the margin on the wheat (hard white winter) futures were reduced from 10 percent to 5 percent.[16] In addition, the daily price limits for mungbean was lowered at the same time. According to the ZCE, it was the CSRC who mandated the exchange to increase the margin rate of mungbean step by step and lower the margin rate of wheat futures.[17] As expected, there was a strong impact on the volatility of both contracts (see Chan *et al.* 2005).

Interestingly, the decision to intervene in the functioning of the market enabled the Exchange and the government to kill two birds with one stone: dampening excessive speculation in the mungbean market while channeling the huge pool of liquidity provided by the mungbean speculators to the wheat futures market which could benefit from such an influx of liquidity. If volume is a good indicator of speculative activities and open interest a good proxy for hedging and arbitrage activities, the disappearing trading volume and open interest in the mungbean futures while increasing for the wheat futures support the conjecture that it might have been a deliberate effort to support one futures market at the expense of another.

THE FUTURE OF THE CHINESE FUTURES MARKETS

Given the expected economic growth in China with huge demand for raw materials, commodities and energy, and the influx of foreign direct investment to China with the scheduled opening of various sectors of China's economy under the WTO agreement, the need for developing the futures markets has never been more important. The prospect for the Chinese futures market is excellent provided careful and immediate attention is given to new product development (especially financial futures), continuing challenges, and foreign participation.

New Product Development

New products to be listed for trading require approval by the CSRC. New products have been approved and launched according to plans orchestrated by the government. Thus, each futures product is allowed to trade only on one exchange so that market activity is concentrated and maximum liquidity obtained. This ensures the success of each contract which has been carefully selected for its strategic importance to the whole economy.[18]

Chinese leaders realize that its voracious demand for commodities can be turned into its advantage by developing world class futures markets so that prices can be set in China. Key Chinese officials believe that China should set the global prices for commodities especially after the lesson they have learned in a cotton crisis.[19] It is clear that China tries to use the futures market as leverage in setting the world prices in major commodities (from oil to metals to cotton) so that it will get the best prices for its consumers (Areddy 2005). Raw material import statistics in Table 3.1 explain China's motivation to hold down prices. China imports almost 30 percent of its oil, 45 percent of its iron ore, and 44 percent of its requirement for ten nonferrous metals according to a report (Areddy 2005). Moreover, China is now the world's leading consumer of copper, using 18 percent of the world supply in 2004 (Table 3.1), or almost one and a half times as much as the US. But, rather than being set in China, global prices are determined on the London Metal Exchange. The listing of metal futures (copper and aluminum) at SHFE is a clear attempt to turn that around.

Will China be successful in its strategy? Chinese officials have been urging the state-owned importers to specify that prices reflect those set on the Chinese exchanges in long-term purchase contracts with foreign suppliers. While the Chinese government can't unilaterally set prices on the exchanges, government entities which trade in the commodities market can exert influence on speculators in these markets, although these government entities may not be the biggest players. China is also arbitraging in the overseas markets, for example, LME and CBOT, in soybeans and grains making the Chinese futures prices move in line with the world markets. Unfortunately, this is sometimes interrupted by trading bans caused by the repercussions of trading abuses, for example, the recent CAO debacle and the copper trading scandal.

Under the WTO agreement, China has pledged to completely open its oil market in five years and thus it is likely that China needs oil futures to hedge the risk of price volatility. There is a need to develop a wide array of energy futures and derivatives for the growing economy. At present, there is only fuel oil futures traded on the SHFE. Acceleration in product development seems warranted despite the recent CAO debacle.

Financial Futures

Each futures exchange in China aspires to become the premier futures exchange by being the first to trade financial futures. Every exchange has done due diligence in researching financial futures. Irregularities in government bond futures trading in 1995, however, have caused the CSRC to continue to be very cautious about the introduction of financial futures. Recently, it has announced that financial futures has been selected for trading in Shanghai in 2006, although the government has not announced where and what products might be introduced (Areddy 2006). According to a report, it will be a new exchange which is a joint venture between the Shanghai and Shenzhen Stock exchanges, the Shanghai Futures exchange, and the Dalian and Zhengzhou commodity exchanges; each exchange will own 20 percent (Silverman 2006). Regarding the type of financial futures to list, some argue that the size of market capitalization for the equity market (3 trillion yuan = US$370 billion) has an urgent need for the development of equity-based derivatives (such as derivatives on stock indexes) for hedging and risk management for institutional investors and funds.[20]

Challenges

There are still some continuing challenges that the Chinese futures market has to overcome. First, despite the need for a futures market for hedging and risk management, Chinese policy-makers and bureaucrats at various levels, for example, municipality or city, are reluctant to be innovative in opening up the cash and futures markets. Probably, they are wary of losing control politically or being held responsible for causing chaos in the financial markets, which is a crime under the national law.

Second, the Chinese futures markets are not yet efficient by standards in the developed capital markets. A few big players, such as state-own enterprises or deep-pocket insiders, can easily manipulate prices in the local market by taking advantage of insider information about possible policy changes. These big players have the edge over small local investors in terms of asymmetric information. These big players do not possess this niche in the international markets, but at least they have the access to international markets whereas the small investors may not.

Third, retail investors lack basic knowledge in investing, let alone futures and derivatives. They tend to be self-indulgent in trading on technicals and rumors. These speculative activities tend to increase the volatility of futures prices.[21]

These challenges continue to roil the market if they are not resolved. Possible solutions to these challenges are common knowledge. For example: it is important to educate the individual investors at large with the basic knowledge; set up fair rules to protect the small investors (for example, market transparency, margin); and put the big and small investors on a level playing field. For example, one source of potential conflict is that the major players in the futures markets control, either politically or on a 'friendship' basis, the major sources of supply of the commodities while having the right to import or export large quantities of commodities. Then, short-squeeze or cornering in the futures and/or spot market can be planted by such big traders. Last, but not least, participation by international investors in the futures markets will help alleviate the problem arising from undue influence of the big players.

Foreign Participation

As mentioned above, it is important to have foreign investors participating in the futures markets, thereby deepening market participation. In addition, access to futures markets is especially important to those foreign investors who are qualified to invest in the stock markets. At present, no person or entity outside China can trade on a Chinese futures exchange. Foreign and domestic banks can undertake over-the-counter derivatives business in China, but for the most part, China's futures markets are closed to foreign participation. Without the access to the derivatives markets, foreign investors are reluctant to invest in China's stock market. At the same time, with foreign participation in the futures markets, China is afraid of losing control of the markets that they have carefully built. This dilemma may be resolved by allowing limited foreign participation in the futures markets through joint ventures with local companies over which the Chinese government has more control.

CONCLUSION

The spectacular growth of the Chinese futures markets since the nation has started to embrace the market-based economy but with a big setback during the mid-1990s make the outlook for the future of the Chinese futures markets cautiously optimistic. China needs to rise up to the challenges that the economy presents. China has amassed decades of experience in terms of regulating the markets through centrally planned schemes in the areas of the non-tradable share reform, experiments in market-oriented interest rates, the exchange rate system, and the floating prices for various financial assets. It doesn't mean that China would be immune to future crises or catastrophes, but at least China would know how to contain the damage should it occur.

With the support from the central government and carefully planned development, the Chinese futures market has handled the challenges well. The two rectifications have laid a solid foundation for a modern futures market. Rules and regulations are now in place and China is ready for the liberalization of the financial markets according to the WTO agreement. The Chinese government and the futures exchanges have relentlessly tackled the challenges as they arise and their performance is commendable given the sheer size of the markets and the number of market participants.

ACKNOWLEDGMENTS

The author is indebted to Owen S. H. Wu and William Ho for valuable discussion.

NOTES

1. Cement and metals are 2004 estimates. *BusinessWeek*, 22/29 August 2005.

2. Following the reporting convention used in China, transaction value (that is, turnover in yuan) and trading volume (that is, number of contracts traded) reported in this chapter are round-trip figures (that is, they include both the buy and sell side of each transaction).
3. Because of rapid development in China, information may be outdated as soon as we finish writing. As such, we refer to 'at present' in this chapter as the time of writing, that is March 2006.
4. See the *Provisional Rules on the Administration of Futures Trading* and the *Measures on the Administration of Futures Exchanges* (CSRC 2004).
5. Wang and Gorham (2002) point out that the criteria for exchange survival in the Second Rectification were not totally transparent, but it was made clear that multiple exchanges within a single city could not continue and must merge as was done in Shanghai. Those exchanges that were not chosen as exchanges could continue to exist as either an order entry site linked to one or more of the three surviving exchanges or converting into brokerage firms.
6. During the development of the Chinese futures markets in the early 1990s, Chinese officials solicited advice from executives of the Chicago Board of Trade in setting up its first futures exchange (Williams *et al.* 1998).
7. See https://English.peopledaily.com.cn.
8. China Aviation Oil (Singapore) Corp, a Chinese state-owned enterprise, traded derivatives in Singapore and produced losses of US$550 million. Directors of the company were indicted for insider trading and for failing to notify the Singapore Exchange and independent members of CAO Singapore's board about the trading losses (Prystay 2006).
9. Outside China, futures contracts can be settled by cash delivery, exchange for physical, or physical delivery.
10. DCE was ranked No. 9 in China by trading volume in 1994.
11. While the DCE leads in trading volume, the Shanghai Futures Exchange has been the leader in terms of turnover. DCE was ranked ninth and SHFE 17th in 2005 in terms of trading volume among the world futures exchanges according to the Futures Industry Association.
12. See *China Daily* (29/5/2005) for a discussion on how Shanghai is becoming an important player in the global price-setting system on base metals.
13. In the aftermath of the copper trading scandal, the State Reserve Bureau, which stockpiles commodities on behalf of the government banned its various departments from trading in overseas markets and in a range of financial instruments including futures (Dyer 2006).
14. Unfortunately, one year later in 2005, ZCE's hard white winter wheat futures experienced an almost 90 percent drop in volume when trading was shifting to strong gluten wheat futures.
15. For example, Yang *et al.* (2001a, b) show that the government plays an important role in aligning futures prices with cash prices.
16. Chan *et al.* (2005) attribute the significant switch in volume between the two futures to the promotion efforts launched by the Exchange including publishing the correlations between the closing prices of wheat futures on ZCE and CBOT.
17. See the exchange's website at www.czce.com.cn
18. Before the rectifications, multiple exchanges (some even in the same city) could offer the same futures contracts. For example, sugar was traded in seven exchanges; steel products in 15 exchanges, copper and aluminum in nine exchanges and gasoline in eight exchanges during the 1990s (Wang and Gorham 2002). Naturally, this caused chaos and confusion and had also created opportunities for unscrupulous market operators to manipulate the market, thus causing systemic instability.
19. For a detail account of the cotton crisis, see Areddy (2005).
20. In 2005, the government approved warrants trading on the two stock exchanges as part of the non-tradeable share reform (Ling and Yau 2005).
21. Chan *et al.* (2005) find evidence that the Chinese futures market was dominated by speculators, while Chan *et al.* (2004) find evidence of the presence of hedgers in the futures market for 1996–2001.

REFERENCES

Areddy, J. T. (2005), 'What China wants, China plans to get', *The Wall Street Journal*, 21 December.

Areddy, J. T. (2006), 'Shanghai Exchange upgrades', *The Wall Street Journal*, 28 February.

Chan, L. H, K. C. Chan and W. K. Leung (2005), 'Institutional interventions and performance of futures markets in China', *Emerging Markets Finance and Trade*, **41**(5) (September-October), 43–55.

Chan, K. C., H. G. Fung and W. K. Leung (2004), 'Daily volatility behavior in Chinese futures markets', *Journal of International Financial Markets, Institutions and Money*, **14**(5), 491–505.

China Securities Regulatory Commission (2004), 'China's securities and futures markets', April.

Dyer, G. (2006), 'Chinese copper scandal agency curbed', 25 January, accessed at www.FT.com.

Fung, H. G., W. K. Leung and X. E. Xu (2003), 'Information flows between the US and China commodity futures trading', *Review of Quantitative Finance and Accounting*, **21**, 267–85.

Ling, T. and J. Yau (2005), 'China's state share reform and exchange traded funds (ETFs)', *China & World Economy*, **13**(6) (November-December), 52–65.

Prystay, C. (2006), 'Three CAO Singapore officials are fined in derivatives case', *The Wall Street Journal*, 3 March.

Silverman, E. J. (2006), 'China plans financial derivatives exchange in Shanghai for 2007', 23 January, accessed at www.riskcenter.com.

Wang, X. and M. Gorham (2002), 'The short dramatic history of futures markets in China', *Journal of Global Financial Markets*, (Spring), 20–28.

Wang, H. Holly and B. Ke (2005), 'Efficiency tests of agricultural commodity futures markets in China', *Australian Journal of Agricultural and Resource Economics*, **49**(2), 125–41.

Wang, X. and N. Ronalds (2005), 'China: the fall and rise of Chinese futures, 1990–2005', *Futures Industry Magazine*, (May/June), accessed at www.futuresindustry.org/fimagazi-1929.asp?a=1038&iss=153.

Williams, J., A. Peck, A. Park and S. Rozelle (1998), 'The emergence of a futures market: mungbeans on the China Zhengzhou Commodity Exchange', *Journal of Futures Markets*, **18**, 427–48.

Yang, J., D. A. Bessler and D. J. Leatham (2001a), 'Asset storability and price discovery of commodity futures markets: a new look', *Journal of Futures Markets*, **21**, 279–300.

Yang, J., M. S. Haigh and D. J. Leatham (2001b), 'Agricultural liberalization policy and commodity price volatility: a GARCH application', *Applied Economics Letters*, **8**, 593–8.

Yao, C. (2004), 'Traders upbeat about futures', *China Business Weekly*, 19 October, accessed at www.chinadaily.com.cn.

4. The small- and medium-enterprise stock market

Hung-gay Fung and Qingfeng 'Wilson' Liu

INTRODUCTION

Before 1978, China's economy had been controlled by a central-planning system in which all enterprises were either state-owned or collectively-owned, with all aspects of operations directly administered by the government. The financing of these enterprises was managed by the government through the state-owned banking system, which granted loans in accordance with policy priorities.[1] Since the late leader Deng Xiaoping began the economic reforms in 1978, many small and medium-sized private enterprises (SMEs) have emerged. An example was the large number of countryside textile workshops that sprang up in the coastal provinces of Jiangsu and Zhejiang. For these private businesses, it was difficult to obtain a loan from the state-owned banking system, limiting their business development potential. Out of the large number of private businesses, only a small proportion were able to grow into mature enterprises and achieve economies of scale.

The stock market was formally established in the early 1990s with the opening of the Shanghai on 19 December, 1990 and Shenzhen Stock Exchanges on 3 July, 1991. Chinese companies that were able to get listed on exchanges and sought financing by issuing stocks were mostly state-owned or partially privatized state-owned enterprises. The strict listing requirements and quota restrictions made it impossible for many private businesses to raise funds through stock exchanges, especially for those cash-thirsty new high-tech firms.

With the advent of the information age in the mid- to late-1990s, many high-tech firms emerged. For example, Beijing's Zhongguancun Science and Technology Zone was known as China's 'Silicon Valley' because of the large number of high-tech firms launched in the 1990s and early 2000s. Some other major cities also designated similar high-tech zones where a certain number of high-tech ventures were initiated.[2] These capital-intensive high-tech firms typically needed a large amount of financing in their early stages of development. In Western countries, high-tech firms usually resort to venture capital or initial public offerings (IPOs) to fulfill financing needs. But in China, the burgeoning venture capital industry (Fung *et al.* 2004) was not able to offer much assistance. Therefore, it is important for China to set up a NASDAQ-type stock market from which small- or medium-size enterprises (SMEs) can seek financing.

In addition to the stock exchanges, the Chinese government has established numerous regional assets and equity exchanges within the last decade, through which SMEs can obtain capital by selling part of their ownership stake, and foreign investors can invest in domestic companies. These financing activities are comparable to private placements before IPOs in the US. The assets and equity exchanges help organize and facilitate these transactions and allow effective oversight and monitoring by administrators.

The rest of the chapter is organized as follows. The next section examines the evolution and development of the SME stock market in China. The third section focuses on the characteristics of the recently established small- and medium-enterprise bloc (SMEB) by comparing it to the main board of China's stock markets and Hong Kong's Growth Enterprise Market. The fourth section discusses some current issues facing the SMEB development. The fifth section describes the regional assets and equity exchanges and the steps for foreign investors to acquire domestic enterprises. The final section offers some concluding remarks.

THE DEVELOPMENT OF THE SME STOCK MARKET

This section documents the evolution of China's SME stock market from the late 1990s, when the idea was first proposed to the Chinese authorities in December 2005, when the Small- and Medium-Enterprise Block index was compiled.

China's SME market development was closely linked to the NASDAQ's performance in the late 1990s and early 2000s. In March 1998, in light of the remarkable success of the NASDAQ in raising capital for high-tech firms in the US, the China National Democratic Construction Association (CNDCA), a small domestic political party, proposed to the government that policies should be enacted to encourage the development of the venture capital industry and related financing sources for the high-tech industries, including a NASDAQ-type stock market. In response, in August 1998 the then CSRC chairman stressed the need to support the development of high-tech industries by providing financing through a high-tech block in the stock market in his visit to the Shenzhen Stock Exchange, suggesting that the central government was seriously considering the CNDCA proposal. Then in December 1998, the State Council requested the CSRC to research and to provide suggestions on the establishment of a small- and medium-enterprise stock market. Between December 1998 and March 1999, a number of government agencies and the Guangdong provincial government provided advice to the CSRC, and a research report and proposed implementation schemes were submitted by the Shenzhen Stock Exchange. Premier Zhu Rong-ji, in his April 1999 state visit to the US, made NASDAQ one of his destinations and asked many related questions during his visit there. It was apparent that high-level officials were also impressed by the success of NASDAQ and thus interested in setting up a similar market in China.

Because the Company Law, issued in 1993, set strict requirements for companies that were allowed to issue IPOs and get listed, the Standing Committee of the People's Congress at the end of 1999 specifically removed these requirements for high-tech corporations and left them at the discretion of the State Council. In April 2000, the CSRC submitted a proposal on the establishment of a 'second board' and the listing requirements, stock circulation, and risk control measures. This proposal was approved by the State Council within a month and the 'second board' was named the Growth Enterprise Board (GEB). It appeared that, after two years of research, discussion, consideration and preparation, such a NASDAQ-type market had collected considerable momentum and were soon to materialize.

However, the NASDAQ took a major right turn at this moment, so did the development of China's Growth Enterprise Board. After reaching a historic high index level of 5047 in March 2000, NASDAQ dropped 49 percent to close the year at 2557, and eventually plunged to a low of 1114 on 9 October 2002. Some other regional growth-oriented stock markets experienced similar crashes during the same period, exposing the risks of excessively relaxing listing and information release requirements, and having too many listed firms concentrated in a few industries. These events raised concerns among top government officials and considerably slowed down the development of GEB. In September 2000, the CSRC chairman said the preparation for the GEB was under way but the timetable could not be predicted, which hinted at the suspension of GEB. In the meantime, many major stock indices in China began a prolonged retreat, prompting the Shenzhen Stock Exchange to impose a moratorium on IPOs on 15 September 2000. This created another roadblock for the GEB. During the following three years, there were still discussions about it but the preparations work appeared to have halted. Premier Zhu Rong-ji made some revealing remarks during this period that China's stock markets should learn from the lessons of Hong Kong and other financial markets, and that the conditions for setting up such a board was found to be 'immature'.

It might be coincidental that the government's interest in the GEB increased again when the NASDAQ began to recover in 2003. In November 2003, CSRC Chairman Shang Fu-lin stated that the GEB should be developed in multiple steps, with the first step on the small- and medium-enterprise board to accumulate experience. In February 2004, the State Council promulgated the Several Opinions on Promoting the Reform, Opening, and Stable Development of the Capital Market, widely known among investors as the Nine Opinions, which stressed the need to use a multiple-step approach to develop the GEB and establish multi-level stock markets where small- and medium-enterprises can seek financing. Soon after this, the Shenzhen Stock Exchange twice tested the system for the sale of new shares as part of the final preparation work. With the approval of the State Council, the CSRC issued the Implementation Scheme of the Establishment of the Small- and Medium-Enterprise Block on the Shenzhen Stock Exchange (the 'Implementation Scheme') on 17 May, 2004. Ten days later, on 27 May, 2004, the SMEB was formally launched. Although the SMEB was different from the GEB in many ways, it was regarded by many as a step forward in the development of the GEB. The CSRC, however, insisted that the SMEB was a component of the main board and it allowed high-growth and high-tech companies to get listed.

As of December 2005, 50 companies had been approved to go public and get listed on the SMEB. About 80 percent of these firms are privately-held and the remainder state-owned. Because the SMEB followed the main board's strict listing requirements, few information technology companies (for example, dot-com's) were listed, whereas many listed ones are from traditional industries like pharmacy, utilities, appliances, machines, and so on.

The division of circulated and non-circulated stocks has been a major perennial issue for China's stock markets.[3] It was viewed as one of the most important drivers behind the bearish performance of the stock markets in the early years of the 2000s. The CSRC in August 2005 approved the proposal to allow the SMEB to implement the stock circulation reform. By 21 November, 2005, all 50 stocks listed on the SMEB had completed the reform converting non-tradable stocks to tradable stocks. The reform has been well received by the market.

The SMEB index was compiled using Laspeyres' concept of a weighted arithmetic average and all the outstanding shares of the 50 component stocks. When the index was first released on 1 December, 2005, it was 43.9 percent higher than the base date of 7 June 2005 when the 50th stock was issued and the index was set at 1000. The large percentage price increase is

Table 4.1 Development timeline of the small- and medium-enterprise block at the Shenzhen Stock Exchange

Date	Event
Mar. 1998	China National Democratic Construction Association, a domestic political party, proposed to the central government the establishment of a market where high-tech enterprises can seek financing
Aug. 1998	Zhou Zheng-Qing, then CSRC chairman, in his visit to the Shenzhen Stock Exchange, stressed the need to support the development of high-tech industries by providing financing through a high-tech block in the stock market
Dec. 1998	The State Council requested that the CSRC research and provide suggestions on the establishment of a small- and medium-enterprise stock market
Apr. 1999	Premier Zhu Rong-ji visited the NASDAQ
Dec. 1999	The People's Congress revised the Company Law to remove the strict requirements for high-tech coporations to issue IPOs and get listed on a stock exchange
Jan. 2000	The State Council requested the CSRC design and propose detailed rules on underwriting and trading share of this type
Apr. 2000	The CSRC submitted to the State Council a proposal on the establishment of a 'second board' and its listing requirements, stock circulation, and risk control measures
May 2000	The State Council approved in principle the CSRC proposal, and named the 'second board' the growth enterprise board
Sep. 2000	CSRC Chairman Zhou Xiao-chuan said the preparation for the 'second board' was under way but the timetable could not be predicted
Nov. 2001	Premier Zhu Rong-ji said that China's stock markets should learn from the lessons of Hong Kong and other financial markets, and that only after the main board had been straightened out would the growth enterprise board be launched
Oct. 2002	Premier Zhu Rong-ji revealed that the original plan for the growth enterprise board was a bit 'hurried and overoptimistic', but that the conditions for setting up such a board was later found to be 'immature'
10 Nov. 2003	CSRC Chairman Shang Fu-lin stated that the growth enterprise board should be developed in multiple steps, with the first step on the small- and medium-enterprise board to accumulate experience

Table 4.1 (continued)

Jan. 2004	The State Council promulgated the Several Opinions on Promoting the Reform, Opening, and Stable Development of the Capital Market, a.k.a. the Nine Opinions, which stressed the establishment of multi-level stock markets to meet the financing needs of different types of enterprises
Feb. 2004	The Shenzhen Stock Exchange twice tested the sale of new shares, which was regarded as making essential technical preparation for the launch of the SMEB
17 May 2004	The State Council approved the establishment of the SMEB at the Shenzhen Stock Exchange. The CSRC issued the Implementation Scheme of the Establishment of the Small- and Medium-Enterprise Block in Shenzhen Stock Exchange
27 May 2004	The Small- and Medium-Enterprise Block was formally launched

Source: Adapted from Zhang (2005).

remarkable when compared to the 4.25 percent increase for the main board in Shenzhen and 6.63 percent for Shanghai during the same period.[4] This reflects the high expectations of market investors for the SMEB and the impact of resolving the stock circulation problem.

THE CHARACTERISTICS OF THE SMEB

Since the late 1990s, many investors had been expecting a 'second board'-type GEB, which was set up for small- and medium-enterprises, especially high-tech and high-growth companies, with significantly more lenient listing requirements than those for the main board. The SMEB did not meet these expectations, as the government apparently became more prudent after the NASDAQ stock market crash.

The Implementation Scheme laid out six principles for the SMEB. First, the law and regulations that govern the SMEB stay the same as those for the main board. Second, the listing conditions and information release requirements remain the same as those for the main board. Third, the SMEB will use an independent trading system. Fourth, the SMEB uses an independent monitoring system. Fifth, the SMEB employs an independent coding system for listed stocks. Finally, the SMEB compiles an independent index.

The first two principles ensured that the SMEB remained a section of the main board without any changes to existing laws, regulations, rules, or listing requirements and procedures. The last four principles granted a certain level of independence to the SMEB from the main board, providing the crucial flexibility needed for changes in the future. After all, making changes to a small and independently-operated section of the stock market is far easier and has fewer repercussions than doing the same things to the entire main board. In addition to serving as a 'first step' toward the GEB, the SMEB can potentially be used as a guinea pig to test new policies and rules by the authorities. Next we compare the SMEB to the main board and the Hong Kong Growth Enterprise Market (GEM) respectively.

Comparing the SMEB to the Main Board

Although generally the SMEB was by design a section of the main board and applied the same laws, regulations, listing and information disclosure requirements, with regard to the specific transaction rules, the SMEB was different from the main board in some features. Table 4.2 provides a snapshot of these differences.

First, the open price for the SMEB is determined by an open batch auction between 9:15 a.m. and 9:25 a.m. while the main board's open price is established by a closed batch auction during the same time span. The open batch auction process of the SMEB reports real-time indicative open price, matched trading volume and unmatched volume continuously between 9:15 a.m. and 9:25 a.m. The closed batch auction process of the main board resembles a 'black box' – trading orders go in from one side between 9:15 a.m. and 9:25 a.m. and the matching price which results in the maximum trading volume comes out of the other side at 9:25 a.m. Liu (2003) finds evidence that small investors are less willing to be involved in the closed batch auction because of the increased risk associated with the 'black box', while large investors are more inclined to use batch auction as a means of price manipulation. Following the batch auctions, there are no new orders accepted for both boards between 9:25 a.m. and 9:30 a.m. At 9:30 a.m. the entire market opens and begins continuous auctions.

Second, the close price for both markets is determined in a different way. The SMEB's close price is established by a closed batch auction process during the last three minutes of the trading day (2:57 p.m.–3:00 p.m.) in order to avoid market manipulation and reach one single close price without a bid-ask spread. If the batch auction process cannot produce a close price, then the last transaction's trading price will be used as the close price. The main board, on the other hand, employs a weighted average price of all transactions within one minute of the last transaction, which might be more prone to manipulation as large investors can give extremely large buy and sell orders within one minute of market close at 3:00 p.m. From

Table 4.2 Comparison between the SMEB and the Main Board

Category	SMEB	The Main Board
Open price determination	Open batch auction between 9:15 a.m. and 9:25 a.m.	Closed batch auction between 9:15 a.m. and 9:25 a.m.
Close price determination	Open batch auction during the last three minutes (2:57 p.m.–3:00 p.m.), or the last transaction's price	Weighted average price of all transactions within one minute of the last transaction
Trading position disclosure	The first three stocks with daily price increases or decreases of ± 7 percent; the first three stocks with daily price fluctuations of 15 percent; the first three stocks with daily turnover of 15 percent	The first five stocks with daily price increases or decreases of ± 7 percent
Abnormal price fluctuations	Daily price increases or decreases reach ± 20 percent for three consecutive days; daily average turnover reach 20 percent for three consecutive days; for ST* stocks, daily price increases or decreases reach ± 15 percent for three consecutive days	Daily price increases or decreases reach ±10 percent for three consecutive days; daily price fluctuations reach 15 percent for three consecutive days; daily trading volumes increase by over 50 percent for five consecutive days

Source: Wang (2005), and http://finance.sina.com.cn, 22 December 2005.
* See Footnote 5 for an explanation of ST stocks.

the rules for open price and close price determination, it appears that the authorities are indeed experimenting with new and probably better rules on the SMEB. If the results turn out in a satisfactory fashion, these rules will likely be used on the main board in the future.

Third, in terms of trading-position disclosures, the SMEB discloses the first three stocks with daily price increases or decreases of 7 percent, the first three stocks with daily price fluctuations of 15 percent, and the first three stocks with daily turnover of 15 percent. In comparison, the main board only discloses the first three stocks with daily price increases or decreases of 7 percent. Because the SMEB contains generally smaller and higher-growth corporations than the main board, the authorities impose more extensive disclosure rules.

Lastly, the abnormal price fluctuation, which is an important parameter for the monitoring system, is defined differently between the two boards. For the SMEB, the abnormal price fluctuations include the following three conditions. First, daily price increases or decreases reach ±20 percent for three consecutive days. Second, daily average turnover reach 20 percent for three consecutive days. Third, for special treatment (ST) stocks, that is, stocks with poor financial performance, daily price increases or decreases reach ±15 percent for three consecutive days.[5] For the main board, the abnormal price fluctuations are defined as: (a) Daily price increases or decreases reach ±10 percent for three consecutive days; (b) Daily price fluctuations reach 15 percent for three consecutive days; (c) Daily trading volumes increase by over 50 percent for five consecutive days. Obviously, rule-makers took into account the characteristics of the SMEB listed stocks and allowed them to fluctuate within wider ranges.

Comparing the SMEB to the Hong Kong GEM

Since the 'second board' or the GEB never came into being, we do not know its exact rules and regulations. Many investors, however, assume that it resembles the Hong Kong GEM as a number of Chinese companies have been listed there. Table 4.3 provides a comparison between the SMEB and the GEM, which should shed light on how far the SMEB has to go to become the GEB.

First, the SMEB has much more stringent listing requirements than the GEB as the SMEB follows the same laws, regulations, rules and requirements as the main board on Shenzhen Stock Exchange. The GEM does not require net profits for recent fiscal years, while the SMEB requires the company to at least have net profits for the three most recent fiscal years. The GEM requires the companies to have two years of operations records and 100 stockholders, or one year of operations records and 300 stockholders, whereas the SMEB needs at least three years of operations records and 1000 stockholders with stocks of at least RMB1000 in face value. In addition, SMEB implements the main board's listing requirements that listed companies cannot have less than RMB50 million in equity capital, their net equity as a percentage of total assets cannot be lower than 30 percent, and their intangible assets, like patents and royalties, as a percentage of net assets cannot exceed 20 percent. As a result, a high-tech company in its early stage of development, which is in desperate need of capital financing, has a very low chance of getting listed on the SMEB. This helps explain why only a small fraction of the 50 listed stocks on the SMEB as of December 2005 are information technology companies, while some of

Table 4.3 Comparison between the SMEB and the Hong Kong Growth Enterprise Market (GEM)

Category	Hong Kong GEM	SMEB
Net profit requirement for listing	No net profit requirements for listing	Net profits for the most recent three consecutive fiscal years
Operations records for listing	At least 24 months of operations records (can be reduced to 12 months, see below)	At least three years of operations records
Number of stockholders	At least 100 upon listing. If the firm only has 12 months of operations records, the number of public stockholders needs to exceed 300	At least 1000 stockholders, each of whom owns stocks of at least RMB 1000 in face value
Main investors and stock preferences	Mainly international institutional investors. Listed firms are typically large international-oriented companies	Mainly individual investors. The SMEB is suitable for firms that are less international-oriented
IPO price-to-earnings ratio	No restrictions. Typically between eight and 12	Required to be below 20
Stock circulation	All stocks can be circulated	Stocks are divided into circulated and non-circulated stocks*

Source: Wang (2005), and http://finance.sina.com.cn, 29 November 2005.
* As of 21 November 2005, all SMEB listed stocks had completed stock circulation reform, and all SMEB stocks became circulated stocks.

them are from traditional industries like pharmacy, utilities, appliances and machines.

Second, because Hong Kong is a well-established international financial center with few restrictions on capital flows and foreign exchange conversion, the GEM attracts mainly international institutional investors who are interested in firms conducting business in both domestic Chinese markets and overseas markets. The SMEB, on the other hand, are subject to China's foreign exchange control and capital flow restrictions, and thus attract mainly domestic individual investors. The listed firms on the SMEB mostly focus their business on domestic markets.

Third, there are no restrictions on the GEM's price-to-earning ratios, though they are typically between eight and 12. On the SMEB, the authorities impose a restriction of 20 on the IPOs' Price-to-Earnings ratios to prevent irrational investors from bidding up the prices to very high levels. Therefore, the red-hot IPO market on the NASDAQ in the late 1990s is impossible to replicate on the SMEB, unless this restriction is removed.

Lastly, when the SMEB was launched in May 2004, the listed companies followed the main board's tradition to divide the stocks into circulated and non-circulated stocks. Circulated shares can be freely traded on stock exchanges whereas non-circulated shares cannot. Non-circulated shares come from three sources: (a) The state-owned shares converted from state-owned assets when the listed company was transformed into a share-holding company; (b) the shares of company founders; and (c) the shares obtained by other organizations through private placements. As non-circulated shares constitute as much as two-thirds of the total shares of many listed companies, converting non-circulated shares into circulated ones may lead to an over supply of shares or a market crash, which occurred in 2001 when the government attempted to sell the state-owned shares.

Beginning mid-2005, the administrators restarted the circulation reform, mostly by allowing non-circulating shareholders to compensate circulating shareholders with shares or other types of distributions. As of 21 November 2005, while more than half of all listed stocks on the two stock exchanges have not completed the stock circulation reform, all 50 listed stocks on the SMEB have, which means all stocks on the SMEB can be circulated, just like those on the GEM. This is a big step the SMEB takes toward the GEB and is a particularly significant move for the venture capital industry. Before this reform, venture capitalists cannot sell their shares even when the firm they finance goes public, because their stocks are categorized as non-circulated shares. The reform essentially removes one important roadblock in the venture capitalists' exit mechanism and should help invigorate the development of the venture capital industry in China.

CURRENT ISSUES

Although many investors regard the SMEB as a step toward the GEB, especially after the SMEB became the first to complete the stock circulation reform, and the SMEB does use an independent stock index, an independent trading system, an independent coding system and an independent monitoring system than the main board, strictly speaking, the SMEB remains largely a homogeneous section of the main board as of early 2006.

From our perspective, there are three important current issues facing the SMEB.

First, the first two principles laid out by the Implementation Scheme require the SMEB to abide by the same laws and regulations as those for the main board, and use the same listing and information release requirements. Companies intending to be listed on the SMEB cannot have less than RMB50 million in equity capital. Their net equity as a percentage of total assets cannot be lower than 30 percent, and their intangible assets, like patents and royalties, as percentage of net assets cannot exceed 20 percent. In addition, some transaction monitoring and information release requirements for the SMEB are stricter than those for the main board. Therefore, in its development process, the SMEB is currently much closer to the main board than to the GEB. For small- and medium-enterprises, it may not make much difference for them to get listed on the main board or on the SMEB. There is a long way to go for the SMEB to be able to provide good financing opportunities to high-growth businesses. At present, it appears only mature companies with a high market share and thus relatively low growth potential are able to get listed on the SMEB.

Second, it was believed that the Shenzhen Stock Exchange imposed a moratorium on A-share IPOs in September 2000 in order to prepare for the launch of the GEB. Now that a main board-like SMEB has been initiated to lift the moratorium, there may be less pressure on the CSRC to set up the GEB. Because the SMEB is basically a section of the main board, it is impossible to grow the GEB out of the SMEB. As a result, the establishment of the SMEB may actually lengthen the process and time it takes to create the GEB.

Lastly, the majority of listed stocks on the SMEB are private and family-based businesses, which might make it more difficult to monitor and guarantee the integrity of financial statements and corporate decisions. As of December 2005, at least seven listed stocks on the SMEB have had corporate scandals like cooking the books, concealing material information, distributing exceptionally high dividends to original stockholders and so on. It is vital for the development of the SMEB to have a complete and thorough monitoring and controlling system to minimize corporate malfeasance and protect the interests of public investors.

REGIONAL ASSETS AND EQUITY EXCHANGES

Given the strict requirements for listing on a stock exchange, many SMEs resort to private financing. The government has set up many regional assets and equity exchanges within the last decade or so to facilitate these financing activities. These exchanges enable SMEs to find investors, such as venture capitalists or enterprises in the same industry, which are interested in buying a stake in their business. For instance, among the most influential ones, the China Beijing Equity Exchange (CBEX) and Shanghai United Assets and Equity Exchange (SUAEE) were both established in 1994. The CBEX was formed as a comprehensive equity transaction platform authorized by the Beijing Municipal Government after the restructuring and merger of the former Beijing Equity and Assets Exchange and Zhongguancun's China Technology and Equity Exchange (CTEE), which was once deemed as an embryonic form of an over-the-counter stock market for high-tech firms such as Zhongguancun was the hub of high-tech firms and nicknamed 'China's Silicon Valley' (Fung and Liu 2006). Since the merger, the CBEX has taken over the role of the CTEE as the trading center for high-tech firms' equity transfer and private placement.[6] The SUAEE, on the other hand, has consistently been the largest assets and equity exchange in terms of trading volume over the past 11 years and derives most of its trading volume growth from the increasing equity transfer by state-owned enterprises in the Yangtze River Delta. Its trading volume of RMB82.52 billion in 2005 exceeded that of the Shanghai Stock Exchange (RMB60.68 billion).[7] Counterparts of these regional exchanges in Western countries are rare as investment bankers with enormous networks and information typically take these roles and help private businesses conduct private financing.

Assets and equity exchanges at both the provincial and municipal levels across China are listed in Table 4.4. At the provincial level, nearly every province and centrally administered municipalities have its own exchange, with some, like Shandong Province, having two or more such exchanges. At the municipal level, many cities across the country have set up their own exchange, and economic powerhouse provinces like Guangdong, Jiangsu and Zhejiang, have more municipal exchanges. By the end of 2005, the government had allowed 64 regional exchanges to be set up and conduct equity transactions.

There are mainly three reasons why the authorities want to establish such an extensive network of regional assets and equity exchanges. First, the government wants to maintain close oversight of private financing activities. If necessary, the administrators can step in and directly influence the terms and patterns of these activities in accordance with new policies or regulations. This is consistent with the government's prudent attitude toward other parts of the financial system, like the inter-bank market.

Second, private enterprises are just one type of client that these exchanges serve. There are a large number of state-owned enterprises that trade their assets and equity, hoping to obtain more capital for development, or just to

Table 4.4 China's regional assets and equity exchanges

Provincial level assets and equity exchanges	Municipal level assets and equity exchanges
China Beijing Equity Exchange	*Guangdong Province*
Shanghai United Assets and Equity Exchange	Guangzhou Assets and Equity Exchange
Tianjin Assets and Equity Exchange Center	Shenzhen Assets and Equity Exchange Center
Chongqing United Equity Exchange	Shenzhen International High-Tech Assets and Equity Exchange
Northern Assets and Equity Exchange and Common Market	Zhuhai Assets and Equity Exchange Center
Hebei Assets and Equity Exchange	Dongguan Assets and Equity Exchange Center
Henan Technology Assets and Equity Exchange	*Jiangsu Province*
Jiangsu Assets and Equity Exchange	Nanjing Assets and Equity Exchange
Jilin Changchun Assets and Equity Exchange Center	Lianyungang Continental Bridge Assets and Equity Exchange Center
Gansu Assets and Equity Exchange	Yangzhou Assets and Equity Exchange
Heilongjiang Assets and Equity Exchange Center	Huaian Assets and Equity Exchange Center
Yellow River (Huanghe) Regional Assets and Equity Exchange and Common Market	Nantong Assets and Equity Exchange
Sichuan State-Owned Assets and Equity Exchange Service Center	Huaihai Assets and Equity Exchange Market
Luxin (Shandong Province) Assets and Equity Exchange Center	*Zhejiang Province*
Lucai (Shandong Province) Assets and Equity Exchange Center	Hangzhou Assets and Equity Exchange
Jiangxi Assets and Equity Exchange Net	Yiwu Assets and Equity Exchange Co. Ltd.
Hua-er Assets and Equity Exchange	Ningbo Assets and Equity Exchange Center
Fujian Assets and Equity Exchange Information Center	Jinhua Assets and Equity Exchange
Shanxi Assets and Equity Exchange	Shaoxing Assets and Equity Exchange Center
Yunnan Assets and Equity Exchange	*Hubei Province*
Western Assets and Equity Exchange	Wuhan Assets and Equity Exchange
Hubei Assets and Equity Exchange Center	Shiyan Assets and Equity Exchange Center
	Jingmen Assets and Equity Exchange
	Xiangfan Assets and Equity Exchange

Table 4.4 (*continued*)

Provincial level assets and equity exchanges	Municipal level assets and equity exchanges
Shenyang (Liaoning Province) Assets and Equity Exchange Center	
Hunan Assets and Equity Exchange	*Shandong Province*
Yangtze River (Changjiang) Regional Assets and Equity Exchange and Common Market	Jinan Assets and Equity Exchange
Guangxi United Assets and Equity Exchange	Weifang Assets and Equity Exchange Center
Guangdong Assets and Equity Exchange Center	Qingdao Technology Assets and Equity Exchange
Xinjiang United Assets and Equity Exchange	*Liaoning Province*
Hainan Special Economic Zone Assets and Equity Exchange Center	Dalian Assets and Equity Exchange,
Guizhou Sunshine Assets and Equity Exchange	Liaoyang Assets and Equity Exchange Center
Inner Mongolia (Neimenggu) Assets and Equity Exchange Center	Benxi Assets and Equity Exchange Net
Ningxia Assets and Equity Exchange Center	*Jiangxi Province*
Huarong Assets and Equity Exchange	Ganzhou Assets and Equity Exchange Center
	Jiujiang Assets and Equity Exchange
	Shangrao Assets and Equity Exchange and so on

Note: Beijing, Shanghai, Tianjin and Chongqing are four centrally administered municipalities and have the same political ranks as the provinces. Therefore, their exchanges are at the provincial level instead of the municipal level.

Source: http://www.zjpse.com/, Zhejiang Property and Stock Exchange, 9 February 2006.

avoid bankruptcy. The establishment of many of these exchanges was related to former Premier Zhu Rongji's campaign to transform the numerous large and money-losing state-owned enterprises in the late 1990s. As an example, Huarong Assets Management Company, which specializes in handling the non-performing loans of the Industrial and Commercial Bank of China,[8] one of the 'Big Four' state-owned banks, has its own assets exchange.

Third, China so far has not established an advanced financial information network and a competitive investment banking industry. These regional exchanges essentially serve as an information center where potential buyers and sellers can find relevant information and meet together to discuss possible merger and acquisition (M&A) deals.

These assets and equity exchanges can also provide services to foreign investors. As the authorities have gradually realized that introducing foreign investment is essentially a shortcut in transforming money-losing state-owned enterprises by bringing international standard practices and management expertise, more and more M&A deals that involve foreign investors have been approved and successfully completed in regional assets and equity exchanges. With regard to the detailed steps, Figure 4.1 provides a flow chart for such international M&A transactions at the CBEX. As Beijing is the political center where the most important policies and regulations are formulated, steps and procedures in other regional exchanges are similar. There is an important step which is not included in Figure 4.1, however. If the M&A target is a state-owned enterprise, the foreign investor needs to obtain approval from the level of government that has jurisdiction over the enterprise. And for both state-owned and private enterprises, consent of the relevant government department that oversees the M&A target's industry is required. And lastly, foreign share ownership of a domestic enterprise is usually capped at 49 percent.

CONCLUDING REMARKS

There have been significant changes and development in China's 'second board' stock market since it was first proposed in the late 1990s. Due to the wild fluctuations in other countries' second board markets in recent years, especially those of the NASDAQ, and the administrators' prudent attitude, the resulting SMEB was essentially a certain hybrid form of the main board and a real second board. While with regard to its characteristics the SMEB is arguably closer to the main board than to a second board stock market, the fact that it maintains a certain level of independence from the main board, and that all component stocks have completed circulation reform, allows the government to speed up the transformation process of the SMEB to a NASDAQ-type market which enables SMEs to gain access to more capital financing.

China's extensive network of regional assets and equity exchanges, which were set up to facilitate private equity transfer and non-performing loans transactions, seem to partially fill the void. SMEs that cannot get listed on the stock exchanges resort to private financing through these regional exchanges. Also foreign investors can invest in non-listed domestic state-owned and private businesses through these exchanges. However, in comparison to

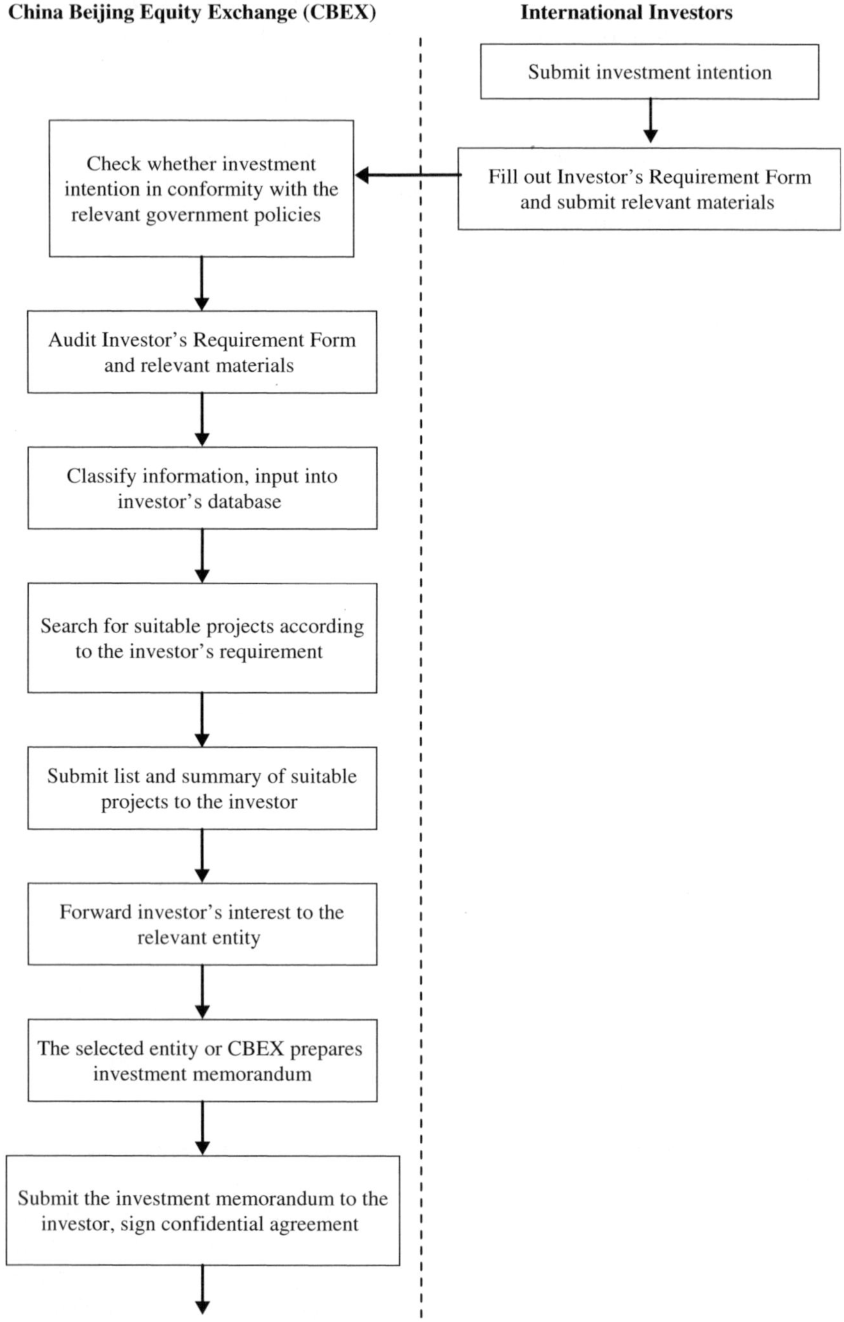
China Beijing Equity Exchange (CBEX)
International Investors
Submit investment intention
Fill out Investor's Requirement Form and submit relevant materials
Check whether investment intention in conformity with the relevant government policies
Audit Investor's Requirement Form and relevant materials
Classify information, input into investor's database
Search for suitable projects according to the investor's requirement
Submit list and summary of suitable projects to the investor
Forward investor's interest to the relevant entity
The selected entity or CBEX prepares investment memorandum
Submit the investment memorandum to the investor, sign confidential agreement

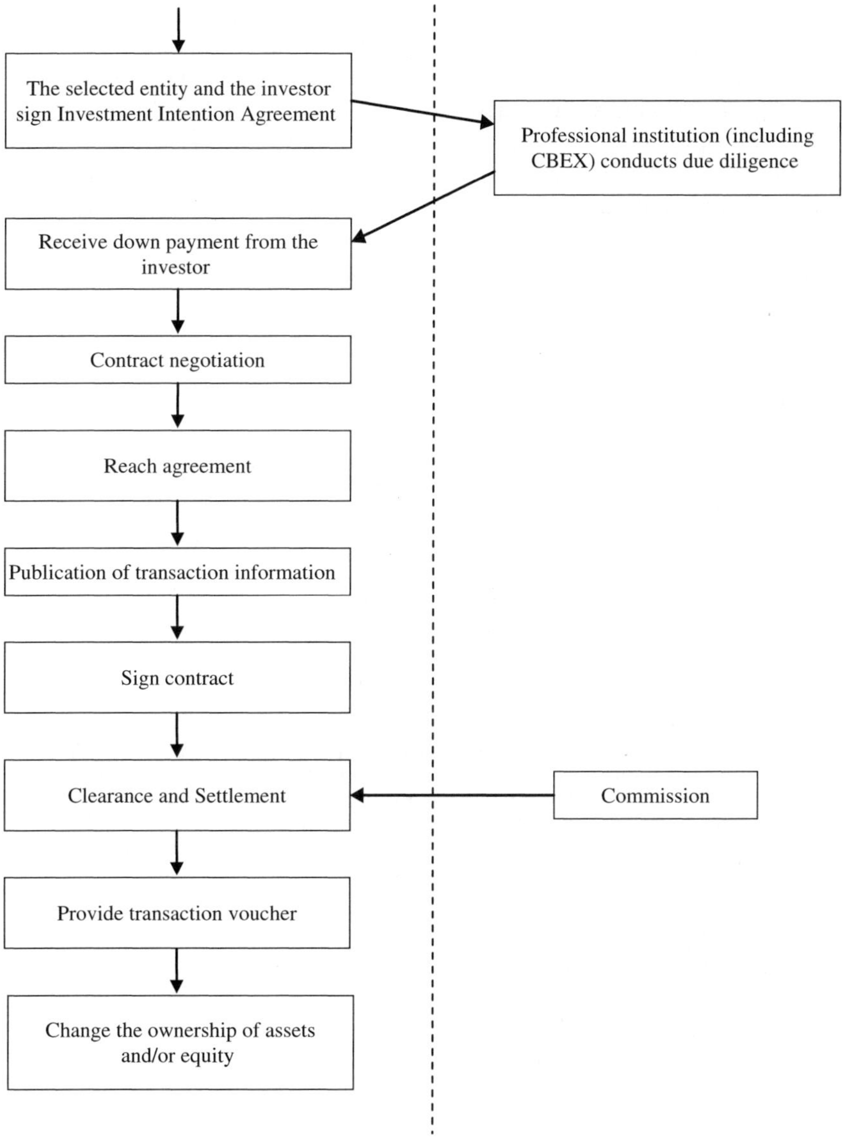

Source: http://www.cbex.cn/e_about04.shtml, China Beijing Equity Exchange web site, 23 February 2006.

Figure 4.1 Flow chart for international merger and acquisition at the China Beijing Equity Exchange

issuing stocks or bonds to raise capital, private financing is not a very efficient or effective way in obtaining capital due to the limitations in information dissemination and the high costs involved. Given that China's larger stock exchange, the Shanghai Stock Exchange, has lower trading volume than the assets and equity exchange located in the same city – the SUAEE, it appears advisable that the government should, to a certain extent, loosen the strict listing requirements, and speed up the transformation of the SMEB to a real second board, so that more SMEs and other businesses can utilize the equity and bond financing channels on stock exchanges instead of having to rely on private financing activities.

NOTES

1. China's banking system has been dominated by state-owned banks. The first and only private bank, China Minsheng Bank, was established in Beijing on 12 January 1996. See the banking chapter for more details.
2. For example, in Shenzhen City, Guangdong Province, the establishment of Shenzhen High-Tech Industrial Park was credited for the fast-growing high-tech sector, which accounted for 31 percent of the city's GDP and contributed to 35 percent of the economic growth in 2002 (http://www.southcn.com/, 16 July 2003).
3. For more details, see Fung and Liu (2006).
4. http://info.chinanasdaq.com, 1 December 2005. The main board's growth rate is calculated using the Shenzhen Composite Stock Index and the Shanghai Composite Stock Index.
5. Beginning 22 April 1998, Shanghai and Shenzhen Stock Exchanges designated stocks with two types of special financial situations as ST (Special Treatment) stocks. These two types of financial situations include: (a) The listed firm has had audited net losses in two fiscal years; (b) The listed firm's audited net worth per share is below the stock's face value. The special treatment the stock receives are: (a) The daily price increase and decrease limits are reduced to ±5 percent from ±10 percent; (b) The name of the stock adds a prefix 'ST'; (c) The mid-term reports need to be audited (http://finance.sina.com.cn/2000-08-16/6539.html).
6. http://www.chinadaily.com.cn, 5 April 2004.
7. SUAEE's trading volume is obtained from the First Financial Journal (in Chinese), 20 January 2006. Shanghai Stock Exchange' trading volume figure includes the 2005 total turnovers of A-share, B-share, Securities Investment Funds, T-Bond Spot, T-Bond Repo, Financial and Corporate Bond and Convertible Bond.
8. The Industrial and Commercial Bank of China is the largest bank in China. Most of its non-performing loans originate from money-losing state-owned enterprises.

REFERENCES

Chen, Wei (2005), 'A study of the Batch Auction System for market close on the Small- and Medium-Enterprise Board', Shenzhen Stock Exchange research series 0109, accessed at www.szse.com.cn/main/research/Default.aspx.

Fung, H. G. and Liu Q. (2006), 'China's financial reform in banking and securities markets', in *China and the Challenge of Globalization: The Impact of WTO*

Membership, in H. G. Fung, C. H. Pei and K. Zhang, (eds), New York: M.E. Sharpe, pp. 145–63.

Fung, H. G., Q. Liu and X. Shen (2004), 'Venture capital cycle, opportunities, and challenges in China', *The Chinese Economy*, **37**(4), 28–49.

Liu, Wei (2003), 'Changing closed batch auction to open batch auction', *China Securities Daily*, 6 March, accessed at www.htdqsec.com.

Wang, Li (2005), *A Guide to Listing on and Investment in the Small- and Medium-Enterprise Board*, Beijing: The China Machine Press.

Zhang, Yujun (2005), *The New Shenzhen Stock Exchange*, Beijing: The China Finance Press.

PART II

Banking, insurance and foreign exchange markets

5. The banking system – development and current issues

Hung-gay Fung and Qingfeng 'Wilson' Liu

INTRODUCTION

In the three decades before Deng Xiaoping's reform and open-up policies began implementation in 1978, the state-owned banks had almost made up the entire financial system in China's economy. Under a central-planning system, all enterprises, including the banking sectors, are under the directives of the government. That is, firms received production orders from the authorities that were also responsible for distributing the products. The funds for acquiring raw materials, buying machines and parts, and paying workers' salaries were allocated to the enterprises by the government, usually through the state-owned banks. They were required to hold their financial balances as bank deposits, and to keep only enough cash to meet daily expenses. Payments for transactions were conducted by debiting the account of the purchasing unit and crediting that of the selling unit, which essentially reduced the need for currency.[1] Replacement, expansion, and new venture project decisions were mostly not made by the enterprises themselves, but by officials of the overseeing government agencies, who also had the authority to issue financing directives to the state-owned banks to allocate the required funds.

The banking system then was actually a branch of the government serving the fiscal and account functions and a policy tool designed to carry out economic plans of the Central Government. As many decision-making officials did not have adequate financial expertise and skills to make informed sound financial decisions, and those who did might well be hampered by political considerations like their own political careers and higher-ranking officials' intentions, funds in the banking system ended up in places where they could not be used efficiently, giving rise to the non-performing loan problem that still plagues the financial services industry today. Other problems that stemmed from the old system include corruption, fraud, lack of transparency and mismanagement, among others (Fung 1999).

Almost another three decades have passed since the reform began and the most recent GDP data showed that China had surpassed the UK to become the fourth biggest economy in the world after the US, Japan and Germany, but the footprints of the first three decades' central-planning system, the dominance of the banking sector, still characterize China's economy. As presented in the overview chapter of this book, China's bank credit was 141 percent of GDP in 2004, far exceeding the 104 percent in the similarly banking-dominated Euro Area countries, as well as Japan's 94 percent, South Korea's 80 percent, US's 46 percent, and India's 37 percent. Thus, China's financial system is characterized as a bank-based system in which the banks play a far more important role than the securities markets (Allen *et al.* (2002), and Levine (2002)).

In general, China's commercial banks can be divided into four layers as shown in Table 5.1. The first layer is the 'Big Four' – Bank of China (BOC), China Construction Bank (CCB), Industrial and Commercial Bank of China (ICBC) and Agricultural Bank of China (ABC). These four state-owned banks dominate the banking system and each has more than 10 000 branches all over the country.

The second layer includes China CITIC Bank, Bank of Communi-

Table 5.1 The structure of China's banking system

Overseeing Authority	The People's Bank of China, the central bank, and the China Banking Regulatory Commission
Policy Banks	The China Development Bank, China Agricultural Development Bank, China Import-Export Bank
Commercial Banks	
Layer 1 State-Owned Banks	The 'Big Four': Bank of China, China Construction Bank, Industrial and Commercial Bank of China, and Agricultural Bank of China
Layer 2 Commercial Banks Controlled by Local Government or State-Owned Enterprises	China CITIC Bank, Bank of Communications, China Merchants Bank, China Everbright Bank, Guangdong Development Bank, Shenzhen Development Bank, Shanghai Pudong Development Bank, China Post Bank, Huaxia Bank, Fujian Industrial Bank, etc.
Layer 3 Collectively-Owned Share-Based Cooperative Banks	Rural Credit Cooperatives, Urban Credit Cooperatives, the numerous municipal commercial banks
Layer 4 Private Banks	Minsheng Bank

Source: Kang (2005) and http//countrystudies.us/China/96.htm, retrieved 22 January 2006.

cations, China Merchant Bank, China Everbright Bank, Guangdong Development Bank, Shenzhen Development Bank, Shanghai Pudong Development Bank, China Post Bank, Huaxia Bank, Fujian Industrial Bank, and so on. These banks are either controlled by local governments, like Guangdong Development Bank, Shenzhen Development Bank, Shanghai Pudong Development Bank, and Huaxia Bank,[2] or controlled by some large state-owned enterprises, like China CITIC Bank and China Everbright Bank.[3]

The third layer is collectively-owned share-based cooperatives, which include the Rural Credit Cooperatives and Urban Credit Cooperatives. In many cities, a number of urban credit cooperatives have merged together to form municipal commercial banks, like Shenzhen Commercial Bank, Shanghai Commercial Bank, and so on. There were 113 such municipal commercial banks across China as of September 2005.[4]

Lastly, the fourth layer, the private banks, is only represented by Minsheng Bank. Although Minsheng bank is a private bank, its policy is still under the strong influence of the Chinese government because governmental officials sit on the board of the bank. In recent years, there have been talks about the establishment of another private bank, the Nanhua Bank, in Guangdong Province. So far this has not materialized, probably due to the fear of authorities that private banks may weaken the government's control on the financial system, and that private companies may use these banks as an 'ATM' machine. Table 5.2 provides a brief description of each of these Chinese banks' history and characteristics.

In addition to these four layers of commercial banks, the government has also set up several policy banks to implement specific policy initiatives, including the China Development Bank, China Agricultural Development Bank and China Import-Export Bank. Above all these banks are the People's Bank of China (PBOC), the central bank and the China Banking Regulatory Commission (CBRC). They are the government agencies that oversee and regulate the banking system. As China will allow open and free competition from foreign banks by the end of 2006 in line with its World Trade Organization (WTO) accession agreements signed in 2001, the PBOC and CBRC have introduced a number of initiatives to address perennial problems including non-performing loans, information transparency and capital inadequacy and boost the competitiveness and efficiency of Chinese commercial banks.

In the following sections, we will examine new developments in China's banking system, and then discuss the current issues and opportunities. The last section offers some concluding remarks.

Table 5.2 A brief description of Chinese commercial banks

Bank	Brief description
Bank of China (BOC)	Established in 1912, BOC handles the majority of China's foreign exchange dealings through its global network of over 560 overseas offices in 25 countries in all major continents
China Construction Bank Corporation (CCB)	Incorporated in 1954, CCB manages state appropriations and loans for capital construction
Agricultural Bank of China (ABC)	Created in 1953, ABC facilitates and oversees financial operations in the rural areas, handles state appropriations for agriculture, and directs the operations of rural credit cooperatives
Industrial and Commercial Bank of China (ICBC)	Founded in 1984, ICBC is the youngest and largest in assets of the 'Big Four' and extends loans to state-owned industrial and commercial enterprises, city and town collective enterprises, and private industry and commerce
Bank of Communications	Established in 1908, it was the first Chinese bank to set up branches abroad. As of late 2005, it had an extensive network of over 2800 branches with 45 000 employees
China Merchants Bank (CMB)	Founded in 1987 and headquartered in Shenzhen, CMB was the first share-holding commercial bank wholly owned by corporate legal entities
China Post Bank	The Chinese postal savings service was converted by the CBRC into China Post Bank, which manages 9 percent of China's total deposits and has 31 500 branches (70 percent in rural area)
China CITIC Bank	It was founded in 1979 and controlled by China International Trust and Investment Corporation (CITIC)
China Everbright Bank	Established in 1992 and controlled by the Everbright Group, Everbright Bank was the first state-owned bank with shares held by international financial institutions
Guangdong Development Bank	Set up in 1988 in Guangzhou City by the Guangdong provincial government, it has 520 branches all over China
Fujian Industrial Bank	Founded in 1988 in Fuzhou City, it has 320 branches in 23 Chinese cities

Table 5.2 (*continued*)

Bank	Brief description
Shanghai Pudong Development Bank	Incorporated in 1993, it is a joint-stock commercial bank with an objective to provide financial services for the development of Pudong, a district of Shanghai City
Shenzhen Development Bank	Established in 1987, it was the first joint-stock owned company to list on the Shenzhen Stock Exchange. It had 237 branches all over the country as of late 1995
Shenzhen Commercial Bank	Set up in 1995 by 16 urban credit cooperatives in Shenzhen, it was the first urban cooperative joint-stock commercial bank in China. There are many such municipal commercial banks in China
Xiamen International Bank	Founded in 1985, it was the first joint venture bank in China
Rural Credit Cooperatives (RCCs)	Small, collectively owned savings and lending organizations, RCCs provide small-scale financial services in rural areas. They are subject to the direction of ABC but act as independent units for accounting purposes
Urban Credit Cooperatives (UCCs)	Created in mid-1980s, UCCs handle deposits and short-term loans for the thousands of individual and collective enterprises that sprang up in urban areas after the reform started in 1978
China Minsheng Bank	Minsheng Bank was founded by non-state-owned enterprises in Bejing in 1996 as the first and only private Chinese bank. It has more than 200 branches across China as of late 2005

Source: http://world.ccavenue.com/content/chinese_banks.jsp, and http//countrystudies.us/China/96.htm, http://www.chinagate.com.cn/english/179.htm, retrieved 22 January 2006.

RECENT DEVELOPMENTS OF CHINA'S BANKING SYSTEM

The enormous potential of China's financial market and China's WTO accession commitment to opening domestic financial market by the end of 2006 have attracted investments from many foreign banking institutions that try to capture the huge domestic market opportunities. The investments from foreign banking institutions speed up the domestic banking reforms and competition.

As of October 2005, 71 foreign banks from 20 countries have set up 238 branches in China, with total assets of US$84.5 billion, or approximately 2 percent of the total assets of China's banking sector. Foreign currency loans made by these foreign banks are about 20 percent of the total amount of such loans in China. Of the 238 foreign bank branches, 138 are allowed to provide Renminbi banking services in the cities where they are located, 15 are allowed to offer online banking, 41 are engaged in financial derivatives trading operations and five serve as custodian banks for Qualified Foreign Institutional Investors (QFII). In addition, 173 banks from 40 countries have opened representative's offices in 23 cities in China.[5]

As the WTO commitment date approaches, these numbers are expected to rise further, posing ever-increasing competition to domestic banks. To prepare Chinese banks for the upcoming challenge, the authorities have taken steps that include privatizing domestic banks, loosening restrictions on foreign investment in domestic banks, reducing non-performing loans, and encouraging financial innovations.

Bank Privatization and Foreign Ownership

To obtain more capital and enhance market oversight, the government has expanded the traditional four layers of banks into five layers by first allowing two commercial banks to issue A-shares on domestic stock exchanges since the early 1990s. Shenzhen Development Bank was the first bank to list shares through an initial public offering (IPO) on the Shenzhen Stock Exchange in 1991. Shanghai Pudong Development Bank was the second bank listed on the Shanghai Stock Exchange on 23 September 1999. China's only private bank, the Minsheng Bank, went public on 19 December 2000, followed by Beijing-based Huaxia Bank and Shenzhen-based China Merchants Bank.

Because of China's prolonged bearish stock market since 2000 and lack of sophisticated institutional investors, the government's two objectives for listing domestic banks to obtain capital and improving market oversight, were not completely achieved. As a result, the authorities turned to the nearby Hong Kong stock market. On 23 June 2005, Shanghai-based Bank of Communications, one of China's oldest banks and a state-owned shareholding commercial bank, became the first mainland bank to go public offshore and issued H-shares on the Hong Kong Stock Exchange.[6] It appeared that the government used the Bank of Communications IPO as an experiment to test the water and gain experience. Shortly after this, on 27 October 2005, one of the 'Big Four', the CCB (China's

Construction Bank) also went public on the Hong Kong Stock Exchange (HKSE).

The CCB was the first among the 'Big Four' to list overseas because of its lowest non-performing loan (NPL) ratio, at 3.7 percent at the end of 2004, in comparison to 5.12 percent in BOC, 19.6 percent in ICBC and 26.31 percent in ABC.[7] The IPO of CCB was the largest in the world in 2005, raising over US$8 billion in new capital with 14 percent of CCB's shares.[8] The IPO was priced at HK$2.35 (US$0.30), near the top of its indicative price range of HK$1.90 to HK$2.40, due to overwhelming market response with institutional subscriptions exceeding fours times the shares offered. The price was 1.95 times CCB's expected book value for 2005, a premium to listed peer Bank of Communications which sold a US$1.9 billion IPO for 1.6 times book value. Investors largely factored in the almost double digit economic growth in China, which was expected to boost CCB's earnings prospects.

After the IPO, CCB stock (HKSE stock code: 00939) became one of the most actively-traded stocks on the HKSE, and its price rose steadily. As Figure 5.1 shows, the market close price of CCB went up from HK$2.38 on 27 October 2005, to HK$3.25 on 9 February 2006, a 36.55 percent jump in less than four months. This far exceeded the 7.18 percent growth of the Hang Seng Index during the same period from 14381.06 to 15413.43 points. In view of CCB's successful debut, the BOC and ICBC plan to issue

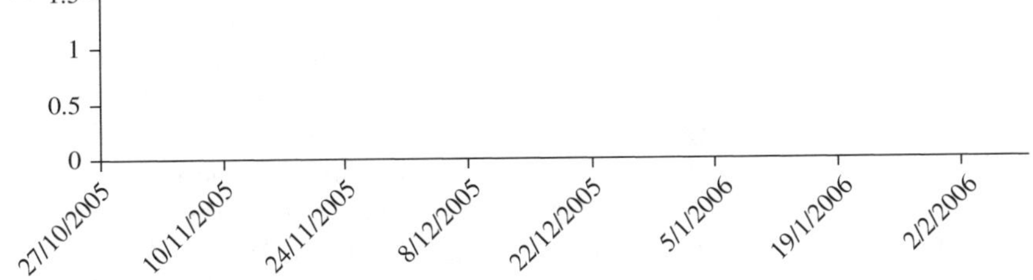

Source: http://finance.yahoo.com (ticker symbol: 0929.hk), retrieved 11 February 2006. These prices are all market close prices, HK$2.38 on 27 October 2005, and HK$3.25 on 9 February 2006.

Figure 5.1 China construction bank stock price and trading volume, 27 October 2005 – 9 February 2006

IPOs on the HKSE as well in 2006, but possibly concurrently with an A-share IPO on the Shanghai Stock Exchange.

In addition to allowing state-owned banks to go public in domestic or overseas stock markets, the government also loosened the restrictions on foreign ownership of domestic bank shares. The BOC and ICBC both have plans to introduce investments from the so-called 'strategic investors', which refer to foreign financial institutions that can provide not only equity capital, but also banking and management expertise. These investors are required to invest in at least 5 percent of the bank's shares. In August 2005, the BOC announced that it would sell 10 percent of its shares at US$3.1 billion to a consortium comprising the Royal Bank of Scotland (RBS), Merrill Lynch, and Hong Kong's Li Ka-Shing Foundation. According to the agreement, RBS will also appoint a representative to serve on the board of directors of the BOC. It was one of the largest foreign investments in China's banking sector, and helped establish a strategic cooperative relationship between the BOC and the RBS, Europe's second largest and the world's sixth largest banking group.

The two banks will enter into broad cooperation in a range of areas including credit cards, wealth management, corporate banking and personal lines of insurance. In addition, the two banks intend to cooperate in major banking managerial areas, including corporate governance, risk management, financial management, human resources management and information technology. Through strategic cooperation with RBS, the BOC hopes to transform its operational structure, enhance the internal management and corporate governance, improve its competitiveness, and promote profitability in preparation for its IPO. For the RBS, the large customer base and vast distribution channel of the BOC will help strengthen its presence in China's banking market.[9]

Other strategic cooperation investors include Temasek Holdings, a Singapore government-owned investment company, which will spend US$1.52 billion to buy a 5 percent stake in the BOC, Bank of America, which will spend US$3 billion on CCB stocks,[10] and a consortium made up of Goldman Sachs, Allianz AG, Europe's biggest insurer, and American Express, which will spend US$3.78 billion to acquire a 10 percent stake in China's largest commercial bank, the ICBC, in the largest foreign investment in the banking sector so far. As of the end of 2005, foreign financial institutions have obtained control of 14.1 percent, 16.8 percent and 10 percent of the shares in the CCB, BOC and ICBC respectively.[11] Without the WTO agreement, these large foreign investments would have been impossible given the prudence and conservativeness Chinese banking regulators have exhibited over the years.

In a more dramatic move, the government put up the NPL-plagued Guangdong Development Bank for auction in late 2005. The bank had been the second largest regional bank in Guangdong Province, the richest province in China, with NPL of RMB35 billion. Citigroup and the Carlyle Group, a private equity firm, of the US, Société Générale, a French bank, and some other financial institutions are vying for an outright control stake of over 85 percent of stock ownership in the insolvent bank. Although the Guangdong Development Bank is in deep financial trouble, its location in China's most developed region, with over 500 branches in southern China, and its national banking license all make it a desirable acquisition target. Most important of all, it is the first domestic bank ever that is approved by the authorities to sell its majority control rights. The successful bidder will be able to install its own management team, and will not have to contend with political considerations and institutional resistance that foreign minority investors have had to deal with in other banks.

Municipal commercial banks could become attractive targets for foreign investments, too. These banks were mostly founded in the last two decades through mergers of urban credit cooperatives. According to CBRC statistics, there were 113 municipal commercial banks in China with total assets of RMB1.9 trillion as of September 2005, but their capital adequacy rate was merely 2.7 percent, well below the average of around 9 percent for the 'Big Four'. In view of these banks' relatively weak finances, the CBRC seems to allow more room and flexibility for their development, merger, restructuring, expansion across regions, and foreign investment. In 2005, Singapore-based Overseas Chinese Bank spent RMB0.57 billion to acquire a 12.2 percent stake in Ningbo Commercial Bank. Some other foreign banks are expected to follow suit in the near future.

Although restrictions on foreign ownership of domestic banks seem to have been loosened, those for foreign banks' business in China have not. If the total foreign ownership of a domestic bank exceeds 25 percent of the total shares, the domestic bank will be categorized as a foreign bank which is subject to CBRC regulations on the scope of operations, services and clients.[12] This, however, does not apply to listed banks. For instance, after the CCB's IPO on the Hong Kong Stock Exchange, the CCB's foreign ownership has surpassed 25 percent, but it is still regarded by the CBRC as a domestic bank.

Non-Performing Loans

China's state-owned commercial banks, especially the 'Big Four', inherit extremely large amounts of non-performing loans (NPLs) from the pre-1978 old system, and keep making more each year as their lending decisions are still heavily influenced by various levels of governments. As recent as

June 2003, the NPL ratio of 12.91 was reported for the CCB, 19.16 percent for BOC, 22 percent for ICBC and 26.54 percent for ABC.

The NPL ratio of the Agricultural Bank of China (ABC) has consistently been the highest among the 'Big Four' due to a large rural-urban income gap and pervasive financial problems in rural areas.[13] But one and half years later at the end of 2004, according to official statistics, these ratios have been reduced to 3.7 percent in CCB, 5.12 percent in BOC, 19.6 percent in ICBC and 26.31 percent in ABC.[14] While the NPLs apparently concentrate in the ICBC and ABC, those of the CCB and BOC have shrunk so quickly that they have received approval from the State Council to issue IPOs on the Hong Kong Stock Exchange; CCB did just that in October 2005 and BOC is expected to follow suit after May 2006. At the end of 2005, the overall NPL ratio of China's commercial banking system has gone down to a single digit for the first time, at 8.9 percent, and 53 commercial banks have reached the 8 percent standard set by the authorities.

The government mainly uses three approaches to address the NPL problem. First, the Chinese government has injected US$259 billion of capital into the national state-owned banks since 1998.[15] For instance, the government issued RMB270 billion of Treasury bonds in 1998 specifically for the 'Big Four', and injected US$45 billion from the foreign exchange reserves into the BOC and CCB in late 2003, which helped explain the aforementioned sharp decrease in these two banks' NPL ratios between mid-2003 and late 2004.

Second, the four national financial asset management companies (AMCs), Huarong, Oriental (Dongfang), Cinda, and Great Wall (Changcheng), which were specifically set up in 1999 to manage the NPLs of commercial banks, have been largely effective (Fung and Liu 2005). Since 1999, the authorities have transferred over US$325 billion worth of NPLs to these four AMCs.[16] Table 5.3 provides a snapshot of the amounts of NPL disposed and cash recovered by September 2005. While the cash recovery rate ranges from 10.54 percent (for Great Wall AMC affiliated with ABC) to 34.66 percent (for Cinda AMC affiliated with BOC), the four AMCs together have disposed of a total of RMB736.6 billion of NPLs and recovered RMB155.0 billion in cash, which, to a certain extent, has lessened the NPL burden for state-owned commercial banks.

Third, the authorities have strengthened oversight of the banks' lending operations by establishing the CBRC and its local branches in 2002, and setting up a five-level loan-classification system that divide all loans into five levels – normal, watched, inferior, suspicious and lost. The system helped improve the transparency of bank operations and pinpoint loans that have the highest likelihood of becoming NPLs for closer and better monitoring. The CBRC also initiated a campaign in recent years to fight

Table 5.3 The four asset management companies

Asset management company	Affiliated bank	Bad loan disposed/Cash recovered/Percentage recovered (RMB billion) by September 2005	Examples of companies affected
Oriental (Dongfang)	Bank of China	113.5 / 27.8 / 24.48%	Jiangxi Phoenix Optical Appliance
Cinda	China Construction Bank	164.4 / 57.0 / 34.66%	Beijing Cement Plant
Huarong	Industrial & Commercial Bank of China	223.8 / 45.5 / 20.34%	Cooperate with Ernst & Young to repackage & market NPL overseas
Great Wall (Changcheng)	Agricultural Bank of China	235.0 / 24.8 / 10.54%	Hualu Electronic

Source: *The Wall Street Journal*, 9 March 2004, and http://finance.sina.com.cn,5 January 2006.

banking corruption, embezzlement and other crimes, and achieved some results. For instance, the ABC alone found 805 cases of banking crimes and 15 provincial-level branch leaders were punished in 2005.[17] Overall, the three approaches seem to have contributed to the decline of NPLs while the first one, injection of government capital at the expense of taxpayers, is definitely the most effective and achieves the quickest results.

Financial Innovations

In recent years, bank deposits in China have been rising rapidly due to the almost consistently double-digit GDP growth rates, a bearish stock market, a declining real estate market in many cities, and lack of a well-constructed retirement protection system. The savings rate of Chinese citizens has long been above 40 percent, far higher than the world's average of 25 percent. Domestic total deposit balance broke the RMB12 trillion mark in January 2005, the RMB13 trillion mark in May 2005, and then the RMB14 trillion mark in December 2005, representing a jump of over 18 percent within the year.[18] The number of individuals with a net worth of US$1 million or more exceeded 300 000 in 2004, doubling the figure seven years ago. As the savings interest rates remain at a low level,[19] there is a growing need for commercial banks' financial innovations. As a result, many new financial products have emerged from commercial banks, which can be divided into the following three types.

The first type helps domestic investors invest indirectly in overseas financial markets and thus circumvent the foreign investment restrictions. For instance, China Merchants Bank offers the so-called 'Diamond 2' wealth management programs to specific high-wealth clients. The duration of the investment program is three years. At maturity, the principal will be returned in RMB, whereas returns will be paid in US dollars.

The second type combines the features of existing banking products to create a hybrid one. For example, the CITIC Bank cooperated with the Southern Fund Management Company to launch the 'CITIC Southern Mutual Fund Credit Card', which combines mutual fund investment with credit card transactions and allows investors to invest in mutual funds automatically through extra credit card payments. There are also hybrid wealth management products that integrate an RMB and a US dollar account together in an integrated wealth management program and provide profit potential from exchange rate fluctuations.[20] These hybrid products are able to take advantage of the features of each individual financial product and provide added convenience and return potential to investors.

The third type of financial innovation is tied to financial securities with saving deposits. That is, the investments combine semi-savings products that provide guaranteed returns higher than the savings interest rate in the same period with stocks-related products that help investors indirectly invest in the stock market with professional assistance and short-term-bond-related products that invest in commercial papers, mutual-fund-related products that allow retail investors to invest in mutual funds with high investment thresholds, and exchange-rate-related products that invest in foreign currencies and have expected returns of at least 3 percent.

In addition to these three types, some new financial products offer added liquidity and flexibility by allowing investors to redeem before maturity with a small penalty in return. These new products prove to be attractive to people who expect sudden and erratic cash needs.

As of early 2006, most financial products offered by commercial banks have a minimum limit of RMB50 000. Investments below this amount cannot purchase these financial products. To circumvent this limitation, some banks help retail investors sign agreements to group smaller amounts of investments together to purchase financial products under the name of one investor.[21]

Many domestic and foreign banks have planned to increase their stakes in this fast-growing segment of the banking market. Minsheng Bank, the only domestic private bank, intends to increase the weight of its personal financial services in all banking services from 10 percent in 2005 to 30 percent in 2007.

London-based Standard Chartered Bank has opened a wealth management center in its branch in Shenzhen City, and some other foreign banks are expected to follow soon.

Although we cannot find any official comments on these emerging financial products, it appears the authorities have adopted an open and positive attitude toward their development and do not intend to impose any regulations or restrictions in the foreseeable future. After all, financial innovations can make domestic banks more competitive and better prepared for the market-opening reforms after December 2006.

CURRENT ISSUES AND CHALLENGES

Recent initiatives taken by the authorities exemplify the determination and willingness of the government to address perennial problems and strengthen the competitiveness of the banking sector. However, some new issues have emerged which may weaken the effect of the government's efforts. They include the new NPLs from the real estate market, competition from a developing underground banking system, lack of investment channels for the fast-increasing deposits, and corruption. Next we will examine each of these issues.

NPLs from the Real Estate Industry

In recent years, real estate prices across China have consistently outgrown inflation. As Table 5.4 shows, for both residential and non-residential real prices, growth rates were much higher than the reported inflation rate of 1.2 percent in 2003, and the 5.2 percent year-on-year consumer price index (CPI) in September 2004.[22] The index started to rise sharply in the fourth quarter of 2003 and the first quarter of 2004, a result showing signs of overheating in the housing market. In some cities in the booming southeastern coastal area, real estate prices have been rising so fast that apartments have become unaffordable for the average double-income family. For instance, the average price of apartment units in metropolitan Shanghai more than doubled in less than three years, from below RMB5000 per square meter in 2001 to RMB12 000 in the third quarter of 2004.

To address the so-called 'real estate bubble' for fear that decreasing housing affordability may give rise to social problems, Chinese authorities, instead of allowing the market to cool down by itself, began to adopt some austerity measures, or so-called macro-adjustments, in mid-2004. These administrative measures included real estate tax hikes for second homes and houses sold within two years of purchase. The impacts were quick and

Table 5.4 Real Estate Price Indices (%, Quarter I, 2003 – Quarter III, 2004)

	Quarter I, 2003	Quarter II, 2003	Quarter III, 2003	Quarter IV, 2003	Quarter I, 2004	Quarter II, 2004	Quarter III, 2004
Housing price index[a]	4.8	5.0	4.1	5.1	7.7	10.4	9.9
Residential	5.2	4.8	5.9	7.0	7.6	10.1	8.6
Economy	3.8	3.0	1.2	2.5	5.2	2.8	2.0
Ordinary	5.8	5.2	6.6	7.3	7.7	10.6	9.2
Luxury	2.3	3.3	2.9	7.6	7.9	11.1	8.4
Non-residential	2.5	2.4	3.4	2.6	7.4	6.0	7.7
Office	3.8	2.4	3.7	3.6	7.8	9.3	8.6
Commercial	1.5	1.3	3.1	2.2	8.2	5.1	7.5

Source: *China Economic Indicators Monthly Report*, January 2003–September 2004.
[a] The housing price index also reflects changes in the sale prices of units subsidized by the government.

drastic. The increase in the index for the economy's residential market, which was closely controlled by the government, dropped the earliest – in the second quarter instead of in the third quarter, and by the biggest margin, from 5.2 percent in the first quarter of 2004 to 2.8 percent in the second quarter. According to Wang (2005), Shanghai's housing prices dropped by over 20 percent and transaction volume by 60 percent as of the end of 2005 from their peaks in 2004.

This downturn in the real estate market created serious problems for domestic commercial banks. Since the late 1990s, many banks, including the 'Big Four', have been lax and lenient in granting mortgage loans as they mistakenly viewed these loans, with real estate as collateral, as almost default risk-free. Mortgage loans as a percentage of total loans rose from 4 percent in 1999 to 15 percent in 2005, crossing the internationally-recognized red line for the weight of such loans. An estimate by Ernst and Young (China) put the figure at 30 percent. In addition, bad mortgage loans that are hidden in the second level of the aforementioned five-level bank loan classification system, which need to be 'watched' closely, have amounted to RMB525 billion, which might ignite a new wave of NPLs. The second-level loans increased sharply over the last two years due to a surge of problematic mortgage loans.[23] As Wang (2005) points out, most mortgage loans finance 70 percent of the house purchase price. As real estate price decline approaches 30 percent, more and more mortgage default and negative individual wealth emerge, thereby raising the NPL level of the lending banks. This problem is a side effect of heavy-handed policies, which the authorities might not have expected when they tried to cool down the over-heated real estate market. Some analysts predict that, if the rising mortgage loan default amounts to a financial crisis, the government will have no choice but step in to reverse its macro-adjustment policies. But these government interventions in financial markets could probably be replaced, at least partially, by natural market self-adjustment by the so-called 'invisible hand' to achieve better results and reduce losses.

Competition from the Underground Banking System

Underground banking emerged in China shortly after the reform and opening up policies took effect in 1978, mainly due to the need of citizens to convert currencies before they went abroad to study or do business. The tight foreign exchange control made it difficult for these people to obtain all the foreign currencies needed, so they resorted to underground banks, which have grown substantially for two reasons.

First, in the 1980s and 1990s, tens of thousands of factories were set up by overseas investors in coastal areas to produce goods which were exported to foreign markets, and many of these manufacturers paid their workers with foreign currencies, which also needed to be converted to RMB at underground banks.

The second reason that gave rise to underground banking was the lending preferences of the commercial banking system, which was dominated by state-owned banks. Banks officials, who were also Communist Party officials, directed most of the loans to state-owned or collectively-owned businesses to avoid making political mistakes and secure their own careers. It has been difficult for the fast-growing private sector, represented by the large number of small- and medium-size private businesses that sprang up in both the rural and urban areas, to obtain bank financing.[24] So they, too, had to turn to underground banks.

The macro-adjustment, which started in mid-2004 to prevent the economy from overheating, seemed to have no end in sight and created more room for underground banks' development. With regard to the source of funds, the high savings rates, more than 20 years of high economic growth, and lack of alternative investment channels have left many Chinese citizens with large amounts of cash at hand. And they are willing to take some risk in exchange for higher returns by depositing their cash at underground banks.

The interest rates of underground financing vary widely. In the Pearl River Delta in Guangdong Province, interest rates ranged from 12 percent to 24 percent depending on how well the borrower operates and whether there is collateral. In most cases, factory equipment, company shares, and even intangible assets can be used as collateral for underground financing. In Shanghai, underground loans backed by collateral usually charge interest rates between 8 percent and 12 percent. The sharp decline in the local real estate market and strict macro-adjustment policies forced many real estate developers to turn to underground banks. Their desperate need for cash have driven up the interest rate as high as 20 percent to 25 percent. Although regular commercial banks can offer loans at much lower interest rates, their inflexible loan terms, low quality services, red tape in loan approval process, and limitations and restrictions imposed by the government have made them less competitive and lost many potentially lucrative opportunities to their underground peers.

According to a study, financing provided by the underground banking system is estimated to be between RMB740.5 billion and RMB816.4 billion, representing about 28 percent of the total financing obtained from normal banking channels as of late 2005. For China's small- and medium-size businesses, approximately one-third of their financing comes from underground banking. In rural areas, more than 55 percent of the farmer's financing also comes from underground. And this percentage is even higher in less developed areas. Between 3 percent and 4 percent of the total currency amount in M2, the sum of cash, checking and savings accounts, and short-term assets, is used by the underground banking system.[25] Due to its size and rapid growth, underground banking has, to a certain extent, neutralized the effect of the macro-adjustment policies and created considerable competition to China's commercial banking system. In view of the upcoming opening-up of the banking market, the authorities need to find a way quickly to legalize and integrate the underground banking system and take advantage of its ingenuity, flexibility and adaptability to strengthen China's commercial banking system.

Lack of Investment Channels

While depositing money at a commercial bank remains the first choice for most Chinese and the deposit balance kept breaking historic marks in 2005, commercial banks were faced with a new problem – how to deal with the growing pile of cash? Due to macro-adjustment policies that limit bank lending in order to cool down the economy, and fast-growing competition from the underground banking system, the lending-deposit (loan balance divided by deposit balance) ratio across domestic banks dropped to 51.83 percent as of October 2005. This means that almost half of the RMB14 trillion-plus deposits is left sitting in the bank while the bank is obligated to pay the PBOC-set interest rates on these deposits, which would not have happened had the banks been given more autonomy and decision-making power. This low usage of funds leads to a sub-optimal allocation of resources. While the banking system is having trouble dealing with the piles of cash, the stock markets remain bearish and listed companies cannot obtain enough financing by selling stocks and corporate bonds.[26] Furthermore, such a low lending-deposit ratio would inevitably cut into the profitability of commercial banks, weakening their financial strength at an inopportune time right before they have to face much tougher competition from foreign banks after 2006. To address this issue, the PBOC issued directives to, in principle, allow commercial banks to buy corporate bonds in December 2005, and the new version of Securities Law that took effect on 1 January 2006, also removed the restrictions on banks' investment in stocks. However, the situation may not change much before the detailed implementation rules are announced, which could take quite some time.

Corruption and Fraud

Although the CBRC has stepped up its efforts in fighting corruption and fraud, new shocking cases still keep emerging. One of the most conspicuous involved a huge amount of US dollar funds at BOC. Table 5.5 provides a list of banking scandals in recent years. All of the 'Big Four' enter the list. CCB and BOC, the two banks that report the lowest NPL ratios and go public on the HKSE, actually had more scandals. This will definitely hurt the confidence of potential investors. In addition, the fact that most scandals involve internal bank employees indicates that there is huge room for improvement with regard to the operations transparency, corporate governance, internal audit and control of China's banking system.

CONCLUDING REMARKS

There have been significant developments and changes in China's pivotal banking system in recent years as a result of the growing pressures from the WTO accession agreement to open the banking market by the end of 2006. While the financial system remains dominated by state-owned banks, the government has undertaken gradual deregulation measures and loosened restrictions on foreign investments and other areas in the banking market, which may offer potentially lucrative opportunities to foreign banking institutions. For policy makers of developing countries that intend to restructure their banking systems, these changes may provide valuable experience and lessons.

Although there have been some positive results, like the declining NPL ratios, new issues arise which need to be dealt with quickly, including

Table 5.5 Recent banking scandals

Time	Bank affected	Location	Brief description
March 2005	CCB	Jilin Province	A branch was defrauded of RMB320 million. A bank manager fled abroad with US$8 million
March 2005	CCB	Beijing	CCB Chairman, Zhang Enzhao, was investigated for bribery and corruption charges
March 2005	ABC	Inner Mongolia	Criminals colluded with bank clerks to defraud a branch of RMB115 million
January 2005	BOC	Heilongjiang Province	An audit found RMB800 million had disappeared from a branch in Harbin; branch manager fled to Canada
August 2004	BOC	Hong Kong	Two vice presidents of BOC (HK) were arrested for transferring funds for personal use
June 2004	ICBC	Guangdong Province	A private business owner colluded with bank clerks to obtain RMB7.4 billion with fraudulent financial statements
December 2003	CCB & BOC	Beijing	A former top executive of CCB and BOC, Wang Xuebing, was convicted of bribery and corruption
November 2003	Shantou Commerical Bank	Guangdong Province	Top bank executives were convicted for collecting illegal deposits and granting illegal loans
September 2003	Huaxia Bank	Beijing	A publicly-traded bank, Huaxia allegedly cooked the books on NPL level. Top bank executive was arrested
February 2002	BOC	Shanghai	Former vice chairman of BOC board of directors was arrested for mishandling loans and corruption
October 2001	BOC	Guangdong Province	Three consecutive branch managers stole US$483 million between 1993 and 2001, fled to the US

Sources: http://finance.news.tom.com/, 6 December 2005; http://www.chinatimes.com/, 2 February 2006; http://www.scol.com.cn/, 17 November 2003.

surging bad mortgage loans, the fast-growing underground banking system, low lending-deposit ratios, and rampant corruptions. We believe that more in-depth measures are needed to address deep-rooted structural issues that give rise to many perennial problems, and to prepare the relatively inefficient domestic commercial banks for the upcoming open market competition.

One important area for the Chinese government to implement is to encourage and motivate commercial banks to help small and medium size enterprises (SMEs) for financing. SMEs are the engine of China's future growth and they create employment opportunities for China's huge unemployed labor force. Like the Small Business Administration loans in the US, China needs to set up such loans for helping SMEs rather than relying on underground banking. This of course poses challenges for Chinese commercial banking.

Recently, China's Banking Regulatory Commission has designated Citibank of the US, Bank of Montreal, HSBC of Hong Kong/UK, Standard Chartered Bank of the UK, and ABN AMRO Bank of the Netherlands, along with eight domestic commercial banks, as RMB spot foreign exchange market makers. These market makers serve as dealers in RMB foreign exchange transactions and help establish open and closed market exchange rates each day. Given that foreign exchange trading has long been a closely guarded area for the authorities, this move represents a substantial shift in the government's attitude, and is expected to provide further momentum to the ongoing changes in China's banking market.

NOTES

1. This remains one of the most popular ways to transfer funds today. As checks are still scarce, parties involved in transactions usually transfer money between their bank accounts. Many people either memorize their long bank account numbers or carry the numbers with them.
2. Guangdong Development Bank is currently controlled by Guangdong provincial government, Shenzhen Development Bank by Shenzhen city government, Shanghai Pudong Development Bank by Shanghai city government, and Huaxia Bank by Beijing city government.
3. China CITIC Bank is currently controlled by China International Trust and Investment Corporation (CITIC), and China Everbright Bank by China Everbright Group.
4. http://www.chinatimes.com, 16 January 2006.
5. Liu, Mingkang, Chairman of CBRC, speech at a State Council press conference on 5 December 2005.
6. Bank of China (Hong Kong) issued IPO on the Hong Kong Stock Exchange. It was not, however, regarded as a mainland bank since this branch of BOC did most of its banking business in Hong Kong and was treated as a separate unit for accounting purposes. The stocks issued by mainland-registered companies on the Hong Kong Stock Exchange are called the 'H-shares', with 'H' referring to Hong Kong. Along the same

line, 'N-shares' mean Chinese stocks listed on American stock exchanges, with 'N' standing for New York.
7. http://www.chinatimes.com, 28 January 2006.
8. http://www.chinesenewsnet.com, 29 December 2005.
9. http://www.atimes.com, 20 August 2005.
10. As a byproduct of the deal, Bank of America has earned large underwriting fees from CCB's IPO.
11. http://www.chinatimes.com/, 12 January 2006.
12. Liu Mingkang, Chairman of CBRC, speech at a State Council press conference on 5 December 2005.
13. One of the most popular political terms in China is 'San Nong Wen Ti', or 'three rural problems' that refer to the issues associated with rural areas, rural businesses, and rural residents. Due to the graveness of these problems, it has become a tradition that the State Council's first official policy document each year focuses on rural problems.
14. http://www.chinatimes.com, 28 January 2006, http://www.xinhuanet.com/, 18 January 2006.
15. *Business Week*, 23 January 2006. While the government has injected huge amounts of capital to clean up the national state-owned banks, it has been reluctant to do the same with regional banks, which explains why the Guandong Development Bank was put up for sale.
16. http://www.chinatimes.com/, 23 November 2005.
17. http://www.xinhuanet.com/, 18 January 2006.
18. http://www.chinatimes.com/, 17 January 2006.
19. As of January 2006, the one-year fixed-term savings interest rate was 2.25 percent.
20. http://www.chinatimes.com/, 13 February 2006.
21. http://www.chinatimes.com/, 13 February 2006.
22. Yahoo! Financial News, 10 December 2004, http://au.biz.yahoo.com/041210/33/2fif.html.
23. http://www.chinatimes.com, 23 November 2005.
24. The authorities attempted to meet these needs for small-scale financing by setting up rural credit cooperatives and urban credit cooperatives. But obviously this attempt has not been very successful.
25. http://www.xinhuanet.com/, 6 December 2005.
26. In China a large quantity of corporate bonds are traded on the two stock exchanges in Shanghai and Shenzhen.

REFERENCES

Allen, Franklin, Jun Qian and Meijun Qian (2002), 'Comparing China's financial system', University of Pennsylvania working paper.

Fung, Hung-Gay (1999), 'Chinese banking: challenges and opportunities in the new millennium', *Business Forum*, **24**(3, 4), 2–6.

Fung, Hung-Gay and Qingfeng Liu (2006), 'China's financial reform in banking and securities markets', in H. G. Fung, C. H. Pei and K. Zhang (eds), *China and the Challenge of Economic Globalization: The Impact of WTO Membership*, New York: M.E. Sharpe, pp. 145–63.

Kang, Shusheng (2005), *Banking Systems Comparison and Trend Research*, Beijing: China Finance Press.

Levine, Ross (2002), 'Bank-based or market-based financial systems: which is better?', NBER working paper no. 9138.

Wang, Chentao (2005), 'The Shanghai sample of China's housing price war', *Chinese News Weekly*, accessed at www.chinesenewsnet.com

6. Investment banking in China: past, present and future

Alan V. S. Douglas and Alan Guoming Huang

INTRODUCTION

This chapter briefly describes the history and current status of China's investment banking industry. We focus on three narrowly defined categories of investment banking activities: underwriting, brokerage and financial advisory services. These three lines of business closely resemble the business scope of investment banks in China to date. Underwriting services include public offerings and private placements of equity and debt securities; brokerage services include commission-based security transactions, and financial advisory services include advice on mergers and acquisitions (M&A), divestitures, spin-offs and other corporate finance activities.

The investment banking industry in China is fairly young. The first investment bank was founded in 1987. Investment banks in China predominantly call themselves 'securities companies', for example, 'Guangfa Securities Co., Ltd'. Following the growth of the Chinese economy and its capital markets, the industry has grown exponentially over the years, both in terms of firm numbers and firm assets. By the end of 2004, there were a total of 128 securities firms, with total and net assets of RMB458 billion and 100 billion, respectively.[1] However, the industry remains in its early stages of development, even though the growth has been phenomenal. The size of the industry and individual firms is relatively small by the standards of developed financial markets.

The industry's growth to date can be broken into three distinct periods, based on legislative milestones and the speed of growth. These three periods are the arising period (1987–1990), the rapid growth period (1991–1999), and the adjustment period (1999–present). Briefly, the first period witnessed the birth of some 50 securities firms spreading geographically across the country. As startups, these firms were typically very small. A distinct feature of this period is that the securities firms had to operate in an extremely immature legal and regulatory environment. In the rapid growth period, the sector grew exponentially, mainly due to an exploding capital market during the period. For example, the number of companies listed on the stock exchanges grew from 14 in 1991 to 720 in 1997, a 50-fold increase. As a result, the number of securities firms doubled, and total assets grew 15-fold. During this growth period, the China Securities Regulatory Commission (CSRC), China's regulatory counterpart to US Securities and Exchange Commission, was established to regulate the securities industry. The establishment of the CSRC coincided with the enactment of key new laws, such as The Company Law. The third distinct period began in 1999, and is characterized by broad-based adjustment related to two major events: the enactment of The Securities Law in 1999, and China's accession to the World Trade Organization (WTO) in 2001. The Securities Law aims at creating a level legal playground for industry participants; and the WTO membership requires China to open up its financial service sector within a few years. These events led to profound changes. To abide by the new law and prepare for the imminent competition, there has been wide-spread consolidation in the securities industry, either through mergers and acquisitions or through liquidations associated with investment banking fraud that occurred in the previous expansion periods. Furthermore, the state has initiated a key reform agenda aimed at floating what were originally non-traded state-owned shares on China's stock exchanges. These efforts are designed to mitigate the major differences between Chinese and western financial markets, and have set the stage for another growth period in the Chinese investment banking industry.

Currently, the industry is heavily concentrated. Geographically, most of the big players are headquartered in three major cities: Beijing, Shanghai and Shenzhen. The reason is apparent: Beijing is the capital city where much of the regulatory power resides, and Shanghai and Shenzhen host the country's only two stock exchanges. As of year end 2004, 51 out of 128 securities firms were based in these three cities. From a market share perspective, the investment banking industry is dominated by the top five to ten players. For example, in 1997, the top five securities firms account for a third of the industry's total assets, 50 percent of the industry's underwriting income, and 15 percent of the industry's brokerage income.[2] Industry revenues are also heavily clustered within the limited business lines of underwriting, brokerage, and principal trading. Zheng *et al.* (2003) document that underwriting spreads, brokerage commissions, investment gains and interest revenue account for 96.53 percent of industry revenue in 1999. Huang and Fung (2004) corroborate this by illustrating that other revenues, such as M&A advising fees, are negligible. It is noteworthy that, as might be expected, industry revenues are strongly correlated with the ups and downs of the markets. Overall, industry revenues show a strong increase during the rapid growth period from 1991 to 1998, but have since stagnated in the adjustment period from 1999 to the present.

In addition to delineating the industry by firms and growth, this chapter describes the development of the industry in the context of transitive legal environment and regulatory framework. The evidence indicates that the Chinese legal system improves with industry growth. To understand why the investment banking industry operates the way it does, it is necessary to recognize the changing legal constraints faced by investment banks in China. Over the years, three major pieces of legislation, namely the Company Law, the Securities Law, and the Investment Companies Law, have come into existence and shaped the legal environment for the industry. These three laws regulate most of the operating scope of the securities industry, from setting up a company to insider trading. Bound by these laws, securities firms must also operate under various stipulations from the regulatory bodies and government policies, which sometimes can set the ground for financing activities and investment banking business. For example, the CSRC maintains a policy specifying the types of securities that firms can issue, and in the past has rationed the security issuance activity to provinces. Policies such as this can greatly affect the structure of investment banking income.

The development of the investment banking industry is positioned as a key factor in achieving the goals of Chinese reforms. Two areas in which investment banks are expected to play a vitally important role are economic growth and reforming state-owned-enterprises (SOEs) into market-oriented modern corporations. The tasks seem more urgent than ever as the WTO accession requires China to open critical service sectors such as banking, insurance, asset management and securities to foreign direct investment. In light of such transition, this chapter also offers some foresight into the industry. In particular, it examines the causes and possible impacts of the current undertaking to move toward the full floatation of state-owned shares. By and large, the full-floatation experiment is the state's response to one of the many challenges brought by the WTO accession. For the securities industry, WTO membership means opportunities as well as challenges. The opportunities reflect the state's push for SOEs to be market-oriented, such as the full-floatation undertaking, which will deepen the capital market. The challenges come from direct outside competition for both expansion opportunities and existing business, following WTO membership. Chinese securities firms will need to expand their capabilities to fend off these challenges.

The rest of the chapter is organized as follows. The next section generalizes the development of the investment banking industry. It first breaks the history of China's investment banking industry into the three development periods and then discusses industry concentration. The third section discusses the industry's operating constraints. The fourth section provides some thoughts on the challenges faced by the industry. The final section concludes.

AN OVERVIEW OF THE CHINESE INVESTMENT BANKING INDUSTRY

Based on the legislative and regulatory environment, and on industry growth, the brief history of China's investment banking industry can be divided into three periods: the arising period, the rapid-growth period and the adjustment period. In what follows, we outline the milestone events in each of the three stages, and provide some up-to-date statistics. Overall, the industry can be characterized by three features: fast growth, heavy concentration, and small absolute size. The analysis suggests that the industry is evolving quickly, and that the state is making strong efforts to ensure the young industry develops into a strong one.

Three Stages of Development

The arising period: 1987–1990

The modern Chinese securities market emerged slowly in response to the 'opening and reform' policy of 1978. The central government issued the first Treasury bond in 1981. Firms started to issue, mainly through commercial banks and trust companies, corporate bonds and stocks to institutions and individuals to raise the much needed capital. The financing activities gained a great deal of momentum, particularly in the so-called Special Economic Zones that served as model opening cities to the outside world. Gradually, the building momentum led to the establishment of firms specializing in the securities business. The first securities firm, Shenzhen Special Economic Zone Securities Co., Ltd, was established in 1987 in Shenzhen, a special economic zone city bordering Hong Kong. Its main business then was to conduct over-the-counter Treasury bond transactions and shortly after, over-the-counter stock issuance and trading. Within a year, 23 more securities firms were founded throughout the country, and the number climbed to 52 within four years (see, for example, Ma, 2004).

Although the first securities firm was established in Shenzhen, most of the major players during the period emerged in Shanghai, which was the Far East financial center in the early 20th century. The biggest players at the time were Wanguo, Shenyin, and Haitong, each with starting registered capital of RMB1 billion. Shenyin was a pioneer in market innovations. Its predecessor, a non-independent unit of the Industrial and Commercial Bank of China Shanghai Branch, issued the first Chinese stock in 1984, established the first transaction counter in 1986, and compiled the first stock index in 1987. Wanguo, on the other hand, became the de facto king of the markets. Established in 1998, Wanguo expanded aggressively, becoming the preeminent trader in the Treasury bond market. At its peak, Wanguo captured half of the nation's securities business. Facing an inevitable bankruptcy due to trading fraud in the Treasury bond markets, it was later acquired (in 1995) by Shenyin.

During the arising period, the industry was regulated by various state institutions. The securities firms were owned by state-owned enterprises or state departments, such as the People's Bank of China (the central bank) or the Treasury Department. As a result, they were regulated by the People's Bank of China and local governments, as well as other state institutions such as the Treasury Department. There was, however, no unified regulatory body – the different government institutions simply extended their existing functions to monitor the industry.

For most of this period, the industry's business was confined to primary securities issuances and over-the-counter secondary securities transactions. This was not to be changed until late 1990 and 1991, when the country's two stock exchanges were established in Shanghai and Shenzhen respectively. The two stock exchanges started, for the first time in the nation's history, open consolidated transactions for listed companies' stocks and bonds. Undoubtedly, this gave a boost to the brokerage and underwriting business. At the same time, the existing over-the-counter markets were consolidated into a nationwide computerized trading system called the Securities Trading Automated Quotations system (STAQ), modeled on the US NASDAQ system. By creating a unified national trading framework, the two stock exchanges and STAQ signified the formal emergence of Chinese securities markets. Subsequently, the securities industry embarked on rapid growth.

The rapid growth period: 1991–1999

The investment banking industry grew impressively from 1991 to 1999. The size of the industry, as evidenced by the number of securities firms, income, assets and number of products, reached heights that dwarfed the 1991 levels. During this time, the industry grew toward a boom in 1996, and peaked in 1998. The number of securities firms grew to 87 in 1992, and another ten had emerged by 1994. Securities firms also expanded their trading branches[3] to smaller cities throughout the country. There were some 1500 trading branches in 1994, and 2419 branches two years later. The expansion in trading branches was accompanied by a huge increase in brokerage commission: the equity trading volume increased almost 1000 times from 1991's 4 billion yuan to 1999's 3 trillion yuan (See, for example Ma 2003). Boosted by the growing capital market activity, the securities industry experienced phenomenal growth in total assets, net assets, and net income. From 1995 to 1999, the securities firms' total assets increased four times from 83 billion to 308 billion yuan; their net assets grew seven times from 7 billion to 49 billion yuan; and their net income increased seven times as well from 80 million to 560 million yuan.

There was also an increase in the variety of services offered by investment banks. In the arising period (prior to 1991), securities firms offered only the standard IPO underwriting and commission-based brokerage services. As the markets exploded in 1991, however, securities firms began to offer many new types of services to satisfy financing demands. The number of listed companies grew almost 100 times from 1991's 14 to 1999's 949. With an ever larger market, the demand for initial public financing and continuous financing became enormous. New financing tools, including rights offerings, secondary equity offerings and convertible bonds, emerged only to become main stream financing activities as the period progressed. By 1999, the investment banks were involved in virtually all forms of equity financing that exist in the western markets, and their brokerage services had expanded to include discount internet trading.

The biggest players in the growth period included the 'national three' (namely China, Southern and Guotai, all founded by various national institutions in 1992), the major banks such as Shenyin and Wanguo, and a limited number of regional-transformed firms such as Junan and Guangfa. Junan and Wanguo were later acquired by Shenyin and Guotai respectively. These few firms dominated the primary markets and captured a large fraction of the secondary markets.

The rapid growth in this period reflected profound changes in China, including a solid infrastructure developing in the capital markets. The preceding decade of economic growth created enormous demand in these markets, and the establishment of the two stock exchanges created a unified platform that facilitated capital transactions. Aided by the growth of the capital markets, the legal environment also improved significantly. In particular, a unified SEC-like regulatory framework was created, and new laws and regulations were introduced to support the primary and secondary markets. The State Council Securities Commission and China Securities Regulatory Commission (CSRC) were created in 1992 as regulatory bodies – the former set industry standards, while the latter monitored the execution of these standards. Over the next few years the two bodies effectively merged. By 1998, the CSRC emerged as the sole regulatory entity, taking over the functions of the State Council Securities

Commission, as well as the remaining securities-industry regulatory functions from the People's Bank of China. In addition, a number of key laws and regulations were enacted during the growth period, including the Interim Stipulation on Stock Issuances and Transactions of 1993, the Corporate Debt Regulation of 1993, the Company Law of 1994 and the Commercial Banking Law of 1995. The Interim Stipulation on Stock Issuances and Transactions regulated on the qualification of stock issuance, stock trading and insider trading. The Company Law defined for the first time the rights and liabilities of a limited-liability company, and the Commercial Banking Law, which separates the operation of commercial banking, securities industry and insurance industry, gave the securities industry the identity of independence. Taken together, the regulatory framework and legal system provided the infrastructure needed to foster the growth of the securities industry.

Some major problems also emerged during the rapid growth period. Market wise, the ownership of listed companies was split between a non-tradable state-owned majority and a tradable private minority. The tradable shares were often worth a large premium over the non-tradable shares (see, for example, Huang and Fung 2005). In place from the establishment of the markets, this ownership structure created a significant misalignment of objectives between majority shareholders and minority shareholders, because majority shareholders, holding non-floatable shares, faced interests other than maximizing stock prices. This incentive conflict was accompanied by relatively weak corporate governance (see, for example, Clarke 2003) and quite often, led to fraud by insiders. Industry wise, securities firms offered homogeneous products, and had a hard time soliciting new capital to meet their own financing needs, partly due to regulations that limited their financing capabilities. Indulged by the market boom, then, they were reluctant to develop innovative products, lacked sufficient governance, and often participated in market fraud. Eventually, the overall effect of these problems was to significantly hinder the market performance – by 1999, the markets had lost considerable steam. The markets subsequently entered a prolonged bearish period, to the detriment of the investment banking industry.

The adjustment period: 1999–present

The adjustment period began with an air of optimism, which was soon replaced with a prolonged period of pessimism. Encouraged by a major market boom during 1996–1998, additional securities firms were established and existing firms pursued additional financing to increase their equity capital. For instance, Haitong expanded its registered equity capital from 1 billion to 4.06 billion yuan in 2001, at which time the number of securities firms reached over 100. The industry's net equity increased almost two-fold from 1999's 49 billion to 2001's 86 billion yuan, mostly due to external financing of registered capital.

Despite the brief spike in 1999–2000, the market suffered a downward trend that pushed the investment banking industry into an adjustment period. The major indices stalled at 1999 levels for several years: in 2005, the major indices are close to 1999 levels. The stagnation of the markets curtailed both transaction volume and firm financing activities, which greatly reduced the investment banking income. The industry further lost income from two reforms during the period that would reshape their business models: the underwriting process reform and the liberalization of the brokerage commissions. Traditionally, the number and amount of IPOs were rationed to various provinces and state departments. In 2001, the rationing system was formally abandoned and replaced by a qualification system, in which any firm meeting the issuing threshold could issue equity. Similarly, the universally imposed 3.5 percent round-trip trading commission was lifted in 2002, leaving brokerage firms free to charge the commissions they wish. These two reforms led to heated competition among securities firms, as they exercised their new-granted ability to undercut each other. This typically led to lower commissions in both underwriting and brokerage. It is not hard to imagine that the stiffened competition, in particular the lowering of commissions, inevitably lowered revenues for securities firms. Indeed, the industry as a whole started to lose money in 2002. By 2004, despite a slight increase in operating revenues, the net income for the industry was −20.63 billion yuan. Total and net assets also declined by 2004, and the prolonged bearish period now has many people worrying about the survival of the industry.

It seems that the regulatory bodies were less concerned about market decline than harnessing and fixing the market framework. A major factor underlying the regulatory action is China's accession to the WTO in 2001, in which China promised to fully open its securities industry by 2005. It appears that a serious house-cleaning is needed in the investment banking industry to properly face the challenges created by the WTO accession. Some very difficult issues must be addressed on several fronts, including legislative issues, the tradability of state-owned shares, the governance and openness of the industry and money management practices. On the legislative side, the state enacted a system of laws to fully cover the operation of the industry. In particular, the Securities Law was enacted in 1999 and the Investment Companies Law was enacted in 2005. Replacing the 1993 Interim Stipulation and related regulations, the 1999 Securities Law provides a single platform to oversee the entire industry, covering areas from the set-up of share-holding companies to insider trading. The Investment Companies Law regulates the mutual fund industry and money management practice. Along with the CSRC, the Securities Law sets the legal norm by which the industry operates – the Securities Law articulates the 'cans' and 'cannots' for the industry, and the CSRC exercises its regulatory power according to the Securities Law.

The house-cleaning effort goes far beyond building legal infrastructure. Floating state-owned shares was next on the agenda. After years of debate, in 2005 the CSRC started to allow for full floatability of state-owned shares at a discount price to tradable shares. This helps to align the objectives of the different shareholders, and is expected to have a major impact on both corporate governance and the market pricing of securities. Also on the house-cleaning agenda are the operating procedures for the markets and the securities industry. Delisting procedures were installed for the first time, with the first delisting in 2001. At the same time, securities firms with unsalvageable fraud problems were ordered to close their doors – the most famous incidents being the liquidations of Southern and China, two of the once 'big three'. These measures seem to have helped reclaim investor confidence. Lastly, the regulatory bodies started to open the investment banking and money management industry to foreign and domestic private ownership on a scale never before seen. By 2004, there were four joint venture securities firms, and 13 joint venture mutual funds, many of which were affiliated with world-class names such as Goldman Sachs. In addition, several small securities firms are now privately owned, and foreign capital firms have made open acquisitions in the market.

Finally, the adjustment period witnessed significant change in the money management industry. The first open-end mutual fund was established in 2001, and by 2003, there were already 56 open-end mutual funds managing 120 trillion yuan. This links directly to the securities firms discussed above, who are typically the controlling shareholders of these mutual funds.

A generalization of the industry's development, 1987 to 2004

This section generalizes the development of the securities industry over the three periods. We focus on the growth after the establishment of the two stock exchanges and emphasize more recent statistics, including size, top players and comparison with the industry size of a mature market. Table 6.1 provides some general statistics relating to the investment banking industry during 1990–2004. Panel A describes the size and profitability of the industry in three metrics: total assets, net equity and net income. Panel B provides background information on general market growth during the period. From Panel B, the number of listed firms in China increased by about 100 every year, whereas the trading volume peaked in 2000 at 6 trillion yuan. The

Table 6.1 *An overview of the Chinese investment banking industry: 1990–2004 (in billion RMB yuan where applicable)*

Year	1990	1991	1992	1993	1994	1995	1996	1997	1998	1999	2000	2001	2002	2003	2004
Panel A: The industry															
Number of firms	44	52	87	91	91	97	94	90	84	87	94	102	125	127	128
Total assets	7	19	49	56	63	83	159	216	227	308	530	582	539	533	458
Average firm total assets	0.2	0.4	0.6	0.6	0.7	0.9	1.7	2.4	2.7	3.5	5.6	5.7	4.3	4.2	3.6
Net equity	–	–	–	–	–	7	18	32	35	49	71	86	115	125	100
Average firm net equity	–	–	–	–	–	0.08	0.19	0.35	0.42	0.56	0.75	0.85	0.92	0.98	0.78
Net income	–	–	–	–	–	0	5	8	–	8	–	–	−1	−3	−19
Number of trading branches	–	–	–	–	1500*	–	2419	–	2412	2541	2623	2704	2900	2976	–
Panel B: The markets															
Number of listed firms	9	14	53	183	291	323	530	745	851	949	1088	1160	1224	1287	1457
Trading volume	–	4	68	367	813	440	2132	3072	2355	3132	6083	4026	2916	3280	4234

Sources: China Securities Regulatory Commission (CSRC), www.p 5w.net, www.cncapital.net, The Securities Association of China, Shanghai Stock Exchange, Shenzhen Stock Exchange, and Feng (2005). If there are inconsistencies among these sources, the CSRC data are used.
*Estimate.

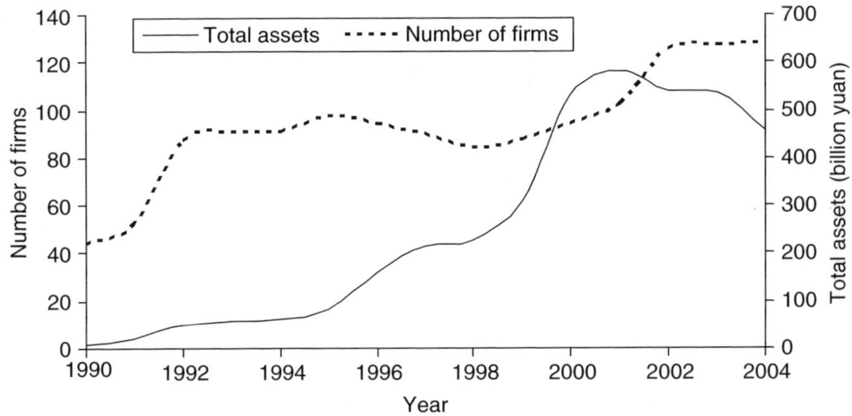

Figure 6.1 *Growth of the investment banking industry over 1990–2004: firm number and total assets*

industry growth, and particularly the increase in total assets, closely matches that of the general markets. Across the period, the number of securities firms tripled, and the industry's total assets increased by more than 60 times. Figure 6.1 illustrates this growth. Overall, total assets and net equity, as well as the number of firms, show positive growth over time.

The trends in Figure 6.1 and Table 6.1 reflect the growth phases previously described. Prior to 1999, the growth in size, as proxied by total assets and net equity, was primarily due to generic business growth – that is, it was largely achieved through growth in existing businesses rather than external financing. In contrast, from 1999 and 2002, the industry engaged in substantial equity financing (that directly increased industry equity and assets). Following the reduction in market volume (seen in panel B of Table 6.1), net income fell into negative territory in 2002. Total assets and net equity shrunk as well.

To better understand whether the growth reflects the addition of firms or the growth of incumbents, we also examine the average size of Chinese securities firms in Figure 6.2. The rapid growth in the average total assets and net equity disappears in 2000. Excluding the effect of external financing in 1999–2000, average industry growth has been virtually stagnant since 2000, as visualized in Figure 6.2.

Table 6.2 lists the ten largest securities firms in 2003 and 2004, in terms of total assets and operating revenues. Most of the top investment banks from the rapid growth period of 1991–1999 managed to maintain their rankings in the adjustment period, notably Guotai Junan Securities Co. Ltd, Shenyin Wanguo Securities Ltd., and Haitong. Some notable second-tier

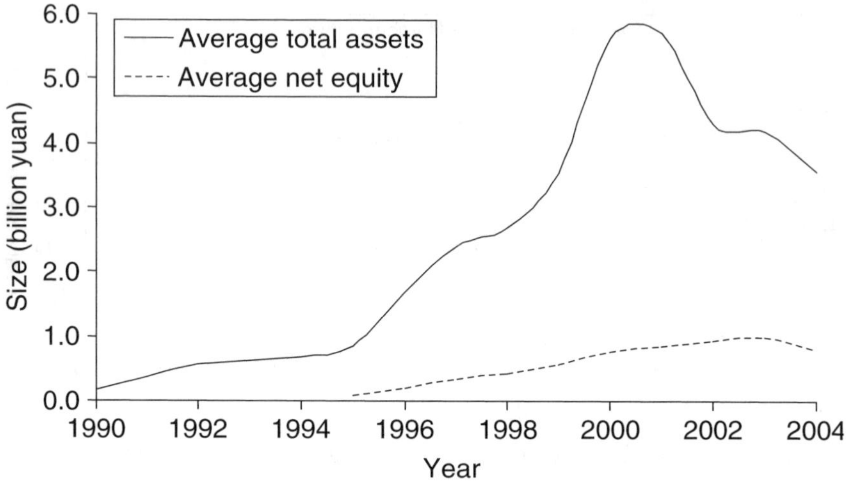

Figure 6.2 Firm average total assets and net equity: 1990–2004

investment banks are Guangfa, Citic and Everbright, which also ranked consistently over the years among the top ten banks. As of 2004, the biggest bank, ShenyinWanguo, had total assets of 20 billion yuan and operating revenue of 1 billion yuan.

Compared to the US, the Chinese securities industry and individual firms are very small. Table 6.3 provides industry and firm size for the US securities industry from 1998 to 2004, based on four statistics: total assets, firm average total assets, net assets, and firm average net assets. For comparison purposes, it also shows the averages of Chinese counterparts during the same period. From this perspective, the Chinese industry seems tiny: the total assets and net assets of the US securities industry are respectively 482 times and 81 times those of China; similarly, average total and net firm assets are, respectively, 208 and 35 times. Comparatively speaking, the Chinese industry is in the early stages of its life cycle, and has a long way to go before reaching a size comparable to that of the US.

Industry Concentration

China's securities industry is also quite concentrated. In particular, there is a relatively large dominance by the top banks, a heavy reliance on brokerage commissions for revenues, and a disproportionate amount of equity underwriting in the underwriting and corporate finance business. We elaborate on this concentration below.

Table 6.2 Top ten investment banks in 2003 and 2004 (in billion yuan)

Rank	2004				2003			
	Total assets		Operating reveue		Total assets		Operating reveue	
	Company	Total assets	Company	Operating revenue	Company	Total assets	Company	Operating revenue
1	ShenyinWanguo	20.1	GutaiJun'an	1.6	GuotaiJun'an	32.4	China Galaxy	1.4
2	GuotaiJun'an	18.9	ShenyinWanguo	1.0	ShenyinWanguo	30.6	GuotaiJun'an	1.2
3	Haitong	16.2	Guangfa	1.0	China Galaxy	28.5	ShenyinWanguo	1.1
4	Citic	12.0	Haitong	0.9	Haitong	26.4	China	1.0
5	Guangfa	9.3	China Merchant	0.7	China	20.8	Citic	0.8
6	Huatai	6.8	Citic	0.6	Citic	17.3	Haitong	0.8
7	Guosen	6.3	Everbright	0.6	Guangfa	12.9	Guangfa	0.7
8	Everbright	6.0	Eastern	0.5	Tiantong	11.8	China Eagle	0.5
9	Bank of China Int'l	5.9	China Int'l Capital	0.5	Xiangcai	10.6	Guosen	0.5
10	China Merchant	5.7	Western China	0.5	Everbright	9.6	Xiangcai	0.5

Source: The Securities Association of China. The statistics include all member firms of the Association. The vast majority of firms are members.

Note: China Galaxy was not included in the 2004 statistics. China and Eagle were liquidated in 2004.

Table 6.3 Size of the US investment banking industry and comparison with China (in billion yuan)

Year	1998	1999	2000	2001	2002	2003	2004	US average	Chinese peer average: 1998–2004 from Table 1	Multiple: US average/ Chinese average
Total assets	145 261	164 103	194 576	225 350	219 732	263 508	318 816	218 764	454	482
Average total assets	513	586	718	863	916	1126	1392	874	4.2	208
Net equity	4740	5861	6933	7226	6889	7463	7980	6728	83	81
Average net equity	17	21	26	28	29	32	35	27	0.75	35
Number of firms included	283	280	271	261	240	234	229	257	–	–

Source: The Securities Industry Association (www.sia.com). The US numbers are multiplied by a USD/RMB yuan exchange rate of eight.

Asset and market share concentration by the top banks

Overall, the top players in the industry garner a large share of the business. Table 6.4 shows the absolute size (proxied by total assets and net equity) and market share (proxied by revenue) of the top five and top ten securities firms in 2003 and 2004. The table also shows the industry share of the top banks in terms of size and market share. Note that the top five or ten in Table 6.4 refer to the largest five or ten cross-sectional observations for a particular variable. For example, the top five in total assets refers to the sum of the five largest total assets observations across securities firms. From Table 6.4, the top five firms account for roughly 20 percent of the industry's assets, net equity and revenue over 2003–2004, while the top ten firms account for more than 25 percent. This indicates that the industry is heavily concentrated in terms of size and market share, with the top ten firms incorporating roughly a quarter of the industry's size, and capturing a quarter of the business.

Panel B of Table 6.4 provides market shares of the top ten firms in terms of commission and underwriting income during the five-year period from 1996 to 2000. On average, the top ten firms generate some 30 percent of the industry's commission income and more than three-quarters of the underwriting income. This distribution implies that the underwriting business is heavily concentrated within the top ten. The brokerage business is also quite concentrated, but to a far lesser degree. This is reflective of the industry dynamics: over the years, most securities firms develop into pure brokers. Only a few, however, develop into broker-dealers with the ability to generate the more sophisticated underwriting business.

While there is considerable concentration in China, the degree of concentration is significantly lower than in the US. From 1990–1999, the top ten US firms accounted for 59.92 percent of the total capital and 52.55 percent of the total revenue in the US industry.[4] In terms of total capital and revenue of the top ten firms, the degree of concentration in the US is almost double that in Chinese markets. This suggests that Chinese markets are less dominated by the 'top-tier' players – although the top securities firms enjoy a relatively high market share in Table 6.4, there remain a number of second-tier players that are able to challenge the first-tier's dominance.

Revenue sources concentration

The securities industry's revenue sources are highly skewed towards brokerage income. The three major services provided by the Chinese securities firms are brokerage, underwriting and related services and principal trading. Over the industry's history, the most important single source of revenue has been brokerage commission, which accounts for about half of

Table 6.4 Size and market share by the top five and ten firms (in billion RMB yuan where applicable)

Panel A: Size and revenue by top firms: 2003–2004

	2003					2004				
	Industry	Top 5		Top 10		Industry	Top 5		Top 10	
		Absolute	Percentage	Absolute	Percentage		Absolute	Percentage	Absolute	Percentage
Total assets	533	139	26.0	201	37.7	458	76	16.7	107	23.4
Net equity	125	19	15.1	28	22.4	100	17	17.4	28	27.7
Revenue	29	6	19.3	9	29.9	30	5	17.4	8	26.4

Panel B: Percentage of industry revenue received by Top 10 firms: 1996–2000

	1996	1997	1998	1999	2000	Mean
Brokerage commission[a]	28.4	28.5	28.9	33.1	37.8	31.4
Underwriting income[a]	83.3	79.5	74.4	73.7	77.5	77.7

Sources: The Securities Association of China and China Securities Regulatory Commission (CSRC).
[a] Adapted from Feng (2005).

Table 6.5 Revenue distribution for the industry, and for the top ten firms, 1996–2000 (in billion yuan where applicable)

	1996	1997	1998	1999	2000	Mean
Trading volume	2132	3072	2355	3132	6083	3355
Underwritten amount	29.4	85.6	77.8	89.7	154.0	87.3
Estimated commission income	14.93	21.51	16.49	21.92	42.58	23.48
Estimated underwriting income	0.74	2.14	1.95	2.24	3.85	2.18
Commission income/ Total revenue (%)[a]	41.2	38.4	40.4	48.8	55.4	44.8
Underwriting income/ Total revenue (%)	2.0	3.8	4.8	5.0	5.0	4.1

Note: The estimated commission income is calculated as the trading volume times twice of the imposed uni-lateral commission rate of 0.35 percent, or 0.7 percent. Buyers and sellers both pay this uni-lateral rate. A 2.5 percent of underwriting spread is used to calculate the estimated underwriting income. This is consistent with the CSRC-imposed 1-2.5 percent of underwriting spread and with Huang and Fung's (2004) finding that banks tend to charge the higher end of spread in their business practice.

Sources: China Securities Regulatory Commission (CSRC), www.p 5w.net, The Securities Association of China, and Feng (2005).

[a] Adapted from Feng (2005).

total revenue. The industry has not been able to diversify their revenue: underwriting revenue has been small, and capital gains from principal trading have been unreliable due to market fluctuations.

Table 6.5 decomposes the distribution of revenue in the industry, illustrating the importance of brokerage commissions. The revenue from commissions was 44.8 percent of total revenue on average during the five years depicted (1996–2000). Underwriting revenue accounts for a significantly smaller portion – less than 5 percent of industry revenue. As documented by Feng (2005), this pattern is shared by other time periods. Overall, the industry relies heavily on brokerage income as the single most important source of revenue.

Table 6.6 illustrates the revenue distribution for the top three and top ten firms in 1999, reinforcing that commission income is the most important source of revenue. Again, the top ten and top three firms draw about 50 percent of their revenue from brokerage commission. This percentage is similar to that for the industry as a whole. It is interesting, however, to note that the top firms derive a significantly higher percentage of their income from underwriting business than the industry as a whole. Underwriting

Table 6.6 *Percentage of revenue from commissions and underwriting for the top ten and top three Chinese firms: 1999*

	Top 10	Top 3
Brokerage commission	44.6	52.7
Underwriting	5.7	10.7
Other		
Principal trading income	29.5	
Interest income	5.1	36.7
Other	15.1	

Source: Adapted from Feng (2005).

income accounts for 11 percent of revenue for the top three firms, 5.7 percent for the top ten firms, and 4.1 percent for the industry as a whole. This further supports the evidence in Table 6.6 that the underwriting business is concentrated in the top few.

Concentration in equity underwriting revenues

There are three major lines of corporate financing business: (a) equity offerings, including IPOs, SEOs and rights offerings, (b) bond offerings, including straight bond offerings and convertible bond offerings; and (c) M&A advisory services. Chinese securities firms engage in all three types of activity, which produce underwriting or advisory revenues. Despite the wide range of participation, the evidence shows that the industry's corporate finance revenue is highly concentrated in equity underwriting. Huang and Fung (2004) document that more than 90 percent of all underwriting revenue in China is generated by equity underwriting during the period 2001–2003, as compared to just 24 percent in the US from 1980–2002. The same authors also report that the majority of the underwriting revenue in the US stems from underwriting bond issues and providing M&A advice. In sharp contrast, bond offerings and M&A advising are minor sources of income for investment banks in China.

This extreme skewness of underwriting revenue may reflect the optimal financing behavior of Chinese firms. Bond markets are a lot smaller than the equity markets, with a very limited number of listed corporate bonds. Investors are averse to the bond market because it is small and illiquid. Issuers tend to stay away from issuing bonds because it involves as much work as filing a stock issue, yet is not as value-enhancing (Huang and Fung (2004)). Another factor may be that bond issues typically cannot take advantage of the price differential between floatable and non-floatable controlling shares. In contrast, issuing equity at the market price will increase the book value of the non-floatable shares, since the market-to-book equity ratio is substantially greater than one. For non-floatable shareholders to increase their wealth proxied by book value, issuing equity or instruments with equity features (such as convertible bonds) is a preferred choice as long as they are feasible. By the same argument, M&A activities are typically non-value enhancing. Controlling shareholders, who hold non-floatable shares, typically cannot increase their value through M&A activities, unless investment banks can provide sufficiently valuable advisory services. Nonetheless, with issuing firms demanding less bond financing and M&A services, China's securities firms appear to focus on equity underwriting.

To summarize, we have described in this section the three periods of development in the Chinese securities industry. We also document that the industry has enjoyed superior growth, and is quite concentrated with respect to the size and market share of the top few firms. Finally, we have illustrated that the industry's revenues are most heavily dependant on brokerage commissions. We now turn our attention to the operating environment within the Chinese securities industry.

OPERATING ENVIRONMENT AND CONSTRAINTS

Legal Constraints

The securities industry operates within state law, and is regulated by the China Securities Regulatory Committee (CSRC). Currently, three national laws govern the operation of the industry: Company Law, Securities Law, and Investment Companies Law. The Company Law of 1999 defines the structure of the firms and sets the operating limits for all companies. The Securities Law, passed in 1999, sets the rules for virtually all operations in the securities industry. These rules cover the regulatory system, security issuances and transactions, mergers and acquisitions, exchanges and intermediaries, fiduciary duties, etc. Finally, the Investment Companies Law enacted in 2005 governs institutional investment activities and the money management industry. The principal trading and asset management components of the securities business fall into this category and are regulated by the Investment Companies Law. Together, these three pieces of legislation cover the entire industry, from underwriting to principal trading.

The CSRC, like the SEC in the US, is the main regulatory body of the securities industry. It receives authority from the State Council, and the national laws above, to regulate all participants in the industry, including exchanges, intermediaries and individuals. Much of its power is exercised by judging various filings in the industry, such as IPO or other types of financing filings, listed firms' reports, trading rule changes, new licenses, and so on. To exercise its wide-range of regulatory functions, it has established offices nationwide and delegated regulatory power to various internal departments. The major departments include new issues, institutions, listed companies, accounting, and legal departments.

Neither the CSRC nor the State Council has legislative power. Nonetheless, their regulatory power allows them to draft stipulations that amend or materialize major laws. These stipulations concern numerous aspects of the industry, and many are temporary (subsequently replaced by further stipulations or new laws). Current stipulations address the qualification and procedures for securities issuing, the financing and asset fiduciary duties of securities firms, various aspects of corporate governance and reporting, and the tradability of state-owned shares. These stipulations lay out the interpretation of the law by the regulatory body, and are strictly adhered to.

Political Constraints

Government policies in China play an important role in firms' financing activities and investment banking business. Given the ubiquity of central government policies, the Chinese markets are very often regarded as policy-driven. Although not officially part of the law, many policies set the implicit directions of the regulation. For example, in 2004, the State Council set the tone for floating state-owned shares and protecting minority shareholders through an influential memo called 'Several Opinions on Furthering Capital Market Reforms and Growth'. The memo, as in its title, was aimed at pulling the capital markets out of the adjustment period that has been lingering for years. Shortly after its release, the CSRC established six task forces to handle a wide range of initiatives discussed in the memo, such as capital gains taxation, trading of state-owned shares and bond market activities. Given the power of the central government, it is important for investment banks to understand the implications of the government policies.

Two examples help to illustrate the importance of policy considerations for the Chinese investment banking business: the IPO quota system from 1993 to 1997, and the segregation between ownership and floatability of shares. From 1993 to 1997, the State Council rationed IPO quotas to provinces and various state departments. The aggregate number of issues and the aggregate issue size were specified by the quota system. Only those who received a quota allotment could issue an IPO. The aggregate issuing quota was small and (somewhat arbitrarily) held constant during that period. Such a system created a scarcity of IPOs in 'hot' markets (for example, in 1996–1997). The rationing, in addition to creating a hotbed of rent-seeking behavior, greatly restricted the availability of financing channels because many qualified firms couldn't issue IPOs to tap into the capital markets. It was not until 1998 that the quota system was changed to a qualification system, which allows any firms that are qualified, as defined under the Company Law and Securities Law, to issue IPOs.

A second example of the influence of government policy is the dichotomous floatability of firm shares. This dichotomy refers to the fact that two-thirds of outstanding shares in China are not tradable on either of its two stock exchanges. As per Company Law, prior to initial public offerings, firms were typically initialized through a promoting shareholder, who holds promoter shares. The firms were founded after a round of 'private' placements to specific shareholders, who obtained placed shares. The majority of these shares are owned by the state, and government policies prohibit the sale of state shares to the public during an IPO. The process of going public, then, involves only the public subscription of new shares – only the new shares issued in an IPO are publicly traded. The pre-IPO shares, even though they have the same claim to dividends and the voting rights, are not allowed to trade on the exchanges. As a result, corporate ownership is segmented between non-floatable and floatable shareholders, and the holders of the non-floatable shares are typically the controlling shareholders. For example, Huang and Fung (2004) document that 65 percent of the shares outstanding were non-floatable from 1998 to 2003.

CHALLENGES

China's full WTO membership, which allows China's securities firms to compete domestically and internationally presents both opportunities and challenges. Given the small size and limited expertise of the relatively young industry, it will likely take time for Chinese firms to become effective international competitors. For now, it seems more realistic for the domestic firms to focus on growth opportunities in domestic markets. Of course, the accession to the WTO brings foreign competition to the domestic markets in full force. As such, it will dramatically affect the operating environment in the industry. In this section, we focus on the challenges that the domestic industry faces post WTO, and the regulatory implications.

WTO Accession

China became a WTO member at the end of 2001. The WTO membership in principle requires that member countries adopt open market policy towards the supply of goods and services from other member countries. With respect to the securities sector, the foreign commercial presence in China will be unrestricted, except for a grace period of three years, as stated in the formal accession document.

> Upon accession, foreign service suppliers will be permitted to establish joint ventures with foreign investment up to 33 percent to conduct domestic securities investment fund management business. Within three years after China's accession, foreign investment shall be increased to 49 percent. Within three years after accession, foreign securities institutions will be permitted to establish joint ventures, with foreign minority ownership not exceeding 1/3, to engage (without Chinese intermediary) in underwriting A shares and in underwriting and trading of B and H shares as well as government and corporate debts, launching of funds. Criteria for authorization to deal in China's financial industry is solely prudential (that is, contain no economic needs test or quantitative limits on licenses).[5,6]

The accession to WTO means that Chinese securities firms will have to compete directly against much bigger and more accomplished foreign peers on all fronts. Domestic firms, however, have a comparative advantage in understanding domestic markets, including the politics involved in the sector and the unique cultural environment. Domestic and foreign firms are likely to complement each other: domestic firms can take advantage of foreign capital and expertise, while foreign firms can take advantage of domestic guides. Indeed, joint ventures have emerged during the grace period in the three main lines of the investment banking business – underwriting, brokerage, and money investment. Prior to the accession, there were no joint-venture securities firms. By 2005, four joint-venture securities firms and 20 joint-venture mutual funds have formed, including the likes of Paribas, Goldman Sachs, CFSB and ING.

Inevitably, Chinese securities firms compete directly with their foreign peers, as seen in the institutional money management business. In December 2002, China began to allow Qualified Foreign Institutional Investors (QFII) to invest in its domestic markets, previously open only to domestic investors. These QFII's will be fully foreign owned and compete directly with domestic investment companies. By 2005, the markets experienced an inflow of 34 QFIIs, many of whom are associated with industry behemoths such as Citigroup, HSBC, UBS, Nomura Securities, Deutsche Bank, Morgan Stanley, Goldman Sachs and JP Morgan. As China's WTO grace period ended in 2005, Chinese securities firms encounter face-to-face competition from very formidable foreign firms in underwriting, brokerage and the other advisory services. For domestic securities firms, there are three possibilities: continue to be independent but grow more market-driven;

become takeover targets for foreign or domestic firms; or perish in the competition. Thus, challenges abound in the face of enormous uncertainty.

Full-Floatability

The Chinese securities market commingles aspirations to a mature market, as evidenced by the accession to the WTO, with substantial remnants of the planned economy. As previously mentioned, one of the biggest remnants is the separate ownership of floatable and non-floatable shares. There is a key difference between these types of shares – the non-floatable shares are worth less due to poor liquidity. There is no public market for non-floatable shares; they can only change hands, typically in big blocks, through bilateral agreements. As documented in Huang and Fung (2004), non-floatable shares are typically exchanged at their book value, while the floatable shares trade at a much higher market price. Indeed, the market to book equity ratio of floatable shares is typically two to three times (for example, in October 2002, even after an extended market decline, the average market to book ratio remained at 3.02).

Several adverse effects of this ownership segregation have been identified. The objective of non-floatable shareholders may deviate from maximizing market value. Instead, they may wish to increase book value as a way of improving their bargaining position during block transfers (Huang and Fung 2004), demand excessive dividend payments, or pursue other self-serving actions (Clarke 2003). The incentive conflicts can lead to severe corporate governance problems, as pointed out by Allen *et al.* (2002). For investment banks, Huang and Fung (2004), among others, point out that a firm's financing behavior is likely to cluster in equity financing due to the non-floatable shareholders' incentive to increase book value. In the past, rampant equity financing through the open market has indirectly reduced the price differential between the two classes of shares.

It seems apparent that a market that prohibits trading of two-thirds of the shares outstanding may suffer from pricing inefficiencies. Without proper pricing, it is difficult to attract foreign investors, which is a major goal of the accession to the WTO. No other modern financial market has this widespread segregation of ownership. A movement toward full floatability is an important step toward a proper price-discovery mechanism, financial innovations and sustainable growth in Chinese markets.

The movement toward full-floatability and its time line have been debated for years. It appears that the expiration of the WTO grace period has expedited the process. The state initialized full-floatability experiments in early 2005, and aims to implement full-floatability market wide by 2006. At the time of writing, this remains an ongoing challenge. A typical full-floatability scheme would have two components: a subsidy to floatable shareholders from non-floatable shareholders, and a lockup period for non-floatable shareholders to trade their shares in the open market. The subsidy works as follows. As a condition for non-floatable shares to become floatable, floatable shareholders will typically receive a side payment of shares from the non-floatable shareholders. The number of total shares outstanding will remain unchanged, and the net effect will be redistribution of shares from the holders of non-floatable shares to the holders of floatable shares, with an increase in floatable shareholders' ownership in the firm. While the magnitude of this redistribution has yet to be finalized, the completion of a full-floatability reform is a major milestone for China's securities market. Many merits of modern securities markets can be gained. Full floatability allows for fair pricing of the securities, by and large an aligned shareholder body, and an ownership transaction market in the real sense. For the investment banking industry, the implementation of full floatability may imply that they can finally move from brokerage business to a wide-range of deeper corporate financing services.

CONCLUDING REMARKS

In just 15 years, China has progressed enormously toward establishing a large securities market and a burgeoning investment banking industry. In this short period, its investment banking industry grew to an enviable size by many metrics: assets, revenue, number of domestic competitors, lines of business and geographical depth. Furthermore, China has managed to regulate the industry following the model of larger, mature markets. Key new laws govern a wide range of activities, and an SEC-like unified regulatory body, the CSRC, executes governing power. Squarely speaking, China has successfully developed an important financial service sector in a well-regulated environment, and is well on its way to fulfilling its reform agenda.

During its brief history, the industry has seen numerous ups and downs, and remained fairly concentrated. We identify three basic periods of development: the arising period, the rapid growth period and the adjustment period. The industry arose and enjoyed rapid expansion prior to 1999. The period from 1999 has witnessed a long period of adjustment, with the industry experiencing some major house cleaning and adjusting for the challenges brought on by China's accession to the WTO. At present, the industry is concentrated along three dimensions: (a) the top few firms comprise a large fraction of the industry's size, dominate the underwriting business, and garner a disproportionate fraction of the brokerage business, (b) brokerage commission is a disproportionately large source of revenue for the industry; and (c) equity underwriting is the dominant form of corporate finance service.

The accession to the WTO brings both challenges and opportunities. As the Chinese securities industry prepares for a direct competition from formidable foreign investment banks, Chinese firms have the opportunity to learn from their peers' expertise. The WTO membership has also accelerated China's house cleaning efforts. In addition to the industry consolidation, the ongoing full floatability reform will greatly bridge the gap between Chinese and western markets. A predictable result of the ongoing reforms is to increase the size of the Chinese securities markets impressively in the next few years. Already there has been a large inflow of foreign firms. We believe that with the introduction of mature market standards, more and more foreign competitors will pursue the Chinese securities industry. Since domestic firms possess useful expertise regarding domestic markets, the Chinese industry is likely to grow significantly despite the tougher competition. In the foreseeable new round of growth, however, only the best firms are likely to survive and grow into international brands.

ACKNOWLEDGMENTS

We thank Hung-Gay Fung and Guobang Leng for help and advice. All errors are ours.

NOTES

1. Data source: China Securities Regulatory Commission, 2005. 1 US dollar approximately equals RMB8 at the end of 2005.
2. See, for example, Chen (2004).
3. A trading branch is a physical trading location linked with the securities firm's central trading system where investors place orders.
4. Calculated from the data provided by the US Securities Industry Association (www.sia.com).
5. Authors' note: A shares are the domestically listed shares denominated in yuan. The majority of shares listed are A shares. B shares are the domestically listed shares denominated in US or Hong Kong dollars. H shares are listed in Hong Kong, which is generally treated as a separate market.
6. The accession documents can be found at WTO's website at http://docsonline.wto.org/.

REFERENCES

Allen, F., J. Qian and M. Qian (2003), 'Comparing China's financial system', University of Pennsylvania Wharton School working paper.

Clarke, D. C. (2003), 'Corporate governance in China: an overview', University of Washington School of Law working paper.
Chen, X. (2004), 'A comparative study on the capital accumulation of China's securities industy', Guangfa Securities Co., Ltd. China working report.
Feng, E. (2005), *A Research on the Scale Economy of Securities Firms,* Beijing: China Financial Publishing House.
Hu, T. C. and O. Yang (2004), 'An investigation on allocation and efficiency of control rights on listed companies', Guangdong Securities Co., Ltd. China working report.
Huang, A. G. and H. G. Fung (2004), 'Stock ownership segmentation, floatability, and constraints on investment banking in China', *China & World Economy*, **12** (2), 66–78.
Huang, A. G. and H. G. Fung (2005), 'Floating the non-floatables in China's stock market: theory and design', *Emerging Markets Finance and Trade*, **41**, (5), 6–26.
Ma, Q. (ed.) (2003), *A History of the Chinese Securities Industry: 1978–1998*, Beijing: Citic Publishing House.
Securities Association of China (2005), *The Annual Report on China's Securities Industry*, Beijing: China Public Finance and Economics Publishing House.
Zheng, D., W. Duan, and Z. Liu (2003), 'EVA evaluation of capital allocation of China's securities firms', Guangzhou Securities Co., Ltd. China, working report.

7. China's insurance market: challenges and opportunities

Hung-gay Fung, Fei Liu and Yanda Xu

THE MACROECONOMIC ENVIRONMENT

Since China's economic reform started in late 1978, it has been shifted from a centrally planned economy to a market oriented economy. China's GDP (gross domestic product) has increased by 8.5 percent annually from 2000 to 2004 and reached a new record of US$2.26 trillion in 2005, which placed China as the fourth largest economy in the world after the US, Japan and Germany. Corresponding to the growth of the Chinese economy, the insurance premiums increased 39.6 percent annually from 1980 to 1998, a higher growth rate than the GDP growth rate over the same period.[1]

With respect to savings deposits, China also experiences tremendous growth. Urban disposable income per capita had a steady annual increase of 10 percent over 2000–2004. Personal deposits reached RMB14 trillion (US$1.7 trillion) at the end of 2005, an increase of more than 20 percent over the same period one year earlier. Table 7.1 shows the general economic indicators in China between 2000 and 2004. All variables including GDP growth, industrial output, retail sales and disposal income indicate rapid growth. With fast-growing wealth, Chinese consumers gradually deviate from the traditional consumption style which focuses on necessities, and begin to increase their spending on durable consumer goods such as housing and automobiles. These durable consumer goods have become popular among the rich and middle class in recent years. Consumption growth directly generates higher demand for homeowner and auto insurance.

Table 7.1 China's economic indicators, 2000–2004

	2000	2001	2002	2003	2004
GDP (RMB billion)	8946.80	9731.50	10 517.20	11 725.20	13 651.50
Real GDP growth (%)	8	7.5	8.3	9.3	9.5
Fixed-asset investment	10.3	13	16.9	27.7	25.8
Value-added industrial output[a]	17.8	11.6	16.5	27.3	16.7
Retail sales	9.7	10.1	11.8	9.1	13.3
Consumer price index (%)	0.4	0.7	−0.8	1.2	3.9
Urban disposable per capita income (RMB)	6280.00	6859.60	7702.80	8472.20	9422
Rural net per capita income (RMB)	2253.40	2366.40	2475.60	2622.20	2936
Urban unemployment rate (%)[b]	3.1	3.6	4	4.3	4.3

Notes:
[a] Of enterprises with sales of more than RMB5 million.
[b] According to official NBS figures, which do not include under-employment or the migrant population.

Source: PRC National Bureau of Statistics (NBS, http://www.stats.gov.cn) *China Statistical Yearbook*, 2004.

HISTORICAL TRANSFORMATION OF THE INSURANCE INDUSTRY

Development of Governmental Authority and Supervision

Before 1998, the governing body for the insurance industry had been the Insurance Administration Department of the People's Bank of China (PBOC). An insurer must obtain an operating license from PBOC before it can write any insurance policies in China. Before 1984, the only insurance company, the People's Insurance Company of China (PICC) was part of the PBOC and represented the whole insurance industry. In 1984, the State Council separated the PICC from the PBOC to allow the PICC to operate on its own, while the PBOC was to focus on issuing licenses and overseeing insurance company operations. From 1949 to the late 1980s, the state-run PICC was the insurance monopoly in China. During this period, the insurance industry in China, essentially, did not exist. Few Chinese owned personal property, and almost all business enterprises were government-owned and thus 'self-insured'. Since economic reforms were launched in 1979, two other state-run insurance companies, Ping An in

Shenzhen and China Pacific in Shanghai, were established in 1988 and 1991, respectively.

In 1992, the industry opened its doors to foreign companies, with the granting of an insurance license to American International Group (AIG) in Shanghai. In 1994, the Japanese insurer Tokio Marine and Fire Insurance was also granted a license to conduct insurance business in Shanghai. At the end of 2005, there were 41 foreign insurers, including AIG and Royal & Sun Alliance, which are running business across China. Within this short period, China's insurance industry has grown to more than RMB50 billion (US$5.9 billion) in terms of premiums per year, with over US$1 billion of that coming from life insurance sales as of 1994.

In 1993, a team called the Financial Surveillance and Administration Department was established to develop insurance regulations in China. This team spent two-and-a-half years studying the industry at Lloyd's in London, the US National Association of Insurance Commissioners (NAIC) in New York, and various insurance organizations in Tokyo and Munich. It cooperated with PBOC and PICC to formulate and issue the 1995 Insurance Law and subsequent regulations, which reshaped the insurance industry, provided opportunities for both domestic and foreign insurance companies to develop and compete with each other, and set the tone for the ensuing market evolvement.

In 1998, the PICC was dissolved and split into three different companies – China Life Insurance, China Property Insurance (PICC), and China Reinsurance. In the same year, the China Insurance Regulatory Commission (CIRC) was established, and has been serving as the watchdog of the insurance industry under the authority of the State Council ever since. By the end of 2004, there were in total 86 insurance companies in China. Among them, 45 companies are China-funded insurance companies and the others are foreign-funded.

GROWTH OF THE INSURANCE MARKET

Chinese insurance companies offer various insurance products to Chinese residents, which cover life, health, accidental, and property insurance. Foreign insurance companies have introduced new types of insurance products. For instance, Groupama SA opened a branch in Chengdu in Sichuan Province in 2004 and provided a highly popular agricultural insurance policy to farmers.

Table 7.2 shows the insurance income and asset composition of the insurance industry in China. The country's insurance premiums were RMB492.73 billion in 2005 and RMB431.81 billion in 2004. Life insurance

Table 7.2 China's insurance income and asset compositions

	Unit: RMB billion		
	2003	2004	2005
Premium	**388.04**	**431.81**	**492.73**
1. Property	86.94	108.99	122.99
2. Life	301.10	322.82	369.75
(a) Accidental	9.96	11.71	14.09
(b) Health	24.19	25.99	31.23
(c) Life	266.95	285.13	324.43
Benefit and claims	**84.10**	**100.44**	**112.97**
1. Property	47.63	56.75	67.17
2. Life	36.47	43.69	45.79
(a) Accidental	3.06	3.94	4.35
(b) Health	6.99	8.91	10.79
(c) Life	26.41	30.84	30.65
	0.00	0.00	0.00
Operation expense	**36.12**	**43.58**	**52.60**
Bank deposit	**454.97**	**496.88**	**524.14**
Investment	**382.89**	**571.19**	**889.44**
State bond	140.69	265.17	358.83
Equity funds	46.33	67.32	109.92
Total Assets	**912.28**	**1185.35**	**1522.60**

Source: CIRC Statistics from http://www.circ.gov.cn.

is more important than the property insurance in terms of market share of premiums. Life insurance premiums and the growth rate were RMB369.75 billion and 154.5 percent in 2005, RMB322.82 billion and 7.22 percent in 2004, and RMB301.1 billion and 20.75 percent in 2003. Property insurance premiums reached RMB122.99 in 2005 and RMB108 billion in 2004 with a growth rate 12.8 percent. The total assets of the insurance industry were RMB1.52 trillion in 2005 compared to RMB1.19 trillion in 2004, representing a growth rate of 28.4 percent.

The size of the insurance industry has become an important component of the capital market in terms of the asset size. The investment options for the insurance companies have expanded to include bonds and equity funds. The total equity investment was RMB109 billion in 2005 as compared to RMB46.33 billion in 2003, representing an average annual growth rate of 68.6 percent for the two years in between.

The monopoly of the insurance business by the government has become history as there are currently 86 insurers across China. Among them are

Table 7.3 China life insurance company premium, 2005

Category	Company	Unit: RMB billion	
		Premium	%
State	China Life	160.68	44.1
State	China Pacific Life	36.21	9.9
State	China Life Annuity	25.12	6.9
Foreign	General China Life Insurance Co. Ltd	19.97	5.5
State	Taiping Life	7.85	2.2
Foreign	AIA	6.44	1.8
Foreign	CITIC-Prudential Life Insurance Co. Ltd	1.04	0.3
Foreign	Aviva-COFCO Life Insurance Co. Ltd	0.89	0.2
Foreign	Pacific-Aetna Life Insurance Co. Ltd	0.71	0.2
Foreign	Manulife-Sinochem Life Insurance Co. Ltd	0.70	0.2

Source: CIRC Statistics from http://www.circ.gov.cn.

45 state-owned, all others are joint-stock, Chinese-foreign joint ventures, and subsidiaries of foreign insurers. The insurance brokerage and the insurance agency market have also grown at a fast pace. At the end of 2005, there are about 1800 insurance brokers and agencies in China's insurance market. Agency and other types of middle market players took 4.16 percent of total premiums in 2005.

Table 7.3 shows the key insurance companies that received the largest insurance premiums in China's 2005 insurance market. China Life Insurance Company Ltd, the largest insurance company in terms of premiums, enjoys the leadership role in China's rapidly growing life insurance market. It was initiated by China Life Insurance (Group) company. On 30 June 2003, with a registered Capital of RMB20 billion, the company conducted three lines of business: life insurance, accidental insurance and health insurance.

China Life successfully went public on both the New York Stock Exchange and Hong Kong Exchange in December 2003, making it the first Chinese financial enterprise to list in both the US and Hong Kong. China Life received US$3.5 billion in its initial public offering (IPO), which was the world's largest IPO in 2003. In 2005, China Life's life insurance premium took a 44 percent share of the total life insurance market in China.

Ping An followed the steps of China Life to list its shares in Hong Kong in 2003. In addition to raising capital via the stock market, CIRC also permitted insurance firms to issue subordinated bonds, starting from October 2004. The measures will give insurers more means to replenish their capital base and have more ties with the capital market. The subordinated bonds are

Table 7.4 China property and casualty insurance market

	Unit: US$ billion growth 1998–2003		
	1998	2003	%
Panel A: Premium Income			
China	6.04	14.47	140
South Korea	11	17.76	61
Japan	92	97.53	6
US	387.93	574.57	48
Panel B: Premium per capita			
China	4.8	11.3	135
South Korea	264.4	371.7	41
Japan	709.4	751.1	6
US	1425.7	1988.2	39

Source: Pilla, D., 2005, Penetrating the Mist, *Best's Review*, **106**(1), 28–32.

to have maturities no shorter than five years, and the bonds are subordinated to all other issuers' liabilities. Creditors are prohibited from filing bankruptcy charges if an issuer does not repay the bond. The regulatory obstacle for creditors to file bankruptcy charges against an insurance company is an additional hurdle to integrate insurance companies with other financial institutions. CIRC also stipulates that it would not allow insurers to issue subordinated bonds for three years if they violate issuing guidelines.

Table 7.4 shows details of insurance premiums in China, South Korea, Japan and the US over 1998–2003, providing a comparison of premiums across these countries. The size of the insurance sector in China was small relative to other countries. It seems apparent that China's insurance industry still has much room to expand. In particular, the premium per capita in China is the lowest among South Korea, Japan and the US. However, insurance in China has experienced tremendous changes in the past years. From 1998 to 2003, China property and casualty insurance has increased by 139 percent to US$14 billion in terms of premium income, close to South Korea's market size. However, the premium per capita was only 3 percent of South Korea's. It indicates that there is still tremendous growth space in China's market.

The growth rate of the insurance premiums between 1998 and 2003 was about 140 percent, higher than South Korea (61 percent), Japan (6 percent) and the US (48 percent) The rapid growth rate in China clearly illustrates the beginning of the insurance product cycle, which offers challenges and opportunities for policymakers and the insurance industry.

Table 7.5 2005 property insurance company premium detail (RMB billion)

Category	Company	Premium	%
State	PICC P&C	65.94	51
State	China Pacific Property	14.44	11
State	Ping An	12.67	10
State	China United	10.40	8
State	Tian An	6.35	5
State	Da Di Property	3.82	3
State	Yong An	3.16	2
State	Export Insurance	2.24	2
State	Hua An	2.12	2
State	Taiping Property	1.39	1

Source: CIRC Statistics from http://www.circ.gov.cn.

Table 7.5 reports the rankings of 2005 property insurance premiums in China. The PICC's P&C is the largest property insurance company. It has more than half of the total market share of the property insurance market. Auto insurance business dominates roughly two-thirds of the market in terms of premium volume. It is driven by the fast growth of the economy and the growing acceptance of the demand for insurance. The largest non-life insurer PICC takes control of over half of the market share in terms of premium volume at present. The company was listed on the Hong Kong stock market at the end of 2003.

There are three major categories of health insurance products. They are medical expense related, critical illness, and accident insurance. Each category can be purchased by an individual or on a group basis. Many life insurers in China are offering health insurance products. In addition, over 30 non-life insurers are moving toward accident insurance and health insurance. Currently, China life, Ping An and China Pacific are the key players in China's health insurance market. China Reinsurance Company has a strong client relationship and a large market share, and it has been successful in selling new commercial business and is active in life reinsurances.

RELAXED REGULATIONS FOR FOREIGN INSURERS

By 2020, China's middle class population could reach 600 million.[2] The standard for middle class is an annual income of 75 000 yuan and owning

310 000 yuan of assets on average for a household. As of 2002, it was estimated that the middle class population was about 50 million. The potential growth of the middle class indicates huge opportunities for foreign insurers who are willing to take calculated risks because they have the available income and a need to buy insurance. China has to fulfill its WTO market-opening commitments, allowing foreign insurers to provide health, group and pension fund insurance, lifting all geographical restrictions on foreign insurers, and allowing foreign firms to hold majority shares in joint ventures. Thus, doors are open to insurance brokers and agents.

In 2005, foreign life insurers could obtain a license to operate insurance business anywhere in China. Previously, they were restricted to a couple of selected cities from a short list of more economically advanced urban areas. For life insurance, a maximum of 50 percent foreign-equity interest in a joint venture was allowed upon accession (it is worth noting that this restriction on foreign equity participation in life insurance business has now been clarified and re-instated in the Implementing Rules).

For non-life insurance, joint ventures in which the foreign partner's equity interest does not exceed 51 percent will be permitted upon accession; and wholly foreign-owned enterprises providing non-life insurance services (except for statutory insurance business) would be permitted within two years after accession from December 2003.

There are two ways for international firms to enter China's insurance industry. First, it is possible to establish wholly-owned companies or joint ventures in China, such as AIG. Statistics from the China Insurance Regulatory Commission shows that there are 34 foreign-funded insurance companies and 54 operation institutions in inland China. The requirement of direct capital investment is about RMB5 billion.

Second, a foreign insurance company can enter into the China insurance sector indirectly by acquiring an existing insurance company. Last year, HSBC entered the Chinese insurance market by acquiring 19.9 percent of outstanding shares of Ping An. The deal was the largest foreign investment in the Chinese insurance market to date. Xinhua Life Insurance Co. and Taikang Life Insurance also introduced foreign stockholders. The amounts of these indirect investments are approximately RMB10 billion.

Domestic insurers can sell up to 24.9 percent of their equity to foreign investors. For instance, Carlyle Group (US) has agreed to invest $400 million for a 24.9 percent stake of China Pacific Life Insurance Co. The requirements for the foreign group are: (a) the assets at the end of the previous year must reach US$5 billion; (b) their representative offices in China must be over two years old; and (c) the companies should be the ones that have engaged in insurance businesses for over 30 years. Individual foreign investors would be allowed to own no more than 5 percent of the company.

RISK AND OPPORTUNITY

According to a joint study by Reuters and KPMG, only 4 percent of China's 1.3 billion people hold insurance policies. China indeed represents a vast, untapped market for foreign insurers. Yet, it also carries challenges and risks. The joint ventures (JVs) with foreign ownership generally have developed policies to target clients with annual premiums of about US$300 per individual client. The targeted customers are relatively affluent with an annual income of over US$6000 and usually live in bigger cities such as Shanghai, Beijing or Shenzhen.

After the establishment of a joint venture insurance company, there are still major challenges, such as the lack of suitable investment avenues. Restrictions on investment lead insurers to put most of their money in savings accounts and government bonds, creating a challenging asset-liability mismatch dilemma. Insurance policies need to target liability with durations of 20 to 30 years, but there is a scant supply of long-term bonds and very few high-quality corporate bonds with a long maturity.

Weak mechanisms of corporate structure are also an issue that foreign investors face when they explore the possibility of a joint venture. CIRC expects that foreign investment and involvement in the operation of China insurers so that efficiency of the insurance industry can be improved and can provide input to the Chinese insurers for improving their performance. As of December 2004, China allowed foreign life insurance companies to provide health insurance, group insurance and enterprise pension insurance service to Chinese individuals. China will no longer limit the business areas of foreign insurance companies.

Table 7.6 displays the market percentages of the domestic and foreign insurance companies in China's insurance market in 2005. State-owned insurance companies are the dominant players in both life and property insurance markets. In terms of total premiums, domestic state-owned insurance accounts for 93 percent of the total markets. That is, they represent 91 percent of the total life insurance market and 99 percent of the property insurance market. Although foreign insurers took about only 7 percent of the market share in terms of premiums in 2005, they kept a faster growth pace than domestic counterparts. Official statistics from CIRC show that foreign insurance companies account for half of the insurance companies in China. From 1999 to 2003, their total assets increased 3.5 times while their premiums increased 2.7 times. They have more than 10 percent of the market share in booming cities like Shanghai and Guangzhou (capital of south China's Guangdong province).

In terms of the life insurance market, half of the top ten insurers were foreign funded by the end of 2005. Wu Ding Fu, Chairman of CIRC, has

Table 7.6 China insurers' premium details 2005

	Property RMB billion	%	Life RMB billion	%	Total RMB billion
State Owned Insurance Company	126.43	28	332.18	72	458.61
%	99		91		93
Foreign Insurance Company	1.68	5	32.44	95	34.12
%	1		9		7
Total	128.11	26	364.62	74	492.73

Source: CIRC Statistics from http://www.circ.gov.cn.

confirmed that China would continue to regularize the operation of both the domestic and foreign insurance companies in line with the related laws and regulations and provide a good environment for their development. China would make use of both the international market and domestic market to promote the internationalization of the Chinese insurance industry.

Risk Consideration

When the insurance market expands at the current high speed, it undoubtedly brings various types of risks to market participants in China as follows.

Business risk

Some insurers overlook the cost control within the competition process. Stiff competition gives rise to low pricing, high reward, high commission, and illegal side agreements, representing substantial insurance business risk to the insurers. For example, for the auto insurance industry, domestic insurers do not have operational profits even though it takes 60 percent of property insurance business.

Investment risk

When insurance funding has the chance to invest in the capital market, particularly in the stock market, it is necessary for the insurers to set up a risk control mechanism. In recent years, China's stock market has been in a down turn. The average dividend yield has been low and in fact, it was lower than the saving interest rate in the bank. Poor stock price performance hurts the insurance industry because dividends are nearly the sole investment income from stock investments.

Personnel risk

Insurance is a new profession in China in light of its short development period. Education and professional training are lagging behind in comparison to the growth rate of the industry. According to statistics by CIRC, over 1.5 million insurance sales representatives have acquired the profession licenses to date. In light of the booming industry and new insurance companies, apparently there is a shortage of experienced and competent managers.

Capital risk

With the tremendous growth of the insurance industry, it becomes clear that the current capital requirement for insurance companies is not sufficient to cover potential capital requirement. In addition, the unhealthy trend of a low profit margin is, no doubt, posing a threat to new inflows of capital into the industry.

Trends

China's insurance is one of the promising industries in China's financial market. Currently, the insurance depth of China (Premium/GDP ratio) was 3 percent, which is less than half of the average ratio worldwide. At the end of 2004, the insurance density (premium per capita) of China was around US$40, one-tenth of the world's insurance intensity. Reform of state and corporate pension arrangements will decide the involvement extent of the insurance industry. Ping An and Tai Ping have been selected to participate in a trial of the new arrangements. With the emergence of more start-up insurance companies, it is more competitive to take a share in China's insurance market.

There are several trends that characterize the relationship between the insurance industry and the capital market. First, the current major investment channel to the individual and institutional investors is to put savings in the bank or in government bonds. Insurance products such as retirement pensions and annuities should provide alternative long term investment options and help diversify the composition of the investment pool.

Second, beginning in October 1999, insurance companies were allowed to enter indirectly into the securities market through the security investment fund. This is a breakthrough in terms of allowing flexibility for insurance companies to invest their collected insurance premiums. As of 2003, investments from insurance companies mainly concentrated on the bonds (governmental bonds, infrastructure bonds and corporate bonds), mutual funds, and structured savings in the bank. While insurance companies can now invest in equities, there are additional restrictions on the scope and quota for their investment. For instance, the maximum investment allowed for state enterprise bonds is 20 percent of the issuance volume in the market.

The yield of China's investment asset was about 3.14 percent in 2002, which is relatively low. The experience from insurance industries in other developed countries suggests that a reasonable return should be around 7 percent for a sound insurance industry.[3] The current investment restrictions in China negatively affect both the scale of economy advantage and imply higher structured risk. The 1995 insurance law clearly states the restrictions of the range as well as the channels for insurance invested assets. In 1996, PBOC issued the regulation that only allows insurers to invest in bank deposits, government bonds, financial bonds and others approved by the State Council.

Third, at the end of 1990, fund management companies started up businesses in China's capital market. CIRC permitted insurance companies to use premiums to purchase equity funds, with a maximum 5 percent of the company's total assets in 1999. CIRC has approved Hua Tai, Tai Kang, and others to increase the limit up to 10 percent of total assets for investing in equity funds in 2006.

In 2001, CIRC allowed Ping An, Xinhua and Manulife-Sinochem to increase from 30 percent up to 100 percent of their investment in equity funds for their unit-linked products. In 2002, the new China Insurance law set up several additional restrictions. First, insurance companies cannot have more than 15 percent of the company's total assets in equity funds. Second, an insurance company is not allowed to purchase more than 10 percent of an individual fund. In terms of product types, premiums for unit-linked products' can be invested up to 100 percent for the investment in equity funds, while premiums of universal products can be invested up to 80 percent in equity funds.

Besides the stock, CIRC has the regulation on purchasing corporate bonds as follows:

- 10 percent or less of the insurer's total assets are allowed in corporate bonds;
- percentage in corporate bonds should be the lower of (a) 2 percent of the company's total asset of the last month, or (b) 15 percent of market share of the bond;
- 100 percent of the unit-linked products' premiums can be invested in corporate bonds; and
- universal products' income can be invested up to 80 percent.

REGULATIONS ON INVESTMENT MANAGEMENT

On 24 October 2004, the China Insurance Regulatory Commission (CIRC) and the China Securities Regulatory Commission (CSRC) jointly promulgated the Administration of Stock Investments by Insurance Institutional Investors Tentative Procedures (the Tentative Procedures), thus coming into effect on the day of promulgation.

The Tentative Procedures allow insurance institutions (including insurance companies and insurance asset management companies) to directly purchase RMB denominated common stock in the primary market or trade it on the secondary market, or to directly purchase convertible corporate bonds and other investment product types stipulated by the CIRC. The insurance industry welcomes the issuance of the Tentative Procedures, which gives more flexibility to the insurance industry to undertake investment activities.[4] There are 61 articles in the Tentative Procedures divided into eight chapters. The regulations mainly focus on the qualification requirements imposed on insurance institutional investors, the scope and proportion of investment, trusteeship of stock assets, conduct of insurance institutional investors, risk control and supervision, and administration.

Insurance asset management companies may invest in stocks without administrative approval as long as they meet certain requirements (Article 5). Insurance companies, on the other hand, must first submit an application to the CIRC to obtain approval before they can make any stock investments, regardless of whether they are planning direct investments or entrustment of stock investments through qualified insurance asset management companies (Articles 6 to 10).

Although insurance funds have been accumulating rapidly in recent years, the income ratios for their utilization decreased over three years consecutively. Income ratio is the total investment income to total investment in assets. The comprehensive income ratio of China's insurance funds' utilization was in a declining trend; it was 4.3 percent in 2001, 3.14 percent in 2002, and 2.68 percent in 2003. In recent years, the People's Bank of China has reduced the interest rates of bank deposits and loans eight times. With heavy investing in bank deposits and other fixed-income (income on interest) products such as government bonds financial bonds and corporate bonds (while only limited investment is made in equity investments such as securities funds and others), it is easy to understand why the income ratio for insurance funds' utilization has to decline. Although the People's Bank of China increased the interest rate for bank deposits and loans recently (in October 2004), this will not help redress the overall imbalance in insurance funds' utilization. Insurance funds need to look for new investment options.

The promulgation of the Tentative Procedures has opened a new and important method in utilizing the insurance funds.

China's stock market would benefit from the Tentative Procedure regulation. Since 2000, the stock market has experienced poor performance. The Tentative Procedures will help to rebuild the market confidence and to improve the market expectations toward a bull market. Insurance companies will supply a relatively stable and large block of funds to the stock market, an important source of support.

Return on investment is very important to insurance companies' profitability. According to relevant data of foreign insurance industries, insurance companies in many countries suffer losses from their insurance businesses. Income from insurance funds investments can make up for such losses in meeting their profit targets. For example, the compensation (losses) incurred by the US property insurance industry from the insurance business were US$22.2 billion in 1994, US$17.7 billion in 1995, US$16.7 billion in 1996, US$5.8 billion in 1997, US$16.8 billion in 1998, and US$23.4 billion in 1999; their income on investments in the corresponding years were US$33.7 billion, US$36.8 billion, US$38.0 billion, US$41.5 billion, US$39.9 billion and US$38.6 billion, yielding net profits of US$11.5 billion in 1994, US$19.1 billion in 1995, US$21.3 billion in 1996, US$35.7 billion in 1997, US$23.1 billion in 1998 and US$15.2 billion in 1999.

In the OECD countries, the average annual income ratio (after making allowance for inflation) during the period from 1970 to 2000 for investments in stocks reached 8.0 percent, while the income ratio of investments in loans was half of that of stock investments, and the income ratio of investments in government bonds was only one-fifth. In the US, the average annual income ratio over the past 20 years for investments in the money market, bonds and stocks was 3.7 percent, 5 percent and 10.3 percent, respectively. In Germany, over the past 30 years, the average annual income ratio for investments in the money market was 3.5 percent, 7.9 percent for bonds and 14.4 percent for stocks. In new market economy countries, the stock investment income ratio was even higher than that of developed countries. These statistics suggest that China's income ratios have been on the low side for the past few years, confirming the need to relax restrictions for insurance investments.

FUTURE CHALLENGES

Since 2003, it has not been easy for medium-size insurers to list on exchanges. Poor market conditions and a cautious securities regulator have caused those listing delays to date. Some companies have turned to other means of raising capital such as subordinated debt or seeking private equity investment.

China is one of several major agricultural countries of the world. However, agriculture insurance is less than 0.04 percent of the whole insurance market. In the next few years, agricultural insurance will be one of the fastest growing insurance categories in China. Export credit and financing insurance are highly encouraged businesses by China's government. For life insurance, it is recommended that cooperation between life insurers and health care providers will combine shares.

To take advantages of the taxation and government supervision, the insurance industry needs to develop corresponding insurance shield products or services, which could include active participation in the long-term construction projects like airport, and highway networks. In addition, the potential to work together among financial institutions (banks, brokerage firms and insurance companies) is great and offers substantial growth opportunities.

CONCLUSIONS

China's insurance industry remains relatively underdeveloped in comparison to other countries, mainly due to the strict regulations and short period of time since the reforms were launched. As China continues to open up its insurance market to foreign players, the monopolistic positions of domestic insurers might be weakened, as foreign companies bring in advanced management expertise, standard international practices, and insurance produce innovations.

The size of the insurance industry has grown considerably over recent decades. Now it plays an important role in China's financial markets. With the deregulations in investment options, funds from domestic and foreign insurance companies (such as those through the Qualified Financial Institutional Investor Programs) will inevitably have an increasing impact on the performance and development of China's stock market and other capital markets.

The insurance industry is expected to continue to grow rapidly in the next few years as an aging population, social security reforms and the low levels of state support for healthcare and pensions serve as key long-term growth drivers. Currently, domestic Chinese insurers dominate the market, but this might change as more and more foreign investors enter the market in view of China's tremendous market potential, rapid economic growth and relaxation in policies and regulations. While foreign insurers have an opportunity to grow beyond a narrow range of products and markets, certain regulatory restrictions still remain even after the WTO clause grants them full access to China's insurance market. Foreign insurers' participation in the market may force large domestic insurers to place more emphasis on profitability, rather than only on market share. For smaller insurance companies, difficulty in obtaining financing remains a major issue.

Recent regulations issued by the CIRC and the State Council relaxed the restrictions on investments and allow insurers to actively participate in the capital markets. The interactive relationship between the insurance industry and capital markets should benefit both by boosting their respective performance and growth.

ACKNOWLEDGMENTS

We thank Johnny Chan and Wilson Liu for valuable comments and Jennifer Dennis for editorial assistance.

NOTES

1. Anonymous (1999), China: Present Situation of China's Insurance Industry, *International Insurance Monitor*, **52**(4), 19–21.
2. See the website, http://www.chinadaily.com.cn/english/doc/2004-06/02/content_335849.htm.
3. Insurance industry research report by Da Cheng Fund, http://www.dcfund.com.cn
4. Stock Market Access Paves the Way for New Utilization of Insurance Funds, 2004.

REFERENCES

Anonymous (1998), 'China – opportunities and obstacles for the insurance industry in an emerging country', *Society of Chartered Property and Casual Underwriters Journal*, **51** (1), 10–19.

Anonymous (1999), 'China: present situation of China's insurance industry', *International Insurance Monitor*, **52** (4), 19–21.

Anonymous (2001), 'Total amount of Chinese insurance market is behind world level', *Asia Info Daily China News*, 24 August, 1.

Anonymous (2004a), 'Stock market access paves the way for new utilization of insurance funds', *China Law & Practice*, December, accessed at http://english.people.com.cn/200411/12/eng 20041112_163756.html.

Anonymous (2004b), 'US China Business Council Forecast Report', accessed at www.uschina.org/statistics/2005economyforecast.html.

Anonymous (2004c), 'Foreign insurance companies to enjoy national treatment at year-end: regulator', *Xinhua World Sources Online,* November.

Anonymous (2004d), 'Deregulation opens doors to some markets', *Asia Today International*, **22** (5) (October), 75–6.

Campbell, D. (2005), 'China opens the door – prospects for investment and growth in China insurance market', *PWC Market Report*, 1-6 September.
Chen, J. and S. S. Thomas (1999), 'China's emerging insurance sector holds foreign participants at arm's length', *US-China Business Council Review*, **3**(4), 38–44.
Chen K. (2004), 'China's party line is capital; market-based blueprint would continue tough approach', *Wall Street Journal*, 12 February, C.20.
Darrel, K. S. (1995), 'China: the next life insurance frontier? Yuen', *National Underwriter*, **99**(21) (May), 2–4.
Pilla, D. (2005), 'Penetrating the mist', *Best's Review*, **106**(1) (May), 28–32.
Wu, X. P. (2004), 'Foreign insurance companies to enjoy national treatment at year-end', *Xinhua World Sources Online,* November.

8. China's foreign exchange market

Gaiyan Zhang

OVERVIEW

China holds a significant and growing place in the international trading system[1] and it is appropriate that China acquire the financial tools available commensurate with its size and presence in the markets. As the country becomes more market oriented and global, China is actively taking steps to modernize its financial infrastructure. A deep and liquid foreign exchange market is a perquisite for a more flexible foreign exchange rate regime and gradual liberalization of the capital account.

Since China's opening-up and reform in 1978, and particularly after the foreign exchange reform in 1994, China's foreign exchange market has witnessed significant progress in a variety of aspects, including market infrastructure, products and services. The market volume has steadily increased over the past decade. The annual turnover reached US$209 billion in 2004, with an average daily turnover of US$829 million, an increase of 411 percent compared to that in 1994 (Figure 8.1).

However, due to the inconvertibility of RMB under capital account and the limited currency flexibility, China's foreign exchange market is still an insulated market that is independent of movements of international foreign exchange markets. The advantage of such a market is that it helps to insulate the Chinese economy from speculative external shocks that can be destabilizing. It also enables Chinese policymakers to have better control of fund inflow and outflow in order to maintain economic stability for the Chinese economy. Nonetheless, the lack of openness and competition renders the market an underdeveloped one with limited market depth and liquidity, concentrated participants and lack of diversity in currencies and products. Presently three main institutional arrangements govern the market development, that is, a mandatory foreign exchange settlement system that restricts foreign exchange holdings for banks and enterprises, a de facto pegged exchange rate, and inconvertibility of the RMB under the capital account. A historical snapshot of the market evolution is useful to better understand the evolution and the current status of China's foreign exchange market.

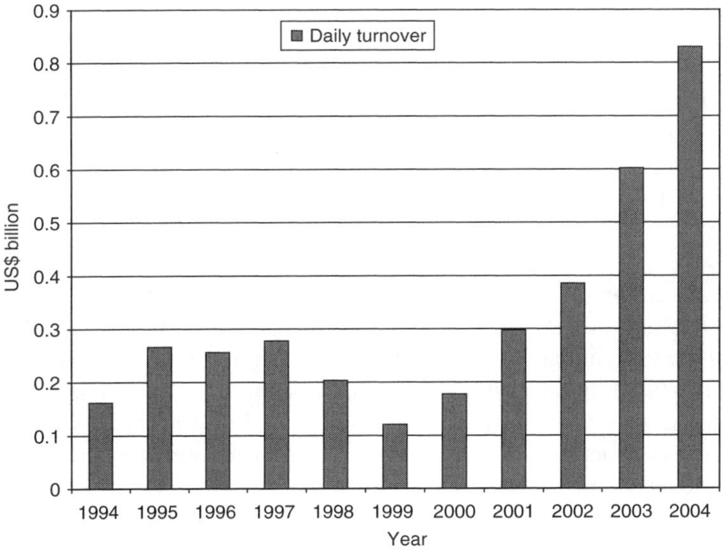

Source: www.chinamoney.com.cn.

Figure 8.1 Daily average turnover in China's foreign exchange market (1994–2004)

EVOLUTION OF CHINA'S FOREIGN EXCHANGE MARKET

Coexisting Foreign Exchange Swap Market[2] and Black Market: 1978–1994

Background

Before the reform and open policy, China implemented the highly centralized planned economy system. Due to limited foreign exchange resources, China continuously implemented the very strict foreign exchange control. Since the implementation of the reform and open policy strategy in 1978, the Chinese foreign exchange reform has made significant progress in cultivating market mechanisms. Founded in 1979, the State Administration of Foreign Exchange (SAFE henceforth) was authorized by the People's Bank of China (PBoC) to regulate foreign exchange management and provide market supervision, ushering in a new era of foreign exchange reform in China.

The RMB exchange rate arrangement experienced two phases. In the first stage (between 1979 and 1984), the country adopted the exchange rate double track system. It was characteristic of the foreign exchange interior settlement price for *trade-related* transactions, and the official exchange rate for *non-trade related* transactions. On 1 January 1985, China abolished the foreign exchange interior settlement price and re-restored the sole exchange rate system at the official rate of 2.8RMB/US$. This is the so-called 'first unification' of exchange rates. In the second stage, from 1985 to 1994, the launch of foreign exchange adjustment centers nation-wide formed the new two-track system, in which the unified official rate and the market-determined adjustment rate coexisted. The 1979–1994 periods also saw frequent adjustments of official exchange rates with a trend of devaluation of RMB against the US dollar. From the early 1979 level of RMB1.50/US$, the official exchange rate adjustment changed on a gradual basis to RMB5.72/US$ by the end of 1993. At the same time, the foreign exchange adjustment rate was allowed to fluctuate based on the market supply and demand. The merging of the official rate and the foreign exchange adjustment rate is usually referred as 'the second unification' (Figure 8.2).

Between 1978 and 1994, China implemented the foreign exchange retaining, submitting and quotas system, which is associated with a high level of foreign exchange control. The enterprises receiving foreign exchange income

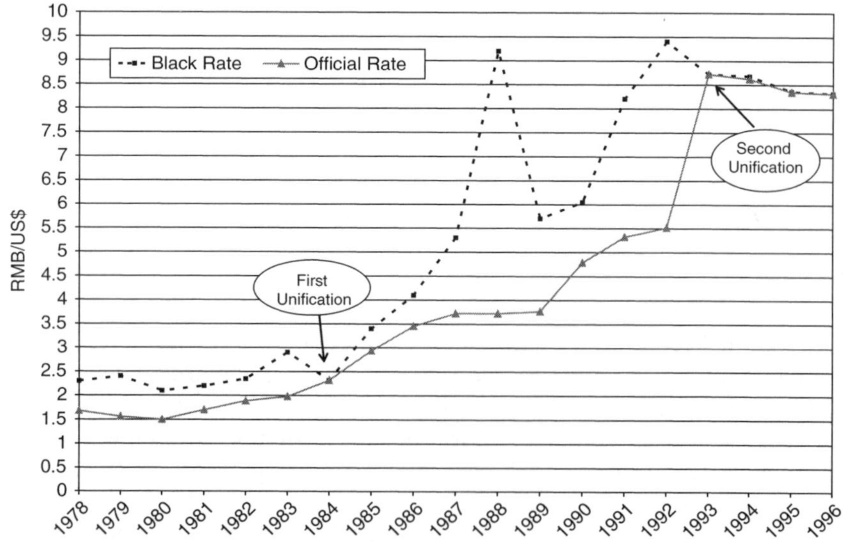

Source: SAFE, Ding (1988).

Figure 8.2 A comparison of the official RMB/US$ rate and the black market rate (1978–1996)

were only allowed to retain a certain proportion of foreign exchange, and the use of the retained foreign exchange must conform to the country stipulation. This system resulted in the imbalance of foreign currency among different enterprises. Some enterprises held redundant foreign exchange and some others never had enough. In such an environment, the absence of a formal exchange market led to the flourishing of black market.

During this period, China implemented the so called 'dual currency system'. The *foreign exchange certificates* (FECs) were issued by the Bank of China on 1 April 1980 to facilitate foreign travelers and prevent the foreign currency from circulation in China. The exchange certificates took the value of RMB. The foreigners, overseas Chinese, the Hong-Kong, Macao and Taiwan travelers and the foreign consulate personnel may use the foreign exchange to exchange the foreign exchange certificates according to the bank's listing price. However, they must use the foreign exchange certificates in the designated stores, airports, hotels or for certain services. Therefore, FECs enjoyed only a limited circulation.[3] The restricted use of FECs in China also channeled a huge amount of foreign currencies to the black market, which traded at a premium against the official rate.

Foreign exchange adjustment center (swap market)

The foreign exchange control and missing foreign exchange market led to the emergence of flourishing black market dealings, which caused great concern to the foreign exchange management authorities. This abnormal phenomenon was not happening incidentally but reflected the conflict between the foreign exchange policy and the reality at the early stage of Reform and Opening-up. To address this issue, in October, 1980 SAFE and the Bank of China started to set up the foreign exchange adjustment center. The word 'transaction' was so subtle at that moment that the trading platform had to be named the Foreign Exchange Adjustment Center, from which we can see the historic trail of Chinese foreign exchange reform. Provincial adjustment centers were successively built later. In March 1988 the national foreign exchange adjustment center was founded in Beijing. The center was fully computerized and consisted of dealers from about 40 local swap centers across the country.

At the primary stage, the adjustment range was limited to state-owned enterprises, collective enterprises and non-profitable institutions; the adjusting rate had to float within 10 percent of the exchange cost with a fixed maximum; all dealings should be finished by the center that is responsible for the matching. The situation changed a lot within one year. The adjustment range was extended greatly, the limit on the adjusting rate is released and the participants could deal face to face. In March 1988 the adjustment rate was allowed to freely float according to the market demand

and supply. Such transactions promoted foreign trades and increased the foreign currency income, and foreign currency reserve.

In June 1992, the Foreign Exchange Transaction Market was set up in Shanghai. The first open exchange market in the modern sense appeared in March 1993 when the commission agent and membership-based systems were adopted. The transaction mode including open outcry and commission mechanism and the principle of 'first bid first served' was set. The whole transaction was electrified. Large-scale electronic displays showed the commission and transaction procedure. By the end of 1993, there were 108 local foreign exchange adjustment centers and 18 foreign exchange markets joined to the nationwide system. With the enhancement of the openness and standardization, the trading amount in the foreign exchange adjustment centers increased gradually, amounting to about $3 billion in 1993. The former administrative measures to control the market were replaced in June 1993 by the 'Foreign Exchange Stabilization Fund' to regulate the foreign exchange market for the first time in its history.

Despite the problems it caused, notably those associated with a dual exchange rate, the adjustment center proved to be a useful transition mechanism for China's foreign exchange liberalization. The existence of the adjustment center caused exchange controls to wither, introduced market forces into exchange rate determination, and facilitated price discovery. This experimental market accumulated valuable experiences for developing foreign exchange markets more in line with international best practices.

A peek at China's foreign exchange black market

Coexisting with the official adjustment centers, the foreign exchange black market was an important outlet of excess foreign exchange and source of foreign exchange demands during this period, which was scattered all over the country. It emerged and flourished due to strict foreign exchange control and inconvertibility of Chinese RMB under both current and capital accounts. The supply side included excess funds from domestic enterprises, remittance from overseas, domestic residents, foreigner's overseas home visits. The demand side included domestic residents, enterprises, and the underground economy.

The black market exchange rate traded at a level higher than an official rate; the premium between the black market rate and the official rate indicated the strictness of government exchange controls. Since this rate reflects the excess demand pressures that foreign exchange restrictions intend to contain, it served as a barometer to measure the deviation of the official rate from market equilibrium. The discrepancy between the official rate and the black market rate was high, especially between 1987 and 1993 (Figure 8.2). For example, the black market rate was RMB11.2/US$ in January 1993, almost double the official rate of RMB5.7/US$ (Ding 1998). The black market exchange rate has shown large fluctuations, and higher volatility than the official rate. The trading volume in the black market was huge. According to the investigation taken by the Chinese People's Bank Shenzhen subsidiary, the enterprises involved in the black dealing are more than 60, the amount reaching $148 million, about 55.8 percent of the export in Shenzhen.[4]

What roles did the foreign exchange black market play during the two unifications in China? Figure 8.2 clearly shows that China's two unifications were the acknowledgment of the 'status quo'. Indeed, the administration did nothing more than admit the truth of the black market rate. The black market exchange rate was already the mature stable rate that the official rate could follow at each unification. For example, under the intervention of the central bank, the foreign exchange adjustment rate was adjusted to RMB8.7/US$ (the prevailing black market rate) from RMB5.72/US$ (the prevailing adjustment rate). The government hesitated to follow the black market exchange rate because frequent devaluation would spur inflation by increasing costs of imports which in turn make exports less competitive. Moreover, devaluation would worsen budgetary conditions given a high level of ratio of external debt in the late 1980s (Ding 1998).

The devaluation of the official rate reduced the black market premium. However, the first unification was a failure since the black market premium continued to grow. The second unification increased the overall attractiveness of the official market and induced a large part of the underground financial activities into the legal economy. It successfully eliminated the gap between the effective exchange rate in the legal market and black market. The black market dwindled after 1994.[5]

Significant Development of the Foreign Exchange Market (1994–2004)

Background

The year 1994 was a milestone in China's foreign exchange reform, along with other macro-economic reforms. The currency was effectively devalued when the official and adjustment rates were unified. Since then, the RMB has appreciated, then stabilized, as the current account has moved into comfortable surplus and FDI inflows have settled at a high level. The authorities are moving gradually toward a less rigidly-controlled exchange rate, with fluctuations allowed within a slightly wider band.

The foreign exchange reform took several dimensions. First, it unified the RMB dual exchange rates and implemented the single, managed floating exchange regime. The exchange rate on 1 January 1994 was settled at RMB8.7/US$, which was the prevalent adjustment rate in the adjustment center (under the central bank's intervention) on 31 December 1993.

Second, China replaced the foreign exchange *retaining, submitting and quotas system* with *the mandatory settlement system*. Enterprises were obliged to sell their foreign exchange income to banks while foreign exchange users could buy it subject to certain regulations. Third, a unified national inter-bank foreign exchange market was set up in 1994 as the times demanded. The China Foreign Exchange Trade System (CFETS) was designed to provide a foreign exchange trading system, to organize national interbank foreign exchange trading, to clear trading, and offer information services. Before the debut of the CFETS, China had over 100 local foreign exchange adjustment centers with varied prices. The establishment of the interbank foreign exchange market unified segmented markets.

The foreign exchange reform was successfully carried out. The RMB had appreciated from RMB8.7/US$ to 8.3 at the end of 1996; the foreign exchange reserves rallied from US$22.4 billion at the end of 1993 to US$107 billion at the end of 1996 (Figure 8.3). On 1 December 1996, China formally accepted Article VIII of the Agreement on International Monetary Funds (IMF), and achieved the RMB's conditional convertibility ahead of schedule. In 1997, when confronted with the Asian financial crisis, the Chinese government declared that the exchange rate of the RMB would remain stable, and the RMB would not be devalued. RMB was

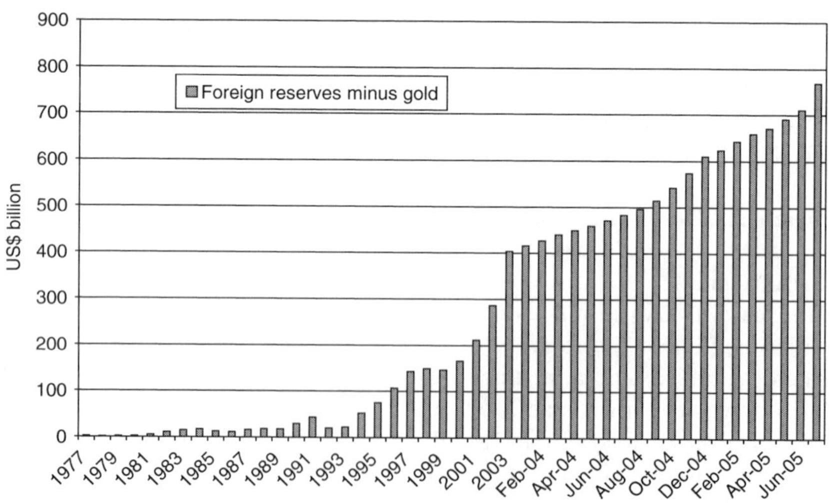

Note: The 1992 figure is lower than the 1991 figure because reserves were redefined in 1992 to exclude foreign-exchange deposits of state-owned entities with the Bank of China.

Source: SAFE.

Figure 8.3 China's Foreign Exchange Reserves, 1977 – Sept. 2005

traded in a narrow floating range of around RMB8.27 to the US dollar. This earned China the applause of the international community. In the new millennium, China is rapidly satisfying its WTO obligations by eliminating quota restrictions and drastically cutting tariffs. On capital account, it has liberalized relatively illiquid FDI flows before eliminating restrictions on shorter term and more liquid financial flows. This decade saw important progress in building the Chinese interbank foreign exchange market.

China's onshore foreign exchange market

An overview: Interbank market and retail market China's Foreign Exchange Trade System (CFETS) is the only interbank foreign exchange market in China.[6] The CFETS provides an electronic bidding system for matching spot transactions of the RMB (RMB) against the US dollar, Hong Kong dollar, Japanese yen and euro. It was established and regulated by PBoC, the central bank of China, and supervised by SAFE. In the interbank market (wholesale market), the major participants are designated foreign exchange banks who make use of an organized exchange trading platform.

Retail transactions are carried out in an over-the-counter (OTC) market. The participants of the retail market mainly include designated foreign exchange banks and their customers, including enterprises and individuals with needs for foreign exchange transactions. Retail transactions are an insignificant component in China's foreign exchange market.

CFETS: A decade's development The CFETS officially started operation on 4 April 1994. From then, China's interbank market has grown steadily and has expanded its business from the mainland to Hong Kong and Macau. Its financial infrastructure improves constantly, and market operational efficiency rises with each passing day. Trading of JPY/RMB was added in 1995, besides previously existed US$/RMB and HK$/RMB; in 2001 the CFETS launched a new foreign exchange trading system, featuring 'new business, new technology and new design'; in 2002, EUR/RMB transactions were launched; in 2003, trading hours were expanded from morning to the whole day, and two-way trading was introduced to facilitate members' rebalancing of positions and fund management. By the end of 2004, the interbank foreign exchange market concluded a record turnover of 209.04 billion in US dollar terms. The average daily turnover reached US$830 million, up 37.8 percent over the previous year (Figure 8.1).

Market organization While the foreign exchange market is an over-the-counter (OTC) inter-dealer market almost everywhere else in the world, an electronic trading system as CFETS is likely to improve price transparency, facilitate access to the market and mitigate settlement risk. An electronic broker automatically in real time matching orders to buy and sell foreign exchange can serve as a more efficient price discovery mechanism than a OTC inter-dealer market. Having the exchange guarantee each leg of the trade not only reduces the risk to participants, it allows banks with weaker credit histories to participate in the market. CFETS has provided an important improvement over the traditional market architecture, by mitigating credit risk from the transaction. The BIS survey (2004) showed that up to 70 percent of spot foreign exchange trading in the major currencies are now traded on electronic broking systems, up from only 10 per cent in 1995. This may indicate future trends in foreign exchange trading.

Market participants The CFETS adopted the membership-based system. With the approval of PBoC, any financial institutions authorized to handle foreign exchange transactions can become a member of the CFETS. Members fall into two categories: dealers, who can trade both for their own accounts and for their customers, and brokers, who serve as matchmakers and do not put their own money at risk. The majority of members are dealers.[7] Members of the CFETS range from domestic commercial banks and their authorized branches, non-banking financial institutions such as insurance companies, securities companies, fund management companies, and financial companies, to foreign financial institutions that are authorized to handle RMB business.[8] By the end of 2004, there is a total of 353 institutions in the interbank market, in which domestic members accounting for 52 percent, and foreign members accounting for 48 percent.[9] The CFETS also handles foreign exchange clearings for all the trading members in its foreign exchange market. The settlement takes place at the second business day. PBoC, the central bank, acting as the sole virtual market maker, enforces the range by trading with members in the foreign exchange market. PBoC set the opening quotes of the foreign rate based on the previous day and allows a narrow range of daily fluctuation.

Technology advancement Over the decade, CFETS devoted itself to establishing and improving a national unified and highly efficient market system. By using advanced electronic information technology, the Internet and leased line, CFETS has set up three service platforms of trading, information and supervision. The CFETS guaranteed the implementation of the foreign exchange settlement system, provided a platform for the central bank's intervention, and constituted a market basis for further reform of the foreign exchange regime.

In June 2004, CFETS announced it would collaborate with the Chicago

Mercantile Exchange (CME) to develop new products to hedge foreign exchange risk using derivatives. CME is the largest US futures exchange and the world's largest regulated exchange marketplace for foreign exchange trading.[10] The collaboration represents a significant move on China's path toward wider exchange reform and greater integration with the world capital market. With the assistance of CME, CFETS will become more familiar with the international foreign exchange derivatives markets practices, products and regulations, and will include derivatives products that fit the need of Chinese enterprises and investors.

Derivatives As the domestic economic principals have been demanding for more and better exchange rate risk hedging services, recent years have witnessed the enhancement of derivatives trading and management in the foreign exchange market. The forward foreign exchange contracts are the major exchange risk management tools provided by banks to customers for hedging these risks. In 1997, PBoC allowed Bank of China to be the first pilot bank to deal in the business of forward sale and purchase of foreign exchange in the OTC market. After the expansion of such pilot businesses both in 2003 and 2004 there are now four state-owned commercial banks and three joint commercial banks licensed to conduct this business. However, the average daily turnover of the onshore outright forwards market is estimated to be less than 5 percent of the spot market turnover by the end of 2002 (Ma 2004).

Offshores RMB markets

Due to strict capital control and a shallow onshore market, the increasing need for hedging the risk of RMB exchange rate fed a fast growing offshore RMB non-deliverable forward (NDF) market. The RMB NDF market offers an alternative hedging tool for foreign investors with RMB exposure or a speculative instrument for them to take positions offshore. The use of RMB NDF markets by non-residents in part reflects restrictions on their access to domestic forward markets. In China, offshore entities are not allowed to participate in the onshore market. The investor base for this market has become broader. This base mainly comprises multinational corporations, portfolio investors, hedge funds and proprietary foreign exchange accounts of commercial and investment banks. Both hedging demand and speculative demand are present in RMB NDF markets.

An NDF contract is similar to an outright forward foreign exchange transaction, with two exceptions. First, it is cash settled and involves no physical delivery. For example, for the RMB NDF in US dollars, the net settlement will be made in US dollars to reflect the difference between the agreed forward rate and the actual spot rate on maturity. Second, NDFs are also distinct from deliverable forwards in that NDFs trade outside the direct jurisdiction of the central bank of China and their pricing need not be constrained by domestic interest rates. The maturity of such contracts ranges from a week, or a month, to 10 years (Fung *et al.* 2004).

Two highly active RMB NDF markets are Hong Kong and Singapore. The RMB NDFs market has deepened over the past few years. As recently as three years ago, daily NDF turnover in the RMB was thought to be less than $100 million per day on average. The turnover in the RMB NDF market has been rising rapidly since, to about $200 million in early 2003 (Ma *et al.* 2003). Estimates of RMB NDF turnover in 2003 vary (Table 8.1), but RMB NDF has become one of six important Asian NDF markets. Judging by reported bid-ask spreads, the RMB NDFs market is comparatively liquid. The bid-ask spread for the one-month contract is 0.05–0.07 percent, and for the one-year contract is 0.12–0.18 percent. Longer maturity is less liquid as compared with maturity less than one year.

There are large and persistent spreads between the onshore yield on RMB and its NDF-implied offshore yield. For example, Ma *et al.* (2003) find that the average spread between three-month onshore money yield and offshore NDF-implied yields was about 260 basis points from January 2002 to February 2004. Wide spreads suggest that capital controls effectively segment the onshore and offshore markets.

The NDF rate may serve as a measure of expectation for the RMB value. Fung *et al.* (2004) find that the forward premium of US dollars becomes discount for various maturities of the NDF after 13 November 2002, which reflects global expectation on RMB appreciation due to the increasingly large China–US trade deficit and mounting foreign reserves.

Table 8.1 Average daily RMB NDF turnover (in millions of US dollars)

Source of estimates	BIS (April 2001)	Lehman Brothers (June 2001)	EMTA (1st quarter)	HSBC (mid-2003)	Deutsche Bank (2003–2004)
RMB	55	50	150	1000	50
Asian six total[a]	7232	920	1890	2250	1140–1680
Percentage	0.76%	5.43%	7.94%	44.44%	2.98%–4.39%

Note: [a] Asian six currencies NDFs include Indian rupee, Indonesian rupiah, Korean won, Philippine peso, New Taiwan dollar and Chinese RMB.

Source: Ma *et al.* (2004).

The RMB NDF offshore market forms an important part of the Chinese foreign exchange markets, equilibrating market demand and supply in the presence of capital controls. Since domestic trading of outright forwards have only recently begun, RMB NDFs amount to about 90 percent of the estimated combined turnover of onshore deliverable forwards and offshore NDFs. Therefore, the importance of NDF markets should not be underestimated, for policymakers and market participants alike. Liquid NDF markets could serve international portfolio investors by affording them an otherwise unavailable means to hedge foreign exchange risk. Ability to hedge currency risk is particularly important for offshore bond investors. Consequently, NDF markets could potentially facilitate foreign investment in China's expanding local currency bond markets and thereby add diversity and liquidity to them.

Links with domestic financial markets

Development of the foreign exchange market goes hand-in-hand with development of other financial markets, especially fixed income markets. Foreign exchange and money markets are integrated to a significant degree – almost perfect substitutes for each other in completely open capital account regimes – through the covered interest parity condition: interest differentials between countries are reflected in forward (or future) foreign exchange premia. Indeed, in many countries the foreign exchange market is actually the source of the most reliable short-term local currency interest rate.

Even with capital account inconvertibility, foreign exchange markets and the bond markets are closely related. Foreign exchange derivatives depend on market participants' ability to borrow and lend in both local and foreign currency. In recent years, China is taking further steps to develop its domestic bond markets. Development of local currency bond markets will reduce the risk to firms' balance sheets of currency fluctuations and give the central bank the tools to move away from a monetary policy framework based on a pegged exchange rate toward a framework where market based interest rates play a greater role in achieving price stability. The market microstructure of CFETS is clearly an advantage, since it is not only the trading platform for the foreign exchange market but also for the money markets. This helps to develop the foreign exchange market and the money market using the same trading platform.

Further moves have been made in China's foreign exchange market and its related areas in 2003 and 2004 (Table 8.2). It developed financial products and markets to support foreign exchange trading and hedging of exchange rate risk. The financial service opening encourages competition in financial and foreign exchange services. Foreign financial institutions

Table 8.2 Significant progresses in China's foreign exchange market and related areas (2003–2004)

Category	Year	Measure
Foreign Exchange Market and Financial Product Development	Aug-04	The Shanghai Futures Exchange (SFE) started to cooperate with NYMEX (New York Mercantile Exchange) on physical delivery futures contracts, clearing and risk management
Purpose: Manage and hedge foreign exchange risk, develop FX derivatives market, and the closely related domestic bond markets	Jun-04	CFETS started to collaborate with the Chicago Mercantile Exchange to develop new products to hedge foreign exchange risk using derivatives
	Jun-04	Permit foreign banks to offer foreign currency financial products to local and foreign businesses
	Feb-04	The Ministry of Finance announced it will expand the maturity structure of its benchmark yield curve, which is needed to price forward contracts
	Nov-03	China announced plans to allow renminbi trading and deposits in Hong Kong
Capital Account Liberalization	Aug-04	Permitted domestic insurance companies to invest up to 80 percent of their current foreign currency holdings in overseas debt and money markets
Purpose: Increase the depth and liquidity of FX markets, reducing the asymmetry of China's restrictions on capital flows	Jul-04	Allow its national social security fund (NCSSF) to invest in overseas capital markets
	2003	Announced policies to encourage foreign direct investment (FDI) outflows
	2003	The limit was raised on foreign currency allowed to Chinese travelers
Current Account Reform	May-04	The retention rate of foreign exchange revenue is raised to 50 percent from 20 percent
Purpose: Reduce upward pressure on balance of payments, facilitating a move toward a more flexible exchange rate	Jan-04	Reform its export tax rebate system to reduce the tax incentives to exporters
Financial Services Opening	Sept. 2004	Streamline the application process for foreign banks regarding new entry or expansion of business and ensure national treatment
Purpose: Encourage competition in FX services by foreign financial institutions with expertise in managing FX risk	Aug-04	Permit GMAC and its Chinese partner's joint venture to start operations to extend auto-loans
	2003	Permit foreign banks to open multiple bank branches a year (rather than just one)
	Dec. 2003	Allow foreign banks more local currency business and larger stakes in joint venture banks

also bring in state of the art expertise in managing foreign exchange risk. China has also reduced barriers to capital flows to increase the depth and liquidity of foreign exchange markets, making them more efficient at transmitting price signals. In the meantime, China has taken important steps to strengthen its banks and bank supervision help ensure that removing controls on capital flows is done in a manner that safeguards financial stability. The regulator announced new capital adequacy rules and risk-based guidelines that emphasize adequate governance and internal controls at banks.

The relaxation of capital outflow control was partly made possible by a mountain of foreign exchange reserves in China. The period of 1994 to 2004 witnessed a tremendous increase in China's foreign exchange reserves (Figure 8.3), as exports and foreign direct investments (FDI) posted consistent growth year on year. The asymmetric foreign exchange controls, which are characterized by the strict regulation on capital outflows and the steady entry of foreign capital, have added pressure for foreign exchange regulators to keep the balance of foreign exchange inflow and outflow and maintain the stability of RMB.

To reduce strong upward pressures on the balance of payments, China introduced the qualified domestic institutional investor (QDII) program in 2004. It aimed to free billions of foreign exchange funds for overseas capital markets on a step-by-step basis.[11] In August, domestic insurance companies were allowed to invest up to 80 percent of their current foreign currency holdings in overseas debt and money markets (Table 8.2).

The QDII program will provide new investment channels for mainland institutions and individuals with hefty savings and idle funds. Hong Kong is generally regarded as a natural first choice for mainland funds. Domestic capital has already crossed the border to enter overseas markets through underground channels. Offering legal channels and setting new standards will actually make supervision much easier.

Link with the US bond market

The US bond market is closely related to China's foreign exchange policies due to China's heavy investment of foreign exchange reserves in the US bond market. Economists estimate that as much as 75 percent of China's reserves are held in dollar assets. The Chinese mainland has become the second largest US bond-holder since 2000.[12]

For China, purchasing the US bond is a safe and liquid international investment of its accumulated foreign exchange reserves. For the US with huge fiscal deficits and a current account deficit, such investment greatly supports US economic development, balance of international payments and stability of the exchange rate of the US dollar. However, the concentrated and heavy investment in the US dollar has aroused great concerns in the Chinese academia and authorities. The International Monetary Fund and the World Bank have warned that developing countries face potentially large losses on their holdings of dollar reserves. China is responsible for about 15 percent of foreign purchases of dollar assets. If China were to stop acquiring a large proportion of dollars with its reserves, or diversify away from the US dollar asset, it could put heavy downward pressure on the US dollar and push up the US bond yield, hurting its housing sector. China recently (6 January 2006) indicated that it could begin to diversify its rapidly growing foreign exchange reserves away from the US dollar and government bonds.[13] This will be a potential shift with significant implications for global financial markets.

Latest Developments in China's Foreign Exchange Market (2005–2006)

Background

In 2005, China is taking concrete steps to construct a more mature foreign exchange market, as part of efforts to improve its exchange rate forming mechanism. China has been under pressure from its trading partners to revalue its currency. In the 2004 annual report by PBoC, it announced the country turned in 'double surpluses' – in both current and capital accounts. Current surpluses reached US$70 billion and capital and financial account surpluses reached about US$112 billion. China's foreign reserves jumped to a record high of US$711 billion at the end of June 2005. Foreign trade surplus has rapidly expanded and trade frictions have been further exacerbated since the beginning of this year. In April 2005, finance ministers from the Group of Seven industrial nations stepped up calls for China to ease the RMB's decade-old peg to the dollar. International 'hot money' also flowed into China in two years, as market speculation about an appreciation in the RMB remained unabated, and China's trading partners continue to push for revaluation.

From China's perspective, a more flexible RMB may help China contain inflation and money supply growth amid record foreign-exchange inflows. At a time of heavy inflows of foreign exchange, PBoC has been forced to increase domestic money supply when trying to enforce the RMB trading band, somewhat offsetting efforts to curb the rapid loan increases and prevent excess investment. The pressure was illustrated by excess supply in the interbank foreign exchange market in 2004. As compared with 2003, average daily supply and demand both increased in the interbank market. However, the excess supply over demand increased by US$47.47 billion. The average daily surplus jumped by 37 percent over 2003.[14] A more flexible RMB exchange rate regime is necessary for alleviating foreign trade imbalances and inflation pressures, improving enterprises' international competitiveness, and enhancing the monetary independence of the central bank.

Foreign exchange rate reform in July 2005

On 21 July, China reformed its exchange rate regime by moving into a managed floating exchange rate regime based on market supply and demand with reference to a basket of currencies, instead of the US dollar only. The four main currencies in the basket are the US dollar, the euro, the Japanese yen and the Korean won. China re-valued the RMB exchange rate against the US dollar to 8.11, an appreciation of 2.1 percent against the US dollar.[15] The daily trading price of the US dollar against the RMB in the inter-bank foreign exchange market will continue to be allowed to float within a band of 0.3 percent around the central parity published by the PBoC, while the trading prices of the non-US dollar currencies against the RMB will be allowed to move within a certain band announced by the PBoC. The PBoC will make adjustment of the RMB exchange rate band when necessary according to market development as well as the economic and financial situation.

This reform demonstrates that China is moving toward greater exchange rate flexibility through an improving exchange rate market forming mechanism. While the magnitude of revaluation is minimal, the revaluation carries significance because it is the first important move in the RMB/USD exchange rate since the Asian financial crisis in 1997 (Figure 8.4). It signals Chinese commitment to a more flexible exchange rate in the years ahead. The small change also suggests that China is taking a go-slow approach in achieving this goal rather than a one-step large revaluation called for by its trading partners. As major fluctuations in the RMB exchange rate would create a great impact on China's economic and financial stability, caution has been taken in the reform of the RMB exchange rate regime.

Importantly, the reform also indicates less dependence on the value of RMB on the US dollar. The size of the US current account deficit, its monetary policy, and the possibility of a slowdown in the US economy may lead to downward pressure on the dollar. After the reform, the RMB is no longer pegged to the US dollar. Instead, adjustments will be made with reference to the exchange rates of a basket of major currencies. The relative changes in the exchange rates of major currencies on the international market can help reduce the volatility of the RMB exchange rate. This potentially allows the RMB to rise against the dollar. The recent announcement by SAFE on a potential shift in Chinese reserve accumulation policy away from US assets might be part of a policy to allow the RMB to rise gradually against the dollar.

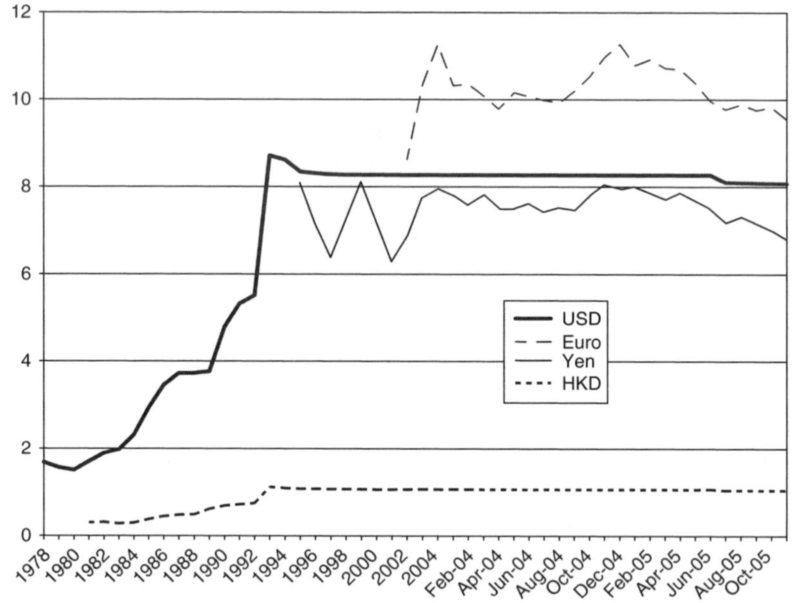

Source: SAFE, *China Statistical Yearbook*.

Figure 8.4 RMB exchange rates against USD, euro, yen and HKD (1978–2005)

The July reform is a signal that institutional restrictions such as rigid exchange rate and other foreign exchange regulations will gradually phase out and China's foreign exchange market will be given more latitude to gain momentum in its growth. The increasing volatility of RMB rate makes it imperative to provide more instruments in the market for enterprises to hedge foreign exchange risk.

Latest moves to develop the foreign exchange market

A prerequisite to creating a fair RMB exchange rate forming mechanism is a foreign exchange market with healthy price discovery functions. In 2005 and early 2006, the authority speeded up the construction of the nation's foreign exchange market, including launching OTC dealer market, running the US dollar market maker system and introducing derivatives.

Over-the-counter operations The first move in 2006 demonstrates China's commitment to moving to greater efficiency and flexibility, and less direct intervention by PBoC in the foreign exchange market. On January 4, 2006, China launched the long-signaled move to over-the-counter (OTC) operations and a market-maker system. 'China's increasing market participants and trading volume and more diversified demand for transactions and risk control have created the need for the introduction of OTC', PBoC said on its website[16]. OTC deals allow for two parties to mutually agree a price without the intervention of a third party. Under the new regime, participants will be able to choose the earlier automatic price-matching system or move to more direct OTC transactions. The creation of over-the-counter trading is an essential counterpart to market-making, with this form of dealing accounting for the bulk of spot transactions in currencies around the world.

Market maker system Market-makers are large institutions that continuously offer prices and carry out currency dealing so that trades can be made at any time, with this greater liquidity in turn helping to smooth out volatility and allow more exchange rates to be set more efficiently. Market maker systems enable makers to base their trading behavior on their judgments about exchange rates, and therefore help fulfill the price discovery function. This will help boost the turnover and increase market liquidity by continuous trading.

After it signed up Bank of China as the first market maker in March 2005, CFETS selected a further eight banks to act as market makers for the new products it planned to launch in May. The list includes one Chinese bank and seven foreign banks. In November 2005, the US dollar market maker system was adopted based on CFETS platform.[17] SAFE invited qualified members to apply to become market makers for RMB spot trading in November 2005. As qualified members become market makers, they will buy dollars if they see the dollar drop sharply against the RMB, giving regulators the confidence to loosen restrictions on currency trading. In December 2005, 13 domestic and foreign market makers were named by SAFE to act as market makers for RMB on the interbank foreign exchange market. ABN AMRO Bank, Citibank, HSBC, Bank of Montreal and Standard Chartered are among those foreign banks who received approval from SAFE.

The introduction of a market-making system in early 2006 is a step intended to promote deeper and more liquid currency markets – conditions that are essential if RMB is to be allowed to float freely on global foreign exchanges. Market makers, including China's big domestic commercial banks and foreign banks, will be able to provide continuous buy and sell prices. Rather than being determined by the closing price for the previous trading day, the new parity rate is more market-orientated as it is a summary from market markers by CFETS, which is authorized by PBoC to determine the central parity of RMB against the dollar, euro, yen and

Hong Kong dollar at 9:15 a.m. each day. To form the central parity, CFETS will first ask prices from all 13 market makers before the opening of the market, and then calculate out the central rate of the RMB against US dollar for the day. The rate will also be the basis for CFETS to determine the central parity of the RMB against other currencies. However, it is still capped by the central bank's limit for RMB's exchange rates. The RMB value will be allowed to fluctuate up and down by a mere 0.3 percent against a daily 'parity' versus the dollar, while it will continue to be restricted to daily moves of no more than 3 percent against other currencies. This move fits in with China's repeated determination that it will liberalize RMB at a slow pace, so as not to risk any destabilizing effect.

Market participants In August 2005, PBoC expanded the scope of transaction participants. Non-financial institutions and enterprises that meet the relevant requirements of PBoC are invited to participate in the foreign exchange market, largely increasing the number of participants. This will better reflect the de facto demand and supply in the foreign exchange market. Previously, only a few financial institutions, mainly the Bank of China, can trade foreign exchange. Other institutions, even though they have a large amount of foreign exchange reserves, are kept out of the door. Therefore, the previous mechanism can hardly mirror the true situation.

Technology advancement On 18 May 2005, CFETS launched its multi-bank portal built with foreign exchange technology from Reuters (www.reuters.com), the global information company. CFETS member banks will benefit from a real-time, internet-based foreign exchange multi-bank portal, thereby facilitating the growth of foreign exchange trading in China. The financial institutions which have the permission to trade foreign currencies will be able to trade streaming executable foreign exchange prices contributed by ten market makers.[18] The ten liquidity providers contribute competitive executable prices on a 'best bid' and 'best offer' basis. With Reuters Electronic Trading, CFETS can now offer its member banks access to executable prices from leading global liquidity providers and thereby allow domestic financial institutions, that may otherwise not have the credit, to trade in the international currency markets. CFETS also offers a full trading, settlement and clearing facilities to all its members and market makers. Domestic banks in China can leave orders, request a price or execute foreign exchange transactions with a single click for any of the non-RMB currency pairs quoted on the portal. This system will help the banks to conduct their foreign exchange activities more effectively and improve the liquidity of the foreign exchange market in China.

New price query system In August 2005, besides the existing ways of dealing, such as centralized, real time matching of orders, a new price query system, the so-called Request for Quote is introduced. The standard OTC dealer market based on RFQ (Request for Quote) enables freedom in choosing counter-parties, broad market access and continuous trading, all generally believed to bring about fairness and consistency in pricing. However, there is still a difference compared with the standard practice in the international markets where fluctuation of trading currencies are mostly not bottomed or capped. The daily trading price of the US dollar against the RMB in the inter-bank foreign exchange market will float within a narrow band of 0.3 percent around the central parity published by PBoC, while the trading prices of the non-US dollar currencies against the RMB will be allowed to move within a certain band announced by the central bank.

New products In 2005, PBoC introduced new products in the spot market with transactions of eight foreign currency pairs, including the US dollar against the euro, yen, Hong Kong dollar, Sterling, Swiss franc, Australian dollar and Canadian dollar, plus the euro versus the yen.

Importantly, PBoC also loosened the restriction on forward foreign transactions and RMB to other currencies swaps in August 2005. Banks operating in China with licenses to trade RMB against foreign currencies on the inter-bank market, including foreign banks such as HSBC Holdings Plc, can apply to SAFE for permission to trade RMB forwards and RMB swaps.

With more flexibility of the RMB exchange rate, the domestic enterprises have been demanding more and better exchange rate risk hedging products and services. The forwards and swaps of RMB against foreign currencies allow banks to offer instruments to clients to help them protect against currency swings. The Bank of China, the nation's largest foreign currency trader, was allowed to trade RMB forwards in a pilot program in 1997. The program was extended to include all four of China's biggest State-owned lenders and three commercial banks in 2004 and is now open to most banks in the country.

As PBoC is recognizing that the demand for this kind of transaction will be increasing, more banks are allowed to engage in forward foreign exchange business. Banks can make quotations to customers based on their own capacity in terms of business management and risk control so as to enhance the price discovery function, facilitate trading and provide better service to customers. The terms of trading have been relaxed so that banks can decide at their discretion the maturity of trading and the number of extensions. The scope of trading has been expanded. In addition to the present Balance of Payments (BOP) items of trade in goods and service and investment income, all kinds of current account transactions including transfer under current account have been relaxed. In addition, banks are also allowed to engage in RMB swaps against foreign currencies (excluding interest rate swaps for customers) six months after they are approved to engage in forward transactions. The trading scope for swaps is also enlarged to some extent.[19]

The central bank carried out on 26 November 2005 its first currency swap deals with local banks in a move that could help bring more flexibility to the market. The central bank offered one-year currency swaps worth $6 billion at 7.85 Chinese RMB per dollar. Ten major banks, including the big four state lenders – Bank of China, Industrial & Commercial Bank of China, China Construction Bank, and Agricultural Bank of China – were involved.

On 28 December 2005, Bank of China introduced RMB forwards with maturity over one year, in response to the needs of enterprises to lock in exchange rate in a longer horizon. These are the first forwards with over one year maturity in the onshore market.

Overall, 2005 is another landmark in China's foreign exchange reform. RMB was revaluated. Measures to boost the development of foreign exchange market were introduced one after another in preparation for a more flexible RMB forming mechanism. Looking into the future, the only certainty will be an increasing volatility of RMB rate.

MARKET DEFICIENCIES AND POLICY SUGGESTIONS

While the Chinese foreign exchange market witnessed tremendous changes and progresses in the past 25 years, there are many market deficiencies in its depth, width, and liquidity. Ma (2003) compared China's foreign exchange market with major world markets and found the Chinese market to be small, segmented and concentrated in US dollar trading with a nascent market for forwards and a missing swap market. Wang (2004) identified several structural problems such as the small trading volume, high market concentration, poor liquidity, limited transaction instruments and significant settlement risk. He traced the problems back to a 'super stable' RMB/US dollar exchange rate and pointed out that in China, for flexibility of the exchange rate to increase, the foreign exchange market must expand considerably from its current depth and scope. In sum, China's foreign exchange market is characterized by lack of market depth and scope, restricted participation, and limited transaction types and currencies.

Lacking of depth and scope

(a) The average daily turnover in China's inter-bank foreign exchange market is very low compared to that on the world's major markets. Up to 2004, the average turnover in the Chinese foreign exchange market amounts to a trivial US$0.83 billion per day, when compared to US$753 billion in the United Kingdom market, US$461 billion in the US market, and US$199 billion in the Japanese market (Table 8.3).

(b) Market activities remained highly concentrated among a small number of members. Only designated banks licensed by the PBoC and SAFE to conduct retail foreign exchange trade are eligible to become members in CFETS.

(c) The products traded on China's foreign exchange market are limited mainly to spot trading in US dollars. The lack of mature forward, futures and swap markets limits the risk-hedging function to Chinese enterprises and restricts the overall growth in the market.

Concentrated participants

(a) Although CFETS currently has over 350 members, the trading activities are mainly concentrated among a small number of members. The major participants include: state banks, commercial banks, other non-bank financial institutions authorized to engage in foreign exchange transactions, foreign financial institutions qualified for foreign exchange transactions, and PBoC. Trading is dominated by the Big Four state-owned banks plus the China International Trust & Investment Corporation (CITIC). These large banks are usually net sellers in the market with the rest as net buyers. The Bank of China itself is estimated to account for more than half of net foreign exchange selling in 2003 (Ma 2003). On the buy side, PBoC's net purchase of foreign exchange accounted for two-thirds of the total inter-bank market turnover. The concentrated participants and limited amounts of foreign exchange result in an illiquid market with low competition.

(b) The market is dominated by dealers, while brokers played a limited role (Yang and Yao 2002). This contrasts with the global foreign exchange market where brokers play an important and active role. For example, a large fraction of the inter-bank transactions in the United States is conducted through brokers, specialists in matching net supplier and demander banks. These brokers receive a small commission on all trades. Brokers supply information at which rates various banks will buy or sell a currency; they provide anonymity to the participants until a rate is agreed to; and they help banks minimize their contracts

Table 8.3 *Daily average turnover and market share in top global foreign exchange markets and China's foreign exchange market (daily averages in April, in billions of US dollars and percent)*

	1992		1995		1998		2001		2004	
	Amount	Share	Amount	Share	Amount	Share	Amount	Share	Amount	Share
United Kingdom	291	27	464	29.5	637	32.5	504	31.2	753	31.3
United States	167	15.5	244	15.5	351	17.9	254	15.7	461	19.2
Japan	120	11.2	161	10.2	136	6.9	147	9.1	199	8.3
Singapore	74	6.9	105	6.7	139	7.1	101	6.2	125	5.2
Germany	55	5.1	76	4.8	94	4.8	88	5.5	118	4.9
Hong Kong	60	5.6	90	5.7	79	4	67	4.1	102	4.2
Australia	29	2.7	40	2.5	47	2.4	52	3.2	81	3.4
China[a]	0	0	0.26	0.02	0.21	0.01	0.30	0.02	0.83	0.03
Global Total	1076	100	1572	100	1958	100	1612	100	2406	100

Note: [a] Spot transactions only.

Source: BIS (2005), www.chinamoney.com.cn.

with other traders. With the advancement of technology and telecommunications, electronic brokers have significantly increased their share of the foreign exchange business.[20]

(c) The role of PBoC in the foreign exchange market as a supervisor is distorted. Under the pressure of RMB appreciation, PBoC was forced to play the super market-maker role in the foreign exchange market. It was the net purchaser of US dollars and had to sterilize these operations to control the domestic money supply. The effectiveness of the central bank's intervention in the foreign exchange market is lower. Moreover, the central bank loses monetary policy independence.

Sparse financial products

For a long time China's inter-bank market offered spot transactions only. There is a nascent onshore forward market which is estimated to have a trivial market share of 5 percent (Figure 8.5). Foreign exchange swaps in the retail market weren't allowed until August 2005. While Bank of China was allowed to offer forwards beginning in 1997, the highly stable relationship

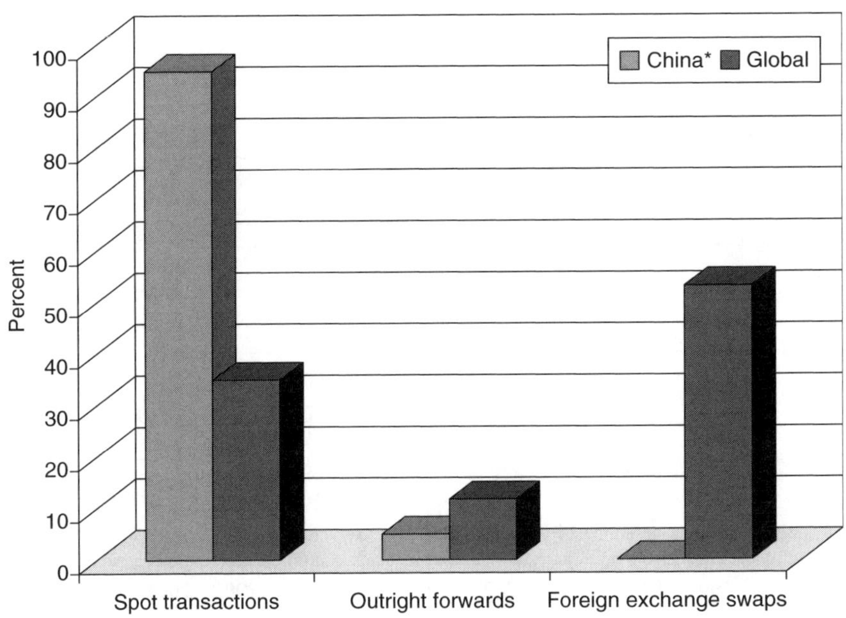

Source: BIS (2005), CFETS.

Note: China data is for onshore foreign exchange markets only.

Figure 8.5 Breakdown of daily turnover by product types (2004)

between the RMB and the US dollar since the Asian Financial Crisis made the need to hedge risk diminished and the forward market contracted. Lack of motivation to hedge two-way exchange risks also prevented participants from building up professional skills in exchange risk management and retarded the development of foreign exchange derivatives. This may turn out to be one of the most important fragilities when exiting from the current peg. In contrast, the offshore market in RMB shows a much higher share of trading in forwards (NDF), indicating a demand for hedging instruments that China's domestic market is not able to serve.

Dominance of the US dollar

Furthermore, the market is characterized by the over-concentration in the US dollar, which accounts for over 90 percent of the overall trading in the market since 1994 (Figure 8.6), while the shares of the Hong Kong dollar and yen have been rather small and tend to shrink. In contrast, the US dollar is comprised of 44.35 percent in the global market (Figure 8.7). The dominance of the US dollar actually strengthened during the late 1990s,

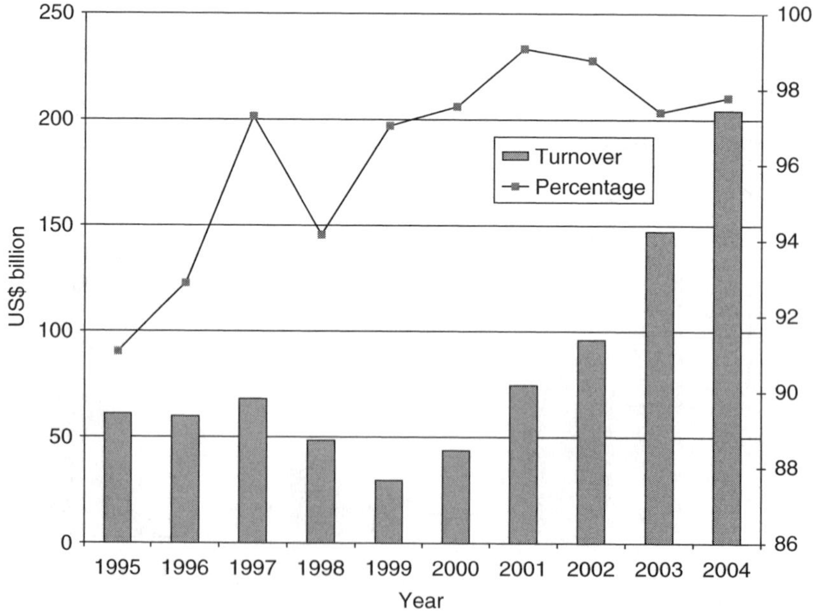

Source: www.chinamoney.com.cn.

Figure 8.6 Turnover and percentage of the US dollar in China's foreign exchange interbank market

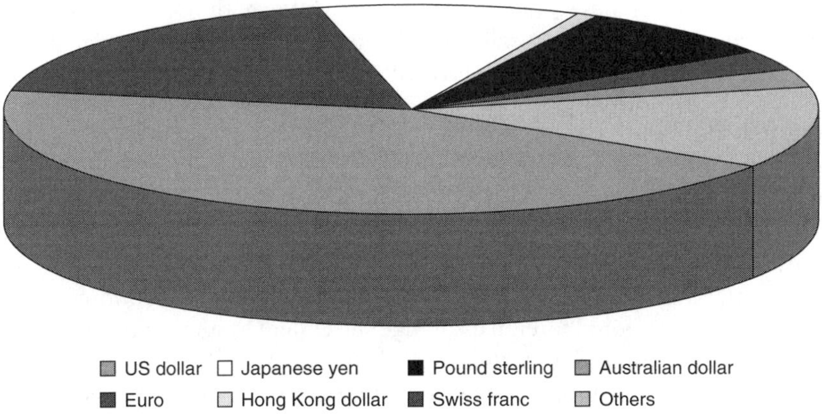

Source: BIS (2005).

Figure 8.7 Percentage of major currencies in global foreign exchange market (2004)

and was little influenced by the introduction of the euro in 2002. Even with the introduction of eight foreign currency pairs in 2005, the domination of RMB/USD trading is unlikely to be changed in the near future.

There are at least two reasons for the brisk trade in the US dollar. First, most of the foreign trades in China are settled in USD. Under the mandatory settlement system, the interbank foreign exchange market cannot balance supply and demand automatically, and the central bank, as an equilibrium force, often enters USD/RMB trading to adjust market supply and demand to stabilize the exchange rate. Second, the poor liquidity of JPY/RMB, EUR/RMB and HKD/RMB trade is due to their inferior status in the RMB exchange rate determination compared to USD. The central bank didn't enter these trades to artificially stabilize these rates as for the US dollar. Therefore, compared to the RMB/USD rate, the fluctuations of EUR/RMB and JPY/RMB were much higher (Figure 8.4).

Policy Suggestions

A sound foreign exchange market plays an essential role in paving the way to achieve more flexible exchange rate arrangements. The mandatory foreign exchange settlement system, as well as the restrictions on the capital account, distorts market supply and demand. The rigid exchange rate regime constrains exchange rate flexibility and reduces the central bank role to one of passive intervention. Because these institution arrangements evolve gradually, the Chinese government has to reform the foreign exchange market at a pace commensurate with the macroeconomic environment.

First, the current mandatory foreign exchange settlement system should be reformed gradually to the *optional* settlement system, in order to broaden the market basis for determining the exchange rate. Presently, exporters and foreign investors must surrender a majority of their foreign exchange earnings to the designated banks, and these banks in turn must sell their foreign currency receipts on the inter-bank foreign exchange market subject to an allowable working position. Demand and supply are subject to strict regulations, rather than determined by the economic force. Moving to an optional foreign exchange settlement system, through gradually lowering 'surrender requirements', is one key element to facilitate exchange rate determination based on market force, and it is essential to boost the volume and liquidity of the foreign exchange market. This will also help to rationalize the exchange rate determination mechanism, and reduce central bank's risk. For corporations, it can reduce transaction risk and costs. Scrutiny should be exercised to prevent firms from participating in the foreign exchange market for speculation purposes and avoid the capital account transactions to be mixed into the current account.

Second, allowing a wider range of institutions to access the foreign exchange market would increase market turnover and liquidity. The expansion of CFETS membership to include more foreign banks and small domestic banks as well as the recent official permission to include non-bank financial institutions and non-financial enterprises in the inter-bank market showed a trend in the right direction. This would aid the market clearing process and support the exchange rate formation mechanism based on market demand and supply, freeing the PBoC from overly market intervention. It would also spread the fixed costs of the trading platform among more members thereby lowering transactions costs. In addition, if the function of market maker system is brought into full play, the problems of poor liquidity, unreasonable price and big fluctuation of JPY/RMB and EUR/RMB trade would be solved.

Third, it should be of priority for CFETS to introduce *futures contracts* for forward delivery as China moves to a more flexible exchange rate. Any effort on the part of banks or corporations to manage their foreign exchange exposures requires an ability to trade today for future delivery. Such contracts, therefore, are integral to banks' and corporates' efforts to manage their foreign exchange risk. In the mature markets, two-thirds of foreign exchange market turnover is in the forwards and swaps markets (Figure 8.5), which can be replicated in China by futures and spot contracts. By giving trading companies the ability to lock in prices at which they transact at dates beyond the current date, CFETS can make an important contribution to helping firms and banks to manage their foreign currency exposures as the authorities move toward capital account convertibility and greater currency flexibility. Trading tools for major currencies other than the US dollar should be developed as well. In the meantime, CFETS must undergo major transformation with respect to market-orientation, services offered, technology, efficiency and risk management, through collaboration with the mature market such as CME. At the same time, the central bank needs to improve fine-tuning methodologies and enhance supervision and market transparency to ensure stabilities of foreign exchange markets.

Fourth, broaden the range of currency pairs traded on CFETS to include the major three currency pairs – USD/EUR, USD/JPY, EUR/JPY – and then others as they are permitted. The most developed foreign exchange markets in the world are the markets for the US dollar/euro and US dollar/yen currency pairs, which claimed a global market share of 28 percent and 17 percent, respectively (BIS survey). Including these currency pairs on CFETS seems not only a natural extension of the current suite of products, but also allows the central bank's policy to be put into effect.[21] As RMB rate is determined with the reference of a basket of currencies, the price discovery function for other contributing currencies has become an important task for CFETS.

CONCLUSION

As China prepares to move to exchange-rate flexibility and domestic enterprises prepare to hedge exchange risk, technical facilities is ever more important, so that a well-developed foreign exchange market is critical in China's foreign exchange reform. The current structural problems in China's foreign exchange market will hurt or delay future exchange rate reform. It is imperative to develop the foreign exchange market with diversified trade bodies, multiple trading methods and varied trading tools. Significant reform measures have been introduced in 2005 and early 2006 to address some of the structural problems.

It is obvious to all that China's foreign exchange market is undergoing constant transformations. With China's entry into the WTO, the opening-up process has entered a new stage, in which RMB is becoming an important currency for pricing, payment, transaction and settlement in both Asian and international foreign exchange markets. Foreign exchange trading volumes are expected to increase dramatically in the next five years as global trade with China continues its rapid ascent.

For a large economy like China's, a progressive development of the foreign exchange market is important for financial stability and economic growth. China has to take into full account macroeconomic conditions, the risk management capacity of the financial system, and the impact on domestic and regional economies in its foreign exchange reform. Accordingly, the deepening of the foreign exchange market will proceed in stages. It may take years for the Chinese foreign exchange to be integrated into global markets. Looking further down the road, there is a trade-off between efficiency and stability in deepening foreign exchange markets. As always, the Chinese authorities need to strike a delicate balance in between.

NOTES

1. China's external trade reached US$1155 billion, ranked third in the global economy. China's foreign reserves, the world's second-biggest after Japan's, jumped to a record high of US$769 billion at the end of September 2005, as current account and capital account posted 'double surpluses'. Source: http://www.tdctrade.com/main/china.htm
2. It is also referred to as *the foreign exchange adjustment center*. The swap market is a misnomer since there is only spot transaction in the market.
3. In 1995, China ended the circulation of FECs.
4. http://www.shenzhenwindow.net/20years
5. Although China's foreign exchange black market withered to nothing after the second unification, the market still exists as long as there is strict capital control.
6. Through the National Interbank Funding Center (Chinese money market), the CFETS also operates markets for RMB interbank lending and RMB bond trading.
7. Yang and Yao (2002), page 312.
8. On 5 November 2002 the China Securities Regulatory Commission (CSRC) and the People's Bank of China (PBOC) introduced the QFII (Qualified Foreign Institutional Investor) program as a provision for foreign capital to access China's financial markets (RMB denominated A-share and bond markets). Chinese QFII regulations relax some capital controls and allow foreign institutions to invest in RMB denominated transactions. More than US$1 billion of overseas capital has flowed into A shares and bonds over 2004 through the QFII arrangement. As of 31 December 2005, a total of 34 foreign institutions have received QFII licenses with quotas ranging from $50 million to $800 million (www.chinamoney.com.cn).
9. Source: www.chinamoney.com.cn (CFETS)
10. CME moved about $1.5 billion per day in settlement payments in the first quarter of 2004 and managed $38.1 billion in collateral deposits at 31 March 2004 (www.cme.com).
11. The National Council of Social Security Fund (NCSSF), which operates nearly RMB140 billion (US$16.9 billion) of strategic social security reserve funds, is a pioneer in the sector. The NCSSF obtained State Council approval to invest in overseas capital markets in 2004 and it has acquired US$500 million of initial overseas investment quota. Source: www.chinadaily.com.cn/english/ doc/2004-06/14/content_339240.htm
12. By the end of May 2002, the balance of overseas US government bonds reached US$1032.8 billion, of which Japan held US$321 billion, Chinese mainland US$80.9 billion (plus Hong Kong's US$42 billion and Taiwan's US$32.9 billion added up to a total of US$155.8 billion), and Britain US$51.4 billion. Source: http://english.people.com.cn/200208/09/eng 20020809_101194.shtml
13. China foreign exchange reserves reached nearly US$800 billion at the end of 2005 and is expected to be near US$1000 billion in 2006. On 1 January 2006, Yu Yongding, chief adviser to the PBoC warned that China should scale down its purchases of US dollars and bonds. Yu warned that the new Fed chief Ben Bernanke might start lowering US interest rates in 2006 and start guiding the dollar downward, and putting upward pressure

on the yuan. More seriously, China's economy would take a big hit if the US dollar weakened sharply due to such factors as a bursting of the US property bubble. So it is important for China to diversify as more pressures are imposed for RMB to appreciate against the US dollar. Source: http://news.ft.com/cms/s/f39fa8e4-7. . .00779e2340.html

14. Source: www.chinamoney.com.cn
15. On 25 November Bank of China, the country's largest foreign exchange bank, and some other banks quoted a 7.9997 RMB buying price for the dollar in cash, the first time the currency had passed a psychologically sensitive line of 8 to 1.
16. Source: www.pboc.gov.cn
17. Source: www.safe.gov.cn
18. Ten leading global institutions include: ABN AMRO, Bank of China, Bank of Montreal, Citic, Citibank, Deutsche Bank, HSBC, ICBC, ING and the Royal Bank of Scotland.
19. Notice on Issues Regarding Expanding Designated Banks' Forward Sale and Purchase of Foreign Exchange Business to Customers and Launching RMB Swaps against Foreign Currencies (www.pbc.gov.cn)
20. Shapiro (2005).
21. While the central bank has authorized banks to deal in other important bilateral currency pairs, for many banks, an inability to access credit from dealing banks has prevented them from being able to enter that market.

REFERENCES

Bank for International Settlements (BIS) (2005), *Triennial Central Bank Survey of Foreign Exchange and Derivatives Market Activity in 2004*.

Ding, J. P. (1998), 'China's foreign exchange black market and exchange flight: analysis of exchange rate policy', *The Developing Economies*, **36**(1), 24–44.

Fung, H. G., W. K. Leung and J. Zhu (2004), 'Nondeliverable forward market for Chinese RMB: a first look', *China Economic Review*, **15**, 348–52.

Ma, G., C. Ho and R. N. McCauley (2004), 'The market for non-deliverable forwards in Asian currencies', *BIS Quarterly Review*, June, 81–94.

Ma, G. (2004), 'China's foreign exchange market: an international perspective', *BIS Quarterly Review*, January.

Shapiro, A. C. (2005), Foundations of Multinational Financial Management, 5th edn, New York: John Wiley & Sons, Inc.

Wang, X. (2004), 'Problems and countermeasures in China's foreign exchange market', *China & World Economy*, **12**(1), 62–74.

Yang, S. G. and X. Y. Yao (2002), *Theory and Principles of Foreign Exchange Trading*, Beijing: China Financial Publishing House.

PART III

Regulatory and other issues

9. China's Qualified Foreign Institutional Investor and Qualified Domestic Institutional Investor programs

Hung-gay Fung and Qingfeng 'Wilson' Liu

INTRODUCTION

China's Qualified Foreign Institutional Investor (QFII) program is a transitional arrangement aimed to introduce foreign capital to domestic financial markets at a measured and controlled pace. The QFII approach has been commonly used in emerging markets, such as Korea and Taiwan, to gradually open up their domestic financial markets to foreign institutional investors that have been 'qualified' by the local government. Historically, the QFII program was first initiated in Taiwan in 1990 and soon spread to other emerging financial markets such as South Korea, Brazil and India. The results varied by the country, but overall the program proved to be quite successful in opening up domestic securities markets to foreign capital investment in a timely fashion. In the late 1990s, some financial practitioners and researchers recommended that China adopted the program to grant QFIIs limited access to the domestic A-share market, which had initially been designed for domestic investors only.

The number of QFIIs approved in China increased rapidly in 2004 and 2005. They are from all across the globe. The approval process through which a foreign financial institution becomes a QFII takes time as the future trading transactions have to go through a custodian bank designated by the Chinese government. As of the end of 2005, there were 34 QFIIs, most of whom had invested in common stocks. A few had investments in convertible bonds and investment fund securities as well. QFIIs are selective in their investments. As their investment quota increases, their impact on China's capital market will become greater. Their investments will act as a signal to the market concerning the quality of the underlying securities because of their better investment skills, analysis, and technologies.

The Qualified Domestic Institutional Investor (QDII), on the other hand, allows domestic investors with foreign currency to invest in overseas financial assets through qualified financial institutions. It was first proposed by the Hong Kong government to China's State Council in light of the bearish stock markets across the world in 2001. Although QDII might reduce the capital available to the domestic market and have a temporal adverse effect on market performance, in the long run, it should actually benefit the domestic market because it serves to link the Chinese economy closer to the outside world.

In this chapter, we will examine and discuss these two programs and their historical and future development in China .

THE QUALIFIED FOREIGN INSTITUTIONAL INVESTOR (QFII) PROGRAM

The evolution and development of many emerging financial markets indicated that there are usually three phases in the course of opening up the domestic securities markets to foreign capital investment. The first is the indirect investment phase, in which foreign investors are allowed to indirectly invest in the securities markets through country-specific mutual funds, securities deposit receipts, or special securities set up for foreign investors. In China, the establishment of B-shares in China is a case in point.

The second phase is limited direct investment, and the third phase is complete direct investment, with no formal restriction for foreign investments in the domestic market. China's QFII program belongs to the second phase of the investment cycle of opening up the financial market, and thus it offers foreign investors limited access to the domestic A-share market (equity market) and domestic bond market.

Since the establishment of the Shanghai Stock Exchange (SHSE) in December 1990 and the Shenzhen Stock Exchange (SZSE) in April 1991, there have been A- and B-shares listed on the two exchanges. Initially, A-shares are restricted to domestic Chinese investors and B-shares to foreign investors. Similar to the different classes of common stocks in the US established to protect the control rights of the corporation's founding family, the a dual-class system in China was designed to keep the control of the listed firms in the hands of domestic parties. This system, nevertheless, caused many problems. One of which was the substantial price gaps between A- and B-shares, that have generated substantial interest in academicians and policymakers in understanding the price differential and development of the two markets. The price of a company in the A-share market is typically higher than the price of the same company in the B-share market.

On 11 February 2001, the Chinese authorities allowed domestic investors who held foreign currencies (as hard foreign currencies can be exchanged to Chinese currency, yuan in China, but not the other way around) to buy B-shares listed on the two exchanges (B-shares are denominated in US dollars on the Shanghai Stock Exchange and in Hong Kong dollars on the Shenzhen Stock Exchange). The policy change appeared to have reduced a lot the prices gaps, and marked the first step toward removing the dual-class system of the two markets. The more recently implemented QFII program, which authorized specific foreign institutional investors to invest in A-shares, was another step in integrating the two segmented markets resulting from differences in ownership.

The QFII program was formally implemented on 1 December 2002 in accordance with the Provisional Measures on Administration of Domestic Securities Investments of Qualified Foreign Institutional Investors (the 'Provisional Measures'), jointly issued by the Securities Regulatory Commission (CSRC) and the People's Bank of China. Many believed that the program was aimed to boost the bearish domestic stock markets at the time, which had been on the decline in sharp contrast with the rapid growth of the overall economy. Soon after that, the State Administration of Foreign Exchange, the two securities exchanges, Securities Registration and Clearing Corporation, and the People's Bank of China issued supplementary guidelines on the handling of the foreign exchange, securities transactions, securities investment registration and clearing, and custodian bank applications.

Main Features of the QFII Program

The Provisional Measures established high qualification requirements for QFIIs, which are limited to commercial banks, insurance companies, securities firms, and fund management institutions (private or government). All QFIIs need to have managed securities assets over US$10 billion in the latest fiscal year. For commercial banks, the total assets have to be ranked among the top 100 in the world. For insurance companies, the paid-up capital has to exceed US$1 billion, and the company has to have been in the insurance business for over 30 years. For securities firms, the paid-up capital requirement is the same as that for insurance companies. The brokerage firm needs to have been in the securities business for over 30 years. For fund management institutions, the institution has to have been in the fund management business for at least five years. These requirements are more stringent than those of most other QFII programs in the world, reflecting the prudent mentality of the authorities. Table 9.1 shows the requirements of different types of QFIIs.

Table 9.1 Requirements for Qualified Foreign Institutional Investors (QFIIs)

Type of QFIIs	History	Capital	Assets under management
Funds	> 5 years	–	> US$10 billion
Insurance	> 30 years	> US$1 billion	> US$10 billion
Brokerage	> 30 years	> US$1 billion	> US$10 billion
Banks	–	Top 100 globally	> US$10 billion

Source: www.hk-lawyer.com/2003-1/Jan03-cover.htm.

QFIIs are allowed to invest in listed A-shares, national treasury bonds, and any other financial assets approved by the CSRC. However, 'national security-related' industries such as television media, cable network, electricity network and operations, book publication and distribution, telecommunication, securities and financial derivatives, are off limits. With regard to the amount of investment, or the approved foreign exchange quota, the lower and upper bounds are US$50 million and US$800 million respectively. Any QFII cannot hold more than 10 percent of any firm's outstanding shares, and the total QFII investment in one firm cannot exceed 20 percent.

Concerning the control of capital flows in and out of the country, the Provisional Measures require the QFIIs to remit in the capital within three months of qualification. The capital has to stay in China for at least one year. After that, each outbound remittance cannot exceed 20 percent of the total amount, and the time interval between two remittances cannot be shorter than three months. For investment in close-end funds, the capital has to stay for three years, and the outbound remittance interval cannot fall below one month. In addition, the investment quota can be transferred among QFIIs upon approval, and the capital gains can be converted back into foreign currencies once a year.

The Role of the Custodian Bank

The custodian bank is typically a domestic commercial bank, or a foreign bank's domestic branch, sanctioned by the CSRC. Foreign institutions apply to the CSRC for QFII status through a custodian bank. Upon approval, the custodian bank acts as a trustee for the QFII to manage the capital. In addition, as a commercial bank familiar with the operations of China's financial system, the custodian bank is able to provide the QFII with valuable information and investment advice obtained from various channels including domestic securities firms. Thus QFII rarely establishes direct contact with securities firms without the involvement of the custodian bank.

With regard to the conditions of becoming a custodian bank, a commercial bank is required to have the following:

- specific fund custody department;
- paid in capital of more than RMB8 billion;
- sufficient number of professionals familiar with a custody;
- the ability to manage entire assets of the fund safely;
- qualifications to conduct foreign exchange and RMB business; and
- no material breach of foreign exchange regulations in the preceding three years.

By October 2005, ten commercial banks had been granted QFII custodian bank status, which include the Big Four – Bank of China, China Construction Bank, Industrial and Commercial Bank of China and Agricultural Bank of China – three smaller domestic commercial banks – the China Merchants Bank, the Bank of Communications, and the China Everbright Bank – and three foreign bank branches – the Shanghai branches of Citibank, HSBC and Standard Chartered Bank. The majority of QFIIs have chosen one of the three foreign bank branches to be their custodian bank.[1]

QFII Transaction Process

Figure 9.1 provides an example of the transaction process for QFIIs. First, the QFII gives a transaction order to its securities broker. After receiving the order, the securities broker needs to verify whether there is sufficient cash (for buying order) or securities (for selling order) with the QFII's custodian bank. If the response from the custodian bank is positive, the broker will go ahead and execute the order through the transaction system in the securities exchange. The securities exchange then sends transaction data to China Securities Depository and Clearing Corporation (CSDCC) to update the QFII's securities account with the CSDCC. At 5 p.m., the transaction confirmation is sent to both the broker and the custodian bank. All these take place on the same trading day (T + 0).

On the second day (T + 1), the CSDCC sends payment notices to both the custodian bank and the clearing bank. With the notice, the custodian bank deposits into (for selling order) or deduct from (for buying order) QFII's cash account for the transaction amount, and correspondingly collects from or pays to the clearing bank the same amount at 5 p.m. Lastly the clearing bank will adjust the QFII's account with CSDCC.

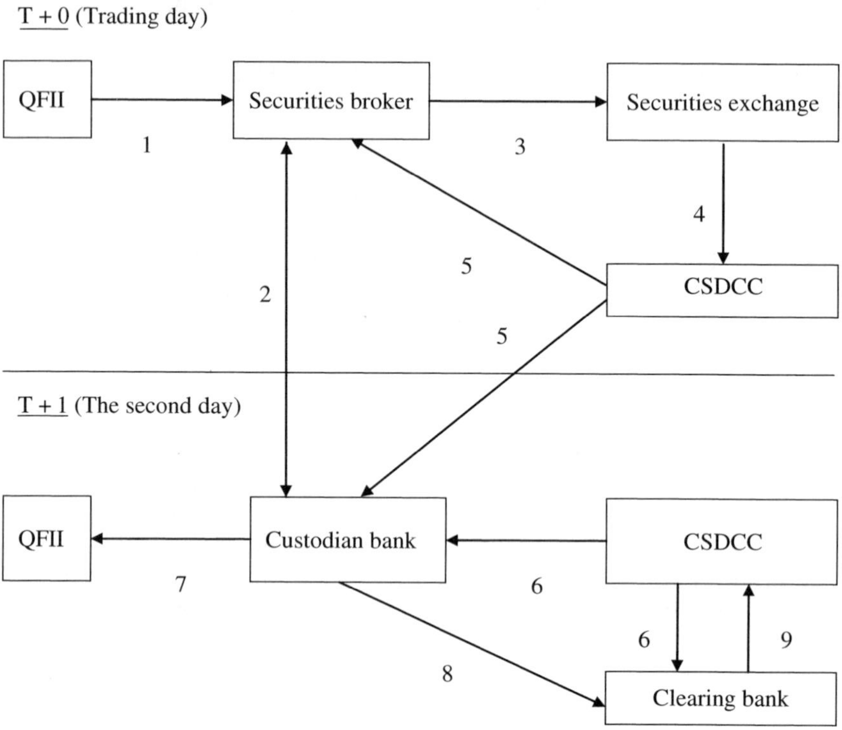

Steps:
1. QFII gives transaction order to broker.
2. Broker verifies usable cash and securities with custodian bank.
3. Broker executes order through the transaction system in securities exchange.
4. The securities exchange sends transaction data to CSDCC.
5. QFII's securities account at CSDCC is updated. Transaction confirmation is sent to both the broker and the custodian bank at 5 p.m. on trading day.
6. On the second day, CSDCC sends payment notices to both the custodian bank and the clearing bank.
7. Custodian bank deposits into or deduct from QFII's cash account.
8. Custodian bank pays to or collects from the clearing bank the transaction cash amount at 5 p.m.
9. Clearing bank adjusts QFII's accounts with CSDCC.

Source: Adapted from *A Closed View of Qualified Foreign Institutional Investors*, Morgan Stanley, 2003.

Figure 9.1 QFII transaction process – an example

In this process, it is clear that the QFII makes decisions on buying or selling securities, and that the custodian bank facilitates the transactions on behalf of the QFII.

QFII Investments

By October 2004, the CSRC had granted QFII status to 27 foreign financial institutions with a total investment quota of US$4 billion, but the quota recently increased to US$10.[2] However, for about one year since then, no more QFIIs or investment quota were added, which, from our perspective, was due to the mounting pressures on the Chinese currency to appreciate. The US$4 billion investment quotas had been used up by June 2005 and the CSRC promised to increase it to US$10 billion, but it gave no timetable for that increase.[3]

Table 9.2 provides the names of all QFIIs, their approval date, custodian bank, location of headquarters, and their investments in major industries. The first approved QFII was UBS Limited, which was set up in May 2003. Citibank was the custodian bank for UBS. Many QFII come from the US, Europe and Asia (such as Hong Kong, Japan and Singapore). The table shows investments of QFII are in a variety of industries.

Table 9.3 reports the characteristics of investment of some QFII. Many of them have investment in stocks, while some in convertible bonds and investment funds. Many QFII do not disclose their investment portfolios.

Several points about the QFII investments should be noted here from Tables 9.2 and 9.3. First, repeated holdings seemed to be a feature among QFIIs. For example, Wuhu Conch Profile and Science Company stock was held by four QFIIs – UBS, HSBC, Standard Chartered Bank and ING Bank, with the first three banks among the top ten stockholders.[4] Jiu Zhi Tang Pharmaceutical Group Company stock was held by four QFIIs – Citigroup, Credit Suisse First Boston, Merrill Lynch and ING Bank and ZTE Corporation, Golden Eagle Textile, Chang-jiang Electric, Rebecca Hair Products and Pudong Development Bank stocks were also held by multiple QFIIs. This, to a certain extent, reflected that there was a lack of high-quality stocks in China's A-share markets, which was consistent with fact that many high-quality firms had been listed in overseas stock exchanges, such as the Hong Kong Stock Exchange and NASDAQ in the US market.

Second, QFIIs seemed to concentrate their investments on energy, metal, transportation, textile, pharmaceutical and banking industries. The stocks chosen were typically the industry's leading companies, like Golden

Table 9.2 Some characteristics of QFIIs

Company	Approval time	Custodian	Geographical	Major industries invested (2005/9/30)
UBS Ltd	23/5/2003	Citibank Shanghai branch	America	Metals and non-metals
Nomura Securities Co. Ltd	23/5/2003	Citibank Shanghai branch	Japan	Metals and non-metals; Estate; Textiles, fashions and Furs Electrics; Trader; Machines
Morgan Stanley & Co. International Ltd	5/6/2003	HSBC	America	Transportation; Electric utilities, steam and hot water manufacturers and distributors; Machines and equipment; Minerals mining; Metals
Citigroup Global Markets Ltd	5/6/2003	Standard Chartered Bank	America	Metals and non-metals; Beverages and food; Minerals mining; Coal mining; Machines and equipment; Agriculture; Petroleum, petrochemicals, plastics
Goldman, Sachs & Co.	30/7/2003	Citibank Shanghai branch	America	Metals and non-metals
Deutsche Bank Aktiengesell-schaft	30/7/2003	Citibank Shanghai branch	Europe	Electrics; Metals and non-metals; Electric utilities, steam and hot water manufacturers and distributors
HSBC	4/8/2003	China Construction Bank	Europe	Machines and equipments; Pharmaceuticals; Metals and non-metals; Petroleum, petrochemicals, plastics
ING Bank N.V.	10/9/2003	Standard Chartered Bank	Europe	NA
J.P. Morgan Chase Bank	30/9/2003	HSBC Shanghai Branch	America	NA

Table 9.2 (*continued*)

Company	Approval time	Custodian	Geographical	Major industries invested (2005/9/30)
Credit Suisse First Boston (Hong Kong) Ltd	24/10/2003	Chinese Industry and Commerce Bank	Hong Kong	Beverages and food; Minerals mining; Coal mining; Machines and equipment; Air delivery and freight services; Textiles, fashions and Furs; Metals and non-metals
Standard Chartered Bank (Hong Kong) Ltd	11/12/2003	Bank of China	Hong Kong	Machines and equipment; Beverages and food; Petroleum, petrochemicals, plastics; Agriculture; Estate
Nikko Asset Management Co. Ltd	11/12/2003	Bank of Communi-cations	Japan	Machines and equipment; Petroleum, petrochemicals, plastics; Variety stores; Metals and non-metals; Hotels
Merrill Lynch International	30/4/2004	HSBC Shanghai Branch	America	Machines and equipment; Communication and communication equipment; Electrics; Estate; Beverages and food; Pharmaceuticals;
Hang Seng Bank	10/5/2004	China Construction Bank	Hong Kong	Finance; Computers
Daiwa Securities SMBC Co. Ltd	10/5/2004	Industrial and Commercial Bank of China	Asia	Electrics; Petroleum, petrochemicals, plastics; Metals and non-metals
Lehman Brothers International (Europe)	6/7/2004	Agricultural Bank of China	Europe	Petroleum, petrochemicals, plastics; Coal mining; Machines and equipment; Traveling
Bill & Melinda Gates Foundation	6/7/2004	HSBC	America	Machines and equipment; Wood and Furniture; Agriculture; Metals and non-metals;

Table 9.2 (continued)

Company	Approval time	Custodian	Geo graphical	Major industries invested (30/9/2005)
INVESCO Asset Management Ltd	4/8/2004	Bank of China	America	NA
ABN AMRO Bank N.V.	2/9/2004	HSBC	Europe	NA
Societe Générale	14/9/2004	HSBC	Europe	NA
Templeton Asset Management Ltd	14/9/2004	HSBC	Singapore	NA
Barclays Bank PLC	15/9/2004	Standard Chartered Bank	Europe	Petroleum, petrochemicals, plastics, Civil engineering
Dresdner Bank Aktiengesell-schaft	27/9/2004	Industrial and Commercial Bank of China	Europe	NA
Fortis Bank SA/NV	29/9/2004	Bank of China	Europe	NA
BNP Paribas	29/9/2004	Agricultural Bank of China	Europe	Petroleum, petrochemicals and plastics
Power Corporation of Canada	15/10/2004	China Construction Bank	North America	NA
CALYON S.A.	15/10/2004	HSBC	Europe	NA
Goldman Sachs Asset Management International	11/2005		North America	NA
Government of Singapore Investment Corporation	11/2005		Singapore	NA

Table 9.2 (continued)

Company	Approval time	Custodian	Geographical	Major industries invested (2005/9/30)
Martin Currie Investment Management Ltd	11/2005		Europe	NA
Danmaxifudun Investment Management Co. Ltd	18/11/2005		Singapore	NA
AIG Global Investment Corporation	18/11/2005		North America	NA
JF Asset Management	12/2005		Asia	NA
The Dai-ichi Mutual Life Insurance Co.	12/2005		Asia	NA

Data resources: www.jrj.com/QFII, and www.csrc.com.cn. *As QFIIs have neither invested nor invested enough to be one of the big ten shareholders of the company data are not available.

Eagle Textile or a fast-growing company, like Pudong Development Bank. Some industries chosen by QFIIs possess unique Chinese characteristics. For example, the textile industry has China's comparative advantages over foreign competitors, and the three pharmaceutical companies in Table 9.1 – Jiu Zhi Tang, Ma Ying Long and Yibai, are located in different provinces but all produce unique Chinese traditional medicines with good market shares.

Third, in addition to investing in stocks, some QFIIs have made investment in corporate convertible bonds and close-end funds, which have been largely ignored by domestic investors. For instance, out of 54 close-end funds, there have been 34 funds of which QFIIs have entered the top ten holders.[5]

Table 9.3 Investment Analysis of QFIIs ($ million)

Company	Investment Quota	Stocks Investments 2005/9/30	Convertible Bond Investment 2005/3/31	Investment Fund 2005/6/30
UBS Ltd	800	62.93	103.49	36.97
Nomura Securities Co. Ltd	50	15.47	NA	NA
Morgan Stanley & Co. International Ltd	550	164.24	2.39	NA
Citigroup Global Markets Ltd	400	293.86	155.91	46.13
Goldman, Sachs & Co.	150	46.14	NA	14.27
Deutsche Bank Aktiengesellschaft	400	13.95	NA	2.36
HSBC	400	61.49	NA	NA
ING Bank N.V.	100	NA	NA	NA
J.P. Morgan Chase Bank	50	NA	NA	0.95
Credit Suisse First Boston (Hong Kong) Ltd	300	268.62	NA	5.11
Standard Chartered Bank (Hong Kong) Ltd	75	19.02	0.46	NA
Nikko Asset Management Co. Ltd	250	41.50	NA	NA
Merrill Lynch International	300	28.90	NA	NA
Hang Seng Bank	100	16.48	NA	NA
Daiwa Securities SMBC Co. Ltd	50	7.14	NA	NA
Lehman Brothers International (Europe)	75	16.20	NA	NA
Bill & Melinda Gates Foundation	100	8.96	NA	NA
INVESCO Asset Management Ltd	50	NA	NA	NA
ABN AMRO Bank N.V.	75	NA	NA	9.19
Societe Générale	50	NA	19.11	NA
Templeton Asset Management Ltd	100	NA	NA	NA
Barclays Bank PLC	75	1.10	NA	NA
Dresdner Bank Aktiengesellschaft	75	NA	NA	NA
Fortis Bank SA/NV	400	NA	NA	NA
BNP Paribas	75	1.19	NA	2.58
Power Corporation of Canada	50	NA	NA	NA
CALYON S.A.	75	NA	NA	NA
Goldman Sachs Asset Management International	200	NA	NA	NA
Government of Singapore Investment Corporation	100	NA	NA	NA
Martin Currie Investment Management Ltd	120	NA	NA	NA

Table 9.3 (*continued*)

Company	Investment Quota	Stocks Investments 2005/9/30	Convertible Bond Investment 2005/3/31	Investment Fund 2005/6/30
Danmaxifudun Investment Management Co. Ltd	100	NA	NA	NA
AIG Global Investment Corporation	50	NA	NA	NA
JF Asset Management	NA	NA	NA	NA
The Dai-ichi Mutual Life Insurance Co.	NA	NA	NA	NA

NA for QFII implies their investment figures were: (a) either not available; or (b) their investments not sufficient enough to be one of the big ten shareholders of the companies.
Data resources: www.jrj.com/QFII

THE QUALIFIED DOMESTIC INSTITUTIONAL INVESTOR (QDII) PROGRAM

Given the speed at which foreign reserves have piled up in recent years due to a large trade surplus, China can now afford to allow domestic companies to invest overseas. Through the QDII program, Chinese companies can invest overseas to acquire foreign competitors to gain market share and expand globally. There have been remarkable changes regarding the QDII scheme in recent years (Brown and Browne, 2004). In 2003, overseas investment by Chinese companies rose 5.5 percent to $2.85 billion. State-run oil firms and mining companies were vanguards in overseas investments.

The Ministry of Commerce has established new rules to encourage smaller firms to invest overseas and recently set up a web site to allow all Chinese companies to apply and receive approvals for investing overseas (Fung, 2005). The three objectives for allowing Chinese domestic firms to invest abroad are: (a) to gain access to foreign technology; (b) to acquire research and development skills; and (c) to find new markets.

Under the QDII program, Chinese companies are allowed to expand overseas, but at the same time they need to be aware of the risks associated with the global business, as well as the rules of games that govern international business activities. For example, China Aviation Oil, a Chinese company listed on the Singapore Stock Exchange, has created headlines. The company mismanaged oil derivatives trading and incurred over $550 million in losses. It also caused concerns on alleged illegal insider trading of the company's stock.

Table 9.4 Selected China's foreign investments abroad

Date	Company and country
11 June 2001	Beijing Orient Electronics Group acquired Hyundal Display Technology in South Korea for $650 million
18 January 2002	China National Offshore Oil Corp acquired Repol-YPF (Indonesia oil assets) for $591.9 million
8 December 2004	Lenovo Group acquired IBM, a US personal computer business for $1750 million
12 April 2005	CNOOC acquired 17 percent of Alberta oil-sand concerns of MEG Energy in Canada for US$124.2 million, China's first acquisition in oil sands
14 April 2005	Canadian pipeline operator Enbridge announced plan to develop US$2.07 billion pipeline with PetroChina International to provide China access to crude oil from Canada's oil sands
31 May 2005	China Petroleum and Chemical, or Sinopec, paid US$124.2 million for 40 percent stake in Northern Lights in Canada
28 October 2005	China National Petroleum Corp. (China's largest oil producer) acquired Canada-based PetroKazakhstan Inc. in Kazakhstan for $4.18 billion

Source: *Wall Street Journal*, various issues – 23 August 2005, 15 July 2005 and 24 June 2005.

China's foreign investment was $2.9 billion in 2003 and its total overseas investments since the early 1980s were $33.2 billion (*Knight Ridder Tribune Business News*, 1 November 2004). Table 9.4 shows the selective deals that Chinese companies invest overseas.

Table 9.4 shows that there are more foreign investments by Chinese companies recently, particularly in the oil drilling industry, indicating China's desire to secure more oil for its domestic consumption. China's acquisition of a US-based computer business, IBM, in 2004 has received much attention and signifies the outreach of Chinese firms for external growth and market. The deal made in the acquisition of PetroKazakhstan implies that China increasingly focuses its attention on other parts of the world where it can leverage its influence in order to counteract the negative effects of the failed bid by China's CNOOC Ltd to acquire a US oil producer Unocal Corp, because the deal was rebuffed by the US Congress.

The QDII would indeed enable domestic residents with foreign currencies to invest in overseas financial securities through qualified financial institutions. It is apparent that the QDII program would have negative impacts on the already-bearish domestic stock markets. The QDII program has been popular among domestic residents.[6] This is likely due to a flourishing underground banking industry in Shenzhen, a city that borders on Hong Kong, and other coastal cities. These underground banks provide banking services to residents to convert Chinese Renminbi to foreign currencies and help them forward the money through Hong Kong.

In addition, travel was relaxed to Hong Kong by residents of several mainland provinces and cities in 2003. Coupled with the fact that the amount of Chinese and foreign currencies that are allowed across the border has been increased by the Foreign Exchange Administration in recent years, it has become easier for affluent domestic residents to invest in financial and real assets in Hong Kong and other places. The recent IPO, H-share and real estate investment frenzy in Hong Kong could all be traced to the massive inflow of mainland capital through the QDII.[7]

Another factor that contributes to the rapid growth of the QDII is the bearish domestic financial markets, which have been hampered by the reform on non-circulating shares, the moratorium on IPOs in recent years, and the lack of investment instruments. Even though the QDII involves additional risks due to the unsanctioned capital flow channels, with the overall economy and private savings growing at high speeds, many domestic residents are willing to take the risk to invest abroad.

On September 11, 2005, the Insurance Regulatory Committee issued the Implementation Rules for the Provisional Measures on the Administration of Insurance Foreign Exchange Capital, which essentially allowed insurance companies to buy or sell stocks of Chinese enterprises listed on overseas exchanges with their foreign currencies. Although this move did not involve the conversion between the Chinese Renminbi and foreign currencies, it was viewed by many as a step to expand the QDII program beyond foreign direct investments.

CONCLUDING REMARKS

This chapter discusses the various issues related to the QFII and QDII programs. These programs were in fact transitional steps to open up China's restricted domestic markets, as foreign capital had not been able to directly invest in the domestic markets and domestic capital had not been able to directly invest overseas. If this transition proves successful, more financial liberalization is expected to follow.

This chapter discusses the development of QFII, the qualification requirements, and approval process. The Chinese government has expanded the investment quota of the QFIIs in order to increase their impact on the Chinese market. At the same time, the QDII may have adverse effect on China's capital market because it potentially speeds up capital outflow to foreign financial markets. Thus, it appears the Chinese government has been taking a more prudent approach in implementing it. Since the programs are still relatively new in China, whether and to what extent they work and how they impact China's financial markets are important topics for future research.

NOTES

1. Beijing Securities, http://www.bjzq.com.cn/news/, 1 October 2005.
2. Chinalawinfo.com, http:// article.chinalawinfo.com/, 20 September 2005.
3. *People's Daily*, http://english.people.com.cn, 4 August 2005.
4. Beijing Securities, http://www.bjzq.com.cn/news/, 25 April 2005.
5. Beijing Securities, http://www.bjzq.com.cn/news/, 25 April 2005.
6. Yi, Xianrong, http://finance.sina.com.cn, September 21, 2005.
7. Yi, Xianrong, http://finance.sina.com.cn, September 21, 2005.

REFERENCES

Brown, Owen and Andrew Browne (2004), 'China opens doors for its companies to invest overseas', *Wall Street Journal*, 13 October, A2.

Fung, Hung-Gay (2005), 'China trade and investment: an overview and analysis', *China and World Economy*, **13**, 3–16.

Newman, Gray and Luis Arcentales (2003), *A Closed View of Qualified Foreign Institutional Investors*, New York: Morgan Stanley.

10. A primer on the securities investment fund industry in China

Xiaoqing Xu

INTRODUCTION

China's emerging securities investment fund (SIF) sector represents one of the fastest growing fund markets in the world. In 1999, China only had ten fund management companies (FMCs) and an industry asset base of RMB51 billion (or US$6 billion), accounting for 6 percent of China's tradable stock market value (see Table 10.1). By the end of 2005, 52 FMCs had set up 218 funds with an asset base of RMB471 billion (or US$59 billion), accounting for 44 percent of the country's tradable stock market value. In addition, China's fund industry has attracted capital and talents from many of the world's leading fund managers. By the end of 2005, 20 joint venture (JV) FMCs had been set up by leading international asset management firms and Chinese domestic financial institutions.

Securities investment fund, an investment intermediary that gathers funds from investors and collectively invests in a portfolio of publicly-traded stocks and bonds, is a natural byproduct of the security market development. Through the collective investments of the SIF, each investor shares in the return from the fund's portfolio while benefiting from professional investment management, risk diversification and enhanced liquidity. There are two major types of SIFs: closed-end funds (listed and traded on the stock exchange with a fixed number of shares) and open-end funds (unlisted shares open to investors for purchase or redemption at Net Asset Value). Closed-end funds raise the capital for security investments through an IPO, while open-end funds (also called 'mutual funds') are subject to redemptions from investors and must therefore pay closer attention to fund management, performance and service. Unlike the closed-end fund which has a fixed number of exchange-traded shares, an open-end fund stands ready to issue new shares and redeem old shares at Net Asset Value (NAV). The price of a closed-end fund may increase or decrease depending on the market demand for shares, and they are generally traded at a discount to the fund's NAV.

Table 10.1 Size of the securities investment fund industry in China relative to its stock market

	Dec. 1999	Dec. 2002	Dec. 2005
Panel A: Stock market			
Number of listed companies	949	1224	1378
Stock market value (RMB billion)	2647.1	3832.9	3243.0
Stock market value (US$ billion)	319.3	462.4	402.4
Stock tradable market value (RMB billion)	821.4	1248.5	1063.1
Stock tradable market value (US$ billion)	99.1	150.6	131.9
Panel B: Securities investment funds			
Market value of fund assets (RMB billion)	51.0	131.9	471.4
Market value of fund assets (US$ billion)	6.2	15.9	58.5
No. of fund management companies	10	20	52
No. of securities investment funds	22	71	218
No. of open-end funds	*0*	*17*	*154*
No. of closed-end funds	*22*	*54*	*64*
Fund assets/stock negotiable market value total	6.2%	10.6%	44.3%

Sources: Shanghai Stock Exchange, Shenzhen Stock Exchange, China Securities Regulatory Commission (CSRC), *China Securities and Futures Statistical Yearbook* (2003).

Table 10.2 Comparison of the size and structure of securities investment fund industry in China and the US as of December 2005

	China	US
Stock tradable market value (US$ billion)	131.9	16 990.0
No. of securities investment funds	218	8616
No. of closed-end funds	*64*	*646*
No. of open-end funds	*154*	*7970*
Market value of fund assets (US$ billion)	58.5	9182.5
Market value of closed-end fund assets	*11.5*	*277.0*
Market value of open-end fund assets	*47.0*	*8905.5*
Fund assets/stock negotiable market value	44.3%	54.1%

Table 10.2 presents comparative statistics on the open-end and closed-end funds for China and the US. The US fund industry is much bigger than that of China, with US$8.9 trillion assets under management by 7970 open-end funds (dominant form of SIFs in the US) and another US$277 billion assets under management by 646 closed-end funds. Close-end fund was the

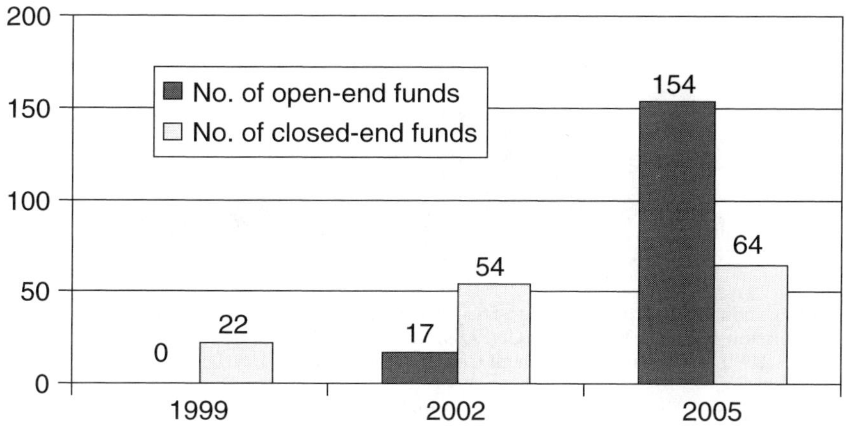

Figure 10.1 Number of open-end and closed-end funds in China

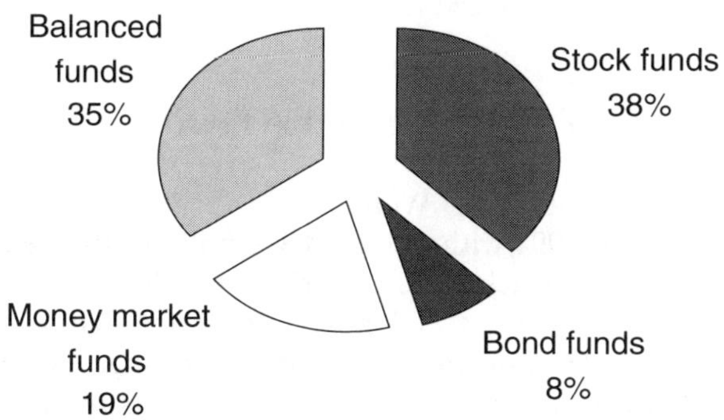

Figure 10.2 Number of open-end funds by types in China

original form of SIFs in China due to the ease of management, but the industry has shifted its growth toward the open-end fund structure since 2000. As of December 2005, 71 percent of the SIFs in China are structured as open-end funds, which control 80 percent of the SIF assets under management. Among the 154 open-end funds operating in China, 37 percent, 35 percent, 19 percent and 8 percent are stock funds, balanced funds, money market funds and bond funds, respectively (see Figure 10.2). In contrast, the US has a stronger focus on stock funds (57 percent) and bond funds (25 percent), and pays less attention to balanced funds (6 percent) (see Figure 10.3). Given the large number of funds available in the US, mutual fund investors often customize their own asset allocation among

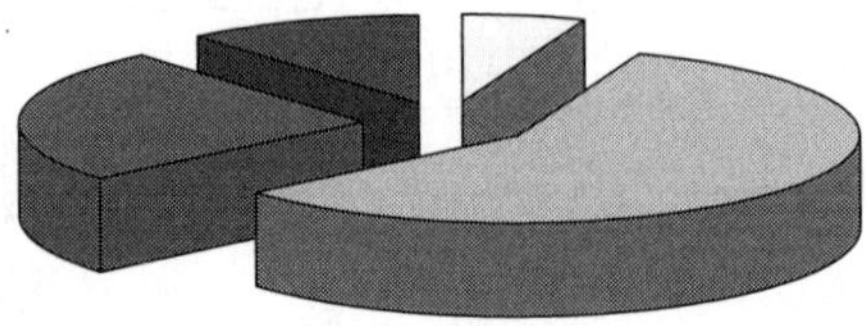

Sources: Shanghai Stock Exchange, Shenzhen Stock Exchange, China Securities Regulatory Commission (CSRC), http://www.CNFUND.CN, New York Stock Exchange, NASDAQ, American Stock Exchange, Investment Company Institute.

Figure 10.3 Number of open-end funds by types in the US

stocks, bonds and money market assets within the same fund family, instead of investing in balanced funds.

DEVELOPMENT AND REGULATIONS

China's first investment fund, Wuhan Securities Investment Fund, was launched in October 1991 with only RMB10 million. By the end of 1993, the number of funds reached 70 and the total dollar amount reached RMB8 billion, although only 27 of those funds were listed on the Shanghai Stock Exchange (SHSE) or Shenzhen Stock Exchange (SZSE) while the rest were traded over-the-counter. These early funds often structured as closed-end funds and invested in a small portion in publicly-traded securities and a large portion on unlisted investments, such as real estate.

China's fledgling fund industry was largely unregulated with significant operational problems until the promulgation of the *Interim Measures for the Management of Securities Investment Funds* (the 'Measures') on 14 November 1997. The measures stipulate that FMCs must have a minimum registered capital of RMB100 million and closed-end funds must have a minimum capital of RMB200 million. No more than 10 percent of a fund may be invested in any single company, and no more than 10 percent of a company's stocks may be held by the fund. Furthermore, 80 percent of assets held by the funds must be invested in stocks and bonds, and at least 20 percent must be invested in government bonds. By the end of 1999, 22 closed-end funds were approved according to the 1997 measures. In May 2000, the new SHSE Fund Index was introduced to capture the performance of regulated closed-end funds listed on SHSE and to reflect changes in China's growing securities investment fund market.

China had only closed-end funds in the first ten years of its stock market development. By 2000, there was still no open-end fund in China. To broaden the scope and increase the depth of China's SIF industry, the China Securities Regulatory Commission (CSRC) issued the *Provisional Rules for Open-end Funds* in October 2000 (the 'Rules'). According to the Rules, at least 100 investors with a total capital of at least RMB200 million (or US$24 million) are required to set up an open-end fund. In addition, an open-end fund's fees for purchases (front-end load) may not exceed 5 percent of the purchase price, and for redemptions (back-end load) may not exceed 3 percent of the sales price. In September 2001, HUAAN Fund Management became the first Chinese money management firm to launch an open-end fund. By the end of December 2005, China had 154 open-end funds with a total asset base of US$47 billion.

To honor its World Trade Organization (WTO) commitment in opening up the financial industry to foreign competition and to lever on the professional expertise of leading international asset management firms, the CSRC promulgated the *Establishment of Fund Management Companies with Foreign Equity Participation Rules* (the 'Joint Venture FMC Rules') on 1 June 2002. The rules, which took effect on 1 July 2002, permit foreign FMCs to establish JV FMCs in China with the foreign ownership up to 33 percent upon accession, and not exceeding 49 percent until December 2004. It also requires that the foreign FMC has a paid-up capital of at least RMB300 million (US$36 million). On 31 July, 2002, the CSRC officially accepted the first application for a JV FMC from Allianz AG and Guotai Junan Securities. By the end of 2005, 20 JV FMCs have been approved by the CSRC (see Table 10.3 for a complete list of these JVs and their partners), accounting for 38 percent of the total number of FMCs in China. Three of the JV FMCs (Fullgoal, Guotai, and Harvest) are among the top ten FMCs in China (see Table 10.4).

On 28 October 2003, the Standing Committee of the National People's Congress adopted the *Securities Investment Funds Law* (the 'Law'), which took effect on 1 June 2004. The 2003 law replaces the 1997 measures (on closed-end funds) and 2000 rules (on open-end funds), and provides a comprehensive legal framework for China's SIF industry and strong basis to ensure investor protection. The law covers six areas of regulations for both open-end and closed-end funds in China: the sales and marketing of SIFs; management of FMCs; fund operations; information disclosure; a code of practice for FMC executives; and criteria for fund custodian banks. Table 10.5 summarizes the key differences between the 2003 law and the 1997 measures. According to the law, an FMC's registered capital must

Table 10.3 List of all 20 joint venture fund management companies (JV FMCs) in China as of December 2005

	Name of JV FMCs	Major domestic and foreign partners
1	China Merchants Fund	China Merchants Securities; China Power Finance; China Hua Neng Finance COSCO Finance; ING Group
2	Fortune SGAM Fund Management	Fortune Trust & Investment SG Asset Management
3	Guotai Junan Allianz Fund Management	Guotai Junan Securities Allianz AG
4	Fortis Haitong Investment Management	Haitong Securities Fortis Investment Management
5	INVESCO Great Wall Fund Management	Dalian Shide Group; Great Wall Securities; Kailuan Group AMVESCAP
6	Fullgoal Fund Management	Haitong Securities; Shenyin & Wanguo Securities; Huatai Securities; Shandong Intl Trust & Inv. Co.; Fujian Intl Trust & Inv. Co. BMO Financial Group
7	ABN AMRO Xiangcai Fund Management	Xiangcai Securities; Shandong Xinyuan Holding ABN AMRO
8	Everbright Pramerica Fund Management	Everbright Securities Pramerica Investment Management
9	SYWG BNP PARIBAS Asset Management	Shenyin & Wanguo Securities BNP Paribas Asset Management
10	China International Fund Management	Shanghai International Trust and Investment J.P. Morgan Asset Management (UK) Ltd
11	BOC International Investment Managers	BOC International (China) Ltd; BOC International Holdings Ltd Merrill Lynch Investment Managers
12	Franklin Templeton Sealand Fund Management	Sealand Securities Franklin Templeton Investments
13	AIG-Huatai Fund Management	Huatai Securities; Suzhou New District Hi-tech Industrial; Guohua Energy Investment Corporation (China); Jiangsu Communications Holding AIG Global Investment Corp

Table 10.3 (continued)

	Name of JV FMCs	Major Domestic and Foreign Partners
14	UBS SDIC Fund Management	State Development & Investment Corp UBS
15	Harvest Fund Management	China Credit Trust; Lixin Investment Deutsche Assets Management
16	ICBC Credit Suisse Asset Management	Industrial and Commercial Bank of China; China Ocean Shipping (Group) Co Credit Suisse First Boston
17	Bank of Communications Schroder Fund Management	Bank of Communications; China International Marine Containers (Group) Schroder Investment Management Ltd
18	CITIC Prudential Fund Management	CITIC Trust & Investment; China-Singapore Suzhou Industrial Park Venture; Suzhou New District Economic Development Group Prudential Group
19	CCB Principal Asset Management	China Construction Bank; China Huadian Corporation Principal Financial Services, Inc.
20	HSBC Jintrust Fund Management	Shan Xi Trust & Investment Corporation HSBC Investments (UK) Ltd

Source: China Securities Regulatory Commission (CSRC).

not be less than RMB100 million (US$12 million) and the FMC's principle shareholders (with 25 percent or more ownership in the fund) must have at least RMB300 million (US$36 million) in registered capital. Unlike the 1997 measures, the law does not make explicit restrictions on the asset allocation on stocks and bonds, but states that the fund's asset allocation must be restricted to publicly-traded stocks and bonds, and in accordance with the fund's prospectus. The law has detailed and unambiguous requirements on information disclosure, requires that disclosed information be truthful, accurate and complete, and prohibits misleading statements in predicting future fund performance. The most striking difference between the new law and the old measures is the strong emphasis on investor protection by imposing more rights on fund shareholders and more obligations on fund managers and bank custodians. The law establishes a solid national legal foundation to foster the healthy development of SIF industry in China.

Table 10.4 China's top ten fund management companies as of December 2005

Fund management company	No. of funds	Fund assets (RMB bil.)	Fund industry assets (%)
China Southern	10	53.00	11.24
Huaan	8	44.53	9.45
China AMC	12	41.75	8.86
Boshi	11	37.34	7.92
Harvest[a]	10	24.48	5.19
Dacheng	10	13.92	2.95
Penghua	9	11.79	2.50
Changsheng	8	11.25	2.39
Guotai[a]	10	8.87	1.88
Fullgoal[a]	9	8.52	1.81
Top 10 Fund Mgt. Companies	**97**	**255.45**	**54.19**
Other 42 Fund Mgt. Companies	**121**	**215.97**	**45.81**
Total: 52 Fund Mgt. Companies	**218**	**471.42**	**100**

Note: [a] indicates joint venture fund management companies.

Source: China Securities Regulatory Commission (CSRC).

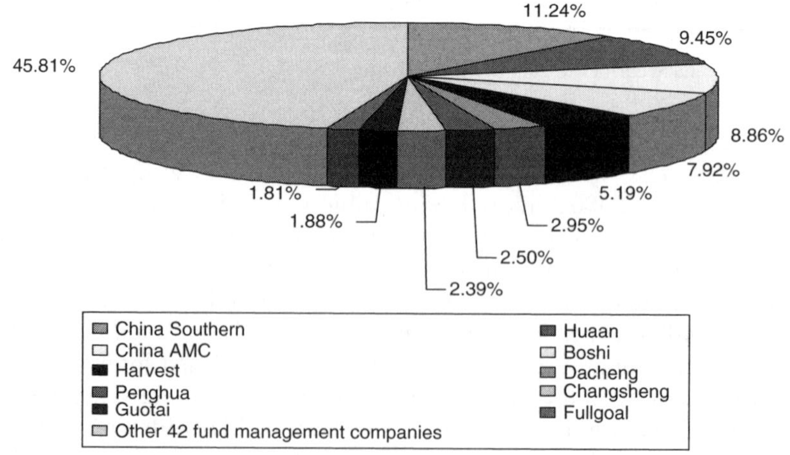

Figure 10.4 China's top ten fund management companies

Table 10.5 Major differences between the 1997 investment funds measures and the 2003 investment funds law

	1997 Investment funds measures	2004 Investment funds law
Capital Requirement	The FMC's registered capital must not be less than RMB100 million (USD12 million)	In addition to the RMB100 million (USD12 million) minimum registered capital requirement for the FMC, the FMC's principal shareholders (25 percent or more ownership in the fund) must have at least RMB300 million (US$36 million) in registered capital
Asset Allocation	No more than 10 percent of a fund may be invested in any single company. 80 percent of assets held by the funds must be invested in stocks and bonds, and at least 20 percent must be invested in government bonds	Fund assets must be restricted to publicly-traded stocks and bonds, and fund investing must be in accordance with the fund's prospectus. There is no explicit restriction on the asset allocation in stocks and bonds
Maximum Fund Share Holding by Investors	A single investor's holding in a particular fund may not exceed 3 percent	Gives investors greater control over the fund by giving the holders with more than 10 percent of the fund shares the right to convene a general meeting
Investor Protection	Not explicit	More detailed and comprehensive provisions on information disclosure. The Law requires that disclosed information should be truthful, accurate and complete. Fund managers are not permitted to predict future fund performance

Source: China Securities Regulatory Commission (CSRC).

OPPORTUNITIES AND CHALLENGES

With the liberalization of the financial services sector mandated by China's access to the WTO, China's fund management industry has received a great deal of attention from global asset management firms. The attraction of

China's SIF industry can be explained by the tremendous market potential as discussed below.

First, China's persistent high economic growth (averaged over 9 percent real GDP growth in the past 15 years) has resulted in rapid wealth accumulation. As of 2004, China's domestic savings and time deposits totaled RMB14.5 trillion (US$1.75 trillion), a size that is equivalent to 45 percent of the savings and time deposits in the US (see Table 10.6), although China's GDP in 2004 was only 15 percent of the US GDP and its fund industry asset was far less than 1 percent of that of the US. The large amount of money in the low-interest-bearing savings and time deposit accounts in banking institutions represents a huge market potential for the further development of SIFs in China.

Second, the potential demand for low-to-medium risk investment channels among retailed investors is tremendous. Many Chinese retailed investors perceive direct investing in the stock market as a rather risky alternative to safe banking deposits, partly due to the risk-averse Chinese culture and the lackluster performance of China's stock markets in recent years. The rapid development of bond markets and money markets, in addition to the stock market, makes asset allocation and risk diversification more practical in SIFs. The risk diversification and professional management offered by SIFs are more appealing to retailed investors than the direct investment in stocks.

Third, the rapid development of institutional investors such as public and private pension funds and insurance companies represent strong institutional demand for SIFs in China. China's modernization from a state-planning economy to a market economy cannot be sustainable until adequate social security and pension benefits are in place. The Social Security Fund (SSF), established in 2000 as the 'fund of last resort' for state government's Social Security payments, controlled about RMB133 billion (US$16 billion) assets as of December 2003 (see Anonymous 2004). New regulations introduced in December 2001 allowed the SSF to invest up to 40 percent in stocks and 10 percent in corporate bonds, in addition to no less than 50 percent in bank deposits and government bonds. In 2002, the government outsourced SSF asset management to six FMCs (China Southern, Boshi, China AMC, Penghua, Changsheng and Harvest). In 2004, four other FMCs (China Merchants, CICC, E-Fund and Guotai) were added to the list of SSF fund managers. The ongoing pension reform in China also calls for the establishment of enterprise-level private pension funds to supplement the severely under-funded SSF. The increasing participation of public pension funds in securities markets and the development of private pension funds represent growing demand for SIFs. Similarly, the explosive growth in China's insurance industry, and thus the rapid growth in insurance premium assets, also results in increasing institutional demand for SIFs.

Table 10.6 A comparison of total savings and time deposits in China and the US

Year	USD/RMB Exchange Rate	Total deposits in China		Total deposits in the US (US$ billion)	GDP in China		GDP in the US (US$ billion)	Total deposits /GDP	
		(RMB billion)	(US$ billion)		(RMB billion)	(US$ billion)		China	US
1990	5.23	749	143	2349	1832	350	5803	0.41	0.40
1991	5.43	929	171	2351	2128	392	5996	0.44	0.39
1992	5.73	1213	212	2293	2586	451	6338	0.47	0.36
1993	5.82	1677	288	2223	3450	593	6657	0.49	0.33
1994	8.45	2246	266	2183	4669	553	7072	0.48	0.31
1995	8.30	3137	378	2280	5851	705	7398	0.54	0.31
1996	8.28	4142	500	2377	6833	825	7817	0.61	0.30
1997	8.27	5037	609	2474	7489	905	8304	0.67	0.30
1998	8.27	5851	708	2627	7900	955	8747	0.74	0.30
1999	8.29	6528	787	2672	8267	997	9268	0.79	0.29
2000	8.29	7102	856	2860	8934	1077	9817	0.79	0.29
2001	8.25	8203	994	3127	9859	1194	10128	0.83	0.31
2002	8.27	9598	1160	3398	10790	1304	10470	0.89	0.32
2003	8.26	11557	1400	3653	12173	1475	10971	0.95	0.33
2004	8.29	14494	1748	3877	14239	1718	11734	1.02	0.33

Source: International Monetary Fund's International Financial Statistics (IFS) Database.

Although full of opportunities and growth potential, the SIF industry in China also faces many challenges. First, the lackluster stock market performance in China has reduced the attraction of its security markets to investors. The SHSE and SZSE Composite Indexes were mainly in the negative return territory for the eight years from 1997 to 2005. The poor financial performance, weak corporate governance, and high percentage of state-owned non-tradable shares for many of the listed firms are to be blamed for this poor domestic equity market performance. To foster the healthy development of the security markets, it is necessary to improve the management quality, information transparency, and corporate governance of the underlying listed firms.

Second, the current Investment Funds Law is solely on the registered investment pools of publicly-traded stocks and bonds. It is silent on the definitions or regulations of the private equity funds (such as venture capital funds or buyout funds) or real estate funds (such as real estate investment trusts). In addition, hedge funds, a popular form of limited partnership investment pool formed by fund managers (general partner) and investors (limited partners), are neither defined nor regulated. Fund of funds is also prohibited under the current law. This limits the innovations and future development of the fund management industry.

Third, the fund industry is still largely fragmented with no centralized database or industry association, making it difficult for investors to make optimal informed decisions on fund selection. China has yet to develop a fund industry association like the Investment Company Institute (ICI) in the US to promote best professional fund management practice, offer industry-wide information and statistics to interested investors, and advocate for better operational environment for FMCs. In addition, China also needs a centralized fund industry rating agency and database system (similar to the Morningstar in the US) that allows investors to access the fund objective, expense ratio, load information, return history, risk profile, portfolio holdings and manager information in one centralized source.

Finally, the present Qualified Institutional Institute Investors (QFII) system in the A-share market presents substantial entry barriers for global asset management firms and limits the A- and B-share market integration. In December 2002, CSRC opened the A-share market to foreign investors via the QFII scheme. Under the QFII rules, each licensed QFII needs to commit a minimum of US$50 million to a special dedicated QFII account and the amount invested must be subject to a one-year lockup period for open-end funds and a three-year lockup period for closed-end funds, in addition to the currency control imposed by the State Administration of Foreign Exchange (SAFE). These rules limit the degree of integration between the A- and B-share markets and result in a fairly segmented dual share class system in China.

FUND PERFORMANCE

Due to the emerging nature of China's fund industry and lack of data, the literature on the structure and performance of securities investment funds in China is limited to Xu (2005). Using daily data on the SHSE Fund Index and the SZSE Fund Index from May 2000 to January 2004, Xu (2005) examines the risk, return, security selection and market timing performance of China's security investment funds, in comparison with the performance of SIFs in the US. Results from the study indicate that China investment funds show superior marketing timing performance while US fund managers display stronger security selection ability. The results imply that the potential synergy for Sino-US joint venture investment funds could be tremendous. Additional analysis of the trading volume on closed-end funds in China illustrates that investors' interests in SIFs are strongly and positively related to fund performance. Results also indicate that Chinese investors favor professionally managed funds more than direct investment in stocks during negative market conditions.

Xu (2005) was based on aggregate index daily return data on closed-end funds up to January 2004. Table 10.7 shows the summary statistics on the quarterly return on SHSE Fund Index (on closed-end funds) and SHSE Composite Index (on the stock market) from the third quarter of 2000 to the fourth quarter of 2005. This period was marked by a negative and volatile stock market performance (mean of –2.04 percent and standard deviation of 8.72 percent on the quarterly SHSE Composite Index return).

Table 10.7 Summary of quarterly returns on the Shanghai Stock Exchange Fund Index (SHFD_R) and Shanghai Stock Exchange Composite Index (SHCI_R): from third quarter 2000 to fourth quarter 2005

Summary statistics	SHFD_R (%)	SHCI_R (%)	SHFD_R minus SHCI_R (%)
Mean	−0.58	−2.04	1.45
Std Deviation	7.71	8.72	4.02
Minimum	−15.58	−17.87	−5.65
Median	0.27	−3.70	1.06
Maximum	16.87	16.11	10.60

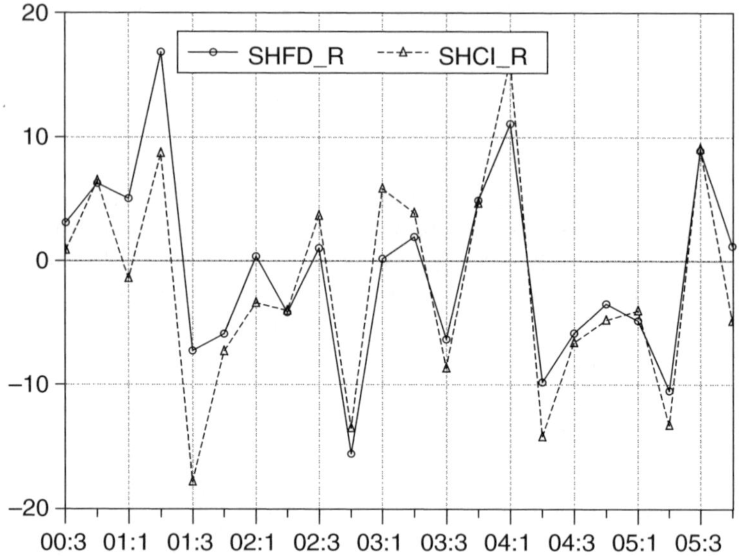

Note: Quarterly returns shown in the above figure are in percentages.

Data source: Bloomberg.

Figure 10.5 Quarterly returns of the Shanghai Stock Exchange Fund Index (HSFD_R) and Stock Exchange Composite Index (SHCI_R)

On the positive side, the SHSE Fund Index had a higher return and lower standard deviation than those of the SHSE composite index, suggesting some value of professional management by the closed-end funds. Tables 10.8 and 10.9 present the total assets, NAV, price, and discount ratio on all closed-end funds traded on SHSE and SZSE, respectively. On average, the 25 closed-end funds listed on SHSE were traded at a 30 percent discount to their NAV as of September 2005, while the 35 closed-end funds listed on SZSE were traded at a 27 percent discount to their NAV as of June 2005.

Although closed-end funds are listed on SHSE or SZSE with easier pricing information access, open-end funds which offer more transparency and flexibility have become the dominant part of China's fund industry. Currently, there is no index tracking the performance of open-end funds in China. Historical data on fund-specific NAV are only available for a few open-end funds in the Bloomberg system. In addition, 90 percent of the open-end funds were setup during the past three years with a very short history, making it difficult to assess the risk-adjusted performance of open-end funds

Table 10.8 Total assets, price, NAV and discount of closed-end funds traded on Shanghai Stock Exchange as of September 2005

Code	Fund name	Total assets (RMB million)	NAV per share	Price per share	Fund price discount to NAV in %
500006	Boshi-Yuyang	2005	1.01	0.58	42.63
500016	Boshi-Yuyuan	1599	1.08	0.91	16.25
500039	Chang S-Tongde	545	1.10	0.91	16.61
500018	China AMC-Xinghe	2840	0.96	0.50	47.84
500008	China AMC-Xinghu	1981	1.00	0.63	37.74
500028	China AMC-Xingye	426	0.86	0.76	11.35
500007	Dacheng-Jingyang	1060	1.06	0.87	18.80
500017	Dacheng-Jingye	428	0.86	0.73	15.57
500056	E Fund-Kerui	3577	1.21	0.73	39.60
500029	E Fund-Kexun	911	1.16	0.95	18.23
500035	Fullgoal-Hanbo	471	0.95	0.79	17.75
500025	Fullgoal-Handing	443	0.91	0.68	25.50
500005	Fullgoal-Hanshen	1985	1.01	0.57	43.39
500015	Fullgoal-Hanxing	2546	0.86	0.47	45.42
500021	Guotai-Jinding	502	1.02	0.85	16.97
500001	Guotai-Jintai	1968	1.00	0.57	43.12
500011	Guotai-Jinxin	2888	0.97	0.52	46.74
500002	Harvest-Taihe	2056	1.03	0.58	43.77
500013	Huaan-Anrui	452	0.91	0.76	17.00
500009	Huaan-Anshun Fund	3284	1.09	0.63	42.33
500003	Huaan-Anxin	2106	1.07	0.65	39.24
500019	Penghua-Purun	473	0.95	0.80	16.22
500038	Rong-Tongqian	1900	0.95	0.52	45.83
500010	Southern-Jinyuan	493	1.00	0.84	16.29
500058	Yingfeng-Sec Inv	2932	1.00	0.55	45.29
	Mean	1578	1.00	0.70	30.25
	Median	1599	1.00	0.73	25.50

Source: Shanghai Stock Exchange, Bloomberg.

in China. As the industry develops and data become more available, future research examining the risk, return, security selection and market timing performance of open-end funds in China should be worthwhile.

CONCLUSION

Securities investment fund (SIF), an investment intermediary that gathers funds from investors and collectively invests in a portfolio of

Table 10.9 Total assets, price, NAV and discount of closed-end funds traded on Shenzhen Stock Exchange as of June 2005

Code	Fund name	Total assets (RMB million)	NAV per share	Price per share	Fund price discount to NAV (%)
160105	Southern Active Allocation Fund	1568	0.91	0.90	1.16
160505	Boshi Theme Sector Fund	1020	0.97	0.96	1.19
161607	Rongtong Juchao 100 Index Fund	511	1.00	0.99	1.40
162605	Invesco Great Wall Dingyi Fund	637	0.93	0.92	1.82
162703	Guangfa Small Cap Growth Fund	1003	0.91	0.90	1.56
163801	BOC Intl. China Opportunities Fund	906	0.96	0.95	1.35
184688	Kaiyuan Fund	1987	0.98	0.57	42.46
184689	Puhui Fund	1812	0.89	0.50	44.33
184690	Tongyi Fund	1923	0.94	0.51	45.71
184691	Jinghong Fund	1766	0.85	0.47	45.33
184692	Yulong Fund	2759	0.90	0.50	44.78
184693	Pufeng Fund	2608	0.86	0.47	45.58
184695	Jingbo Fund	864	0.85	0.65	23.55
184696	Yuhua Fund	507	1.00	0.79	21.12
184698	Tianyuan Fund	3012	0.99	0.56	44.37
184699	Tongsheng Fund	2624	0.86	0.48	45.08
184700	Hongfei Fund	430	0.86	0.67	22.25
184701	Jingfu Fund	2537	0.83	0.45	45.55
184702	Tongzhi Fund	523	1.02	0.86	17.03
184703	Jinsheng Fund	487	0.95	0.67	29.97
184705	Yuze Fund	540	1.07	0.77	29.07
184706	Tianhua Fund	2000	0.78	0.48	39.22
184708	Xingke Fund	501	0.98	0.80	19.59
184709	Anjiu Fund	403	0.78	0.63	21.14
184710	Longyuan Fund	415	0.83	0.69	16.50
184711	Puhua Fund	354	0.69	0.56	19.77
184712	Kehui Fund	983	1.19	0.92	23.87
184713	Kexiang Fund	928	1.12	0.85	25.20
184718	Xiangan Fund	493	0.97	0.76	21.55
184719	Rongxin Fund	793	0.97	0.74	24.33
184720	Jiufu Fund	464	0.90	0.74	18.52
184721	Fenghe Fund	2978	0.97	0.53	45.40

Table 10.9 (*continued*)

Code	Fund name	Total assets (RMB Mil.)	NAV per share	Price per share	Fund price discount to NAV (%)
184722	Jiujia Fund	2061	1.00	0.56	44.91
184728	Hongyang	1804	0.89	0.49	45.45
184738	Rongtong Fund	426	0.83	0.69	17.85
	Mean	1275	0.93	0.68	26.80
	Median	928	0.93	0.67	23.87

Source: Shenzhen Stock Exchange, Bloomberg.

publicly-traded stocks and bonds, is a natural byproduct of the security market development. China's regulated SIF industry started in 1997 with an initial focus on closed-end funds and later introduced open-end funds in 2000. In 2002, China opened the SIF industry to foreign asset management firms by allowing for joint venture fund management companies. In June 2004, China's Securities Investment Funds Law, a comprehensive nation-wide industry regulation with a strong focus on investor protection, entered into effect. As of December 2005, 154 open-end funds and 64 closed-end funds are operating in China with a total asset base that accounts for 44 percent of China's tradable stock market value.

For global asset management firms, China's investment fund industry offers tremendous opportunities, including the high level of domestic savings in low-interest-paying accounts, the increasing demand for low-to-medium risk investment alternatives to direct stock investing among retailed investors, and the rapid development of institutional investors such as public and private pension funds and insurance companies. On the other hand, the industry also faces many challenges, including the lackluster stock market performance, the lack of high-quality listed firms, the prohibition of hedge funds and fund of funds, the lack of a fund rating agency and centralized database, and the lack of market integration due to the present restrictive QFII system.

ACKNOWLEDGMENTS

I thank Hung-Gay Fung for valuable comments and suggestions, Jingqing Xu for excellent data assistance, and the Institute for International Business at Seton Hall University for generous financial support.

REFERENCES

Anonymous (2004), 'The promise of a better tomorrow: China's pension system', *China Law & Practice*, September, 15–22.

China Securities and Futures Statistical Yearbook (2003).

China Securities Regulatory Commission (CSRC), accessed at www.csrc.gov.cn.

Investment Company Institute, accessed at www.ici.org.

Shanghai Stock Exchange, accessed at www.sse.com.cn.

Shenzhen Stock Exchange, accessed at www.szse.cn.

Xu, Xiaoqing Eleanor (2005), 'Performance of securities investment funds in China', *Emerging Markets Finance and Trade*, **41**(5), 27–42.

11. Overseas listing of Chinese companies

Congsheng Wu

INTRODUCTION

Cross-listing and the issuance of new shares in the international markets have expanded enormously since the mid-1980s. Cross-listing refers to a firm having its shares listed on one or more foreign exchanges, in addition to its home country stock exchange. Table 11.1 shows the total number of companies listed on various national stock exchanges in the world and the breakdown of the listings between domestic and foreign companies for 2004. The exhibit indicates that more than 2600 foreign companies have been listed worldwide. All developed stock markets have foreign listings. The top five exchanges with the most foreign companies are the New York Stock Exchange (459), the London Stock Exchange (351), the Nasdaq stock market (340), Euronext (334) and the Luxembourg Stock Exchange (192). Euronext was formed in September 2000 as a result of the merger of the Amsterdam Exchange, the Brussels Exchange, and the Paris Bourse. Additionally, several exchanges have a large proportion of foreign listings. In fact, foreign companies account for 82 percent on the Luxembourg exchange, and more than half of the listed companies on the Mexican exchange are foreign.

Foreign stocks listed on a national stock exchange typically are traded in the form of a depositary receipt, not as ordinary shares. Depositary receipts (or depositary shares) are negotiable certificates issued by financial institutions to represent the underlying shares of the foreign stock, which are held in trust at a foreign custodian bank. Foreign stocks listed in the United States typically take the form of American depositary receipts (ADRs). ADRs are sold, registered, and transferred in the United States in the same manner as any share of stock. Global depositary receipts (GDRs) refer to certificates traded outside the US. GDRs allow a foreign company to simultaneously cross-list on multiple national stock exchanges.

It should be pointed out that depositary receipts are not the only way to cross-list. Foreign stocks can be traded directly on a national stock

Table 11.1 Number of listed companies on national stock exchanges in 2004

Exchange	Total	Domestic companies	Foreign companies	Foreign/Total (%)
Americas				
American SE	575	502	73	12.7
Bermuda SE	58	21	37	63.8
Buenos Aires SE	107	103	4	3.7
Colombia SE	106	106	0	0.0
Lima SE	224	192	32	14.3
Mexican Exchange	326	151	175	53.7
Nasdaq	3229	2889	340	10.5
NYSE	2293	1834	459	20.0
Santiago SE	240	239	1	0.4
Sao Paulo SE	388	386	2	0.5
TSX Group	3604	3572	32	0.9
Europe–Africa–Middle East				
Athens Exchange	341	339	2	0.6
Borsa Italiana	278	269	9	3.2
Budapest SE	47	46	1	2.1
Copenhagen SE	183	176	7	3.8
Deutsche Börse	819	660	159	19.4
Euronext	1333	999	334	25.1
Irish SE	65	53	12	18.5
Istanbul SE	297	297	0	0.0
JSE South Africa	389	368	21	5.4
Ljubljana SE	140	140	0	0.0
London SE	2837	2486	351	12.4
Luxembourg SE	234	42	192	82.1
Malta SE	13	13	0	0.0
OMX Helsinki SE	137	134	3	2.2
OMX Stockholm SE	276	256	20	7.2
Oslo Bors	188	166	22	11.7
Swiss Exchange	409	282	127	31.1
Tehran SE	402	402	0	0.0
Tel Aviv SE	578	573	5	0.9
Warsaw SE	230	225	5	2.2
Wiener Börse	120	99	21	17.5
Asia–Pacific				
Australian SE	1583	1515	68	4.3
BSE, The SE Mumbai	4730	4730	0	0.0
Bursa Malaysia	959	955	4	0.4
Colombo SE	242	242	0	0.0

Table 11.1 (*continued*)

Exchange	Total	Domestic companies	Foreign companies	Foreign/Total (%)
Hong Kong Exchanges	1096	1086	10	0.9
Jakarta SE	331	331	0	0.0
Korea Exchange	683	683	0	0.0
National Stock Exchange India	957	957	0	0.0
New Zealand Exchange	200	158	42	21.0
Osaka SE	1090	1090	0	0.0
Philippine SE	235	233	2	0.9
Shanghai SE	837	837	0	0.0
Shenzhen SE	536	536	0	0.0
Singapore Exchange	633	608	25	3.9
Taiwan SE Corp.	702	697	5	0.7
Thailand SE	463	463	0	0.0
Tokyo SE	2306	2276	30	1.3
WFE Total	38 049	35 417	2632	6.9

Source: Annual Report 2005, The World Federation of Exchanges (www.world-exchanges.org).

exchange. In fact, over 70 Canadian companies are cross-listed on the NYSE, and all of them trade as ordinary shares in both their home market in Canada and the US market.

In November 1998 DaimlerChrysler AG, the result of a merger of Daimler Benz AG and the Chrysler Corporation, surprised the global equity market by being the first company to list on the NYSE using Global Registered Shares (GRSs) rather than ADRs. Prior to the merger, Daimler Benz AG had been listed on the NYSE using ADRs. The primary exchanges for DaimlerChrysler GRSs are the Frankfurt Stock Exchange and the NYSE. However, they are traded on a total of 20 exchanges in different currencies 24 hours around the world. The main advantages of GRSs over ADRs appear to be that all shareholders have equal status and direct voting rights. GRSs are one share traded globally. The shares are fully fungible – a GRS purchased on one exchange can be sold on another. The main disadvantages of GRSs include the greater expense in establishing the global registrar and clearing facility and the larger transaction cost. So far GRSs have met with very limited success. The trading volume of DaimlerChrysler GRSs on the NYSE is much weaker than expected. Very few companies have followed this approach to cross-list. Many companies that considered them opted instead for ADRs. For example, of the ten

European companies listing on the NYSE in 2001, only Deutsche Bank from Germany chose to use GRSs rather than ADRs.

The increase in cross-listing is mainly driven by an investors' desire to diversify their portfolios, reduce risk and invest internationally in the most efficient manner possible. The following have often been cited as reasons for cross-listing:

1. *Improve liquidity and stock prices*. Cross-listing allows a firm to tap the foreign market and expand its investor base. Broader investor base and greater market demand improves the liquidity of the secondary market and increases the stock price.
2. *Provide flexible mechanism for raising capital*. Cross-listing is often accompanied by the issuance of new shares. This is an especially important reason for firms coming from a small, illiquid and partially segmented capital market.
3. *Enhance corporate governance*. Cross-listing into a developed capital market with strict securities regulations and stringent disclosure requirements will discipline the managers to work toward the goal of shareholder wealth maximization. The market often takes it as a signal that enhanced corporate governance is forthcoming.
4. *Increase visibility and name recognition*. Multinational corporations list in markets where they have substantial physical operations. Listing in these markets can enhance corporate image, advertise trademarks and products, and get better local press coverage.
5. *Offer a vehicle for mergers and acquisitions in the foreign markets*. Firms that engage in mergers and acquisitions often use shares as well as cash as a partial payment for the target firms. Offering shares as partial payments in cross-border acquisitions will be more acceptable if these shares have a local, liquid secondary market.
6. *Enable local employees to invest more easily in the parent company*. If a multinational firm wishes to use stock options and share ownership plans for local management and employees, local listing would enhance the perceived value of such plans.

OVERSEAS LISTING OF CHINESE COMPANIES: AN OVERVIEW

Since 1993, when Tsingtao Brewery became the first Chinese state-owned enterprise to tap a foreign market by issuing shares on the Hong Kong Exchange, almost every major state-owned company that has done an IPO has taken secondary listing on an overseas market. The China Securities

Regulatory Commission (CSRC) not only supports large and prosperous Chinese companies to get listed aboard, but also encourages small and medium-sized high-tech companies to go public on overseas second boards.

The majority of them are listed in Hong Kong and the US. In recent years, an increasing number of China-based companies have been listed on the Singapore Exchange as an alternative to the Hong Kong and US markets. At the same time, European exchanges such as the London Stock Exchange have also tried to lobby Chinese executives and government representatives to choose Europe for listing their companies.

By the end of 2005 a total of 287 China-based companies had listed in Hong Kong, the US, Singapore and London (see Table 11.2 and Figure 11.1). Almost half of them were completed within the three years between 2003 and 2005.

Historically, Hong Kong has been the preferred place for large and state-owned companies from the mainland. The exchange has 120 listings from the mainland: 80 on the Main Board and 40 on the Growth Enterprise Market (GEM). The GEM was established in 1999 to provide capital formation opportunities for growth companies. The main advantages of Hong

Table 11.2 Number of Chinese companies listed in Hong Kong, the US, Singapore and London

Year	Hong Kong		US	Singapore	London	Total
	Main board	GEM				
1993	6		3	1		10
1994	9		7	0		16
1995	2		5	1		8
1996	6		6	2		14
1997	15		5	3	3	26
1998	2		1	2	0	5
1999	3		0	4	0	7
2000	3	3	5	2	2	15
2001	3	5	3	4	0	15
2002	4	12	6	0	0	22
2003	10	8	5	16	0	39
2004	8	9	13	33	1	64
2005	9	3	10	24	0	46
Total	80	40	69	92	6	287

Source: Compiled by author based on information provided by the Chinese Securities Regulatory Commission (CSRC), various stock exchanges and banks. The figure for Hong Kong does not include the so-called Red-chips, or shares of Chinese companies registered overseas but listed in Hong Kong.

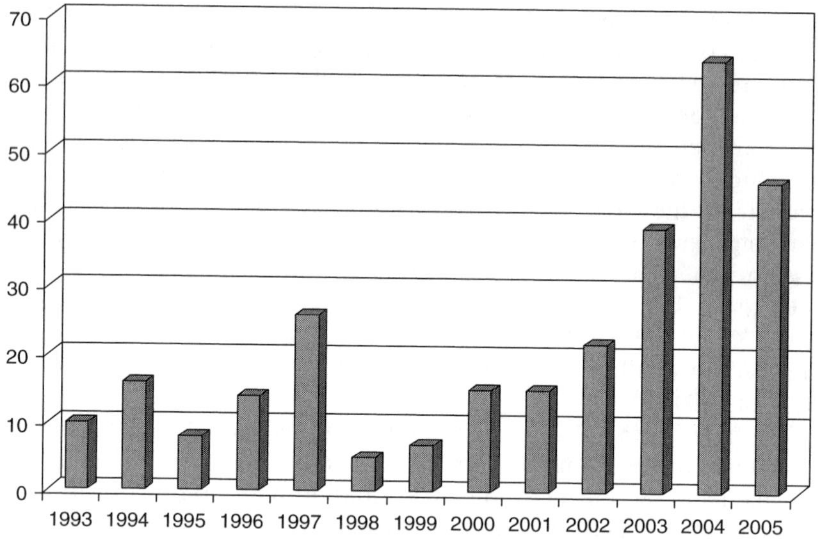

Figure 11.1 Number of Chinese companies listed in Hong Kong, the US, Singapore and London

Kong over other locations appears to be its geographic proximity, sharing the same language and culture. Of the 120 companies listed in Hong Kong, 32 are also listed on one of the two exchanges in mainland China: Shanghai or Shenzhen. Additionally, 12 of those listed in Hong Kong have dual listing in the United States and five have dual listing in London.

By the end of 2005, the Singapore Exchange had attracted 92 Chinese companies, with 80 percent of them completed after 2002. These companies are mostly small- and medium-sized. In addition, 69 Chinese companies have tapped the US capital market with various depositary receipt programs, including private placements. By comparison, only six companies from China have been listed on the London Stock Exchange.

LISTING IN THE UNITED STATES

Listing on a prestigious stock exchange like the New York Stock Exchange (NYSE) and NASDAQ has become increasingly popular among the world's largest companies headquartered outside of the US. Cross-listing in the US commonly takes the form of an American depositary receipt (ADR), which is a kind of negotiable security traded in the US but represents a foreign company's publicly traded equity. ADRs are created when a broker purchases the non-US company's shares on the home stock market and delivers those to the depositary's local custodian bank, which then instructs the depositary bank (such as the Bank of New York) to issue depositary receipts. In addition, depositary receipts may trade freely, just like any other securities, either on an exchange or in the over-the-counter market and can be used to raise capital.

While most investors recognize the benefits of global diversification, they also understand the challenges presented when investing directly in local trading markets. These obstacles include market segmentation, inefficient trade settlements, uncertain custody services and costly currency conversions. For instance, the Chinese domestic A-share market had been closed to foreign investors until 2003 when the government allowed qualified foreign institutional investors that satisfy designated qualifications to invest directly in China's A-share market.

Depositary receipts overcome many of the inherent operational and custodial hurdles of international investing. In fact, cost-benefits and conveniences may be realized through depositary receipt investing, thus allowing those who invest internationally to achieve the benefits of global diversification without increasing expense and complexities of investing directly in the local trading markets. Investors' desire to diversify their portfolios, reduce risk and invest internationally in the most efficient manner attributes to the increasing demand for ADRs.

DR Programs in the United States

Today, more than 2000 foreign companies from over 70 countries have established depositary receipt programs in the US. Depositary receipt programs may be unsponsored and sponsored. Unsponsored depositary receipts are issued by one or more depositaries in response to market demand, but without a formal agreement with the company. Today, unsponsored depositary receipts are considered obsolete and are rarely established due to lack of control over the facility and potential hidden costs.

Sponsored depositary receipts are issued in different 'levels' available in various trading markets by one depositary institution appointed by the company under a Deposit Agreement or service contract. Sponsored depositary receipts offer control over the facility, the flexibility to list on a US or European stock exchange and the ability to raise capital.

Table 11.3 summarizes the characteristics of the four DR programs in the US. It shows three levels of commitment, distinguished by the necessary accounting standards, SEC registration requirement, regular reporting requirements, time to completion, and where they are traded.

A sponsored Level I depositary receipt program is the simplest method for companies to access the US and non-US capital markets. Level I depositary

Table 11.3 Characteristics of depositary receipt programs in the United States

	Level I	Level II	Level III	144a
Public or private	Public	Public	Public	Private
Primary exchange	OTC 'Pink Sheets'	NYSE, Amex, or NASDAQ	NYSE, Amex, or NASDAQ	PORTAL
Accounting standards	Home country standards	US GAAP	US GAAP	Home country standards
SEC registration	Form F-6	Full registration (Form F-6)	Full registration (Form F-1 and F-6)	Exempt
US reporting requirements	Exempt under Rule 12g 3-2(b)	Required (Form F-20)	Required (Form F-20)	Exempt under Rule 12g 3-2(b)
Share issuance	Existing shares only	Existing shares only	New equity capital raised	New equity capital raised
Time to completion	10 weeks	10 weeks	14 weeks	16 days

Source: Excerpted from www.adr.com, a joint project of J. P. Morgan Chase Bank and Thomson Financial, and *Global Offerings of Depositary Receipts, A Transaction Guide* 1995, The Bank of New York.

receipts are traded in the US over-the-counter (OTC) market with prices published in the 'Pink Sheets' and on some exchanges outside the US. Establishment of a Level I program does not require full SEC registration and the company does not have to report its accounts under US Generally Accepted Accounting Principles (GAAP). In essence, a sponsored Level I depositary receipt program allows foreign companies to enjoy the benefits of a publicly traded securities in the US without changing its current reporting process.

The sponsored Level I depositary receipt market is the fastest growing segment of the depositary receipt business. The majority of sponsored programs are Level I facilities. In addition, because of the benefits of depositary receipt investing, it is not unusual for a company with a Level I program to obtain 5 percent to 15 percent of its shareholder base in depositary receipt form. Many well-known multinationals have established such programs. In addition, numerous companies have started with a Level I program and then upgraded to a Level II or Level III program.

Level II applies to companies that wish to list their existing shares on the NYSE, American stock exchange (Amex), or Nasdaq markets. On the other hand, Level III depositary receipt programs are associated with offerings of new shares and as a result, generate the most interest for US investors. Both Level II and III DR programs must meet the full registration requirements of the SEC. This means reconciling their financial accounts with those under the US GAAP, which raises the cost considerably. In general, companies that choose either a Level II or Level III program will attract a significant number of US investors. These types of depositary receipts can also be listed on some exchanges outside the US simultaneously.

In addition to the three levels of sponsored depositary receipt programs that trade publicly in the US, a foreign company can also access the US and other capital markets through the SEC Rule 144a and/or SEC Regulation S depositary receipt facilities without SEC registration.

The SEC adopted its Rule 144a in 1990. This rule permits qualified institutional buyers (QIBs) to trade privately placed securities without the previous holding period restrictions and without requiring SEC registration. A qualified institutional buyer is an entity (except a bank or a savings and loan institution) that owns and invests on a discretionary basis US$100 million in securities of non-affiliates. The SEC has estimated that about 4000 QIBs exist, mainly investment advisors, investment companies, insurance companies, pension funds, and charitable institutions. Simultaneously, the SEC modified its Regulation S to permit foreign issuers to tap the US private placement market through an SEC Rule 144a issue, also without SEC registration. Regulation S programs provide for raising capital through the placement of depositary receipts offshore to non-US investors in reliance on Regulation S.

Rule 144a is developed based on the premise that large, sophisticated investors could look out for themselves and because the US wants to attract more international issuers to its capital markets. Since SEC registration has been identified as the main barrier to foreign issuers wishing to raise funds in the US, Rule 144a placements are proving attractive to foreign issuers of both equity and debt. In fact, this rule has helped many foreign companies that wish to tap the US market but do not want to incur the accounting and legal expenses and to be committed to US disclosure requirements. Such issuers can arrange a private placement to sell their unregistered shares to qualified institutional investors.

A screen-based automated trading system called PORTAL has been established by the National Association of Securities Dealers (NASD) to support the distribution of primary shares and to create a liquid secondary market for these unregistered private placements.

Underwriting Process in the United States

In the investment banking business, underwriting is the process of assuring the issuing firm that an offering will take place for a specified number of shares at a specified price per share. In the US, underwriting is done by forming a syndicate of investment banks that will agree to purchase the entire offering from the issuer and resell the shares immediately to the investors. The new share offering process officially begins with what is typically called an 'all hands' meeting. At this meeting, all members of the team, including the lead underwriter, the accounting firm and the law firm, plan a timetable for the deal and assign duties to each member. If registration with the SEC is needed, the firm must file a preliminary prospectus with the SEC to meet the disclosure requirements. The prospectus must contain, among many other things, a suggested offer price range. The setting of this price range should represent a 'bona fide estimate' of the final offer price based on the expected demand for the deal and other market conditions.

While the filing is being reviewed by the SEC, the issuing company and its underwriters conduct road shows to present the issue to prospective investors. Meanwhile, the underwriters solicit information from their regular clients through non-binding indications of interest. Information gathered in this process will be used to fine-tune the final offer price. At this stage, the customers are not committed to purchase shares unless they accept the final offer price. When demand for the issue is greater than expected, the final offer price will be adjusted upward. Alternatively, if demand is low, the final offer price will be adjusted downward. This process is called 'book building' and is essential to precise pricing efforts. Once the shares are allocated to investors at the offer price on the offer date (typically after the market close), the shares will start trading on the very next day. On Wall Street, a successful priced issue is one in which the entire issue is sold out at the final offer price and the issue opens for trading at a premium of around 10 percent. That is, the offer price is set below the projected market price when the shares are open to the public on the first day of trading. The underwriting syndicate in such an issue is exposed to only a minimal holding period between the purchase from the issuing firm and the confirmation of sales with customers.

Many underwriting agreements contain a 'Green Shoe' provision, which gives the members of the underwriting syndicate the option to buy additional shares at the offer price. The stated reason for the Green Shoe option is to cover excess demand and oversubscription. Green Shoe options usually last for 30 days and involve no more than 15 percent of the newly issued shares. The Green Shoe provision is a benefit to the underwriters and a cost to the issuer. If the market price of the new issue goes above the offer price within 30 days, the underwriters can buy additional shares from the issuer and immediately resell the shares to the public.

The difference between the offer price and the underwriters' buying price is called the underwriting spread. This spread represents the fees paid to underwriters for their underwriting commitment. For a typical issue in the US, the underwriting spread is 7 percent, though it may vary depending on the size of the issue. Large issues can have lower underwriting spread.

As an example, consider the initial public offering of the China National Offshore Oil Corp. (CNOOC) on 20 February 2001. The deal was completed with a simultaneous dual listing on the Hong Kong Exchange and the NYSE, raising US$1430 million. The tombstone advertisement for this deal appeared in *The Wall Street Journal* the next day. The total number of shares sold is 1 856 589 900. Shares offered in Hong Kong are priced at HK$6.01 while the ADRs are offered at US$15.40. Since each ADR represents 20 shares, after adjusting for this ratio and the exchange rate, the two offer prices are identical. On the first day of trading, the close price of the ADR is US$16.12, giving initial investors a first-day return of 4.68 percent.

The three lead underwriters in this deal (called joint global coordinators and joint bookrunners) are BOC International, Credit Suisse First Boston and Merrill Lynch.

There are several methods for achieving international distribution of new issues of equity securities. Issuers may tap foreign equity markets through an international tranche to supplement domestic market liquidity. US companies have been common users of this approach, in which they set aside a proportion of the total shares to be offered to the international tranche that is reserved exclusively for overseas investors while the remaining shares are issued simultaneously in the US domestic market at the same offer price.

There is an equity equivalent of the Eurobond market, called the 'Euroequity' market, that can be used when an issuer wishes to tap a different and larger investor base because its domestic market is too small to absorb the issue or as a way to avoid domestic market regulations and expenses. Privatization issues of large government-owned industrial companies from Western Europe and many emerging markets typically fall into this category because of their large size and the need to attract international institutional investors.

Some of the large Euroequity issues are in reality global equity issues, in which separate but simultaneous tranches are offered worldwide. For example, in July 1993 the Argentine YPF issue raised US$2.76 billion through simultaneous offerings in the Euro-equity market, the US market, and the domestic Argentine market.

ADR Programs Established by Chinese Companies

Based on the comprehensive ADR data base provided by the Bank of New York, by the end of 2005, there are altogether 69 DR programs from China, of which 34 are listed on the NYSE and NASDAQ (Level II or III), 24 are listed on the OTC market (Level I), eight are Rule 144a private issues, and three are unspecified.

Table 11.4 shows the companies listed on NYSE/NASDAQ. The 17 companies listed on the NYSE are mostly large state-owned enterprises that have been privatized through initial public offerings. SINOPEC Shanghai Petrochemical Company is the first Chinese company to tap the US market, which launched its ADR program on the NYSE on 23 July 1993.

On the other hand, the 17 NASDAQ-listed companies are overwhelmingly young, high-tech oriented and are from the private sector. This is consistent with the general pattern in terms of the types of companies listed on NASDAQ. Many analysts argue that NASDAQ investors are more familiar with high-tech stocks and thus listing on NASDAQ can achieve a better valuation for such stocks. For example, Baidu.com – the Chinese Internet search engine – went public on 4 August 2005 by issuing 4 million ADRs offered at US$27 per ADR on the NASDAQ. On the first day of trading, the stock was opened at US$66 and closed at US$122.54.

Though the number of Chinese ADRs has increased in recent years, not a single large state-owned enterprise has raised capital on the NYSE or any other US exchange since late 2003 when China Life Insurance Co. raised US$3.5 billion with a dual listing in Hong Kong and NYSE.

The decline in the number of Chinese state-owned enterprises listing on the NYSE in recent years is largely due to the passage of the Sarbanes-Oxley Act in 2002. This act is intended to enforce corporate governance of public companies traded in the US. The law, among other things, requires CEOs and CFOs to sign off on the accuracy of their companies' financial statements. As such, it has made listing on US exchanges more onerous and expensive. The effect of the new law was reinforced in March 2004 by a class-action lawsuit brought in New York against state-owned China Life. The lawsuit alleges that the firm's officers and directors failed to adequately disclose 'massive financial fraud' at China Life's parent company, China Life Insurance (Group) Corp.

The Sarbanes-Oxley Act and the China Life class-action lawsuit have prompted large state-owned companies to seek listing solely in Hong Kong. For instance, China Construction Bank, whose US$8 billion offering in October 2005 was the world's largest IPO of the year, chose to list its shares only in Hong Kong, as the Bank of Communications did in June of the same year.

Table 11.4 China-based companies listed on NYSE and NASDAQ

DR issuer	Symbol	Capital raised (Yes/No)	Exchange	Depositary bank	Effective date
SINOPEC Shanghai Petrochemical Co., Ltd	SHI	No	NYSE	BNY	July 23, 1993
Jilin Chemical Industrial Co., Ltd	JCC	No	NYSE	BNY	May 19, 1995
Guangshen Railway Co., Ltd	GSH	No	NYSE	MGT	May 16, 1996
China Eastern Airlines Corp., Ltd	CEA	No	NYSE	BNY	January 30, 1997
China Mobile (HK) Ltd	CHL	Yes	NYSE	BNY	October 16, 1997
China Southern Airlines Co., Ltd	ZNH	No	NYSE	BNY	July 24, 1997
Yanzhou Coal Mining Co., Ltd	YZC	No	NYSE	BNY	March 27, 1998
Brilliance China Automotive Holdings Ltd	CBA	No	NYSE	BNY	April 17, 2000
China Petroleum & Chemical Corp.	SNP	Yes	NYSE	CIT	October 18, 2000
China Unicom Ltd	CHU	Yes	NYSE	BNY	June 16, 2000
PetroChina Co., Ltd	PTR	Yes	NYSE	BNY	March 30, 2000
Aluminum Corporation of China	ACH	Yes	NYSE	BNY	December 05, 2001
CNOOC – China National Offshore Oil Corp	CEO	Yes	NYSE	MGT	February 20, 2001
China Telecom Corp., Ltd	CHA	Yes	NYSE	BNY	November 06, 2002
China Life Insurance Co., Ltd	LFC	Yes	NYSE	MGT	December 17, 2003
Huaneng Power International, Inc.	HNP	No	NYSE	BNY	August 19, 2003
Suntech Power Holdings Co., Ltd	STP	Yes	NYSE	BNY	December 13, 2005
Netease.com, Inc.	NTES	Yes	NASDAQ	BNY	June 29, 2000
Ctrip.com International, Ltd	CTRP	Yes	NASDAQ	BNY	December 12, 2003

Table 11.4 (continued)

DR issuer	Symbol	Capital raised (Yes/No)	Exchange	Depositary bank	Effective date
51JOB, Inc.	JOBS	Yes	NASDAQ	MGT	October 04, 2004
China Finance Online Co., Ltd	JRJC	Yes	NASDAQ	MGT	October 20, 2004
eLong, Inc.	LONG	Yes	NASDAQ	MGT	November 02, 2004
Linktone Ltd	LTON	Yes	NASDAQ	BNY	March 09, 2004
Ninetowns Digital World Trade Holding Ltd	NINE	Yes	NASDAQ	MGT	December 08, 2004
Shanda Interactive Entertainment Ltd	SNDA	Yes	NASDAQ	BNY	May 17, 2004
The9 Ltd	NCTY	Yes	NASDAQ	BNY	December 14, 2004
Tom Online Inc.	TOMO	Yes	NASDAQ	CIT	March 11, 2004
Actions Semiconductor Co.	ACTS	Yes	NASDAQ	MGT	December 05, 2005
Baidu.com, Inc.	BIDU	Yes	NASDAQ	BNY	August 04, 2005
China Medical Technologies	CMED	Yes	NASDAQ	CIT	August 15, 2005
China Techfaith Wireless Communication Ltd	CNTF	Yes	NASDAQ	BNY	May 05, 2005
Focus Media Holding Ltd	FMCN	Yes	NASDAQ	CIT	July 18, 2005
Hurray!Holding Co., Ltd	HRAY	Yes	NASDAQ	CIT	February 04, 2005
Vimicro International Corp.	VIMC	Yes	NASDAQ	MGT	November 18, 2005

Source: Bank of New York's web site (www.adrbny.com). Depositary institutions: BNY – Bank of New York; CIT – Citibank; MGT – Morgan Guaranty Trust.

LISTING ON THE HONG KONG EXCHANGE

In July 1993, mainland China-based companies were allowed to list on the Hong Kong Exchange and Tsingtao Brewery became the first state-owned enterprise to be listed there. The shares issued in Hong Kong are commonly named H-shares.

The Hong Kong market is a natural venue for many companies from mainland China because of its geographic proximity. There are two trading platforms of the Hong Kong securities market: the Main Board and the

Growth Enterprise Market. The Main Board is a market for capital formation by established companies with a profitable operating track record or companies meeting alternative financial standards to profit requirement. The Growth Enterprise Market (GEM) is an alternative market established in November 1999 to provide capital formation opportunities for growth companies from all industries and of all sizes.

The listing standards on the Main Board are higher than those on the GEM. To be considered for listing on the Main Board, companies must have a track record of at least three years (with exceptions in certain circumstances). In the case of new applicants to be listed under the 'profit test', the new applicants must have recorded a profit of HK$20 million in the most recent financial year and an aggregate profit of HK$30 million in the two preceding financial years. In the other cases where new applicants are to be listed under 'the market capitalization/revenue test' or the 'market capitalization/revenue/cash flow test', the new applicants must comply with the alternative financial standards tests, including revenue requirement, such as the new applicants must be able to generate substantial revenues for the most recent audited financial year.

Recently, the Hong Kong Exchange has lowered its standards to attract more mainland companies. In April 2004, it changed its listing rules to exempt main-board applicants from the need to show a track record of profitability if they have a market capitalization of at least HK$4 billion and annual sales of HK$500 million.

On the other hand, the GEM does not have a profit record or revenue or other financial standard requirements but companies must have had active business pursuits for the 24 months before listing application (a 12-month active business period is acceptable for companies that can meet certain conditions of size and public shareholding).

The equity raising activities by companies from mainland China are summarized in Table 11.5. By the end of 2005, a total of 120 Chinese companies had been listed on the Hong Kong Exchange. Eighty of them are listed on the Main Board, raising a total capital of HK$362 889.69 million in the initial public offerings (IPOs) and HK$45 939.22 million after the IPOs. Forty companies from mainland China are listed on the GEM, raising HK$5603.98 million through IPO and post-IPO activities.

The market capitalization of China-related companies on the Hong Kong Exchange and their market shares are shown in Table 11.6. The market share of the H-shares has increased to 15.78 percent in 2005 from only 0.61 percent in 1993. If Red chips are included, the market share of China-related stocks exceeded one-third on the Main Board by the end of 2005.

Table 11.5 IPOs and equity funds raised by mainland China-based companies in Hong Kong

Year	Main board				Growth Enterprise Market (GEM)			
	N	IPOs (millions HK$)	Post IPOs (millions HK$)	Total (millions HK$)	N	IPOs (millions HK$)	Post IPOs (millions HK$)	Total (millions HK$)
1993	6	8141.52	–	8141.52	–	–	–	–
1994	9	9879.81	–	9879.81	–	–	–	–
1995	2	2011.35	980.00	2991.35	–	–	–	–
1996	6	6834.16	1037.50	7871.66	–	–	–	–
1997	16	32 037.52	1046.70	33 084.23	–	–	–	–
1998	2	2072.36	1480.16	3552.52	–	–	–	–
1999	3	4263.69	–	4263.69	–	–	–	–
2000	3	51 750.69	–	51 750.69	3	644.18	–	644.18
2001	3	5570.84	497.25	6068.09	5	763.99	–	763.99
2002	4	16 873.60	–	16 873.60	12	1059.60	113.00	1172.60
2003	10	46 252.59	592.04	46 844.63	8	1217.91	204.00	1421.91
2004	8	40 016.78	19 229.95	59 246.73	9	693.60	459.33	1152.93
2005	9	137 184.78	21 075.62	158 260.40	3	175.48	272.90	448.37
Total	80	362 889.69	45 939.22	408 828.92	40	4554.76	1049.23	5603.98

Source: Hong Kong Exchanges and Clearing Ltd. Website: www.hkex.com.hk. This table does not include the so-called Red chips, or shares of Chinese companies registered overseas but listed in Hong Kong.

LISTING ON THE SINGAPORE EXCHANGE (SGX)

The Singapore Exchange (SGX) was inaugurated on 1 December 1999, following the merger of two established and well-respected financial institutions – the Stock Exchange of Singapore (SES) and the Singapore International Monetary Exchange (SIMEX). The SGX divides its company listings into the SGX Mainboard and the SGX SESDAQ. The Mainboard lists companies that meet certain requirements including market capitalization, pre-tax profits, and an operating track record. The SESDAQ, on the other hand, is for newer companies and there are no quantitative requirements for listing. Companies listed on the SESDAQ may apply to be moved to the Mainboard if they have been listed for at least two years and meet the minimum quantitative requirements.

The Singapore Exchange, which received its first overseas application from a Hong Kong company in 1993, has made tremendous efforts to become an international one over the past decade. Singapore had accepted 176 foreign listing companies by the end of 2004, accounting for 27 percent

Table 11.6 Market capitalization of China-related companies on the Hong Kong exchange

Year-end	Main board					
	H shares		Red chips		All	
	Market capitalization (HK$ million)	Market (%)	Market capitalization (HK$ million)	Market (%)	Market capitalization (HK$ million)	Market (%)
1993	18 228.70	0.61	124 129.51	4.17	142 358.21	4.78
1994	19 981.32	0.96	84 279.33	4.04	104 260.65	5.00
1995	16 463.77	0.70	110 701.97	4.71	127 165.74	5.42
1996	31 530.63	0.91	263 330.90	7.58	294 861.53	8.48
1997	48 622.01	1.52	472 970.42	14.77	521 592.43	16.29
1998	33 532.66	1.26	334 966.21	12.58	368 498.87	13.84
1999	41 888.78	0.89	956 942.33	20.24	998 831.11	21.13
2000	85 139.58	1.78	1 203 551.95	25.10	1 288 691.53	26.87
2001	99 813.09	2.57	908 854.82	23.39	1 008 667.91	25.96
2002	129 248.37	3.63	806 407.41	22.66	935 655.78	26.29
2003	403 116.50	7.36	1 197 770.75	21.87	1 600 887.25	29.23
2004	455 151.75	6.87	1 409 357.12	21.26	1 864 508.88	28.13
2005	1 280 495.01	15.78	1 709 960.75	21.08	2 990 455.76	36.86
Growth Enterprise Market (GEM)						
1999	–	–	1255.50	17.35	1255.50	17.35
2000	991.69	1.47	806.00	1.20	1797.69	2.67
2001	1888.75	3.10	1010.60	1.66	2899.35	4.76
2002	2393.01	4.58	830.80	1.59	3223.81	6.17
2003	5063.25	7.21	–	–	5063.25	7.21
2004	6376.35	9.56	727.56	1.09	7103.92	10.65
2005	6420.65	9.64	836.23	1.26	7256.88	10.90

Source: Hong Kong Exchanges and Clearing Ltd. Website: www.hkex.com.hk.

of its total of 625. By 2005, there are over 90 Chinese enterprises listed on the Singapore Exchange. Of the total number of foreign companies listed in Singapore, Chinese companies represent the largest percentage.

However, the recent financial scandal surrounding Singapore-listed China Aviation Oil (CAO) has raised significant concerns over transparency and accountability of mainland China-based companies. China Aviation Oil hit the headlines in November 2004 when it appealed to Singapore's High Court for protection from creditors after losing US$550 million in speculative oil derivatives trading. With a monopoly on importing jet fuel into China's booming aviation industry and having the backing of the Chinese government through a state-run firm owning a majority stake, China Aviation Oil was the darling of investors. Indeed, the Securities Investors Association of Singapore, which acts as a watchdog for small investors, gave China Aviation Oil its 'Most Transparent Company' award in 2003.

The CAO scandal highlights the risks surrounding many mainland China-based and mainland China-related companies as a result of limited transparency. Mainland Chinese companies venturing overseas go to great lengths to appear as if they have the same strict corporate governance standards as those in developed economies, but the changes are often merely cosmetic.

Despite the CAO scandal, lots of Chinese firms remain interested in listing in Singapore. This interest stems from their need to attract huge amounts of funds to sustain their growth momentum. Singapore provides a good alternative to Hong Kong, as these companies find it difficult to get domestic listings due to poor market conditions and regulatory restrictions.

To be sure, Hong Kong is still the preferred market for these Chinese companies. The main reason they come to Singapore is because the pipeline in Hong Kong is full. Hong Kong is preferred because of investment interest in China stocks. Being a bigger and deeper market, Hong Kong, in addition to local funds, also attracts money from all over the world. That in turn attracts more good quality companies to list in Hong Kong despite it having a more stringent set of requirements than those in Singapore.

Nevertheless, Singapore has the niche for smaller companies. The average market capitalization of the China companies listed in Hong Kong is some ten times that of those listed in Singapore.

LISTING ON THE LONDON STOCK EXCHANGE

The London Stock Exchange (LSE) is one of the world's oldest stock exchanges and can trace its history back more than 300 years. Over the centuries following, the LSE has consistently led the way in developing a strong, well-regulated stock market and today lies at the heart of the global financial community.

To lure more Chinese companies, the LSE opened its first Asia-Pacific regional office in Hong Kong in October 2004. The new office demonstrates the Exchange's commitment to the Asia Pacific region, and will enable the Exchange to get closer to its existing Asian customers and to attract further Asian companies to London. With its Hong Kong office, the Exchange will be targeting large privatization deals and the flotations of other medium to large enterprises in China, and will also continue to promote dual listings in London and Hong Kong through a single prospectus.

Table 11.7 Chinese companies listed on the London Stock Exchange

Company	List date	Sector	Ordinary shares	Depositary receipts
Datang International Power Generation	20/3/1997	Electricity	YES	NO
Jiangxi Copper Co.	12/6/1997	Non-ferrous metals	YES	NO
Zhejiang Southeast Electric Power	23/9/1997	Electricity	NO	YES
Zhejiang Express Co.	5/5/2000	Other construction	YES	NO
China Petroleum & Chemical Corp.	18/10/2000	Chemicals	NO	YES
Air China	15/12/2004	Airlines and airports	YES	NO

Source: London Stock Exchange web site (www.londonstockexchange.com).

Despite its efforts, only six relatively small Chinese companies have been listed on the LSE by the end of 2005 (see Table 11.7). The largest of them is China Petroleum & Chemical, which raised US$3.7 billion from a simultaneous listing in Hong Kong, NYSE and LSE in 2000.

The main problem with the LSE is that it has to compete with the Hong Kong and US markets. Initially, London sought to attract Chinese companies in tandem with the Hong Kong exchange. In 2002 the two exchanges announced an agreement in principle to facilitate dual listings by enabling Chinese issuers to tap both markets with a single prospectus. Hong Kong later pulled the plug on the effort in 2004, saying regulatory differences made a single prospectus unattainable.

RATIONALE FOR CROSS-LISTING

Raise Equity Capital

One of the most important objectives of cross-listing is to raise equity capital in the foreign markets. Quite often, firms domiciled in countries with small and illiquid capital markets often outgrow those markets and are forced to raise new capital abroad. Listing on a stock exchange in the market where the new capital is to be raised improves secondary market liquidity, which in turn encourages investors to continue to hold or trade these shares.

Improve Corporate Governance

One often cited motive for overseas listing is based on the agency theory of corporate finance. Researchers have provided evidence in support of the notion that non-US firms cross-list in the US to increase protection of their minority shareholders. Cross-listing on the NYSE or NASDAQ subjects a non-US firm to a number of provisions of US securities law, and requires the firm to conform to US generally accepted accounting principles. It increases the expected cost to managers of extracting private benefits, and commits the firm to protect minority shareholders' interests.

Indeed, corporate governance has been one of the biggest concerns to foreign investors interested in Chinese shares. The majority of China's listed companies are former state-owned enterprises (SOEs). It is hoped that through incorporation and listing, SEOs will finally be separated from the government. In the meantime, however, the government wants to retain share ownership in these companies and a majority shareholding in large companies. Government shares are retained in the state institutions and government departments and are non-tradable. At the national level, the State Council acts as the ultimate owner of SOEs on behalf of the Chinese people, with the State-Owned Property Bureau acting as the agent. Similar bodies exist in provinces and cities. An intermediate tier is composed of provincial- and municipal-level state-asset holding companies. In the new organizational structure, the lines of authority are unclear. In many cases, board members and senior executives are nominated by these government bodies. The lack of clear identification of the owners of government shares undermines corporate governance because it leaves open the issue of who should be monitoring the managers.

It is hoped that corporate governance will be improved through listing on an international exchange. Nevertheless, the CAO scandal in Singapore and the legal troubles of China Life Insurance in the US market highlight the challenges facing Chinese companies listed abroad. Chinese executives must realize that it is not good enough to just appear as if they have the same strict corporate governance standards as those in developed economies.

Overcoming Domestic Listing Restrictions

Another reason why companies choose to list abroad is that some, especially small companies, find it difficult to get domestic listings due to poor market conditions and regulatory restrictions. This is especially true of those that have been listed on the GEM in Hong Kong, the Singapore Exchange, and the OTC market in the US.

Chinese companies that seek a listing on the stock exchanges in Shanghai and Shenzhen need permission from the China Securities Regulatory Commission (CSRC). Small private companies are often discriminated against in favor of large SOEs. Companies that cannot go public in the domestic market have to seek overseas listings to meet their demand for capital.

POTENTIAL PROBLEMS OF CROSS-LISTING

While there are potential benefits to China-based companies listing on foreign exchanges, it is also important to understand the costs and drawbacks associated with overseas listing. The obvious costs include legal, auditing, listing fees, and underwriting fees. Indirect costs include managerial time and efforts to communicate to foreign investors. Other more serious problems are discussed below.

The Commitment to Disclosure and Investor Relations

To maintain a successful cross-listing, companies must commit to full disclosure and a continuing investor relations program. For example, the SEC's disclosure requirements for listing in the US are stringent and costly. Not only are the disclosure requirements stringent, but a continuous timely quarterly information is required by the SEC. Consequently, foreign companies must provide a continuous investor relations program for their US shareholders, including frequent road shows to present to major shareholders.

Class-action Lawsuits

Another unexpected problem is that listing on an international exchange, especially in the US, opens Chinese firms to a far more litigious investor base. China Life Insurance, for example, has been the target of class-action lawsuits on behalf of US shareholders accusing it of failing to disclose a state audit report that showed its predecessor firm breached insurance laws. Its stock price was punished on Wall Street immediately. Managers have admitted that they are unprepared for this kind of lawsuit.

In the wake of corporate scandals such as Enron and Worldcom, the US has adopted much tougher disclosure rules such as the Sarbanes-Oxley Act, which has been fully implemented since 2005. Though this act is intended to improve transparency and corporate governance, foreign firms with established ADR programs might find this corporate responsibility law very demanding and costly.

The Sarbanes-Oxley law and the specter of securities litigation have given pause to Chinese state-owned companies seeking US listing. Rather than list on a US exchange, some Chinese firms have chosen to open trading on a European market or launch in China's Hong Kong alone. A recent example is Air China, which in December 2004 became the first new Chinese company in four years to trade on the London Stock Exchange (LSE). LSE officials have been lobbying Chinese executives and government representatives to choose London over New York for listing their companies, arguing that the London exchange, Europe's largest, offers investors who are focused on international stocks and a regulatory structure that is not as stringent as the US market, given the tough accounting requirements of the Sarbanes-Oxley law.

Valuation Differences

Anyone familiar with the Chinese stock market is aware of the stylized fact that Chinese shares offered to foreign investors (B-shares, H-shares and depositary receipts) trade at a significant discount of the price of A-shares issued by the same company. The Chinese securities laws and regulations explicitly recognize the equal status of shareholders of different share classes of the same stock. For instance, before 19 February 2001 when the China Securities Regulatory Commission allowed Chinese residents to own B-share classes of stock on both the Shanghai and Shenzhen stock markets, on average the A-share price is more than four times that of the B-share price, implying a B-share discount of 75 percent. These shares were previously restricted to foreign investors while domestic investors were only permitted to hold A-shares. Though the regulatory change triggered a dramatic decline of the B-share discount, the discount is still prevailing and significant today.

Similarly, Chinese shares traded in Hong Kong (H-shares) are also traded at a discount of comparable A-shares. The case for ADRs is similar since the Hong Kong market is fully integrated with the US capital market and arbitrage activities ensure that the prices of H-shares and ADRs are the same after adjustment of the ADR ratio and the exchange rate.

This discount is puzzling since the financial literature has documented overwhelming evidence from almost all other countries that shares offered to foreign investors typically trade at a premium, not a discount. For example, researchers find that in general, foreign firms listed in the US are worth more than similar companies listed only in the domestic market.

Chinese shares seem to be a notable exception. The prevailing price discount of shares offered to foreign investors relative to A-shares has been a significant challenge to researchers, regulators, investors as well as issuing firms. Researchers have put forward several potential explanations, including a potential information advantage of Chinese domestic investors, illiquidity, speculation premium for A-share markets and differential demand. The price discount implies that, compared to overseas listing and new equity offering, they could have received a high valuation had they limited their issues to the A-share market.

Why would Chinese firms raise capital in the US at a cheaper price while they can stay in China and issue new shares at a much higher price? One possibility is that the issue is too large to be absorbed in the Chinese domestic market. To be sure, many of the ADRs from China are large state-owned enterprises. The largest issuer, China Unicom, raised a total amount of US$1573.9 million in the US alone, followed by China Life Insurance with a US$1208.7 million ADR offering at the end of 2003. But other offerings are moderate in size. The smallest ADR program, established by Ctrip.com International in 2003, raised only US$75.6 million in equity capital.

This puzzle remains unsolved. It is worth pointing out that the foreign share discount could be significantly reduced once the highly anticipated Qualified Domestic Institutional Investors (QDII) scheme becomes effective. It is well known that the strict exchange and capital control measures imposed by the Chinese government have long prohibited Chinese investors from investing in international capital markets. The QDII scheme is designed to allow qualified domestic investors such as insurance companies and mutual funds to purchase shares in Hong Kong, New York or elsewhere.

The QDII scheme can potentially increase the demand for H-shares and global depositary receipts issued by China-based companies. This will help narrow the gap between the prices of domestic A-share classes and global shares of the same listed companies and thus give more companies the incentive to seek international listing.

CONCLUDING REMARKS

Today, Chinese companies have more alternatives when seeking foreign equity capital, thanks to the increasing demand for Chinese shares by international investors and fierce competition among major foreign exchanges to lure Chinese companies. The costs and benefits of overseas listing and capital raising activities must be fully understood before a firm chooses to list on a foreign exchange.

The US market is the most prestigious but the accounting standards and disclosure requirements are very stringent and costly. The NYSE has been the top choice for large state-owned companies until the introduction of the Sarbanes-Oxley law. Yet young and high-tech oriented companies from the private sector continue to seek listing on the NASDAQ market. This pattern is consistent with the general trend that most young and high-tech firms from other countries also choose NASDAQ over the NYSE.

The Hong Kong market offers unique advantages over others, including geographical proximity, sharing the same culture and language. As a result, Hong Kong investors are more familiar with mainland Chinese firms than are US investors. In recent years, the Hong Kong exchange has shown flexibility such as reducing the listing standards in order to attract more mainland companies.

The number of Chinese companies listed on the Singapore Exchange has increased dramatically in recent years. The SGX has developed itself as a niche market for small- and medium-sized companies from China.

At the same time, other major international exchanges such as the London Stock Exchange, the Tokyo Stock Exchange and the Toronto Exchange have all reached out to China with specific plans. But they have met with very limited success.

As an alternative to formal listing on foreign exchanges, companies can tap the private market through Rule 144a private placements of stock in the US. According to this special SEC provision, foreign companies can raise capital by selling equity to qualified institutional investors while at the same time they can circumvent the SEC disclosure requirements and the Sarbanes-Oxley act altogether.

With the introduction of the Qualified Foreign Institutional Investor (QFII) scheme in late 2002, foreign investors that satisfy designated qualifications can invest directly in China's A-share market. This scheme allows Chinese companies to attract foreign capital without being listed on an international exchange. Regulations covering QFIIs were issued jointly by the CSRC and the People's Bank of China on 7 November 2002 and went into effect on 1 December. According to the provisional measures, QFIIs can invest through initial public offerings, additional share offerings, rights issues, and convertible bond offerings.

On the other hand, the highly anticipated Qualified Domestic Institutional Investor (QDII) scheme will allow qualified domestic investors to purchase shares in Hong Kong, New York or elsewhere. This scheme, once formalized, can significantly reduce the price discount of global shares relative to domestic A-shares of the same listed companies, giving more companies the incentive to list abroad.

No matter where they list, Chinese firms seeking listings on international exchanges must be committed to addressing investors' concerns over accountability, transparency and corporate governance. Corporate governance has been one of the biggest concerns to foreign investors interested in Chinese shares. Shareholder wealth maximization has been widely accepted around the globe as the ultimate goal of management. Chinese companies should learn a lesson from the China Aviation Oil scandal in Singapore and the legal troubles of China Life Insurance in the US market. They must understand that protection of minority shareholders' interests is crucial to a successful overseas listing.

12. Privatization, corporate structure, market transparency and capital markets

Kam C. Chan, Hung-gay Fung and Qingfeng 'Wilson' Liu

INTRODUCTION

The capital market of a country is important because it facilitates efficient allocation of resources and provides an important mechanism whereby signals reflecting underlying information can be assessed by firms and investors. The competitiveness and efficiency of a financial market can be improved through two sources: a competitive goods market and removing market impediments or barriers of a financial market (Mehta and Fung 2004). A financial market is derived from a goods market. A competitive goods market would make the financial market more efficient and competitive. Thus, improving the working of the goods market will help the financial market. Second, removal of financial market impediments or barriers helps a smooth functioning of a financial market and market participants are able to enter and exit the financial market. Consequently, the efficiency of the financial market improves.

This chapter examines how China can improve its goods market. It also discusses various ways to mitigate market impediments in China's financial market. It focuses our attention on China's privatization programs that improves efficiency of Chinese firms. Many state-owned firms were inefficient under China's centrally planned economy before its economic reforms in 1978. The state-owned firms had monopolistic market power and they had no incentive to improve their efficiency. China's privatization programs implemented in the mid-1980s were an important step in getting rid of inefficient state-owned firms. An important process of the privatization program is through the market of mergers and acquisitions (M&As). As privatized firms require external funding for growth and expansion, China will need to provide a sufficient supply of private funds to these small and medium sized private firms by setting up another market of state or privately owned venture capital.

A competitive M&A market is important in mitigating agency problems within the firm (Jensen and Meckling 1976). An active M&A market can replace inefficient incumbent managers with good managers and thus correct underpricings of a financial market. It is clearly seen that active mergers and acquisitions in the 1980s in the US has improved the financial performance of the stock market in the US. China's M&A market through privatization, however, has its own problems despite viewing a transformation of state-owned enterprises to privately own enterprises as successful. We analyse the M&A structure related to China's privatization programs in the following section. It is critical that China establishes a vibrant and competitive M&A market in order to bring on a functioning capital market.

A poor corporate governance structure aggravates the agency cost of a firm because it lacks a well-established mechanism for checks and balances within the organization. We also discuss China's corporate governance structure in this chapter to illustrate issues of agency problems and expropriation of rights for minority stockholders. The conflict between majority and minority stockholders is common among Asian countries and China is no exception.

Having a healthy M&A market is only one facet of the story underlying a good financial market, while a sound corporate governance structure is equally important. The IT bubble in the early 2000s in the US and Enron's ongoing case in manipulating earnings figures illustrate other requirements in ensuring a good financial market besides a good corporate structure.

The traditional view in correcting overpricing of the financial market is through short sales of an asset. Speculators can gain through short sales if their assessments are correct about the overpricing of an asset. Financial theorists thus endorse the ability of short sales in a good, developed financial market. The IT industry in the US had been overpriced since early 2000. Such mispricing was not corrected until several years later after the burst of the IT bubble, leading to a general market downturn in the early 2000s. The unwillingness to short sale by some investors is the result of persistence of market sentiments demanding continued financial performance from the optimistic earnings forecasts. Stock market exuberance stems from a misaligned incentive system in which managers manipulate earnings figures, collusion between firms and analysts of brokerage firms in disclosing information, and investors' interest in short-term earnings as an indicator for success (Jensen 2005).

The lessons for Chinese policymakers' financial policies regarding its capital market are: to improve the transparency of firms, facilitate better disclosure to investors, discourage firms in undertaking earnings management for short-term gains, and to mitigate market impediments (such as regulatory constraints) inhibiting arbitrage. In this regard, we discuss recent developments in China's policies pertaining to corporate transparency, earnings practices and the importance of allowing short sale in the financial market.

M&A AND PRIVATIZATION PROGRAMS

In general, there are three types of mergers and acquisitions activities: inbound, outbound and domestic. An inbound M&A refers to a foreign firm acquiring a Chinese firm, while an outbound M&A refers to a Chinese firm acquiring a foreign firm. A domestic M&A refers to a Chinese firm acquiring another Chinese firm. Outbound M&As have been discussed elsewhere relating to qualified domestic institutional investor (QDII) programs and, thus, will not be analysed here. In the following sections of the chapter, we focus our analysis on domestic M&A and inbound M&A.

Conceptually, M&A activities allow acquirers to take over poorly performed firms and transform these firms into better economic units. In this process, the resources of the economy are allocated efficiently. Firms that are poorly managed and performed become merger and acquisition targets and ultimately ownership changes hands in an active market of corporate control. New owners change the ways of managing these merged firms and make the goods market become competitive and efficient. In a nutshell, M&A activities 'check and balance' firms' management. In the long run, an active M&A market enhances corporate performance and minimizes agency problems, which in turn leads to a more efficient goods market because firms are performing to their best potential.

In China, over the years, there were plenty of inbound and domestic M&As. According to the most recent data, there were 367 transactions worth $17.6 billion of inbound and 1155 transactions worth US$40.2 billion of domestic M&As in China between 1 January 2003 and 25 July 2005 (CSFB 2005). Figure 12.1 reports the year-on-year growth rates of nominal GDP and M&A activities from 1993 to 2004 in China as of September, 2005.[1] Overall, there is a negative correlation between GDP growth and M&A activities growth. This is expected because when the economy slows down, there will be more firms that find themselves mired in financial problems and become M&A targets, thereby boosting M&A activities.

M&A activities grew faster than the nominal GDP in 1995–2000, and reached a peak in 2000. But then they took a precipitous decline in 2001. Since then, the growth in M&As has been relatively stagnant as suggested

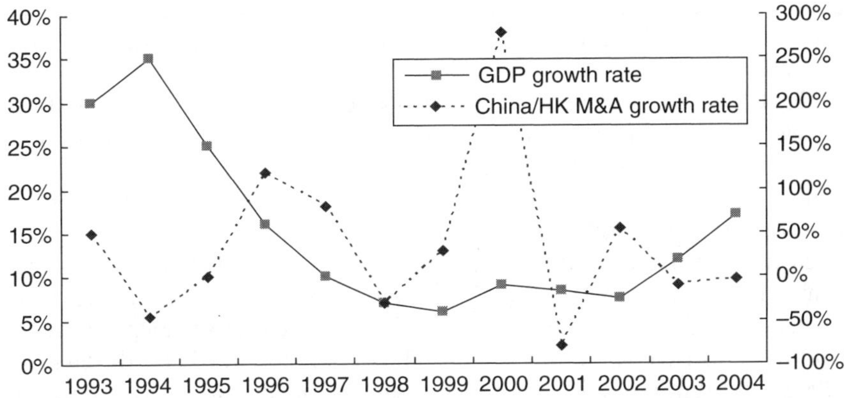

Source: CSFB (2005).

Figure 12.1 China's nominal GDP (left scale) versus M&A (right scale) growth rates

by a negative growth rate in 2003 and an almost zero growth rate in 2004. We attribute the recent slowdown in M&As in China to new (and ambiguous) rules and a general stock market downturn in recent years.

In China, M&A activities have certain unique features that deserve closer examination because China has been in the process of privatizing its state-owned enterprises through its economic reforms. The key to understanding China's M&A market is to understand to what extent the Chinese government intends to privatize its economy and also how the Chinese laws are enforced to accomplish the privatization programs. Thus, the practice of domestic M&A differs from those of the US and other countries as discussed in the following section.

Domestic Mergers and Acquisitions

In China's M&A activity, one striking feature is the dominance of acquisitions over mergers. As China wants to privatize its state-owned enterprises, two approaches have been widely used during its economic reforms. Initially, Chinese state-owned firms were sold to insiders through management buyout as demonstrated in the first wave of privatization. This practice raised serious debates as to whether state-assets were sold deliberately at depressed prices to managers of the firms, and at the same time, triggering huge layoffs of workers after the acquisitions. Second, the

Chinese state-owned firms were sold to outsiders through acquisitions (Fung *et al.* (2006) and Fung (2003)). These practices encourage acquisition over mergers.

The Chinese government opened two stock exchanges to privatize state-owned enterprises so that they can be listed on exchanges. Although these firms are publicly listed, a majority of shares are not tradable and controlled by state-shares (shares owned by the state-government). Listing requirements are tightly regimented to ensure quality of firms, giving rise to earnings management in order to be qualified to get listed. After listing, some of these firms may not be able to satisfy the two-year earning requirements, so they may be put into a special treatment (ST) category, where trading is restricted and they will face the threat of being delisted. Bai *et al.* (2005) find that the paid M&As[2] involving publicly traded firms and privately held firms are heavily motivated by the convenience of getting the privately held firms listing privilege on the stock exchange using the target firms as 'shells' for listing. That is, the M&As are used as a tool to circumvent a time consuming IPO application process in China. After the takeover, acquiring firms usually inject new assets into the new firms that are merged and thus the subsequent financial performance of these new firms is generally improved.

The size of domestic M&A differs from inbound M&As in several ways. First, there were more domestic M&A deals than inbound M&A deals during January 2003 to July 2005 as China intensified its privatization programs. Second, as reported in Bai *et al.* (2005) and Credit Suisse First Boston (CSFB) report (2005), the domestic M&A confined themselves to consolidation activities in fragmented sectors in China.

Inbound M&A

For inbound M&As, there are a number of legal complications. Crooke (2003) discusses the most recent Chinese M&A rules and how these rules may have complicated the M&A activities. The Ministry of Commerce (Mofcom) issued 'the Interim Provisions on the Acquisition of Domestic Enterprise by Foreign Investor' in March 2003 and these provisions became effective on 12 April 2003. The logic of these rules, for antitrust, is to protect the ownership of sensitive industries (for example, telecommunication and banking industries), and for investors and consumers protection in China.[3] According to Crooke, there are three major rules in the new 2003 M&A regulations.

First, a foreign firm must report to Mofcom and the State Administration of Industry and Commerce (SAIC) for approval in the M&As with a Chinese firm if one of the following conditions occur:

- the foreign firm has revenue in China that exceeds RMB 1.5 billion in the current year;
- the foreign firm has merged or acquired more than ten Chinese firms in the associated industry in the current year;
- the foreign firm and its affiliates have already had 20 percent of the market share in the industry; or
- the foreign firm and its affiliates will have 25 percent of market share after the M&A.

Second, the foreign firm has to notify the respective industry regulator before Mofcom and SAIC determine if the M&A will harm domestic competition and consumers. Thus, the respective industry regulators provide the first screening or hurdle in the inbound M&As. Third, the foreign firm may seek exemptions from the rules.

Crooke suggests that the new rules are likely to make the inbound M&As more complicated and there are a number of unanswered questions. Crooke points out some of the unanswered questions:

- How do Mofcom and SAIC determine the market share?
- What documents are required to file with the Mofcom, SAIC, and industry regulator?
- How much time do Mofcom and SAIC need to approve/reject the M&A? If rejected, what is the procedure for appeal?
- What are the standards for exemption?

The China's Securities Regulatory Commission (CSRC), regulator of China's securities market, has the power to approve a merger of a publicly traded firm with a foreign or a domestic firm. After the CSRC's approval, the Mofcom and SAIC then examine the M&A application, a prolonged process imposing higher cost to acquirers and slowing down the M&A activities in China. The process comes from a concern that foreign investors have monopolized many sectors of the Chinese markets in light of China's open-door policy, and it allows Chinese firms to have more time in adapting to the competitive and dynamic environment.

General Economic Issues

We explore two issues in this section. One is related to the pattern of M&A in industry. Second, we ask the question how M&A relates to the general market economy. Table 12.1 displays the top-five sectors in China/Hong Kong-related M&A. The results indicate the top-five outbound M&As are computers, retail, oil and gas, telecommunications and hand and machine tools (Panel A), while the inbound M&As are diversified financials, banks, cosmetics and personal care, beverages and transportation (Panel B). For the domestic M&As, the most important form of M&A is the holding companies as shown in Panel C. This result is not surprising because the holding companies have taken over some failing companies to keep them afloat and are likely to be related to state-owned companies because the Chinese government has been active in trying to consolidate many fragmented industries in different sectors.

Table 12.1 also shows the inbound M&A exceeds that of the domestic M&A, signifying the importance of foreign capital in China's market. The outbound M&As are primarily related to technology and R&A industries in that China wants to acquire those resources overseas.

How does the M&A activities in China relate to the stock market performance? We reproduce the relation between the China M&A activities

Table 12.1 Top-five sectors in China-Hong Kong-related M&A, September 2005

	Amount ($m)	% of Total
Panel A Outbound M&A		
Computers	1833	19.1
Retail	1140	11.9
Oil and Gas	891	9.3
Telecommunications	680	7.1
Hand and machine tools	639	6.7
All industries	*9590*	*100.0*
Panel B Inbound M&A		
Diversified Financials	2473	15.4
Banks	2368	14.8
Cosmetics and Personal Care	2000	12.5
Beverages	1377	8.6
Transportation	1107	6.9
All industries	*16037*	*100.0*
Panel C Domestic M&A		
Holding companies	2033	13.8
Electric utilities	985	6.7
Textiles	905	6.2
Real Estate	893	6.1
Retail	777	5.3
All industries	*14698*	*100.0*

Source: Thomson Financial, CSFB estimates from CSFB (2005).

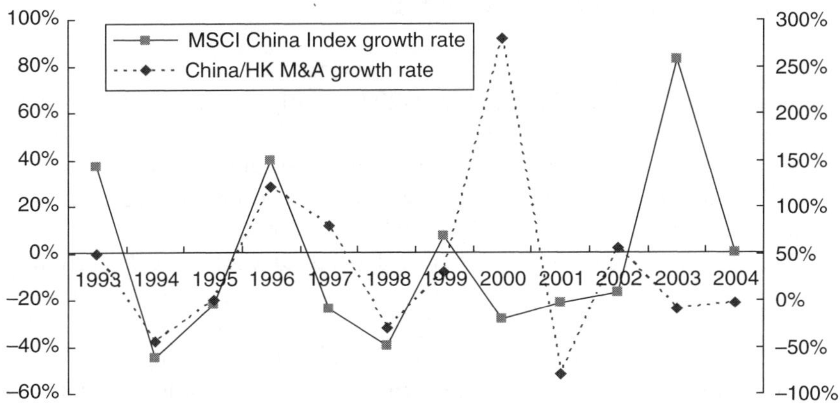

Source: CSFB (2005).

Figure 12.2 MSCI China index (left scale) versus M&A (right scale) growth rates

and Morgan Stanley Composite Index (China) from Credit Suisse First Boston report on China's M&As. Figure 12.2 shows the relations between China's M&A activities and stock market performance as reflected in the year-on-year changes in the Morgan Stanley Composite Index (China).

From 1993 to 1999, the graphical evidence suggests a high correlation between stock market performance and M&A activities as depicted in the high co-movement between the two curves. Given that many M&As are used as a shortcut to getting listed, stronger stock market performance increases the incentives for M&A and thus result in more M&A activities. Since 1999, however, such co-movement has become less conspicuous. That is, the relations between stock market performance and M&A seem to fade away in recent years, when the stock market experienced prolonged decline due to actual and rumored policy changes,[4] corporate scandals, macroeconomic adjustments, and other factors.

While the M&A growth rates in China became stagnant in the past few years, M&A activities in China were at a high level because of China's open-door liberalization policy. The new regulations passed in 2003 limit the size and quantity of inbound M&As. Domestic M&As related to the listing firms, the motivation for the acquirers, appear not to have enhanced the performance of target firms. Rather, it is related to having the ability to list on stock exchanges.

CORPORATE GOVERNANCE

A sound corporate governance practice monitors a firm's performance by reducing agency cost, and hence lowers the cost of capital. Ideally, a sound corporate governance practice follows a competitive goods market driving efficient allocation of scare resources. Corporate governance affects the general business climate and business culture in a country. Corporate governance issues share a number of related characteristics.

Lin (2004) summarizes seven major aspects of corporate governance. They are:

1. rights of shareholders and rules for shareholders' meetings;
2. duties and responsibilities of directors and independence of board of directors;
3. fiduciary duties;
4. performance assessments and incentive and disciplinary systems;
5. information disclosure and transparency;
6. insider information and related party transactions; and
7. the role of the auditor.

These features are a good benchmark for judging a country if there is good corporate governance structure in place.

Evolution and Development of China's Corporate Governance

There had been few corporate governance issues before China's economic reform started in 1978 because the government maintained full control of every aspect of operations in firms. As a market-based economic system gradually took root, it was common (and natural) to find that government officials and agents in the enterprises with monitoring and controlling powers were incapable of making timely and sound decisions in the face of the fast-changing market economy.

Table 12.2 provides a list of milestones in the development of China's corporate governance. In 1984, the ruling Communist Party passed the 'Decision on Reforming the Institution of the Economy', which stated that SOEs should become independent legal entities vested with full self-management authority and a responsibility for its profits and losses.[5] It resulted in the establishment of China's first joint-stock limited company in 1984, which marked the beginning of market-oriented corporate governance.

The 1988 Law of Collective Ownership of Industries further laid out the framework for the separation of ownership and management by stipulating that the property of the SOEs belonged to the people but would be

Table 12.2 Milestones in China's corporate governance

Year	Milestones
1984	China's Communist Party's Decision on Reforming the Institution of the Economy
1988	The Law of Collective Ownership of Industries
1990	Shanghai and Shenzhen Stock Exchanges were established
1992	The China Securities Regulatory Commission (CSRC) was set up
1993	The Company Law of 1993 was issued
1993	The State Council promulgated the 'Provisional Rules on Stock Issuance and Transaction Management'
1994	The CSRC issued the 'Standards on the Contents and Format of Public Disclosure by Listed Firms', which was later revised in 1998 and 1999
1999	The CSRC issued the 'Notices on Enhancing the Quality of Financial Information Disclosure of Listed Companies'
1999	The Company Law of 1999 promulgated
2000	The CSRC launched new corporate disclosure requirements for listed companies
2001	The CSRC issued the 'Code of Corporate Governance' and the 'Guidelines on the Introduction of the Independent Directors System in Listed Companies'
2005	New laws on the issue of new public shares, merger, division, dissolution or alternation of articles of association need an approval of a simple majority of the public shareholders
2006	The government has approved conversion of non-trading shares to trading shares

Source: Chung *et al.* (2005) and Ho (2003) and authors' update.

managed by the firms themselves through a contracting system. That is, the ownership stays with the government while the management rights shift from government officials to one or a group of elite managers who, by contracts with the authorities, are responsible of submitting a certain amount of profit to the government. The managers are allowed considerable latitudes to operate in. However, the 1988 Law also indicates that the primary goal of the firms is to produce according to both *state economic plans* and *market demand*. While the latter conforms to a market-based system, the former enables various levels of the government to supervise the implementation of state directives and allows state plans to override market forces.

In 1990 and 1991, Shanghai and Shenzhen Stock Exchanges were established and began trading. Since then, over 1400 corporations, mostly SOEs, have been listed, helping to privatize SOEs and providing a great impetus for corporate governance reform. The CSRC, set up in 1992, soon issued a number of corporate governance guidelines, while the 1993 Company Law also contained important legal corporate governance requirements for companies. Ho (2003) suggests that the agents of state shareholders in many listed companies had a majority of the seats on the board of directors and thus maintained full control of the firm, and there was a lack of internal checks and balances. The supervisory councils within the board also did not function as expected, which prompted the government to initiate more reforms in later years.

The authorities then made efforts to increase transparency and disclosure of corporate decision-making. Related rules and regulations include:

- the State Council's 'Provisional Rules on Stock Issuance and Transaction Management' of 1993;
- the CSRC's 'Standards on the Contents and Format of Public Disclosure by Listed Firms' of 1994, which was later revised in 1998 and 1999; and
- the CSRC's 'Notices on Enhancing the Quality of Financial Information Disclosure of Listed Companies' of 1999.

While these regulations provide the basic framework for corporate disclosure, the most significant changes occurred in 2000 when the CSRC issued new disclosure requirements for listed companies. Heads of the company, accounting department and the external auditors are required to make public announcements as to the truthfulness and completeness of the reports. The CSRC Code of Corporate Governance further requires that listed companies provide all necessary information to their banks and creditors in order for them to make informed financing or other decisions.

In addition to disclosure requirements, the new Company Law passed in 1999 requires corporations to form three corporate governing bodies: the shareholders' meeting, the board of directors, and supervisory board. The law also allows for two main types of corporations, namely private companies and public companies, which are further classified into wholly-state-owned companies, wholly-foreign-owned companies, Sino-foreign joint ventures and Sino-foreign cooperative companies according to the ownership structure. And the 'Guidelines on the Introduction of the Independent Directors System in Listed Companies' issued by the CSRC required listed companies to appoint at least two independent directors and not less than one-third of independent board members on the board. The Guidelines spell out the qualifications required of independent directors and their duties and power to promote impartiality and independence of the board.

Tunneling

Johnson *et al.* (2000) defined the term 'tunneling' as the practice of transferring profits and assets out of firms for the benefits of controlling shareholders. Shleifer and Vishny (1997) argue that tunneling is a more serious problem than the principal-agent problem, which is particularly true in emerging markets. Claessens (2000) claims that expropriation happens anywhere there are conflicts of interests between controlling shareholders and minority shareholders. As large shareholders' interests do not necessarily coincide with those of other investors, under certain circumstances like inadequate checks and balances in corporate governance, large shareholders have the incentive to expropriate minority shareholders.

Since China's capital market is characterized by ineffective regulatory oversight, opaque legal framework, market segmentation, and concentrated ownership structure among listed firms, tunneling is inevitable. The fact that the Chinese government, the regulator, is itself the controlling shareholder in a majority of the listed firms, exacerbate the problem. Liu and Lu (2004) and Ruan (2004) are two recent studies that provide empirical evidence of China's tunneling issue.

Liu and Lu (2004) find evidence that earnings management in China's listed companies is induced by controlling shareholders' tunneling activity. Using two China-specific situations where earnings management has been identified by previous literature, they document the misallocation of raised capital by controlling shareholders in rights offering, and estimate the size of private control benefits controlling shareholders are able to extract at the expense of minority shareholders. Further, using the data of all listed firms between 1999 and 2001, they find cross-sectional and time-series evidence that earnings management among China's listed companies are linked to corporate governance practices, and that tunneling is the major driver of earnings management in China.

Using Chinese listed firms' 2001 data, Ruan (2004) defines controlling shareholders as those holding more than 30 percent of the ownership of listed firms and finds that over 70 percent of listed firms have controlling shareholders and among them 63 percent are controlled by the government. The corporate value, as measured by Tobin's Q, of listed firms with controlling shareholders is 11 percent – 16 percent smaller than listed firms without in the control sample. Further, if the controlling shareholder is the government, the corporate value is even lower. The finding of negative correlation between the percentage of ownership held by controlling shareholders and corporate value suggests that tunneling is indeed a serious corporate governance issue in China.

Current Issues and Challenges

There are various corporate governance rules and regulations that have been spearheaded by the CSRC, the stock exchanges, and the State Council since 1992, by which to address China's major issues of corporate governance. We discuss some of these rules in earlier chapters in this book.[6] In a nutshell, we find that the 'hardware' for a sound corporate governance structure in China is in place. The key is the ability (and perhaps inability) to effectively execute these corporate governance rules and regulations. Lin (2004) points out a number of potential corporate governance problems in China as:

- highly concentrated ownership structure;
- insider control of corporate affairs;
- weak protection of shareholders' rights;
- frequent insider trading, self dealings and collusions in market manipulations;
- falsification and fabrication of financial data;
- weak independent board of directors and specialized committees;
- weak supervisory board;
- weak auditing profession; and
- weak external governance structure.

Despite the problems mentioned by Lin, there are a number of studies of China's corporate governance revealing the awareness and perhaps promises of sound corporate governance practices in China. For example, Chen *et al.* (2006) study the relation among shareholder ownership structure, corporate governance mechanism, and corporate fraud cases among publicly traded Chinese firms. Chen *et al.* find that ownership structure and board characteristics explain corporate fraud. Specifically, records show that a high proportion of non-executive directors on boards, with a high proportion of foreign shareholders, chairmen with long tenure and the separation of CEO and chairman title, are all associated with less fraud.

Firth *et al.* (2005a) examine the relationship between top management turnover and firm performance. Firth *et al.* show that the turnover of a board chairman is highly associated with the performance of a firm. Using board chairman's turnover as a major indicator of corporate governance, this is in contrast with the general perception that Chinese firms have poor corporate governance. The study by Firth *et al.* (2005a) also reports that a board controlled by non-executive directors is controlling the chairman replacement decision. It appears that some of the western corporate governance norms are also applicable among some Chinese firms.

In a related study, Firth *et al.* (2005b) model the relation among CEO compensation and corporate governance characteristics with Chinese publicly traded firms. Their results suggest that a highly CEO compensated in China is associated with a firm's high return on assets, a large proportion of foreign ownerships, fewer directors, and a large firm size.

The findings by Chen *et al.* (2006) and Firth *et al.* (2005a, 2005b) provide corporate governance policy implications for the Chinese regulators. First, the separation of CEO and chairman of the board is a good policy to implement. Second, foreign investor ownership helps in monitoring CEO compensation, curtail fraudulent activities, and perplex turnover of a poorly performed chairman. Third, the Chen *et al.* and Firth *et al.* studies were done using data found during 1997 to 2000. During this period, the new corporate governance rules were not fully introduced or implemented. Therefore, we anticipate the improvement in corporate governance practices will be better in future years.

It will be some time before China cultivates sound and effective corporate governance practices in China. While marginally improving the rules and regulations or putting together new rules and regulations are helpful, the key continues to be the execution of these rules and regulations.

PRIVATE EQUITY AND VENTURE CAPITAL

Private equity funds refer to investments in equity securities of unlisted companies, which are growing and expanding across the globe. Private equities are generally illiquid and thought of as a medium and long-term investment. Venture capital typically refers to equity investments in start-up firms. Venture capitals are in fact a part of private equity funds.[7] The investment focus of a limited partnership of private equity funds determines the characteristics of the fund. That is, it can be called either private equity fund or venture capital. A venture capital partnership typically focuses on hi-tech companies and on companies driven by emerging and typically tech-linked markets. Buy-out partnerships usually invest in more mature companies, providing funding to finance expansions, consolidations, turnarounds and spin-offs.

Special situation partnerships of private equity funds make investments ranging more broadly to include categories that embody characteristics of both venture and buyout (M&As) and companies in financial distress, besides equity-linked debt and other opportunities. In the US, about two-thirds of the private capital committed to private equity investments in buyouts and special situations and one-third is invested in venture capital.

The private equity investment in China can be best illustrated by a recent example. Standard Chartered Plc's private equity fund invested US$50 million in December 2005 in shares of Dongfeng Motor Corporation, China's third-largest automaker. The private equity fund, under the global leading investment bank, will take advantage of its abundant global resources to fulfill Dongfeng's financing needs for business expansion domestically and internationally. It is the first time an international mainstream private equity fund has entered into the Chinese automobile market.

According to a recent report, the total foreign private equity fund and venture capital flowing into China was about US$5.5 billion in 2005, as compared to about US$2 billion in 2004, an increase of more than twice a year [*Business Week*, 16 January 2006, p. 44]. In 2002, the total foreign funds in China were less than half a billion US dollars. The tremendous growth of foreign fund investments in the Chinese market in recent years reflects the potential size and returns of the market.

When China started its privatization programs in the mid-1980s, venture capital investments were then initiated. The first venture capital firm, China New Technology Venture Investment Company, was set up by the State Council of the Chinese government in September, 1985. In previous years, the Chinese government basically controlled the venture capital industry. In recent years, the Chinese government has adopted a series of policies to encourage the private development of the venture capital industry (Fung *et al.* 2004 and Xiao 2002).

Since the mid-1990s, many government-sponsored venture capital funds have been established to provide financial support for small and medium enterprises (SMEs) at the national, provincial and local levels. International foreign private equity funds can now invest in domestic Chinese businesses either through the establishment of a new venture capital-backed company or by investing directly in an existing Chinese company. While these new policy changes may represent an opportunity to enter this large and potentially-lucrative market, many major challenges remain.

Kambil, Long and Kwan (2006) have suggested seven disciplines for venturing in China. They are:

1. knowledge and appreciation of the importance of social capital networks;
2. understanding of corporate governance and shareholder rights;
3. the ability to manage intellectual property;

4. the ability to adapt business models to local conditions;
5. the ability to add managerial and technical value to young enterprises;
6. knowledge of innovative legal structures; and
7. the ability to navigate complex regulatory environments.

Indeed, private equity funds should also explore domestic debt financing with banks when they invest in Chinese companies.

Foreign-invested venture capital investment enterprises (FIVCIEs) that are allowed to set up in China, may take one of two legal forms: company or non-legal person entity. The non-legal entity is similar to a limited partnership, which is more familiar to foreign private equity investors. Investors of an FIVCIE in the form of a non-legal person entity are jointly liable for its debts, while for each investor of an FIVCIE in the form of a company, the liability is limited to the amount of contributed capital. The establishment FIVCIE needs to satisfy both experiences and minimal capital investments (see Fung *et al.* 2004). New rules on the FIVCIE follow typical international legal practices and standards, representing a significant step forward in the development of venture capital regulatory framework.

On 27 May 2004, the Small and Medium Enterprise Block (SMEB) was formally launched on the Shenzhen Stock Exchange. SMEB is a step forward in the development of the market similar to NASDAQ in the US and allows high-growth and high-tech companies to get listed, in theory. However, it fails in enabling many SME Chinese firms to get listed because of its strict requirements similar to the two other exchanges.

Given the strict requirements for listing on a stock exchange, many SMEs resort to private financing. As a result, the Chinese government has established many regional assets and equity exchanges to facilitate these financing activities, enabling SMEs to find investors, such as venture capitalists or enterprises in the same industry. China's Beijing Equity Exchange (CBEX) and the Shanghai United Assets and Equity Exchange (SUAEE) are two important examples of the asset and equity exchanges. They serve as similar counterparts in Western countries for investment bankers to establish networks enabling private businesses to obtain private financing.

Recent private equity fund policy and regulatory changes are an important part of the ongoing state-owned enterprises (SOEs) reformation and they have started to improve the business environment for the private equity industry to facilitate the development of young and growing companies. In general, China is moving in the direction to establish a more complete legal and regulatory framework and relax the many restrictions imposed on venture capital, creating valuable and potentially lucrative opportunities for domestic and international venture capital investors.

IMPROVING INFORMATION ASYMMETRY IN THE CAPITAL MARKET

Credit Rating

Two forces of credit rating have been developing rapidly in recent years. One is that individual companies have initiated providing credit information about firms to the market while the other is the development of a credit bureau on a regional and national basis, providing credit information at individual and corporate levels.

At an individual firm level, a rating agency such as Xinhua Far East China Credit Ratings has developed a new batch of credit ratings on listed Chinese companies. The list covers companies listed on the Shanghai, Shenzhen, Hong Kong and New York stock exchanges with ratings from 'Triple A' to 'C' where 'Triple A' is the highest rating and 'C' is the lowest. Table 12.3 shows the nine categories of ratings.

Some companies have ratings of 'A' or higher, indicating their credit strength is excellent. Most of these companies are in the oil, gas and utilities sectors, which are protected industries in China and thus relatively insulated from foreign competition. Companies such as PetroChina, Huaneng Power International, and CNOOC Ltd are given 'Triple A' ratings, the highest. The rating depends upon the resulting synergies and how restructuring plans are financed and the rating differentials were continuing to widen, reflecting the increasing gap between the credit risks of various companies as the China economy is liberalized.

Authorities in Shanghai are developing rules for a corporate credit rating system. The plans are part of efforts in China's industrial and business

Table 12.3 Xihua Far East credit rating scale

Long-term rating	Credit strength
AAA, Aaa	Excellent
AA, Aa	Very good
A	Above average
BBB, Bbb	Average
BB, Bb	Below average
B	Weak
CCC	Very weak
CC	Extremely weak
C	Default

Source: Xinhua Finance Limited, http://www.xinhaufinance.com.

center and across the mainland, to help commercial banks make more informed decisions about granting loans to local companies. Shanghai Credit Information Services has already been established to create consumer credit rating systems, which help local banks and financial institutions screen bad debts. At the same time, there is a demand for banking services that are relatively new for the Chinese market, such as credit card, real estate and auto mortgage loans and other secured and unsecured financial services. The Chinese banks realize that consumer credit-rating is a helpful system.

The regulations would determine who can set up a credit bureau, who can have access to the bureau's credit information; and who handles and monitors consumer information so it will not be abused. The Xinhua News Agency recently reported a People's Bank of China official as saying that 3105 Shanghai-based enterprises have so far been given credit ratings over the past few years, which has helped banks reduce bad loans (Anonymous 2002).

The Shanghai credit bureau was set up by the People's Bank of China as a model for other Chinese cities in 2000. Since 2003, the People's Bank of China has set up credit bureaus in other cities, such as the Beijing Credit Bureau in July 2003. These credit bureaus are primarily operating on a regional basis, not on a national level. That is, consumers with a bad credit history may exploit this fragmented credit system to benefit themselves. Currently, China has no law requiring banks to share credit information with regulators or other banks. Without such sharing, any credit bureau would be for decoration, rather than of any worth. Credit information collected by these city-wide credit bureaus contains insufficient credit history data and is far from being complete (Xu and Liu 2006).

The People's Bank of China has been working toward drafting laws for banks to share credit information in developing a national credit database for consumers. Consumer credit history data must include an extensive list of information from income tax, criminal, gas, electric and phone bill payment records. The credit system intends to cover 300 million Chinese consumers, about one quarter of China's population, and will continue to expand over time.

Earnings and Disclosure Requirements

In China, Article 157 of the Company Law requires listed firms with two years of successive negative earnings to be placed in a special treatment (ST) category for a warning. If losses persist for three successive years, the listed firm would be delisted temporarily and be subject to some transfer limitations. For instance, the shares of the firm with 'particular transfer' can be traded on Fridays only.

The intent of the two-year profit requirement is to force Chinese firms to maintain profitability after listing. Such policy creates unintended results. First, it encourages firms to manipulate earnings. Second, it forces the unprofitable firms to solicit mergers and acquisitions with other companies to maintain listing status.

In China, firms are not required to provide management forecasts. But, many Chinese make earnings forecasting in their financial reports. Outside analyst forecasted reports are available for large firms and have become obtainable for more firms only recently. A firm should focus its fundamentals for long-term profitability, not quarter-by-quarter earnings smoothing. According to US experiences, after the IT bubble and Enron's debacle, many US companies have given up the practice of earnings forecast because it misled investors and encourages earnings management practice. At the same time, US regulators have imposed more stringent rules that now separate the analysts from the brokerage firms of many companies.

Other Market Impediments

The regulatory constraints on the separation of tradable and non-tradable shares yield unintended consequences (Huang and Fung 2004). First, controlling shareholders with shares priced at book values will prefer to raise equity financing through the higher-priced public equity market because they will try to increase their book values. Second, stand-alone mergers and acquisitions (M&A) of listed companies on the exchanges are not likely to be seen in China because of the structure of the Chinese economy and government policies. The controlling shareholders for public listed companies with shares not tradable on exchanges will prefer direct equity financing to non-capital-raising activities such as M&A because they will increase their book value of the shares. Thus, the kind of M&A activities for public companies can be explained by the self-interest of the non-trading shares, which can benefit with an increase in book values through M&A, not through market value of the firm. Finally, the study sheds light on a commonly observed sequential financing pattern in China – why Chinese firms restructure through a process of M&A and then refinance through the equity market.

Short sale of an asset is not allowed in China's financial market. The argument against short sale in China is that the possibility of creating speculative activities will destabilize its financial market. One important aspect of a well-developed financial market is the liquidity of a market. Price will not be able to reflect information in a market without depth. A critical function of speculators is their ability to add depth and liquidity to a financial market. Although destabilizing argument appears powerful, there appears no strong empirical evidence supporting this view. The negative evidence on speculative activity in China is the misuse of monopolistic information that would hinder the development.

Chinese policymakers need to rethink carefully how to allow short sale in its financial market as more reforms are put into practice, and at the same time should reduce the monopolistic power of powerful agencies that may exploit information to their advantage. The Chinese government should implement laws to ensure property rights for small investors to avoid tunneling and maintain a transparent and fair forum for all market participants for future development of a sound financial market in China.

CONCLUSIONS

This chapter examines two aspects of the goods market that have significant effects on China's financial market. They are mergers and acquisitions and corporate governance structure. We also discuss some of the market impediments that may hinder the development of an efficient good financial market.

We describe three types of M&A activities – inbound, outbound and domestic. As China moves towards privatization from a centrally planned economy, there are problems in transforming state-owned enterprises into privately owned firms. First, China opened exchanges to let state-owned firms go public and then allowed a large inflow of foreign capitals to buy inefficient firms. Thus, we can see that the volume of inbound M&A exceeds that of the domestic M&A. The Chinese government has to implement policies in order give enough time for domestic firms to improve and then compete successfully with foreign firms.

A vibrant M&A market cannot develop fully without the support of a good private equity market or for an adequate capital supply to finance the growth of firms. This is true particularly in China because of difficulties for small and medium-sized enterprise in China to get listed on its formal stock exchanges. Thus, China has developed many asset exchanges to help out the growth of this private equity market and also allows foreign inflows of private equity funds.

The current corporate governance challenge for Chinese firms is how to ensure a good corporate structure that is transparent and at the same time set up laws that protect minority stockholders from major stockholders. The key issue, of course, is the design of a good incentive system in China that can mitigate the agency cost problem and provide Chinese managers with a proper view for the long-term goal of the firm. In this regard,

Mehta, Dileep, R. and Hung-Gay Fung (2004), *International Bank Management*, London: Blackwell Publishing.
Ruan, H. (2004), 'Tunneling: evidence from China's listed firms', People's University, Beijing, China, working paper.
Shleifer, A. and R. W. Vishny (1997), 'A survey of corporate governance', *Journal of Finance*, **52**, 737–83.
Xiao, Wei (2002), 'The new economy and venture capital in China', *Perspectives*, **3**(6), accessed at www.oycf.org/Perspectives/18_093002/Economy_Venture_China.htm
Xu, E. and J. Liu (2006), 'Consumer credit risk management in an emerging market: the case of China', *China & World Economy*, **14**(3), 86–94.
Xu, Xiaoqing Eleanor (2001), 'Venture capital finance in China', *Journal of Entrepreneurial Finance and Business Ventures*, **1**(1), 11–23.

13. Chinese financial markets: regulators and current laws

Mary Ip

INTRODUCTION

Since 1979 the Chinese economy has undergone extensive transformation from a command model into a socialist market system. Finance is a key branch of a national economy. As part of the overall economic reform, the Chinese financial sector has also experienced significant change. Chinese leaders are aware of the connection between a sound legal regime and investment, especially from overseas, which is vital to the continued economic growth in the country. Without a solid legal environment for business, investors would have no confidence to enter the Chinese market. To translate this awareness into action, the legal system in China has been radically improved in recent decades fostering the economic reformation process. There has been an explosion in the volume of legislation, especially for laws governing business activities. China accessed the World Trade Organization (WTO) in 2001, officially marking the country's integration into the world economy. Benefits flowing from the consequential increment in foreign investment and international exchange would encourage China to further modify its legal structure. Besides, the transparency principle under the WTO agreements is a catalyst for China to move toward a system governed by rule of law. The transparency commitment not only compels China to make available to signatory members the laws it has passed, but also to put them into practice. Development in the financial industry has been accelerated by the WTO membership because, in accordance with the WTO Accord, China is obliged to liberalize its entire financial market for foreign competition by the end of 2006. Undoubtedly, full market accession represents new business opportunities for investors. In order to profit from these business prospects, it is crucial to have a general understanding of the law related to finance so as to identify the legal risk and to manage it in order to make the business opportunities more beneficial and rewarding. This submission is endorsed by Junbo Xiang, the Deputy Governor of the People's Bank of China, who addressed a 'High-level Forum of China's

Law of the People's Republic of China People's Bank of China (Revised) 2003 (Amended Central Banking Law)

The Central Banking Law 1995 formally legalized PBOC's status as the central bank of China, making it responsible for formulating and implementing monetary policies, supervising the financial industry, and exercising macroeconomic control. The significant impact of the Amended Central Banking Law in 2003 is to provide the legal basis for the separation of regulatory responsibility and monetary policy of PBOC. At the outset, the Amended Central Banking Law stipulates that it is formulated to confirm the status and (re)define the duties of PBOC (Article 1). The key role of PBOC being the central bank of China in formulating and implementing monetary policy is highlighted (Article 2) and is enhanced by the extra implementation tool of trading in bonds and foreign exchange in the open market (Article 23(5)). The additional roles in guarding against financial risk and maintaining fiscal stability are encompassed by Article 2. Other major responsibilities of PBOC include issuing renminbi and maintaining its exchange rate at adaptive and equilibrium level, regulating the inter-bank lending market and the inter-bank bond market, implementing foreign exchange control, supervising and monitoring the inter-bank foreign exchange market, regulating the gold market, and managing the State's foreign exchange and gold reserves and treasury (Article 4).

Apart from being a real monetary policy maker, PBOC is also delegated with the duty to guide other banking financial institutions (Article 32(9)) in combating money laundering, to organize actions against it and to check the funds from such dealings (Article 4(10)). This is a duty formerly undertaken by the Ministry of Public Security.

Though PBOC has carved out most of its supervisory functions of financial institutions in the banking sector to CBRC, it reserves a limited right to inspect and supervise certain activities of financial institutions, work units and individuals as stipulated in Article 32 of the Amended Central Banking Law 2003. When required for the implementation of monetary policies and preservation of financial stability, PBOC also has the right to intervene and to make recommendations to CBRC in carrying out investigations or supervision of financial institutions (Article 33). Upon the approval from the State Council, PBOC can directly exercise the right of inspection and supervision of a financial institution when the institution's repayment problem may lead to a financial crisis (Article 34). PBOC and CBRC also have other areas of cooperation. For example, under Article 27 of the Amended Central Banking Law PBOC and the CBRC can jointly formulate payment and settlement rules. PBOC can share with CBRC its supervisory information by virtue of Article 6 of the Banking Regulation Law 2003. In accordance with the revised Commercial Banking Law 2003, both PBOC and CBRC are given authority to penalize commercial banks for committing an illegal act within their jurisdictions.

Law of the People's Republic of China on Banking Regulation and Supervision 2003 (Banking Regulation Law)

The Banking Regulation Law retrospectively legalizes the establishment of the CBRC which came into existence eight months before the law was promulgated. The Banking Regulation Law contains six chapters and 50 articles outlining the structure, goal, responsibilities and operating policies of CBRC. In particular, it verifies the position of CBRC as being the regulatory authority responsible for controlling all banking financial institutions and their business activities throughout the country (Article 2). The Banking Regulation Law clarifies commercial banks, urban and rural credit cooperatives, and policy banks as the types of banking financial institutions subject to the jurisdiction of CBRC (Article 2). It also stipulates the class of entities to be regulated by CBRC, which are financial asset management companies, trust and investment companies, finance companies, financial-leasing companies that are set up in China as well as other financial institutions approved by CBRC (Article 2). It further asserts CBRC's authority over financial institutions it has approved to establish outside China, and overseas business activities of those financial institutions and entities stated-above (Article 2).

As the sole banking sector regulator, CBRC is assigned by the Banking Regulation Law with an array of responsibilities as mentioned earlier (Articles 15–32). The Banking Regulation Law also empowers CBRC to take various measures against a banking institution for its non-compliance of the prudent operation rules. Measures ranging from partial suspension of business, restriction on dividend or other income distribution, curb on asset transfer, order controlling shareholders to assign their equity or restrict relevant shareholders' rights, order readjustment of directors or senior management personnel or if not restrict their rights, and withholding approval of new branches (Article 37). CBRC, the watchdog, also has teeth to mete out penalties on violators, such as command rectification of matters, suspend business for rectification, revoke business permits, confiscate illegal gains, and impose fines (Articles 43–46).

The Banking Regulation Law has moved closer to international best practice by adopting some concepts from the Basle Core Principles for Effective Banking Supervision (Article 21). The Basle Core Principles for Effective Banking Supervision 1997 is a set of rules internationally accepted for banking supervision. They were submitted by the Basle Committee on Banking Supervision, which was established by the central bank Governors of the Group of Ten countries in 1975. Accordingly,

banks in handling of foreign exchange business to seek PBOC permission, or Article 32 requires commercial banks to deposit reserve, according to the ratio specified by the PBOC. Interestingly, the penal provisions of the Amended Commercial Banking Law have re-vested the punishment authority in the PBOC for the violation of those provisions. Article 76 (1) specifies that if a commercial bank handles settlement and sale of foreign exchange without approval, PBOC (instead of CBRC) shall order rectification, confiscation of illegal income, or imposition of a fine. Similarly, Article 77 (3) has given authority to PBOC to mete out similar punishment for commercial banks which fail to place a deposit reserve according to the indicated ratio.

A further example of connection between the pieces of key banking legislation is the appeal procedure specified by Article 47 of the Amended Central Banking Law, which allows a party not satisfied with the imposition of an administrative penalty by the PBOC to initiate an administrative proceeding with the People's Court. Like its peer, Article 90 of the Amended Commercial Banking Law grants a commercial bank or its personnel an appeal right to the People's Court if they are dissatisfied with the PBOC's infliction of punishment or the CBRC's decision. Article 90 has not only echoed what the Amended Central Banking Law has stipulated but also completes the appeal procedure on which the Banking Regulation Law is silent.

THE SECURITIES SECTOR

Regulatory Authority

Despite the official launch of the Shanghai Stock Exchange and the Shenzhen Stock Exchange in 1990 and 1991 respectively, the regulatory bodies, that is, the State Council Securities Commission (SCSC) and the China Securities Regulatory Commission (CSRC), did not come into existence until October 1992. Originally, the SCSC was the primary law and policy making body for the market; whereas the CSRC undertook the supervision and enforcement roles. In April 1998, CSRC was merged with SCSC and became an institution directly under the State Council. The new CSRC marked the segregation of supervision for the securities sector from the POBC and is vested with full authority over the securities and futures market in China.

CSRC derives its jurisdiction from the Securities Law of the People's Republic of China which was revised in 2005 (the revised Securities Law). By virtue of Chapter X of the revised Securities Law, CSRC is the chief regulator of the securities market. Through its 20 respective departments,[3] the CSRC carries out the following duties and functions:

- responsible for supervising and administrating all business dealings concerning securities, such as public issuance of shares, listing, trading, registration and settlement;
- responsible for monitoring and controlling the activities of stock exchanges, listed companies and securities firms and so on;
- responsible for formulating code of conduct and practice and supervising its compliance;
- responsible for investigating and punishing violators for the breach of any securities law and regulations;
- responsible for collaborating with foreign regulatory authorities and other industries' bodies; and
- responsible for publishing new rules, regulations and verdicts of any securities irregularity (in compliance with the WTO obligation of transparency).

Governing Law

The Securities Law of the People's Republic of China was first enacted on 29 December 1998 and took effect on 1 July 1999. However, the original law was promulgated after the Asian financial crisis. Naturally, the law took a conservative approach and contained restrictive provisions to prevent speculative capital market activities. Nevertheless, those restrictive provisions also became a hindrance to the development of the securities market. Consequently, the fast going economy in the country has exposed the inefficiencies of the original Securities Law within two years of its implementation. On 16 June 2003, the Standing Committee of the National People's Congress responded swiftly to the demand for amendment by placing the first Securities Law on the legislative agenda for revision.[4]

In order to appreciate the changes in the revised law, it is important to understand what issues in the Chinese securities sector were identified and addressed. As Zhou Zheng Qing, the deputy chairperson of the Economic and Finance Committee of the National People's Congress, said in the Standing Committee's meeting, the areas of problems subsisting in the financial sector were (Wu 2005, p. 1):

- poor quality of some listed companies;
- irregularity of some securities companies;
- inadequate protection for small or medium investors;
- deficiency in the issuance, listing, registration and settlement system;

Market supervision

The revised Securities Law has also strengthened market supervision through two vehicles, that is, the stock exchange and the CSRC. At the frontline, Chapter V of the revised Law has specified the establishment, function and jurisdiction of the stock exchange. The formation and dissolution of the stock exchange (Article 102) as well as the appointment and dismissal of the stock exchange manager (Article 107) are all subject to the decision of the State Council. Nevertheless the stock exchange is granted with the status of legal person (Article 102) which enables self-regulating administration to be carried out efficiently. Pursuant to relevant laws and regulations, the stock exchange has self-regulating administrative powers to make rules on listing, trading and membership upon CSRC endorsement (Article 118). The stock exchange has also been assigned new powers, which were formerly exercised by CSRC, to approve applications for the listing of any securities (Articles 48), to suspend the listing (Articles 55, 60) or to terminate the listing (Articles 56, 61) under the described circumstances.

While delegating some of the supervisory power to the stock exchange, CSRC has additional responsibilities and new authority from the revised Securities Law to oversee the market. A timeframe of three months and six months has been set for CSRC in carrying out its duty with respect to applications of public offering (Article 24) and applications for establishing a securities company (Article 128) respectively. CSRC is empowered (Article 180) to access extensive information relating to the case under investigation, which include securities accounts or bank accounts of companies as well as of individuals, financial statements, records of communication or registration of property rights. CSRC can also make copies of relevant documentation and collect evidence from related entities or individuals. When there is a risk that evidence or illegal proceeds may be destroyed, damaged, concealed or transferred, CSRC has the power to take further action in sealing up the evidence in question or in freezing as well as closing the accounts without a court warrant. To curb abuse of these 'judicial' powers, prior permission must be sought from the principal of CSRC before the action of preservation (Article 180 (6)) is carried out. Moreover, an investigation must be conducted in the presence of not less than two officers who are equipped with identification or relevant authorization, otherwise the investigation could be declined (Article 181).

Incompatibility between the law and the market requirements

The previous securities law had imposed a number of restrictions in transactions that have been criticized as an impediment to the development of the Chinese capital market. In response to these criticisms, the revised

Securities Law has removed the obstacles and opened up new business opportunities for financial institutions in the following ways:

- permitting mixed model of operation, management and establishment between securities companies and companies in banking, trust and insurance industries (Article 6);
- extending the form of commodities in securities transaction from spot basis to any form, such as trading on futures or options, as prescribed by the State Council (Article 42);
- removing restrictions on bank capital to enter into the stock market. Now the prohibition is only applied to any unqualified capital from going into the stock market (Article 81);
- switching on the green light for state-owned enterprises and state-holding enterprises to participate in listed stock transactions (Article 83); and
- approving securities companies to provide any service of securities financing through securities transactions upon satisfaction of the relevant provision requirements and receipt of approval from CSRC (Article 142).

Working closely and often cross-referencing with the securities law is the Company Law of the People's Republic of China (revised Company Law) which was enacted 27 October 2005 and became effective 1 January 2006, the same date as its 'colleague'. The first Chinese company law was passed in 1993 when the country was in its transition to social-market economy. Naturally, the legislation carried features which were appropriate to the unique market situation at that time but are regarded as obsolete now the Chinese economy has moved on. Accordingly, the first Chinese company law had undergone amendments in 1999 and 2004 so as to bring it in line with the then market needs. The most recent revamp of the Chinese company law is in its third edition. While the scope of coverage basically remains the same as the prevailing versions in governing the establishment, the organizational structure, securities issue and transfer, accounting affairs, merger and acquisition, winding up, and legal liability of a company, the revised legislation has brought in amendments and new provisions as follows:[7]

Barrier of entry

The amount of registered capital required for establishing a limited liability company is no longer distinguished by the nature of its business. It has been standardized as minimum RMB30 000 unless otherwise stipulated by any law or administrative regulation (Article 26). And the minimum registered capital for a company limited by shares has been reduced from RMB10 million to RMB500 000.

weak. To address this, the revised Company Law has strengthened shareholder rights in the following aspects. In addition to the privileges enjoyed by shareholders under the general provisions, Article 34 has given shareholders of a limited liability company an additional right of access to information such as account books, financial reports, records of shareholders' meetings, resolutions of the board of directors' meetings and the board of superiors' meetings. However, shareholders of joint stock limited companies do not enjoy equal rights as they are not allowed to consult the company's accounting book (Article 98).

Furthermore, shareholders of a limited liability company have been given more flexibility in exercising their right of stock transfer (Article 72). For example, consent to transfer is deemed to be given by other shareholders who fail to reply within 30 days upon a shareholder's notice of intent in transferring. Consent to transfer is deemed to be given if the disagreeing shareholders refuse to carry out their obligation to purchase the stock rights in question. The revised Company Law has also set the circumstances under which a shareholder may request the company to buy back his stock rights, for example when a company fails to make any profit distribution to shareholders for five consecutive years despite the fact that the company has made a gain during the same period of time (Article 75).

Pursuant to Articles 41 and 102, shareholders may exercise their rights to call a shareholders' meeting at their own initiative after the board of directors or board of supervisors fail to convene and preside over such a meeting.

Article 152 has newly given a certain percentage of shareholders the right to representative litigation. Shareholder(s) can file a case directly in the People's Court when a director, supervisor or senior manager commits a breach under Article 150, and after the board of directors or board of supervisors fails to lodge a lawsuit within 30 days upon request or refuses to do so; or failure to take immediate court action would bring about irretrievable loss to the company. Such litigation right of shareholders can also be applied to any person who has infringed the company's interests and caused it to suffer loss. Shareholders' right to sue on their own initiative has further expanded by Article 153 which allows shareholders to lodge a lawsuit against a director or senior manager for any violation of law, regulation or company's articles of association.

Article 183 has recently granted shareholders a right of application to court for a company's dissolution if the continuance of the company would subject shareholders to suffer from heavy loss and any other way of dissolution is not feasible. As Ng (2005, p. 3) observes, this right is probably good news for shareholders who are in a deadlocked position with the board of directors over the issue of dissolution while the company is on the brink of bankruptcy.

Obligation of fidelity and diligence

Another means for strengthening creditors' and shareholders' protection is the explicit stipulation with respect to directors, supervisors and senior managers' qualifications and obligations (Chapter VI). Chapter VI is regarded as a vehicle in promoting management conduct and business ethics amongst high ranking personnel of a company which ultimately could fortify investors' welfare. To implement this, Article 147 excludes individuals who are bankrupt, have committed corruption, bribery or embezzlement from taking a major position in a company. At the same time, people who are being found in one of the situations prescribed in Article 147 during their term of office shall be disqualified from the post. Article 148 also lay down fidelity and diligence as the fundamental obligations of the senior personnel of a company. Furthermore, Article 149 specifies a list of proscribed acts for directors or senior managers, such as abusing one's position for self-seeking business opportunity or disclosing company's secrets without permission, and ends with a catch-all proviso stating 'other acts that are inconsistent with the obligation of fidelity to the company'. In addition, Article 149 elucidates that financial gain from those proscribed acts shall be accountable to the company. In order to make company senior personnel further answerable for their unlawful acts, Article 150 imposes on them a liability to compensate for any company loss resulting from their illegal conduct. As discussed above, Article 150 has expanded the class of plaintiffs by allowing qualified shareholder(s) to take legal action directly against a director or senior manager if the board of directors or supervisors decline to do so.

Corporate governance

Extensive bureaucratic control over the internal operations of a company has been a widely debated topic of the previous company legislation. The revised Company Law has taken a few steps to relinquish government interference and to encourage good corporate governance. Corporate governance is supported through using the articles of association as the main authority for administrating corporate affairs. This is demonstrated by Article 13 which allows the articles of association to decide the company's legal representative to be assumed by the chair of the board of directors, the acting director or the manager. It is also evident in Article 16 which authorizes articles of association to stipulate conditions to be satisfied when a company makes investments in other enterprises or providing guarantees for others, both of which are subjected to the resolution at the board of directors' meeting, shareholders' meeting or shareholders' convention.

Social responsibility

Corporate Governance is concerned with economic, social, individual and communal goals and the way of balancing them one against the other. Chinese legislators have taken a proactive approach and, without precedent, introduced into the revised Company Law the requirement of social liability as part of a corporate responsibility. Article 5 states that when a company undertakes business operations it shall abide by the laws and regulations, observe social morality and business proactive ethics, act in good faith, accept government and public supervision, and bear social responsibilities. In fact, such a requirement coincides with the business strategy of most companies which began to appreciate that a corporate social responsibility program could add tangible benefits such as brand name promotion or business relationship enhancement, to their business (Editor 2004, p. 20).

Special provisions on the organizational structure of a listed company

The revised Company Law has added a few special provisions for a listed company, which is defined as a joint stock limited company whose stocks are listed and traded in a stock exchange (Article 121). Apart from the general requirements of a joint stock limited company in establishing a board of supervisors, a listed company is also required to have independent directors (Article 123). Ng (2005, p. 7) casts doubts on the necessity of having independent directors as another overseer given the fact that the listed company has already had a board of supervisors. He suggests further studies should be made of the practicability of this requirement. His suggestion coincides with Article 123 which reserves the authority to the State Council in developing measures with respect to this establishment.

To regulate the conduct of transactions, Article 122 requires a listed company to obtain a shareholders' decision, passed by two-thirds of the votes, when it acquires or sells any material assets or provides security that is worth more than 30 percent of the company's total assets within a year. To supervise the related party transactions, Article 125 removes a director's right to vote for oneself or on behalf of other directors in a board of directors' meeting if the issue to be decided is related to an enterprise in which the director in question is associated. A decision for such transactions shall be referred to the shareholders' meeting if the number of unrelated directors present in the board of directors' meeting is less than three persons.

THE INSURANCE SECTOR

Regulatory Authority

Following the establishment of the People's Republic of China in 1949, Chinese insurance business was developed according to the style of a socialist economy. Hence a state-owned enterprise called the People's Insurance Company of China (PICC) was founded and its operation was supervised by the PBOC. The year 1998 is a landmark for the contemporary Chinese insurance industry because PICC was replaced by three specialized state-owned companies called the China Life Insurance Company, the China Reinsurance Company, and the China Insurance Company Limited. At the same time, the China Insurance Regulatory Commission (CIRC) was created to take over the industry regulatory and supervisory responsibilities from the former Insurance Department of PBOC.

In 2003, the CIRC was upgraded into a ministerial institution directly under the State Council. The internal set up of the CIRC is headed by a chairperson supported by four vice chairpersons and 13 key departments.[8] The CIRC has its head office in Beijing and 35 local branches across the country. Its main functions include:

- devising policies and plans for the development of the insurance business; and formulating laws, rules and regulations for the insurance industry;
- examining and approving the establishment of various insurance institutions; examining and approving the merger, separation, alternation and dissolution of insurance companies;
- examining and approving the credentials of senior personnel in insurance organizations; and formulating basic requirements for the insurance profession;
- examining and approving the categories of insurance schemes; enforcing as well as keeping a record of insurance clauses and premium rates of various insurance schemes;
- supervising the repayment ability and market conduct of insurance companies; overseeing the insurance guarantee deposits; managing the insurance security funds; devising rules and regulations for insurance management funds and supervising its operation;
- supervising the operation of policy-oriented insurance and compulsory insurance; supervising the organizational form and operation of insurance organizations; administering insurance related societies and organizations;

- investigating and punishing insurance organizations and practitioners for their anti-competitive conducts and irregularities; and meting out penalty for the operation of non-insurance and disguised insurance institutions;
- supervising overseas insurance institutions established by domestic insurance or non-insurance institutions in accordance with laws;
- specifying standards for information systems for the insurance industry, establishing insurance risk appraisal, risk warning and risk monitoring systems; tracing, monitoring and forecasting the insurance market business; compiling data and reporting on the whole insurance industry, and disclosing them according to law; and
- undertaking other duties commissioned by the State Council.

Governing Law

The Law of the People's Republic of China on Law of Insurance was passed in 1995 and amended in 2002. The Revised Insurance Law comprises of eight chapters with 158 provisions. Based on the original framework of its predecessor, the Revised Insurance Law has four legislative goals and is amended accordingly as follows:

Compliance with the WTO entry undertaking

In accordance with the WTO obligations, the required 20 percent of reinsurance of each insurance contract underwritten, except life insurance, should gradually reduce to 0 percent within four years of accession, thus the Revised Insurance Law simply edited out the percentage stipulation and states the reinsurance coverage shall be taken out according to the relevant regulations of the CIRC.

Strengthened supervision and administration of the insurance industry

Several amendments in Chapter 5 evidence the reinforcement of insurance companies' supervision. Article 108 requires CIRC to establish a system of benchmark indices for monitoring the minimum payment capability of insurance companies. The next provision empowers CIRC to look into insurance companies' business, financial affairs, funds utilization, and deposits with financial institutions as well as to request submission of relevant reports and information (Article 109). All these rights are buttressed by the second paragraph of the same article which additionally obliges insurance companies to accept CIRC supervision and inspection according to the law.

Strengthening measures are conducted through the operation of insurance companies too. Insurance companies are mandated to appoint professional actuaries certified by CIRC and to establish an actuarial report system (Article 121). Furthermore, business reports, accounting reports, actuarial reports and so on, are required to have truthfully recorded the business activities of the insurance company, and be free from major omission or misleading statement (Article 122). Insurance companies and their personnel who violate the Revised Insurance Law could attract criminal liability or be subject to penalty such as suspension of business, fine, warning or order of replacement (Articles 139–141, Article 150).

Supervision of insurance agents and brokers has also been tightened through their insurers. This approach includes requiring insurers to pay agency fees or brokerage commissions only to legally certified insurance agents or brokers but not any other parties (Article 134); and to provide training to insurance agents or brokers so as to advance their business skills and ethics (Article 136). When the insured makes a reasonable assumption that the agent possesses appropriate authority and enters into an agreement, the insurer shall be liable to the insured for its agent's unauthorized acts but has rights to sue the agent in question for liability according to the law (Article 128).

Strengthened protection for the insured

Apart from fortifying supervision of insurance companies as a means to protect insureds' interests, an insurance guarantee fund has been employed for the same purpose. Article 97 explicitly requires the establishment of an insurance guarantee fund for safeguarding insureds' benefits, and authorizes CIRC to formulate measures for the management and usage of the said funds. Article 32 ensures confidentiality with respect to personal matters of the insured is preserved by the insurer and reinsurance assignee. Furthermore, Article 88 highlights the need to safeguard insureds' rights and interests when life insurance contracts and reserves are transferred to another insurance company or taken over by a CIRC designated insurance company during the winding up or bankruptcy of a life insurance company.

Sustain reform and development of the industry

To maintain continuous reform and development of the insurance sector, some of the outmoded provisions in the former Law have been revised. The new market situation is matched by allowing property insurers to sell short-term health insurance and accident insurance services subject to verification by CIRC (Article 92). While utilization of insurance funds is still limited to bank deposits, government or financial bonds, or other forms of investment specified by CIRC, the former restriction on investing insurance funds has been eased to not running securities firms or enterprises outside the realm of insurance (Article 105).[9] Article 129 narrows the prohibition from accepting commissions from more than one insurer concurrently to individual life insurance agents. As the Chairperson of CIRC, Wu Ding Fu, said in an interview such a ban for corporate life insurance agents or institutions associated with the insurance business has been lifted. To facilitate insurance companies to become true market players, they are allowed to set terms and premium rates for insurance products and are required to file those items with CIRC for record only. However, when the insurance policies have a public interest bearing, as prescribed by law, or are new types of life insurance, then the terms and rates are needed to be pre-approved by the CIRC (Article 107).

CONCLUSION

The Chinese economy has made remarkable development since the formal start of the open door policy in the late 1970s. A growing module is the financial sector which has transformed from a mono-bank system into diverse market structures. To satisfy the need to have a sound and proper financial supervision framework, respective regulatory bodies are created – PBOC for banks, CSRC for securities firms and CSIC for insurance companies – which are assigned different jurisdictional competencies. The Chinese government also recognizes the benefit of laws for the advancement of the country's economic fairs. Therefore, along the economy reform path is the restructuring of the Chinese legal system. In recent decades, Chinese financial laws have been considerably improved in terms of quality and quantity with obsolete legislation being amended or new laws being passed in order to correspond with the financial development in the country. As part of the WTO compliance further construction of laws in the finance area is in the pipeline. Although all the new Chinese finance legislation conforms to international norms, implementation requires further improvement. Apart from that, laws in China are passed by multi-layers of authority ranging from national level to provincial level. Readers should note the necessity of pursuing the above examined legislation in conjunction with the decrees issued by the various financial regulators and other authorities, such as Ministry of Finance and Ministry of Commerce. For instance, Article 105 of the Amended Insurance Law, which restricted insurance companies to invest in fixed income instruments, government or financial bonds, has been relaxed by a series of circulars on stock investment passed jointly and separately by the CSRC and CIRC. Such circulars are the Circular on Relevant Issues of Stock Investments for Insurance Institutional Investors jointly announced by the CSRC and CIRC on the

15 February 2005; together with the Notice on Issues Related to Stock Investment and Tentative Guidelines on the Custody of Stock Assets of Insurance Companies both issued by the CIRC on the 17 February 2005 give effect to the insurers in China to access to Chinese stock market.

Another example is Article 97 of the Amended Insurance Law which, as discussed above, requires insurance companies to participate in an insurance guarantee fund to safeguard the interests of insureds and authorises CIRC to formulate measures for the management and usage of the said funds. Pursuant to this provision, CIRC introduced the Measures for the Administration of Insurance Fund (the Measure) effective on 1 January 2005. With 25 provisions and applicable to both foreign and Sino-foreign insurers, the Measure aims to maintain stability in the insurance market, reduce financial risk and protection of policyholders' interest in case of the bankruptcy of insurance companies.

Further examples can be found in the banking sector regarding the duty of the PBOC in limiting money laundering. As an addendum to the Amended Central Banking Law (Articles 4 and 32), the PBOC has issued three supplementary decrees that were effective on 1 March 2003: The Regulations on Anti-Money Laundering for Financial Institutions (the Regulation), Administrative Measures on Reporting Large and Suspicious RMB Transactions, and Administrative Measures on Reporting Large and Suspicious Foreign Exchange Transactions for Financial Institutions. The Regulation also authorizes the China Banking Association, the China Finance Company Association and other self-regulatory organizations in the financial industry to formulate their own internal guidelines in accordance with the Regulation (Article 24).[10]

An additional example in banking law is Article 40 of the Amended Commercial Banking Law which prohibits commercial banks to grant fiduciary loans to connected persons. Further to the definition of 'connected persons' as stipulated in the Article, the CBRC issued the Administration of Affiliated Transactions Between Commercial Banks and Internal Related Parties or Shareholders Thereof Procedures effective as of 1 May 2004 (the Procedures). The Procedures has not only amplified the description of 'connected persons', but also elucidated what connected persons transactions are and how they are to be supervised.

As for the securities sector, the recently revised Securities Law has a number of open-ended provisions which allow the CSRC to draw up concrete implementation guidelines. To quote a few – Article 11 for the detailing qualification requirement of the recommendation party; Article 22 regards the formation, membership term and work procedure of an issuance committee; and Article 163 about the formulation of measures for raising and managing the securities clearing risk fund in collaboration with

China Through a Lens website (2003a), 'China Banking Regulatory Commission', accessed at www.china.org.cn.

China Through a Lens website (2003b), 'China Insurance Regulatory Commission', accessed at www.china.org.cn.

Duan, Chun Hua (2002), 'Alignment of insurance industry with international practice', Law Library website, accessed at www.law-lib.com/law/lfbj/lfbj_view.asp?id=10181

Fan, Xiangmei, Yanrui Wu and Nicolaas Groenewold (2003), 'The Chinese stock market: development and prospects', University of Western Australia, discussion paper 03.04, accessed at www.donotpublish.weboffice.uwa.edu.au/__data/page/37148/03_04_Fan_Wu_Groenewold.pdf.

Freshfields Bruckhaus Deringer (2005a), 'PRC company law revised', *China Notes*, accessed at www.freshfields.com.

Freshfields Bruckhaus Deringer (2005b), 'PRC securities law amended', *China Notes*, accessed at www.freshfields.com.

Gao, Peiji (2003), 'PRC, People's Bank of China Law', China Law Reference Service Online, CCH Asia PTE Limited, accessed at www.clrsonline.com/.

Hui, Jian (2005), 'Analysis of the revised Securities Law', the National People's Congress of the People's Republic of China website, accessed at www.npc.gov.cn/zgrdw/home/index.jsp.

Insurance Times (2002), 'Getting insurance industry in alignment with international practice – interview with the Chairperson of China Insurance Regulatory Commission', 30 October, sourced from Law-lib website, accessed at www.law-lib.com/law/lfbj/lfbj_view.asp?id=10181.

Jiang, Ping (2005), 'Five aspects of implications that the revised Company Law has bought to a company', Civil Law website, accessed at www.civillaw.com.cn/weizhang/default.asp?id=19100.

Law of the People's Republic of China People's Bank of China (Revised), adopted at the 6th Session of the Standing Committee of the 10th National People's Congress and promulgated 27 December 2003, effective as of 1 February 2004 (Amended Central Banking Law 2003).

Law of the People's Republic of China on Banking Regulation and Supervision, adopted at the 6th Session of the Standing Committee of the 10th National People's Congress and promulgated 27 December 2003, effective as of 1 February 2004 (Banking Regulation Law 2003).

Law of the People's Republic of China on Commercial Banking (Revised), adopted at the 6th Session of the Standing Committee of the 10th National People's Congress and promulgated 27 December 2003, effective as of 1 February 2004 (Amended Commercial Banking Law 2003).

Law of the People's Republic of China on the Law of Insurance, adopted at the 8th Session of the Standing Committee of the 14th National People's Congress 1995; revised at the 30th Session of the Standing Committee of the 9th National People's Congress and promulgated 28 October 2002, effective as of 1 January 2003 (Revised Insurance Law).

Law of People's Republic of China on the Law of Securities, adopted at the 6th Session of the Standing Committee of the 9th National People's Congress 1988; revised at the 18th Session of the Standing Committee of the 10th National People's Congress and promulgated 27 October 2005, effective as of 1 January 2006 (Revised Securities Law 2005).

Law of People's Republic of China on the Law of Company, adopted at the 5th

Session of the Standing Committee of the 8th National People's Congress 1993; revised at the 18th Session of the Standing Committee of the 10th National People's Congress and promulgated 27 October 2005, effective as of 1 January 2006 (Revised Company Law 2005).

Liu, Jun Hai (2005a), 'New approach for the amended Securities Law', the National People's Congress of the People's Republic of China website, accessed at www.npc.gov.cn/zgrdw/home/index.jsp.

Liu, Jun Hai (2005b), 'New approach for the revised Company Law' *Legal Daily*, website, accessed at www.legaldaily.com.cn.

Ng, Kun (2005), 'Twenty-four aspects of amendment in the revised Company Law', *Legal Daily*, website, accessed at www.legaldaily.com.cn/misc/2005-09/13/content_194490.htm.

Perkins Coie's China Practice Group (2004), 'China Legal Highlights', accessed at www.perkinscoie.com/content/ren/dates/china/january2004.htm.

Qian, Andrew Xuefeng (1993), 'Riding two horses: corporatizing enterprises and the emerging of the securities regulatory regime in China', *UCLA Pacific Basin Law Journal*, **12**, 62–97.

Shanghai Business Review (2004), 'Profiting from corporate responsibility', **1**(6), 20–22.

Tokley, I. A. and T. Ravn (1997), *Banking Law in China*, Hong Kong: Sweet & Maxwell.

Tokley, I. A. and T. Ravn (1998), *Company and Securities Law in China*, Hong Kong/Singapore: Sweet & Maxwell.

Tung, An Sang and Li May Sum (2005), 'Some comments regarding the revised Securities Law', *Chinese Financial Review*, **22**, sourced from State Council Development and Research Centre website, accessed at www.drcnet.com.cn.

Wan, Jing (2005), 'The starting point of the revised Securities Law – protecting the legal interest of investors', *Legal Daily* website, accessed at www.legaldaily.com.cn/misc/2005-05/31/content_146865.htm.

Wei, Yuwa (2005), 'The development of the securities market and regulation in China', *Loyola of Los Angeles International and Comparative Law Review*, **27**, 479–514.

Weng, Fen (2005), 'Eighth amendment in the revised Company Law', *Beijing Youth Daily* website, accessed at bjyouth.ynet.com/article.jsp?oid=6169685.

Wu, Kun (2005), 'Significant amendment of the Chinese Securities Law', *Legal Daily* website, accessed at www.legaldaily.com.cn/misc/2005-05/27/content_143084.htm.

Xiang, Junbo (2005), 'Improve the legal system to prevent financial risks', presentation to the 2005 High-level Forum of China's Financial Reform, Shanghai, 26 April 2005, 1–6, sourced from Bank for International Settlements website, accessed at www.bis.org/review/ro50607k.pdf

Xu, Guojian (2002), 'Amended the insurance law: long term policy or expedient measures?', *China Law and Practice*, accessed at www.proquest.umi.com.ezproxy.library.usyd.edu.au/pqdweb?index=8&did=320617861&SrchMode=3&sid=1&Fmt=3&VInst=PROD&VType=PQD&RQT=309&VName=PQD&TS=1140417326&clientId=16331&aid=1.

Zhuang, Cherry (2002), 'The Chinese insurance market', the International Risk Management Institution website, accessed at www.irmi.com/Expert/Articles/2002/Kristensen06.aspx